TWO ESSAYS
ON
BIBLICAL AND ON ECCLESIASTICAL
MIRACLES

THE WORKS OF
CARDINAL JOHN HENRY NEWMAN
BIRMINGHAM ORATORY
MILLENNIUM EDITION
VOLUME VIII

SERIES EDITOR
JAMES TOLHURST DD

TWO ESSAYS ON BIBLICAL AND ON ECCLESIASTICAL MIRACLES

BY

JOHN HENRY CARDINAL NEWMAN

with an Introduction and Notes by

GEOFFREY ROWELL

Gracewing.

NOTRE DAME

First published in 1890
Published in the Birmingham Millennium Oratory Edition in 2010
jointly by

Gracewing
2 Southern Avenue
Leominster
Herefordshire HR6 0QF

University of Notre Dame Press
310 Flanner Hall
Notre Dame
IN 46556 USA

All rights reserved. No part of this publication may be reproduced, stored in a retrieval system, or transmitted in any form, or by any means, electronic, mechanical, photocopying, recording or otherwise, without the written permission of the publisher.

Introduction and Editor's Notes
© Geoffrey Rowell, 2010

The right of Geoffrey Rowell to be identified as the author of the Introduction and Editor's Notes to this work has been asserted in accordance with the Copyright, Designs and Patents Act 1988.

Library of Congress Cataloging-in-Publication Data
Newman, John Henry, 1801-1890.
  Two essays on biblical and on ecclesiastical miracles/by John Henry Newman; with an introduction and notes by Geoffrey Rowell.
    p. cm. — (The works of Cardinal John Henry Newman; v. 8)
  Originally published: Birmingham oratory millennium ed. Leominster, Herefordshire: Gracewing; Notre Dame, IN: University of Notre Dame Press, 2010. With new introd. and notes.
  Includes bibliographical references.
  ISBN 13 978-0-268-03607-2 (cloth: alk. paper)
  ISBN 10: 0-268-03607-1 (cloth: alk. paper)
  1. Miracles. I. Rowell, Geoffrey. II. Title.
  BT97.3.N48 2010
  231.7'3—dc22   2010016599

UK ISBN 978 0 85244 456 6
US ISBN 978 0268 03607 2

Additional typesetting by Action Publishing Technology Ltd,
Gloucester, GL1 5SR

Printed in Great Britain by the MPG Books Group, Bodmin and King's Lynn

CONTENTS

	PAGE
INTRODUCTION	IX
DEDICATION	XLV
ADVERTISEMENT	XLVII
ESSAYS ON MIRACLES	

ESSAY I

THE MIRACLES OF SCRIPTURE

INTRODUCTION	3

SECTION I

ON THE IDEA AND SCOPE OF A MIRACLE	4

SECTION II

ON THE ANTECEDENT CREDIBILITY OF A MIRACLE	13

SECTION III

ON THE CRITERION OF A MIRACLE	49

SECTION IV

ON THE EVIDENCE FOR THE CHRISTIAN MIRACLES	70

ESSAY II

THE MIRACLES OF EARLY ECCLESIASTICAL HISTORY

CHAPTER I

INTRODUCTION	97

CHAPTER II

ON THE ANTECEDENT PROBABILITY OF THE ECCLESIASTICAL MIRACLES	101

CHAPTER III

ON THE INTERNAL CHARACTER OF THE ECCLESIASTICAL
MIRACLES ... 115

CHAPTER IV

ON THE STATE OF THE ARGUMENT IN BEHALF OF THE
ECCLESIASTICAL MIRACLES ... 175

CHAPTER V

ON THE EVIDENCE FOR PARTICULAR ALLEGED MIRACLES	228
SECTION I — THE THUNDERING LEGION	241
SECTION II — CHANGE OF WATER INTO OIL BY ST. NARCISSUS	255
SECTION III — CHANGE OF THE COURSE OF THE LYCUS BY ST. GREGORY	261
SECTION IV — APPEARANCE OF THE CROSS TO CONSTANTINE	271
SECTION V — DISCOVERY OF THE HOLY CROSS BY ST. HELENA	287
SECTION VI — THE SUDDEN DEATH OF ARIUS	327
SECTION VII — FIERY ERUPTION ON JULIAN'S ATTEMPT TO REBUILD THE TEMPLE	331
SECTION VIII — RECOVERY OF THE BLIND MAN BY THE RELICS OF THE MARTYRS	348
SECTION IX — SPEECH WITHOUT TONGUES IN THE INSTANCE OF THE AFRICAN CONFESSORS	369

EDITOR'S NOTES ... 401

NOTE ON THE TEXT
Essays on Miracles
In this Millennium edition, the text on pp. 1–400 follows the edition published by Longmans, Green and Co., London, 1890.

ABBREVIATIONS

AW   *John Henry Newman: Autobiographical*
          Writings, ed. Henry Tristram
L&D   *Letters and Diaries of John Henry Newman*
N&NPF   *Nicene and Post-Nicence Fathers*
ODCC   *The Oxford Dictionary of the Christian Church*
ODNB   *The Oxford Dictionary of National Biography*
US   *Fifteen Sermons preached before the University*
          of Oxford

INTRODUCTION

In 1884 the Revd Ebenezer Cobham Brewer, now mainly remembered for his *Dictionary of Phrase and Fable* (1870), published *A Dictionary of Miracles, Imitative, Realistic, and Dogmatic*, a judicious compilation examining and categorising what Newman would have called 'ecclesiastical miracles' — those recorded in the lives of the saints throughout the Christian centuries. Brewer states in his Introduction that it is not part of his purpose 'either to maintain or to deny the historic truth of the miracles recorded, but simply to reproduce in a compact and handy form, sufficient data to show a mode of religious thought'.[1] Brewer aimed to describe rather than to produce a critical analysis, and he castigates Alban Butler whose *Lives of the Saints*, Brewer suggests, reflects his own subjective position, describing Butler's *Lives* as '*Macbeth* without the dagger, the witches and the ghost.'[2] Brewer notes how miraculous legends reflect the character of the age in which they arose, but

---

[1] E. Cobham Brewer, *A Dictionary of Miracles, Imitative, Realistic, and Dogmatic,* Chatto & Windus, London, 1884, p. xi.

[2] Ibid., l.

believes that far more significant 'was the dogma that God is glorified by miracles, and the more astounding the miracle, the more it exalted the power of the Almighty'.[3] So Brewer believes that the subject of miracles is 'pathologically, theologically, socially, and morally one of the most important and interesting that can be ventilated'.[4]

Brewer's *Dictionary* belongs to a later time than Newman's *Essays on Miracles*, but nonetheless signals the nineteenth-century critical concern to describe, analyse and sift what is true and what is false in the many miracles recorded in the lives of the saints. He does not embark on a similar task in relation to Scripture, using Scripture for the most part as supplying a template for later miracles, what he categorises as 'imitative' miracles. Newman's two essays belong to an earlier period than Brewer's *Dictionary*, but Newman's second essay in particular, with its examination and evaluation of ecclesiastical miracles, inevitably wrestles with some of the same issues with which Brewer was concerned.

Newman's two *Essays on Miracles* are separated in the writing by some fifteen years. The two *Essays* also reflect different theological stances. The first *Essay* (written in 1825–6) focuses on the Miracles of Scripture. In this first *Essay* Newman argues in accordance with the theology of evidences of his time, maintaining that the age of miracles was limited to those recorded in the Old Testament scriptures and then in the Gospels as witnessing to the divinity of Christ, and finally as undergirding the truth of the

[3] Ibid., l, p. xiii.
[4] Ibid., p. xvi.

Gospel in the apostolic preaching. With the end of the apostolic age, the age of miracles came to an end. Miracles of the early ages of the Church are dismissed as suspicious, possibly fraudulent and characterised by 'the apparent needlessness of the extraordinary display'.[5] Newman's early sermons give ample evidence of this position.

> It was *necessary* in the *beginning* of the Church that its foundation should be laid with power – the miracles were the loud voice of God and preaching the loud voice of His servants, to rouse a world slumbering in sin – now the Church is formed, his Spirit speaks neither by miracle nor preaching.[6]

In the first of a series of sermons on Abraham Newman declares that 'From the call of Abraham to the coming of Christ the Church of God was on the whole sustained by *miracles*.'

> God has not wrought miracles at any time (as far as Scripture tells us) to convert or amend this or that person, much less merely to astound us or to gratify our curiosity, but with this one grand consistent object – to introduce into the world *a new religion*, that of the gospel which could not have been introduced without them.

---

[5] *Two Essays on Biblical and on Ecclesiastical Miracles,* London, 1875, (hereafter *Miracles*), p. 41.

[6] *Sermons 1824–1843*, I, 'Sermons on the Liturgy and Sacraments and Christ the Mediator' (ed. Placid Murray), Clarendon Press, Oxford, 1991, pp. 20–1 (1829?).

The disobedience and fall of Adam had introduced disorder into the moral order, and when God sought to remedy that disorder it was through breaking through the 'order of the natural world to repair the disorder of the moral world. The *extra*ordinary *disobedience of man* called forth the *extraordinary* display of divine *power* – but when the evil was remedied, interruptions of the course of nature ceased. – Miracles were *before* Christ's coming not *since*'.[7]

The occasion of Newman's first *Essay* was an invitation to write on the subject for the *Encyclopaedia Metropolitana* – the *Universal Dictionary of Knowledge on an original plan projected by Samuel Taylor Coleridge* in 1817, to which Coleridge had contributed an initial essay on 'Method'. Newman had already contributed an essay to the *Encyclopaedia* in 1824 on 'Marcus Tullius Cicero', which he had written at the request of the editor, Edward Smedley,[8] who had asked Newman's mentor, Richard Whateley, to suggest someone who might write the article in place of an unsuitable one submitted by Julius Hare.[9] This was followed in 1824 by a second article from Newman on 'The Life of Apollonius Tyanaeus, with a

---

[7] Ibid, II (ed. Vincent Ferrer Blehl), Clarendon Press, Oxford, 1993 ('Sermons on Biblical History, Sin and Justification, the Christian Way of Life, and Biblical Theology'), pp. 13–14.

[8] The Revd Edward Smedley, 1788–1836, Fellow of Sidney Sussex College, Cambridge, and editor of the *Encyclopaedia Metropolitana,* in which task he was later assisted by Hugh James Rose and Henry John Rose.

[9] *Letters and Diaries* (hereafter *L&D*), I, p. 176, Smedley wrote: 'Your task has been perhaps the most difficult of any which has passed under my *Editorial* revision, and I speak quite plainly and honestly when I add that none has been more triumphantly executed.'

Comparison of the Miracles of Scripture and Those Elsewhere Related'.[10] Apollonius was a neo-Pythagorean philosopher who lived in Cappadocia in the first century and whose life was written by Flavius Philostratus (*c*.170–247). Apollonius was credited with being the author of many miracles and was used therefore as a pagan rival to the miracles of Christ. Newman notes that this argument was characteristic of earlier ages of the Church, and had been revived by later writers, notably Lord Herbert of Cherbury (1582?–1648) and the free-thinker, Charles Blount (1654–1693), the author of an English translation of the first two books of Philostratus' *Life of Apollonius*. For Newman 'There is not a shadow of a reason for supposing that Apollonius worked miracles in any proper sense of the word; or that he professed to work them; or that he rested his authority on extraordinary works of any kind.'[11] Newman lists nonetheless a series of prodigies ascribed to Apollonius, but judges 'that such marvellous occurrences are wanting either in the gravity, or the conclusiveness, proper to true miracles'.[12] Apollonius' 'miracles' belong for Newman in the category of 'theurgy or magic', and are not characterised by being 'evident innovations on the laws of nature' or with reference to God.[13] 'The miracles of the Gospels' are 'strictly interruptions of physical order, and incompatible with theurgic knowledge'.

[10] Newman's article is reprinted in *Historical Sketches,* I, 1872, pp. 305–31.
[11] Ibid., p. 319.
[12] Ibid., p. 320.
[13] Ibid., p. 325.

> When our Lord and His Apostles declare themselves to be sent from God, this claim to a divine mission illustrates and gives dignity to their profession of extraordinary power; whereas the divinity, no less than the gift of miracles to which Apollonius laid claim, must be understood in its Pythagorean sense, as referring not to any intimate connection with a Supreme Agent, but to his partaking, through his theurgic skill, more largely than others in the perfections of the animating principle of nature.[14]

This is a reminder that Newman's discussion of miracles involved not simply a contrast between 'Scriptural' and 'ecclesiastical' miracles, but a contrast between the biblical miracles understood as undergirding the Christian revelation and the miraculous claims of non-Christian wonderworkers. In the 'Advertisement' to the republication of his two *Essays* in 1872 Newman explicitly characterises his first *Essay* as 'being the sequel to a Life of Apollonius Tyanaeus'.[15] Smedley also asked Newman for a second article on the 'Argument on Miracles', a task which, as Newman told his mother in March 1835, he found daunting.

---

[14] Ibid., p. 326. Samuel Rickards told Newman in 1827 that he thought that in his article on Apollonius 'you have thrashed him and even ground him to powder; but withal you have kicked up such a dust over your job, that one finds much ado to be able to see how well your work is done.' L&D, II, p. 8n. Samuel Rickards to JHN, 15 January 1827.

[15] *Miracles,* p. viii.

It is a very difficult subject, and I hesitated before I accepted it. It requires a *great deal* of reading and much thought. No doubt it will improve me much, but it must be done by September, and cannot be begun until June. I trust God will carry me through it.[16]

Newman accepted Smedley's invitation and, as the *Letters and Diaries* make clear, worked on the two articles – on Apollonius Tyaenus and Miracles – together, beginning his intensive reading for the *Essay on Miracles* at the end of July. The entries, of which the following are but a selection, indicate an extraordinary speed of reading.

> WEDNESDAY 27 JULY 1825 read Hey and Leland on Miracles à priori ...
> THURSDAY 28 JULY 1825 read Jenkins à priori, Locke, Clarke and Tucker on Miracles...
> FRIDAY 29 JULY 1825 read Warburton lib.ix about miracles ...
> TUESDAY 2 AUGUST read Douglas, Monboddo, Tucker, Rutherford, Bryant's Authenticity, Watson against Gibbon, all as far as à priori on miracles is concerned ...[17]

---

[16] *L&D,* I, 1978, p. 216, JHN to Mrs Newman, 4 March 1825. Newman notes in his diaries that he began his work on Miracles on 6 June 1825, telling his sister Jemima two weeks later that the article on Miracles 'is a very alarmingly capacious one – I have begun to nibble at it but nothing more'. (Ibid., p. 237. JHN to Jemima Newman, 15 June 1825.)

[17] *L&D,* I, pp. 248–9.

At the same time Newman was engaged in a correspondence with his atheist brother, Charles, about the truth of Christian revelation, and also about miracles. This personal dimension must never be forgotten in discussing the context and sources of Newman's theological arguments. As well as reading intensively for the *Essay on Miracles* Newman was also reading to inform his response to Charles. Two German theologians are noted: Gottfried Less, whose *The Authenticity, Uncorrupted Preservation and Credibility of the New Testament* appeared in an English translation in 1804, and Johann David Michaelis.[18]

Newman was in correspondence with Edward Pusey in Gottingen about Less, Pusey writing that he had not forgotten to read 'the part of Less which relates to miracles, but I own I was disappointed with the result. Some single points seem well done, others are overstrained, and, though the whole work seems to be prized as the fullest and most satisfactory here, I did not seem to recognise the Master, who is seen in the translated piece'. Pusey promised to 'extract any points, illustrations etc., which may

---

[18] In a letter to Charles of 25 August concerning the reliability of the New Testament, Newman notes that Michaelis and Less maintain that the Canon was settled by fallible men who mistook [the Apocalypse] for an Apostle's writing. 'Other critics reject for different reasons, 2nd and 3rd of St John, 2nd of St Peter etc but they never think that therefore the Christian religion is *false*. Others think part of St Matthew and St Luke spurious who still believe in Christ. Michaelis again thinks Mark and Luke mistaken in some things ...These opinions may be wrong, but there is no inconsistency in them. Let me remind you that the New Testament is not *Christianity*, but the *record* of Christianity.' p. 254.

furnish you with any matter for thought'.[19] Newman clearly needed Pusey's help in engaging with a German text. In a letter to Charles from the end of July 1825, Newman notes that his article on miracles for the *Encyclopaedia* to which Charles had alluded, 'is not yet begun',[20] though a month later he had made sufficient progress to note that he had read the 'essay on Miracles as far as written to Frank' – his other, Evangelical, brother.[21] Edward Hawkins sent a note on 28 August to encourage Newman in his writing: 'I hope by this time your Essay on Miracles, a priori and a posteriori parts, and all the contents of all the books in the window seat, are in a beautiful state of effervescence.'[22]

Newman had enclosed two papers in his 25 August letter to Charles, one on the authenticity of the Gospels and the other on the Egyptians, and returns to a discussion of the former theme in a further letter to Charles on 26 September, which touches on the subject of miracles. Charles had clearly argued that all references to miracles (in which he did not believe) should be cut out of the Gospels as inauthentic. His brother replied that this would destroy the whole of the Gospels, leaving, for instance, only two chapters of St Mark. Charles had also argued that because Paul is silent on the miracles of Christ it is clear they are later interpolations. His brother cogently points out that 'in

[19] Ibid., p. 249, E. B. Pusey to JHN, 19 August [9], 1825; Newman noted that on 18 August he 'went on with Less and began Michaelis with reference to Charles's papers', p. 252.
[20] Ibid., p. 248, JHN to Charles Robert Newman [26 July?] [1825].
[21] Ibid., p. 252 – diary entry for 20 August.
[22] Ibid., p. 255.

most of his Epistles [Paul] speaks of the *resurrection* and that too as the foundation of the Christian's hopes. Let me add that Ignatius (bishop AD 70–100) says, "but the GOSPEL has somewhat in it more excellent, the appearance of our Lord Jesus Xt.".'[23]

Newman resumed work on his *Essay* in November, writing to his mother that he had 'begun the Essay on Miracles in earnest, and think I feel my footing better and grasp my subject more satisfactorily'.[24] He was still writing in December, when he was also engaging with Conyers Middleton's *Free Enquiry into the Miraculous Powers which are supposed to have subsisted in the Christian Church*.[25] Middleton had, in the early part of the eighteenth century, engaged in a controversy with Daniel Waterland about the historical accuracy of the Bible. His *Free Inquiry*, published in 1748, two years before his death, condemned both reports of miracles in the early Church and contemporary instances (such as the convulsionaries of St Médard), concluding with an appeal to 'the right use of our reason and judgement, to raise our minds above the low prejudices and childish superstitions of the credulous vulgar'.[26] On 19 January 1826 he finished the 'first part of the Essay, i.e. life of Apollonius'.[27] A week later he wrote to his sister, Harriett:

> Apollonius is a crafty old knave. After surveying the Essay itself, I took hold of him, thinking to lift him

[23] Ibid., pp. 259–60.
[24] Ibid., p. 268, JHN to Mrs Newman, 14 November 1825.
[25] Ibid., p. 271. Diary entries, 21, 22 December 1825, 3, 4 January 1826.
[26] C. Middleton, *A Free Enquiry,* 1844 edition, p. 177.
[27] *L&D,* I, p. 272.

up to the level of completion without much ado; but the old fellow clung so tight to me that I could hardly get rid of him. He asked me ever so many questions about my authorities for saying this or that of him, made me poke into dusty books, on wild goose chases etc. etc. In fact, instead of despatching him in two days, I was ten.[28]

Newman found himself under pressure and did not finish the *Essay on Miracles* until 20 March.[29] The *Essay* then had to be transcribed in a fair copy, which he completed during a post-Easter visit to Bath, and sent the completed work to Smedley on 29 April, writing to his mother 'I have just despatched my famous Essay by the night coach to Town.'[30] A couple of days later he wrote to his sister Jemima that, although he had got the *Essay* in by the end of the month he had heard that 'The new Number of the Encycl: is published without it – so it has been too late for the coach (a metaphor).'

Smedley is a varlet, to hurry me so when he did not want me – he ought to have written to tell me so. – However I have got it, thank God, off my hands, and it is a great relief – I hope I have written it on the whole with a view to the good of religion and the wellbeing of the church, and trust it will be accepted and prospered. I suppose it will not be published till the middle of the long. The books I took back to the library today, and now my room looks quite *ladylike* – (oh I beg your pardon. -) [31]

[28] Ibid., pp. 273–4. JHN to Harriett Newman, 26 January 1826.
[29] Ibid., p. 280.
[30] Ibid., p. 283.
[31] Ibid., p. 285. JHN to Jemima Newman, 1 May 1826.

In the completed *Essay* Newman sets out to make an extended comparison between the Miracles of Scripture 'and those elsewhere related as regards their nature, credibility and evidence'. His analysis is subsumed under four headings:

§1 On the Idea and Scope of a Miracle.
§2 On the antecedent credibility of a Miracle considered as Divine Interpretation.
§3 On the Criterion of a Miracle, considered as a Divine Interposition.
§4 On the direct Evidence for the Christian Miracles.[32]

In pursuing his argument Newman enters into an ongoing debate between the scepticism of David Hume's *Essay on Miracles* (1770) and a series of Christian apologists who sought to rebut Hume's arguments. Newman notes in the *Apologia* that as early as the age of fourteen, when he was at Walter Mayers' school at Ealing, and just before his 'great change of thought' he had 'read some of Hume's Essays; and perhaps that on Miracles'.[33] Newman also read many of the responses to Hume, particularly Hugh Farmer, *A Dissertation on Miracles* (1771), and *The Criterion or Rules by which the True Miracles recorded in the New Testament are distinguished from the Spurious Miracles of Pagans and Papists* (1774) by John Douglas, Bishop of Salisbury. Douglas was one of a trio of apologists – along with George Campbell, whose *A Dissertation on*

[32] *Miracles*, p. 3.
[33] *Apologia pro Vita Sua,* London, 1864, p. 58.

Miracles (1762) Newman also cites[34] – who argued both against any continual manifestation of miracles and for scriptural miracles being evidence of Divine action. Tom Mozley, in his *Reminiscences*, notes Newman's essay on Apollonius in which he draws 'the line strongly between true and fictitious miracles' and goes on to say:

> He had early faced fairly the question of evidences, by the study of infidel writers. He was one of the few people who could be called thoroughly acquainted with Gibbon's great work. He could recite many long passages of it, particularly the famous one in which Gibbon describes the changelessness of agriculture and the simple arts in the midst of changing governments, religions and manners. He knew well Hume's Essays. He had Tom Paine's works under lock and key, and lent them with much caution to such as could bear the scot. Indeed his carefulness to master the other side of the great question has suggested to some critics that his faith and his scepticism contented for the ascendancy on such equal conditions as to leave the issue sometimes doubtful.[35]

Mozley comments at the end of his *Reminiscences* that Newman 'treated Christianity as a question of evidence as well as probability'.[36]

---

[34] *Miracles,* p. 5.
[35] Tom Mozley, *Reminiscences chiefly of Oriel College and the Oxford Movement,* London, Longman, Green & Co., 1884, I, p. 40.
[36] Ibid., II, p. 438.

Newman's engagement with Hume's scepticism in the first *Essay* on miracles was confirmed in his *University Sermons*, where he is also concerned, as in the *Essay*, to take issue with the continuation of Hume's scepticism in the utilitarianism of Jeremy Bentham, who maintained that 'All evidence for miracles, before it can be received, should be brought into a court of law, and subjected to its searching forms.' As Newman comments in his 1839 Sermon, 'Faith and Reason, contrasted as habits of mind', 'this is to imply that Reason demands exact proofs but that faith accepts inaccurate ones'. [37]

Newman begins by defining a miracle 'as an event inconsistent with the constitution of nature, that is, with the established cause of things in which it is found'. [38] The miracles of Scripture 'are irregularities in the economy of nature, but with a moral end'.[39] A miracle does not, he insists, 'imply a violation of nature … merely the imposition of an external cause' and that external cause is the 'agency of the Deity'. It is important, Newman insists, that 'miracle' is understood as 'a relative term'. The miraculous event may be anomalous in the system of physical laws which are normally accepted as governing the world, but 'The same event which is anomalous in one [system], may be quite irregular in connexion with another.' In a Moral Order, the order of the Providence of God, miracles may have a fitting and appropriate place …

---

[37] J. D. Earnest and Gerard Tracey (eds), John Henry Newman, *Fifteen Sermons preached before the University of Oxford*, Oxford University Press, 2007, p. 132.

[38] *Miracles,* p. 4.

[39] Ibid.

'To consider them as mere exceptions to physical order, is to take a very incomplete view of them.'[40] Revelation itself has a miraculous character, in that prophecy on the one hand, and the capacity of 'illiterate fishermen of Galilee' on the other exceeds expectations built on the conclusions of general experience. The last point was a telling one for Newman as we find it recurring in his 1843 'Sermon on Development' where he remarks on the wonder of the world of thought that constitutes Christian doctrine being 'The expansion of a few words, uttered, as if casually, by the fishermen of Galilee.' As Mary, pondering in her heart the mysteries and experiences of Divine truth, reasons after believing, the reasoning of believing minds, raises 'illiterate peasants into philosophers and divines; it has elicited a meaning from their words which their immediate hearers little suspected. This is a phenomenon proper to the Gospel, and a note of divinity'.[41]

A reductionism which excludes the moral sense is for Newman inadequate as an understanding of human nature including its reasoning capacity. It was a major ground of his critique of the scepticism of Hume and the utilitarianism of Brougham and Bentham. As he put it in a memorandum of 1829 he had 'been forcibly struck with the importance of insisting much on the *moral sense etc.* as a preparatory to religion; in utilitarian writers "*moral discipline* is quite excluded, and bare *knowledge everything*"'.[42]

[40] Ibid., p. 5.
[41] *University Sermons*, (hereafter *US*), p. 214.
[42] Cited in *US*, p. 316 n.

Miracles appeal to that moral sense and that experience of human affairs which already bear witness to [God's] ordinary presence. Although 'miracles are but a branch of evidences', the evidences of revelation are cumulative, and a miracle is not 'a distinct species of evidence for a Creator from that contained in the general nature or order and design in the universe'.[43] 'A miracle is no argument to one who is deliberately, and on principle, an atheist'[44] – a theme Newman underlines in his tenth University Sermon, 'Faith and Reason contrasted as Habits of Mind'; Miracles 'are not wrought to convince Atheists. When they claim to be evidence of a Revelation, miracles presuppose the being of an Intelligent Agent, to whom they may be referred'.[45] 'Miracles, though they contravene the physical laws of the universe, tend to the due fulfilment of its moral laws.' Newman, in this same sermon, readily admitted that 'the system of physical causes' appealed to by Hume, the utilitarians and physical scientists, 'is so much more tangible and satisfying than that of final [causes]: 'a pre-existent and independent interest in the inquirer's mind, leading him to dwell on the phenomena which betokens an Independent Creator; He will certainly follow out those which terminate in the hypothesis of a settled order of nature and self-sustained laws'. He admits that 'It is indeed a great question whether Atheism is not as philosophic-ally consistent with the phenomena of the physical world, taken by themselves, as the doctrine of a creative and governing power.' It is what

[43] *Miracles,* pp. 8, 11.
[44] Ibid., p. 11.
[45] *US*, p. 139.

Introduction

he calls in the first *Essay* on miracles 'certain instincts of mind; such as conscience, a sense of responsibility, and an appropriation of virtue; an innate desire of knowledge, and almost universal feeling of the necessity of religious observances'.[46] As he put it succinctly in a note in his theological papers 'imagination' not reason 'is the basis of Hume's argument against miracles'.[47] As he came to realise Faith both is, and is not, according to Reason. 'Reason, weighing evidence only, or arguing from external experience, is counter to Faith; but admitting the legitimate influence and logical import of the moral feelings, it concurs with it.'[48] Newman agrees with Hume that miracles must have consistency with Divine agency, but they cannot be understood without reference to 'a moral system', which is pointed to by conscience, a sense of responsibility, an approbation of virtue, an innate desire of knowledge, an almost universal feeling of religious observances.[49] Voltaire and Bentham keep the moral government of God out of sight.[50] 'Facts', Newman argues, 'are only so far improbable as they fall under no general rule; whereas it is as parts of an existing system that the Miracles of Scripture demand our attention.'[51] Miracles are not wrought at random.[52]

---

[46] *Miracles*, p. 17.
[47] *US*, p. 366, q. *Theological Papers,* I, p. 47.
[48] *US*, p. 139, Sermon X, 'Faith and Reason, contrasted as Habits of the Mind' (1839).
[49] *Miracles,* p. 17. Cf. The chapter on 'A Moral Sense' in S. A. Grave, *Conscience in Newman's Thought,* Clarendon Press, Oxford, 1989, pp. 30–59.
[50] *Miracles*. p. 21.
[51] Ibid., p. 22.
[52] Ibid., p. 23.

Key to Newman's argument is the principle of antecedent probability.[53] It was an idea which Newman derived in the first instance from Whateley. Thomas Mozley tells how in 1826, contemporaneously with his writing the first *Essay* on miracles, Newman discussed the subject of antecedent probability.[54] Newman was later to say that if he had brought out one truth in anything he had written it was '*the importance of antecedent probability* in conviction. It is how you convert factory girls as well as philosophers'.[55] Miracles, Newman argues, are conforming with what is known of God from 'the Nature of His Providence and Moral Attributes'.[56] He therefore excludes all miracles not attributed to Divine Agency; those, such as those referred to in the apocryphal gospels, which seem to be simply marvels. He admits however that there are some Scriptural miracles which may be held to fall in to this category, such as Eve's temptation by the serpent, Balaam's ass, Jonah and the whale, and the Gadarene swine. The Gospel reference to the descent of an angel to trouble the waters at the

---

[53] Ibid., p. 362 for an extended footnote on Newman's use of antecedent probability in which it is noted that Newman introduced the concept in the first of his contributions to the *Encyclopaedia Metropolitana* on 'Marcus Tullius Cicero'.

[54] Thomas Mozley wrote to his mother on 28 April 1826 telling her that he had 'at last had an interview with my new tutor, Mr Newman, who gave me much good advice on the subject of themes, and gave me a manuscript treatise on composition written by Whately, who is a famous man here. This I have copied, and have all the week been furiously engaged in causes and affects and antecedent probabilities and plausibilities, which, as I have never read a line of logic, have been very abstruse'. *L&D,* I, p. 283n.

[55] *L&D,* XV, p. 381.

[56] *Miracles*, p. 26.

pool of Bethesda to bring healing (John 5:7) is, he notes, following Griesbach, not found in many manuscripts. 'If a Miracle, once wrought, ever after sanctions the doctrines taught by the person exhibiting it, it must be attended by the gift of infallibility, – a sustained miracle, which is inconsistent with the frugality in the application of power which is observable in the general course of Providence.'[57] This comment is noteworthy in two respects – the reference to 'frugality', which is of a piece with the Tractarian sense of 'reserve', and Newman's later distancing from the exuberant devotions of Faber, and Newman's sense that the charism of infallibility, which he did not at this time accept, might be characterised as 'a sustained miracle'. There are reasons, he argues, for not accepting a number of categories of miracles on the grounds of antecdent credibility. In these categories are:

1. miracles whose professed object is trifling and unimportant;
2. miracles wrought for the gratification of mere curiosity;
3. miracles which have a political or party objective;
4. miracles wrought for the conviction of individuals, with a bad or vicious object, or which are simply unnecessary;
5. miracles wrought in attestation of truths already known, e.g. that the sun shines or that vice is blameable;

[57] Ibid., p. 35.

6. miracles which do not tend to the accomplishment of their proposed end;
7. miracles stopped by human authority.

In the second category Newman places miracles associated with relics and tombs, mentioning especially those associated with the tomb of the Abbé Paris, which Bishop Douglas had dismissed in his work on miracles.[58] In this earlier *Essay* Newman notes that 'popish miracles ... occur in popish countries' where they are least wanted.[59] A strong note of anti-Catholic polemic is found in Newman's comment about 'the notorious insincerity and frauds of the Church of Rome in other things are in themselves enough to throw strong suspicion on its testimony to its own Miracles'.[60] Having carefully discriminated amongst claimed miracles he concludes that the 'overpowering majority' point consistently to 'one grand object' and they 'must not be torn from that moral context'.[61]

Newman's second *Essay* rejects the standpoint of his first *Essay* – that 'Claims to supernatural power in the primitive Church are in general questionable.'[62] It was written in 1842–3 as an introduction to the English translation of part of the *Ecclesiastical History* by the

[58] Ibid., p. 33, cf. John Douglas, *The Criterion: or, Miracles Examined with a View to expose the Pretensions of Pagans and Papists; to compare the Miraculous Powers recorded in the New Testament, with those said to subsist in later times, and to shew the great and material Difference between them in Point of EVIDENCE, from whence it will appear that the former myst be TRUE, and the latter may be FALSE,* London, 1754, pp. 119 ff.
[59] Ibid., p. 41.
[60] Ibid., p. 77.
[61] Ibid., p. 47.
[62] Ibid., p. 32.

Abbé Claude Fleury (1640–1723), the first large-scale history of the Church.[63] The *Essay*, designed as a preface, and, as its full title indicates – *The Miracles of Early Ecclesiastical History, compared with those of Scripture, as regards their Nature, Credibility, and Evidence* – discusses significant miracles referred to in the history of the early centuries of the Church with which Fleury deals in the portion of his work that Newman and Albany Christie had translated. As so often, it proved to be a longer undertaking than Newman had envisaged.[64] In the 'Advertisement' to the 1875 reprint of both *Essays* Newman contrasts the different approaches of his two *Essays*.

> In the first of the two, the Miracles of Scripture are regarded as mainly addressed to religious inquirers, of an evidential nature, the instruments of conversion, and the subjects of an inspired record. In the second, the Ecclesiastical Miracles are regarded as addressed to Christians, the rewards of faith, and the matter of devotion, varying in their character from simple providences to distinct innovations upon physical order, and coming to us by tradition or in

---

[63] The translation was a project in which Albany James Christie (1817–1891) took the lead. Christie had been for a time a resident at Newman's 'house for young writers' having been previously a Bible Clerk at Oriel. He took up residence with Newman at Littlemore in 1845, and was received into the Roman Catholic Church in October of that year. He later became a Jesuit. The English translation was published as *The Ecclesiastical History of M.L'Abbé Fleury, from the Second Ecumenical Council to the End of the Fourth Century*. For a fuller note on Fleury see 'Footnotes', p. ii.

[64] See letters from JHN to Jemima Mozley and W. H. Anderdon in *L&D*, IX (ed. Francis J. McGrath), 2006, pp. 50–1.

legend, trustworthy or not, as it may happen in the particular case.[65]

Newman now sees a continuity of sacred history between biblical history and ecclesiastical, and because both are 'sacred history' there is an expectation of miracles in both. 'Miracles are its characteristic, whether it be viewed as biblical or ecclesiastical ... the history of Religion is necessarily of a theological cast, and is occupied with the supernatural.'[66] That having been said, Newman summarises his conclusions at the outset.

> Ecclesiastical Miracles, that is Miracles posterior to the Apostolic age, are on the whole different in object, character and evidence, from those of Scripture on the whole, so that the one series or family ought never to be confounded with the other; yet that the former are not therefore at once to be rejected; that there was no Age of Miracles, after which miracles ceased; that there have been at all times true miracles and false miracles, true accounts and false accounts; that no authoritative guide is supplied to us for drawing the line between the two; that some of the miracles reported were true miracles; that we cannot be certain how many were not true; and that under these circumstances the decision in particular cases is left to each individual, according to his opportunities of judging.[67]

---

[65] *Miracles,* p. vii.
[66] Ibid., p. 97.
[67] Ibid., pp. 99–100.

The position of the 'evidence theologians' – that miracles ceased after the time of the Apostles – is now clearly abandoned. There is no *a priori* exclusion of ecclesiastical miracles; but that does not mean that each and every account of a supposed miraculous event has to be accepted – the judgement of truth or falsity is left to the individual in relation to the evidence in particular cases.

Not surprisingly Newman's second chapter takes up the theme of 'antecedent probability' which, as we have already seen, was fundamental to his theological and philosophical arguments. Ecclesiastical Miracles are not antecedently improbable because the apostolic miracles of Scripture point in the opposite direction. Newman draws on his earlier reading in the eighteenth-century controversies concerning miracles in the works of Conyers Middleton and Bishop John Douglas, noting that the desire of Douglas to argue for the miracles of Scripture but against any 'ecclesiastical' miracles is to 'act towards the miracles of the Church, as Hume acts towards the miracles of Scripture'.[68] Newman goes on:

> Hume judges of professedly Divine acts by *experience;* Bishops Warburton and Douglas by the *probable objects* which a Divine Agent must pursue. Both parties draw extravagant conclusions, and that unphilosophically; but surely we know much less of the designs and purposes of Divine Providence, on which Warburton and Douglas insist, than we know of that physical course of things on which Hume

[68] Ibid., p. 110.

takes his stand. Facts actually come before us; the All-wise Mind is hidden from us. We have a right to form anticipations about facts; we may not, except very reverently and humbly, attempt to trace, and we dare not prescribe, the rules on which Providence conducts the government of the world.[69]

Newman had argued in his first *Essay* that a moral order was as significant as the physical for an understanding of miracles: here he is concerned that, recognising such a moral order in Divine Providence, we should also recognise that that does not mean that we are able to describe the minute particulars of how that Divine Providence operates. It is of a piece with what he wrote in Tract 73 of the *Tracts for the Times,* 'On the Introduction of Rationalistic Principles into Religion':

No revelation can be complete and systematic, from the weakness of the human intellect; *so far as* it is not such, it is mysterious. When nothing is revealed, nothing is known, and there is nothing to contemplate or marvel at; but when something is revealed, and only something, for all cannot be, there are forthwith difficulties and perplexities. A Revelation is religious doctrine viewed on its illuminated side; a Mystery is the self-same doctrine viewed on the side unilluminated. Thus Religious Truth is neither light nor darkness, but both together; it is like the dim view of a country seen in the twilight, with forms half extricated from the darkness, with broken lines, and isolated masses.

[69] Ibid., p. 112.

Revelation, in this way of considering it, is not a revealed *system*, but consists of a number of detached and incomplete truths belonging to a vast system unrevealed, or doctrine and injunctions mysteriously connected together ... such seems to be the meaning of the word Mystery in Scripture.[70]

Newman begins his third chapter by engaging with those, notably Conyers Middleton, whose critique of ecclesiastical miracles was that they were more akin to magic than to the scriptural miracles which witnessed to Divine Revelation. The contrasts adduced by such critics are that the miracles of Scripture are wrought by persons, many ecclesiastical miracles by inanimate material media such as relics or shrines; 'the miracles of Scripture are, as a whole, grave, simple, and majestic: those of Ecclesiastical History often partake of what may not unfitly be called a romantic character, and of that wildness and inequality that enters into the notion of romance'; the miracles of Ecclesiastical History are 'often scarcely more than extraordinary accidents or coincidences' and are often 'only floating rumours, popular traditions, vague, various, inconsistent in detail, tales which only *happen* to have survived'.[71] Having worked through a number of particular examples from the fourth century, Newman turns to earlier writers, such as Irenaeus, and again

---

[70] *Tracts for the Times*, 73, 1839. Newman is arguing against the Scottish lay theologian, Thomas Erskine of Linlathen, in particular his *Remarks on the Internal Evidence for the Truth of Revealed Religion* (1820).

[71] *Miracles*, pp. 116–17. There is a possible parallel in this contrast between Newman's contrasting, in another context, episcopal and prophetic tradition, the latter necessarily having a much more inchoate character.

engages with the dismissive arguments found in Middleton and Douglas. He notes that 'exorcisms, cures, visions, are the chief miracles of the fourth century; and they are equally so of the second and third', though the fourth century accounts are more detailed.[72] Newman notes that in the Fathers themselves there is caution about miracles, and sometimes arguments about why they are not more in evidence, sometimes citing the lack of holiness in the Church as a reason. In particular he quotes at length from Augustine in his work against the Donatists, *On the Unity of the Church,* noting both the deceit of pretending to false visions and miracles, and notable miracles that are known as having taken place in the Catholic Church, even though it is, as Augustine argued in many places, a *corpus permixtum* and not the 'pure' church claimed by the Donatists.[73] He goes on to draw, in Butlerian fashion, an analogy from the animal world in which familiar animals are put in a new perspective when strange animals are encountered in a zoo, an exhibition or a menagerie.[74] Cautioning lest

[72] Ibid., p. 130.
[73] Ibid., pp. 142–6.
[74] Ibid., pp. 148–9. This passage did not quite convince John Keble, who wrote to Newman that he had been 'looking for the second time on your Essay on Ecclesiastical Miracles, where you argue from the Analogy of God's works, especially from the strangeness of certain animals, and it occurred to me whether an objector might not plausibly say, "We do not know how much of what shocks us in God's works may be owing to the intrusion of evil spirits since the fall, there being passages in Scripture which look that way; and perhaps these Church Miracles may have the same origin," Might not this be said? and might it not properly have a distinct answer?' Newman noted in 1878 in reply to this point: 'But I have *also* referred to certain *Scripture* miracles, and certain histories as Samson's, as being in the same sense "*strange*".' (*L&D,* IX, p. 449, John Keble to JHN, 29 July 1843, and n.)

the denial of ecclesiastical miracles, and their possibility, should cede too much to the arguments of sceptics such as Hume, Newman concludes that 'It would not be difficult to show that the miracles of Scripture are a far greater innovation upon the economy of nature than the miracles of the Church upon the economy of Scripture.'[75]

Likewise Newman urges caution in too readily dismissing miracles as the product of 'barbarous and unphilosophical minds', ignorant of 'the beautiful order of nature'. It was such an attitude, he suggests, that led Platonists to acknowledge only 'miracles of knowledge', and, perhaps mindful of his concern always to defend the genuineness and even reasonableness of the faith of believers who do not have the skills or talent of academic, apologetic argument, maintains that the paradigms imposed by 'a liberal education and a cultivated and reflective mind' (the religion of a gentleman?) should not arbitrarily exclude a serious weighing of the evidence in relation to ecclesiastical miracles.[76] The miracles of Scripture provide both pattern and precedent for miracles in the Church, and Newman argues this with particular reference to the case of exorcism. He discerns a pattern of miracles in Scripture – the Mosaic, the Prophetical and the Evangelical – and notes that this may also characterise miracles reported from the early centuries of the Church, in which the fourth century seemed to have a greater abundance than the preceding centuries.

[75] *Miracles*, p. 157.
[76] Ibid., p. 159.

As a gradual revelation of Gospel truth accompanied the miracles of the Prophets, so to those who admit the Catholic doctrines as enunciated in the Creed, and commented on by the Fathers, the subsequent expansion and variation of supernatural agency in the Church, instead of suggesting difficulties, will seem to be in correspondence, as they are contemporaneous, with the developments and additions in dogmatic statements which have occurred between the Apostolic and the present age, and which are but a result and an evidence of spiritual life.[77]

As to the objection that many ecclesiastical miracles, such as those in the apocryphal gospels, have 'a legendary air' in contrast to the sober, grave and exact statements in relation to scriptural miracles, Newman looks to the inspiration of Scripture.

The Scripture miracles were in themselves what they are to us now, at the very time that the world was associating them with the prodigies of Jewish strollers, heathen magicians and astrologers, and idolatrous rites; they would have been thus associated to this day, had not inspiration been interposed; yet, in spite of this, they would have been deserving our serious attention as now, so far as we were able to separate the truth from the falsehood. And such is the state in which Ecclesiastical miracles actually do come to us, because inspiration was not continued; they are dimly seen in twilight

[77] Ibid., pp. 170–1.

and amid shadows; – let us not, then, quarrel with them on account of a characteristic which is but the necessary consequence of external circumstances.[78]

Turning in his fourth chapter to the state of the argument for ecclesiastical miracles, Newman again engages with the scepticism of Hume and the case maintained by earlier controversialists against him. He notes that in many instances those arguing against Hume's scepticism have conceded too much to him.

> Unhappily there is much in Protestant habits of thought actually to dispose our writers to defer to a rationalistic principle of reasoning, the force of which they have managed to evade in the particular case. Hence, though they are earnest in their protest against Hume's summary rejection of all miraculous histories whatever, they make admissions, which only do not directly tell against the principal Scripture miracles, and do tell against all others.[79]

Newman always saw strength in cumulative arguments and is therefore suspicious of the kind of QED proof that seems to characterise arguments such as those of Bishop Douglas.

> It looks like a mere truism to say that a fact is not disproved, because it is not proved; ten thousand

---

[78] Ibid., p. 174. Note the same analogy with twilight as Newman used in relation to revelation and mystery in his argument against Erskine of Linlathen, an analogy which can also be recognised as a reflection of Romanticism.

[79] Ibid., p. 176.

occurrences are ever passing, which leave no record behind them, and do not cease to have been because they are forgotten. Yet Bishop Douglas, in his defence of the New Testament Miracles in answer to Hume, certainly assumes that no miracle is true which has not been proved so, or that it is safe to treat all miracles as false which are recommended by evidence as strong as that which is adducible for the Miracles of Scripture.[80]

Newman sums up his arguments against Bishop Douglas in the following words:

Our feeling towards the Ecclesiastical Miracles turns much less on the evidence producible for them, than on our view concerning their antecedent probability. If we think such interpositions of Providence likely or not unlikely, there is quite enough evidence existing to convince us that they really do occur; if we think them as unlikely as they appear to Douglas, Middleton, and others, then even evidence as great as that which is producible for the miracles of Scripture would not be too much, nay, perhaps not enough, to conquer an inveterate, deep-rooted, and (as it may be called) ethical incredulity.[81]

Such ethical incredulity is a fault, rooted in the misunderstanding that 'Christianity is little more than a creed or doctrine, introduced into the world once for all, and

[80] Ibid., p. 177.
[81] Ibid., pp. 183–4.

Introduction

then left to itself, after the manner of human institutions ... unattended by any special Divine Presence or any immediately supernatural gift.'[82] Once it is recognised 'what stupendous overpowering facts are involved in the doctrine of a Divine Incarnation, we shall feel that no miracles can be great after it, nothing strange or marvellous, nothing beyond expectation'.[83] This echoes what Newman was arguing in his 'Sermon on Development' preached the same year.

> When we pray, we pray, not to an assemblage of notions, or to a creed, but to One Individaul Being; and when we speak of Him, we speak of Person, not of a law or a Manifestation ... Catholic dogmas are, after all, but symbols of a Divine fact, which, far from being compassed by those very propositions, would not be exhausted, nor fathomed, by a thousand.[84]

'Knowledge' in the New Testament is not knowledge of concepts, it is 'the possession of those living ideas of sacred things, from which alone change of heart or conduct can proceed. This awful vision is what Scripture seems to designate by the phrase "Christ in us", "Christ dwelling in us by faith", "Christ formed in us", and "Christ manifesting Himself unto us".'[85]

Newman's ecclesiology had developed considerably between the writing of the two *Essays*, so he can argue in the second *Essay* that 'If we disbelieve the divinity

---

[82] Ibid., p. 184.
[83] Ibid., p. 185.
[84] *US*, pp. 222–3, 'The Theory of Developments in Religious Doctrine'.
[85] Ibid., pp. 223–4.

of the Church, then we shall do our best to deny that the facts attested are miraculous, even admitting them to be true.' 'If the Church be possessed of supernatural powers, it is not unnatural to refer to these the facts reported, and to feel the same disposition to heighten their marvellousness as otherwise is felt to explain it away.'[86] Different underlying philosophies and theologies give rise to differing plausibilities and evaluations of what might be claimed to be miraculous. 'Where there is an admission of Catholic doctrines, there no prejudice will exist against the Ecclesiastical Miracles; while those who disbelieve the existence among us of the hidden Power, will eagerly avail themselves of every plea for explaining away its open manifestations.'[87] 'As the admission of a Creator is necesssary for the argumentative force of the miracles of Moses or St. Paul, so does the doctrine of a Divine Presence in the Church supply what is ambiguous in the miracles of St. Gregory Thaumaturgus or St. Martin.'[88] Newman has no quarrel with the exercise of 'our best powers of inquiry and judgment' on reported miracles – indeed we have a duty to use them – 'yet this is very different from hearing [such reports] with prejudice, and examining them with contempt and insult.'[89] Supernatural powers, Newman notes, are part of the Lord's commission to his Church as found in the last chapter of St Mark's Gospel, and the working out of that is seen in the miracles recorded in the Acts of the Apostles. What

[86] *Miracles*, p. 186.
[87] Ibid., p. 188.
[88] Ibid., p. 189.
[89] Ibid., p. 191.

Bishop Douglas, and even more Conyers Middleton, object to in miraculous accounts from the early Church, are already seen in what Acts records. Just as there was an abiding presence of Divinity on the Ark of the Covenant, so too there was the Church, in which 'The supernatural glory might abide, and yet be manifold, variable, uncertain, inscrutable, uncontrollable, like the natural atmosphere; dispensing gleams, shadows, traces of Almighty Power, but giving no such clear and perfect vision of it as one might gaze upon and record distinctly in its details for controversial purposes.'[90] 'An alleged miracle,' Newman writes, 'is not untrue because it is unproved; nor is it excluded from our faith because it is not admitted into our controversy.' Miracles have different contexts and purposes. 'Some are for our conviction, and these we are to "confess with the mouth" as well as "believe with the heart"; others are for our comfort and encouragement, and these we are to "keep and ponder them in our heart"' – words about Mary from Luke 2:19, the text on which Newman preached his university sermon on the Development of Doctrine.[91] A sifting is required in relation to claimed miracles, and there is nothing strange or startling in the discovery of the 'mixture of fable with truth'. Affirming Augustine's understanding of the Church as a *corpus permixtum* Newman notes that 'as little derogates from the supernatural gift residing in the Church that mira-

---

[90] Ibid., p. 217.
[91] Ibid., p. 230; *US*, p. 211, in which Newman notes how Mary's faith anticipated the miracle at the wedding feast at Cana. Mary does not reason first and believe afterwards but 'from love and reverence, reasoning after believing'.

cles should have been fabricated or exaggerated, as it prejudices her holiness that within her pale good men are mixed with bad'.[92]

Newman finally turns from his general argument in support of the possibility of ecclesiastical miracles to provide what might be called nine worked examples, looking at the evidence for different particular miracles claimed in the early centuries of the Church. These are:

1. The Thundering Legion, referring to an incident in the Danubian campaign of the Emperor Marcus Aurelius (172) when a sudden rainstorm saved the Roman army from defeat, the storm being thought to be the answer to the prayers of Christian legionaries;
2. St Narcissus (a second-century Bishop of Jerusalem) reputed to have provided oil for the lamps when the oil ran out by changing water into oil;
3. St Gregory Thaumaturgus changing the course of the river Lycus;
4. The appearance of the Cross to the Emperor Constantine;
5. The discovery of the Cross by St Helena;
6. The sudden death of the heretic Arius;
7. The frustration by a fiery eruption, of the pagan emperor, Julian the Apostate, in his attempt to rebuild the Jerusalem Temple;
8. The recovery of sight by a blind man at Milan effected by the relics of St Gervasius and St Protasius;

[92] Ibid., p. 238.

9. The African confessors, who had had their tongues cut out by the Vandal king, regaining their power of speech.

In each of these examples Newman presents and assesses the evidence.[93] In his brief conclusion Newman notes that the view he has taken of miracles of the early Church is also applicable to the mediaeval period. 'If the occurrence of miraculous interpositions depends upon the presence of the Catholic Church, and if that Church is to remain on earth until the end of the world, it follows, of course, that what will be vouchsafed to Christians at all times, was vouchsafed to them in the middle ages inclusively. Whether this or that alleged miracle be in fact what it professes to be, must be determined, as in the instances already taken, by the particular case.'[94] Such judgement made in the light of the arguments that Newman has put forward must mean that accounts of mediaeval miracles must be examined without prejudice.

Although the context of Newman's two *Essays on Miracles* are firstly, the rebuttal of the scepticism of Hume and Bentham, secondly the use of miracles as evidence of Divine Revelation, and thirdly, first a rebuttal of ecclesiastical miracles, and then, in the second *Essay*, an acceptance that no hard and fast line could be drawn between the miracles of Scripture and those which were part and parcel of church history, there is an interesting parallel to more recent debates in the context of spiritual gifts in Pentecostalism and

[93] Ibid., pp. 241–87.
[94] Ibid., pp. 389–90.

the charismatic movement in the historic churches. Newman had known this in the early pentecostal revival contemp-oraneous with the Oxford Movement and associated with the name of Edward Irving. A theology of the Holy Spirit in the Church must undergird claims about inspiration, sacraments as mediating Divine life, and healing. Newman, whilst always insistent that miracles must have a reference to the divinely sanctioned moral order, has, by the time of the second *Essay*, grounded his expectation of miracles in the life of the Church in a recognition of the divine character of the Church, and the Christian life as transformation into the likeness of Christ. Newman's movement between the writing of the two *Essays* is essentially a growing into a deeper awareness of the Church as a divine society in whose life miracles and supernatural gifts were to be expected.

TO THE RIGHT HONOURABLE

LORD BLACHFORD, K.C.M.G., P.C.,

IN LOVING REMEMBRANCE

OF OLD DAYS

OF PLEASANT INTIMATE COMPANIONSHIP,

FROM HIS AFFECTIONATE FRIEND,

JOHN H. NEWMAN.

ADVERTISEMENT.

BOTH these Essays were written when the author was Fellow of Oriel College, Oxford.

The former of them, on the Miracles of Scripture, was written in 1825-26 for the "Encyclopædia Metropolitana," being the sequel to a Life of Appollonius Tyanæus.

The latter, on the Miracles of the first age of Christianity, was written in 1842-43, as a Preface to a Translation of a portion of Fleury's Ecclesiastical History.

In the first of the two, the Miracles of Scripture are regarded as mainly addressed to religious inquirers, of an evidential nature, the instruments of conversion, and the subjects of an inspired record. In the second, the Ecclesiastical Miracles are regarded as addressed to Christians, the rewards of faith, and the matter of devotion, varying in their character from simple providences to distinct innovations upon physical order, and coming to us by tradition or in legend, trustworthy or not, as it may happen in the particular case.

These distinct views of miraculous agency, thus contrasted, involve no inconsistency with each other; but it must be owned that, in the Essay upon the Scripture Miracles, the Author goes beyond both the needs and the claims of his argument, when, in order to show their special dignity and beauty, he depreciates the purpose and value of the Miracles of Church History. To meet this undue disparagement, in his first Essay, of facts which have their definite place in the Divine Dispensation, he points out, in his second, the essential resemblance which exists between many of the Miracles of Scripture and those of later times; and it is with the same drift that, in this Edition, a few remarks at the foot of the page have been added in brackets.

With the exception of these bracketed additions in both Essays, and of a Memorandum at the end of the volume, the alterations made, whether in text or notes, are simply of a literary character. As to the latter, no verification has been made of the references which they contain, much pains having been bestowed on them, as it is believed, in the original Edition.

June 20, 1870.

ESSAY I.

THE MIRACLES OF SCRIPTURE

COMPARED WITH THOSE REPORTED ELSEWHERE,

AS REGARDS

THEIR NATURE, CREDIBILITY, AND EVIDENCE.

INTRODUCTION.

ON THE MIRACLES OF SCRIPTURE.

I PROPOSE to attempt an extended comparison between the Miracles of Scripture and those elsewhere related, as regards their nature, credibility, and evidence. I shall divide my observations under the following heads :—

§ 1. On the Idea and Scope of a Miracle.

§ 2. On the antecedent Credibility of a Miracle, considered as a Divine Interposition.

§ 3. On the Criterion of a Miracle, considered as a Divine Interposition.

§ 4. On the direct Evidence for the Christian Miracles.

Section I.

ON THE IDEA AND SCOPE OF A MIRACLE.

A MIRACLE may be considered as an event inconsistent with the constitution of nature, that is, with the established course of things in which it is found. Or, again, an event in a given system which cannot be referred to any law, or accounted for by the operation of any principle, in that system. It does not necessarily imply a violation of nature, as some have supposed,—merely the interposition of an external cause, which, we shall hereafter show, can be no other than the agency of the Deity. And the effect produced is that of unusual or increased action in the parts of the system.

It is then a relative term, not only as it presupposes an assemblage of laws from which it is a deviation, but also as it has reference to some one particular system; for the same event which is anomalous in one, may be quite regular when observed in connexion with another. The Miracles of Scripture, for instance, are irregularities in the economy of nature, but with a moral end; forming one instance out of many, of the providence of God, that is, an instance of occurrences in the natural world with a final cause. Thus, while they are exceptions to the laws of one system, they may coincide with those of another. They profess to be the evidence of a Revelation, the criterion of a divine message. To consider them as mere exceptions to physical order, is to take a very incomplete view of them. It is to degrade them from the station which they hold in the plans and provisions of the Divine Mind, and to strip them of their real use and dignity; for as naked and isolated facts they do but deform an harmonious system.

From this account of a Miracle, it is evident that it may often be difficult exactly to draw the line between uncommon and strictly miraculous events. Thus the production of ice might have seemed at first sight miraculous to the Siamese; for it was a phenomenon referable to none of those laws of nature which are in ordinary action in tropical climates. Such, again, might magnetic attraction appear, in ages familiar only with the attraction of gravity.[a] On the other hand, the extraordinary works of Moses or St. Paul appear miraculous, even when referred to those simple and elementary principles of nature which the widest experience has confirmed. As far as this affects the discrimination of supernatural facts, it will be con-

[a] Campbell, On Miracles, Part i. Sec. 2.

sidered in its proper place ; meanwhile let it suffice to state, that those events only are connected with our present subject which have no assignable second cause or antecedent, and which, on that account, are from the nature of the case referred to the immediate agency of the Deity.

A Revelation, that is, a direct message from God to man, itself bears in some degree a miraculous character; inasmuch as it supposes the Deity actually to present Himself before His creatures, and to interpose in the affairs of life in a way above the reach of those settled arrangements of nature, to the existence of which universal experience bears witness. And as a Revelation itself, so again the evidences of a Revelation may all more or less be considered miraculous. Prophecy is an evidence only so far as foreseeing future events is above the known powers of the human mind, or miraculous. In like manner, if the rapid extension of Christianity be urged in favour of its divine origin, it is because such extension, under such circumstances, is supposed to be inconsistent with the known principles and capacity of human nature. And the pure morality of the Gospel, as taught by illiterate fishermen of Galilee, is an evidence, in proportion as the phenomenon disagrees with the conclusions of general experience, which leads us to believe that a high state of mental cultivation is ordinarily requisite for the production of such moral teachers. It might even be said that, strictly speaking, no evidence of a Revelation is conceivable which does not partake of the character of a Miracle ; since nothing but a display of power over the existing system of things can attest the immediate presence of Him by whom it was originally established ; or, again, because no event which results entirely from the ordinary operation of nature can be the criterion of one that is extraordinary.[b]

In the present argument I confine myself to the consideration of Miracles commonly so called ; such events, that is, for the most part, as are inconsistent with the constitution of the physical world.

Miracles, thus defined, hold a very prominent place in the evidence of the Jewish and Christian Revelations. They are the most striking and conclusive evidence ; because, the laws of matter being better understood than those to which mind is conformed, the transgression of them is more easily recognised. They are the most simple and obvious ; because, whereas the freedom of the human will resists the imposition of undeviating laws, the material creation, on the contrary, being strictly subjected to the regulation of its

[b] Hence it is that in the Scripture accounts of Revelations to the Prophets, etc., a sensible Miracle is so often asked and given ; as if the vision itself, which was the medium of the Revelation, was not a sufficient evidence of it, as being perhaps resolvable into the ordinary powers of an excited imagination ; *e.g.*, Judg. vi. 36—40, etc.

Maker, looks to Him alone for a change in its constitution. Yet Miracles are but a branch of the evidences, and other branches have their respective advantages. Prophecy, as has been often observed, is a growing evidence, and appeals more forcibly than Miracles to those who are acquainted with the Miracles only through testimony. A philosophical mind will perhaps be most strongly affected by the fact of the very existence of the Jewish polity, or of the revolution effected by Christianity. While the beautiful moral teaching and evident honesty of the New Testament writers is the most persuasive argument to the unlearned but single-hearted inquirer. Nor must it be forgotten that the evidences of Revelation are cumulative, that they gain strength from each other; and that, in consequence, the argument from Miracles is immensely stronger when viewed in conjunction with the rest, than when considered separately, as in an inquiry of the present nature.

As the relative force of the separate evidences is different under different circumstances, so again has one class of Miracles more or less weight than another, according to the accidental change of times, places, and persons addressed. As our knowledge of the system of nature, and of the circumstances of the particular case varies, so of course varies our conviction. Walking on the sea, for instance, or giving sight to one born blind, would to us perhaps be a

Miracle even more astonishing than it was to the Jews; the laws of nature being at the present day better understood than formerly, and the fables concerning magical power being no longer credited. On the other hand, stilling the wind and waves with a word may by all but eye-witnesses be set down to accident or exaggeration without the possibility of a full confutation ; yet to eye-witnesses it would carry with it an overpowering evidence of supernatural agency by the voice and manner that accompanied the command, the violence of the wind at the moment, the instantaneous effect produced, and other circumstances, the force of which a narrative cannot fully convey. The same remark applies to the Miracle of changing water into wine, to the cure of demoniacal possessions, and of diesases generally. From a variety of causes, then, it happens that Miracles which produced a rational conviction at the time when they took place, have ever since proved rather an objection to Revelation than an evidence for it, and have depended on the rest for support ; while others, which once were of a dubious and perplexing character, have in succeeding ages come forward in its defence. It is by a process similar to this that the anomalous nature of the Mosaic polity, which might once be an obstacle to its reception, is now justly alleged in proof of the very Miracles by which it was then supported.[c] It is important to keep this remark

[c] See Sumner's " Records of Creation," Vol. i.

in view, as it is no uncommon practice with those who are ill-affected to the cause of Revealed Religion to dwell upon such Miracles as at the present day rather require than contribute evidence, as if they formed a part of the present proof on which it rests its pretensions.[d]

In the foregoing remarks, the being of an intelligent Maker has been throughout assumed; and, indeed, if the peculiar object of a Miracle be to evidence a message from God, it is plain that it implies the admission of the fundamental truth, and demands assent to another beyond it. His particular interference it directly proves, while it only reminds of His existence. It professes to be the signature of God to a message delivered by human instruments; and therefore supposes that signature in some degree already known, from His ordinary works. It appeals to that moral sense and that experience of human affairs which already bear witness to His ordinary presence. Considered by itself, it is at most but the token of a superhuman being. Hence, though an additional instance, it is not a distinct species of

[d] See Hume, On Miracles: "Let us examine those Miracles related in Scripture, and, *not to lose ourselves in too wide a field*, let us *confine* ourselves to such as we find in the *Pentateuch*, etc. It gives an account of the state of the world and of human nature entirely different from the present; of our fall from that state; of the age of man extended to near a thousand years," etc. See Berkeley's "Minute Philosopher," Dial. vi. Sec. 30.

Idea and Scope of a Miracle.

evidence for a Creator from that contained in the general marks of order and design in the universe. A proof drawn from an interruption in the course of nature is in the same line of argument as one deduced from the existence of that course, and in point of cogency is inferior to it. Were a being who had experience only of a chaotic world suddenly introduced into this orderly system of things, he would have an infinitely more powerful argument for the existence of a designing Mind, than a mere interruption of that system can afford. A Miracle is no argument to one who is deliberately, and on principle, an atheist.

Yet, though not abstractedly the more convincing, it is often so in effect, as being of a more striking and imposing character. The mind, habituated to the regularity of nature, is blunted to the overwhelming evidence it conveys; whereas by a Miracle it may be roused to reflection, till mere conviction of a superhuman being becomes the first step towards the acknowledgment of a Supreme Power. While, moreover, it surveys nature as a whole, it is not capacious enough to embrace its bearings, and to comprehend what it implies. In miraculous displays of power the field of view is narrowed; a detached portion of the divine operations is taken as an instance, and the final cause is distinctly pointed out. A Miracle, besides, is more striking, inasmuch as it displays the Deity in action; evidence of which is not supplied in the system of nature. It may then accidentally bring conviction of an intelligent Creator; for it voluntarily proffers a testimony which we have ourselves to extort from the ordinary course of things, and forces upon the attention a truth which otherwise is not discovered, except upon examination.

And as it affords a more striking evidence of a Creator than that conveyed in the order and established laws of the Universe, still more so does it of a Moral Governor. For, while nature attests the being of God more distinctly than it does His moral government, a miraculous event, on the contrary, bears more directly on the fact of His moral government, of which it is an immediate instance, while it only implies His existence. Hence, besides banishing ideas of Fate and Necessity, Miracles have a tendency to rouse conscience, to awaken to a sense of responsibility, to remind of duty, and to direct the attention to those marks of divine government already contained in the ordinary course of events.[e]

Hitherto, however, I have spoken of solitary Miracles; a system of miraculous interpositions, conducted with reference to a final cause, supplies a still more beautiful and convincing argument for the moral government of God.

* Farmer, On Miracles, Chap. i. Sec. 2.

Section II.

ON THE ANTECEDENT CREDIBILITY OF A MIRACLE, CONSIDERED AS A DIVINE INTERPOSITION.

IN proof of miraculous occurrences, we must have recourse to the same kind of evidence as that by which we determine the truth of historical accounts in general. For though Miracles, in consequence of their extraordinary nature, challenge a fuller and more accurate investigation, still they do not admit an investigation conducted on different principles,—Testimony being the main assignable medium of proof for past events of any kind. And this being indisputable, it is almost equally so that the Christian Miracles are attested by evidence even stronger than can be produced for any of those historical facts which we most firmly believe. This has been felt by unbelievers; who have been, in consequence, led to deny the admissibility of even the strongest testimony, if offered in behalf of miraculous events, and thus to get rid of the only means by which they can be proved to have taken place. It has accordingly been asserted, that all events inconsistent with the course of nature bear in their very front such strong and decisive marks of falsehood and absurdity, that it is needless to examine the evidence adduced for them.[f] "Where men are heated by zeal and enthusiasm," says Hume, with a distant but evident allusion to the Christian Miracles, "there is no degree of human testimony so strong as may not be procured for the greatest absurdity; and those who will be so silly as to examine the affair by that medium, and seek particular flaws in the testimony, are almost sure to be confounded."[g] Of these antecedent objections, which are supposed to decide the question, the most popular is founded on the frequent occurrence of wonderful tales in every age and country—generally, too, connected with Religion; and since the more we are in a situation to examine these accounts, the more fabulous they are proved to be, there would certainly be hence a fair presumption against the Scripture narrative, did it resemble them in its circumstances and proposed object. A more refined argument is that advanced by Hume, in the first part of his *Essay on Miracles*, in which it is maintained against the credibility of a Miracle, that it is more probable that the tes-

[f] *I.e.*, it is pretended to try *past* events on the principles used in conjecturing *future;* viz., on antecedent probability and examples. (Whately's Treatise on Rhetoric.) See Leland's "Supplement to View of Deistical Writers," Let. 3.

[g] Essays, Vol. ii. Note I.

timony should be false than that the Miracle should be true.

This latter objection has been so ably met by various writers, that, though prior in the order of the argument to the former, it need not be considered here. It derives its force from the assumption, that a Miracle is strictly a causeless phenomemon, a self-originating violation of nature; and is solved by referring the event to divine agency, a principle which (it cannot be denied) has originated works indicative of power at least as great as any Miracle requires. An adequate cause being thus found for the production of a Miracle, the objection vanishes, as far as the mere question of power is concerned; and it remains to be considered whether the anomalous fact be of such a character as to admit of being referred to the Supreme Being. For if it cannot with propriety be referred to Him, it remains as improbable as if no such agent were known to exist. At this point, then, I propose taking up the argument; and by examining what Miracles are in their nature and circumstances referable to Divine agency, I shall be providing a reply to the former of the objections just noticed, in which the alleged similarity of all miraculous narratives one to another, is made a reason for a common rejection of all.

In examining what Miracles may properly be ascribed to the Deity, Hume supplies us with an observation so just, when taken in its full extent, that I shall make it the groundwork of the inquiry on which I am entering. As the Deity, he says, discovers Himself to us by His works, we have no rational grounds for ascribing to Him attributes or actions dissimilar from those which His works convey. It follows, then, that in discriminating between those Miracles which can and those which cannot be ascribed to God, we must be guided by the information with which experience furnishes us concerning His wisdom, goodness, and other attributes. Since a Miracle is an act out of the known track of Divine agency, as regards the physical system, it is almost indispensable to show its consistency with the Divine agency, at least, in some other point of view; if, that is, it is recognised as the work of the same power. Now, I contend that this reasonable demand is satisfied in the Jewish and Christian Scriptures, in which we find a narrative of Miracles altogether answering in their character and circumstances to those general ideas which the ordinary course of Divine Providence enables us to form concerning the attributes and actions of God.

While writers expatiate so largely on the laws of nature, they altogether forget the existence of a moral system: a system which, though but partially understood, and but general in its appointments as acting upon free agents, is as intelligible in its laws and provisions as the material world. Connected with this moral government, we find certain instincts of mind; such as conscience, a sense of responsibility, and an approbation of virtue; an innate desire of knowledge, and an almost universal feeling of the necessity of religious observances; while, in fact, Virtue is, on the whole, rewarded, and Vice punished. And though we meet with many and striking anomalies, yet it is evident they are but anomalies, and possibly but in appearance so, and with reference to our partial information.

These two systems, the Physical and the Moral, sometimes act in union, and sometimes in opposition to each other; and as the order of nature certainly does in many cases interfere with the operation of moral laws (as, for instance, when good men die prematurely, or the gifts of nature are lavished on the bad), there is nothing to shock probability in the idea that a great moral object should be effected by an interruption of physical order. But, further than this, however physical laws may embarrass the operation of the moral system, still on the whole they are subservient to it; contributing, as is evident, to the welfare and convenience of man, providing for his mental gratification as well as animal enjoyment, sometimes even supplying correctives to his moral disorders. If, then, the economy of nature has so constant a reference to an ulterior plan, a Miracle is a deviation from

[h] See Butler's "Analogy," Part i. Chap. iii.

the subordinate for the sake of the superior system, and is very far indeed from improbable, when a great moral end cannot be effected except at the expense of physical regularity. Nor can it be fairly said to argue an imperfection in the Divine plans, that this interference should be necessary. For we must view the system of Providence as a whole; which is not more imperfect because of the mutual action of its parts, than a machine, the separate wheels of which effect each other's movements.

Now the Miracles of the Jewish and Christian Religions must be considered as immediate effects of Divine Power beyond the action of nature, for an important moral end; and are in consequence accounted for by producing, not a physical, but a final cause.[1] We are not left to contemplate the bare anomalies, and from the mere necessity of the case to refer them to the supposed agency of the Deity. The power of displaying them is, according to the Scripture narrative, intrusted to certain individuals, who stand forward as their interpreters, giving them a voice and language, and a dignity demanding our regard; who set them forth as evidences of the greatest of moral ends, a Revelation from God,—as instruments in His hand of effecting a direct intercourse between Himself and His creatures, which

[1] Divine Legation, Book ix. Chap. v. Vince, On Miracles, Sermon i.

otherwise could not have been effected,—as vouchers for the truth of a message which they deliver.[k] This is plain and intelligible; there is an easy connection between the miraculous nature of their works and the truth of their words; the fact of their superhuman power is a reasonable ground for belief in their superhuman knowledge. Considering, then, our instinctive sense of duty and moral obligation, yet the weak sanction which reason gives to the practice of virtue, and withal the uncertainty of the mind when advancing beyond the first elements of right and wrong; considering, moreover, the feeling which wise men have entertained of the need of some heavenly guide to instruct and confirm them in goodness, and that unextinguishable desire for a Divine message which has led men in all ages to acquiesce even in pretended revelations, rather than forego the consolation thus afforded them; and again, the possibility (to say the least) of our being destined for a future state of being, the nature and circumstances of which it may concern

[k] As, for instance, Exod. iv. 1—9, 29—31; vii. 9, 17; Numb. xvi. 3, 28, 29; Deut. iv. 36—40; xviii. 21, 22; Josh. iii. 7—13; 1 Sam. x. 1—7; xii. 16—19; 1 Kings xiii. 3; xvii. 24; xviii. 36—39; 2 Kings i. 6, 10; v. 15; xx. 8—11; Jer. xxviii. 15—17; Ezek. xxxiii. 33; Matt. x. 1—20; xi. 3—5, 20—24; Mark xvi. 15—20; Luke i. 18—20; ii. 11, 12; v. 24; vii. 15, 16; ix. 2; x. 9; John ii. 22; iii. 2; v. 36, 37; ix. 33; x. 24—38; xi. 15, 41, 42; xiii. 19; xiv. 10, 11, 29; xvi. 4; xx. 30, 31; Acts i. 8; ii. 22, 33; iii. 15, 16; iv. 33; v. 32; viii. 6; x. 38; xiii. 8—12; xiv. 3; Rom. xv. 18, 19; 1 Cor. ii. 4, 5; 2 Cor. xii. 12; Heb. ii. 3, 4; Rev. xix. 10.

us much to know, though from nature we know nothing; considering, lastly, our experience of a watchful and merciful Providence, and the impracticability already noticed of a Revelation without a Miracle, it is hardly too much to affirm that the moral system points to an interference with the course of nature, and that Miracles wrought in evidence of a Divine communication, instead of being antecedently improbable, are, when directly attested, entitled to a respectful and impartial consideration.

When the various antecedent objections which ingenious men have urged against Miracles are brought together, they will be found nearly all to arise from forgetfulness of the existence of moral laws.[1] In their zeal to perfect the laws of matter they most unphilosophically overlook a more sublime system, which contains disclosures not only of the Being but of the Will of God. Thus, Hume, in a passage above referred to, observes, "Though the Being to whom the Miracle is ascribed be Almighty, it does not, upon that account, become a whit more probable, since it is impossible for us to know the attributes or actions of such a Being, otherwise than from the experience which we have of His productions in the usual course of nature. This still reduces us to past observation, and obliges us to compare the instances of the violation of truth in the testimony of men with

[1] Vince, On Miracles, Sermon i.

Antecedent Credibility of a Miracle. 21

those of the violation of the laws of nature by Miracles, in order to judge which of them is most likely and probable." Here the moral government of God, with the course of which the Miracle entirely accords, is altogether kept out of sight. With a like heedlessness of the moral character of a Miracle, another writer, notorious for his irreligion,[m] objects that it argues mutability in the Deity, and implies that the physical system was not created good, as needing improvement. And a recent author adopts a similarly partial and inconclusive mode of reasoning, when he confuses the Christian Miracles with fables of apparitions and witches, and would examine them on the strict principle of those legal forms which from their secular object go far to exclude all religious discussion of the question.[n] Such reasoners seem to suppose, that when the agency of the Deity is introduced to account for Miracles, it is the illogical introduction of an unknown cause, a reference to a mere name, the offspring, perhaps, of popular superstition; or, if more than a name, to a cause that can be known only by means of the physical creation; and hence they consider Religion as founded in the mere weakness or eccentricity of the intellect, not in actual intimations of a Divine government as contained in the moral world. From an apparent impa-

[m] Voltaire.
[n] Bentham, Preuves Judiciaires, Liv. viii.

tience of investigating a system which is but partially revealed, they esteem the laws of the material system alone worthy the notice of a scientific mind ; and rid themselves of the annoyance which the importunity of a claim to miraculous power occasions them, by discarding all the circumstances which fix its antecedent probability, all in which one Miracle differs from another, the professed author, object, design, character, and human instruments.

When this partial procedure is resisted, the *à priori* objections of sceptical writers at once lose their force. Facts are only so far improbable as they fall under no general rule ; whereas it is as parts of an existing system that the Miracles of Scripture demand our attention, as resulting from known attributes of God, and corresponding to the ordinary arrangements of His providence. Even as detached events they might excite a rational awe towards the mysterious Author of nature. But they are presented to us, not as unconnected and unmeaning occurrences, but as holding a place in an extensive plan of Divine government, completing the moral system, connecting Man and his Maker, and introducing him to the means of securing his happiness in another and eternal state of being. That such is the professed object of the body of Christian Miracles, can hardly be denied. In the earlier Religion it was substantially the same, though, from the preparatory nature of the Dispensation, a less enlarged view was given of the Divine counsels. The express purpose of the Jewish Miracles is to confirm the natural evidence of one God, the Creator of all things, to display His attributes and will with distinctness and authority, and to enforce the obligation of religious observances, and the sinfulness of idolatrous worship.º Whether we turn to the earlier or later ages of Judaism, in the plagues of Egypt, in the parting of Jordan, and the arresting of the sun's course by Joshua, in the harvest thunder at the prayer of Samuel, in the rending of the altar at Bethel, in Elijah's sacrifice on Mount Carmel, and in the cure of Naaman by Elisha, we recognise this one grand object throughout. Not even in the earliest ages of the Scripture history are Miracles wrought at random, or causelessly, or to amuse the fancy, or for the sake of mere display; nor prodigally, for the mere conviction of individuals, but for the most part on a grand scale, in the face of the world, to supply whole nations with evidence concerning the Deity. Nor are they strewn confusedly over the face of the history, being with few exceptions reducible to three eras; the formation of the Hebrew Church and polity, the reformation in the times of the idolatrous Kings of Israel, and the

º Exod. iii. xiv.; xx. 22, 23; xxxiv. 6—17; Deut. iv. 32--40; Josh. ii. 10, 11; iv. 23, 24; 1 Sam. v. 3, 4; xii. 18; 2 Sam. vii. 23; 1 Kings viii. 59, 60; xviii. 36, 37; xx. 28; 2 Kings xix. 15—19, 35; 2 Chron. xx. 29; Isaiah vi. 1—5; xix 1; xliii. 10—12.

promulgation of the Gospel. Let it be observed, moreover, that the power of working them, instead of being assumed by any classes of men indiscriminately, is described as a prerogative of the occasional Prophets, to the exclusion of the Priests and Kings; a circumstance which, not to mention its remarkable contrast to the natural course of an imposture, is deserving attention from its consistency with the leading design of Miracles already specified. For the respective claims of the Kings and Priests were already ascertained, when once the sacred office was limited to the family of Aaron, and the regal power to David and his descendants; whereas extraordinary messengers, as Moses, Samuel, and Elijah, needed some supernatural display of power to authenticate their pretensions. In corroboration of this remark I might observe upon the unembarrassed manner of the Prophets in the exercise of their professed gift; their disdain of argument or persuasion, and the confidence with which they appeal to those before whom they are said to have worked their Miracles.

These and similar observations do more than invest the separate Miracles with a dignity worthy of the Supreme Being; they show the coincidence of them all in one common and consistent object. As parts of a system, the Miracles recommend and attest each other, evidencing not only general wisdom, but a digested and extended plan. And while this appearance of design connects them with the acknowledged works of a Creator, who is in the natural world chiefly known to us by the presence of final causes, so, again, a plan conducted as this was, through a series of ages, evinces not the varying will of successive individuals, but the steady and sustaining purpose of one Sovereign Mind. And this remark especially applies to the coincidence of views observable between the Old and New Testament; the latter of which, though written after a long interval of silence, the breaking up of the former system, a revolution in religious discipline, and the introduction of Oriental tenets into the popular Theology, still unhesitatingly takes up and maintains the ancient principles of miraculous interposition.

An additional recommendation of the Scripture Miracles is their appositeness to the times and places in which they were wrought; as, for instance, in the case of the plagues of Egypt, which, it has been shown,[p] were directed against the prevalent superstitions of that country. Their originality, beauty, and immediate utility, are further properties falling in with our conceptions of Divine agency. In their general character we discover nothing indecorous, light, or ridiculous; they are grave, simple, unambiguous, majestic. Many of them, especially those of the later Dispensation, are remarkable for their benevolent and

[p] See Bryant.

merciful character; others are useful for a variety of subordinate purposes, as a pledge of the certainty of particular promises, or as comforting good men, or as edifying the Church. Nor must we overlook the moral instruction conveyed in many, particularly in those ascribed to Christ, the spiritual interpretation which they will often bear, and the exemplification which they afford of particular doctrines.[q]

Accepting, then, what may be called Hume's canon, that *no work can be reasonably ascribed to the agency of God, which is altogether different from those ordinary works from which our knowledge of Him is originally obtained*, I have shown that the Miracles of Scripture, far from being exceptionable on that account, are strongly recommended by their coincidence with what we know from nature of His Providence and Moral Attributes. That there are some few among them in which this coincidence cannot be traced, it is not necessary to deny. As a whole they bear a determinate and consistent character, being great and extraordinary means for attaining a great, momentous, and extraordinary object.

I shall not, however, dismiss this criterion of the antecedent probability of a Miracle with which Hume has furnished us, without showing that it is more or less detrimental to the pretensions of all professed

[q] Jones, On the Figurative Language of Scripture, Lecture x. Farmer, On Miracles, Chap. iii. Sec. 6, 2.

Antecedent Credibility of a Miracle. 27

Miracles but those of the Jewish and Christian Revelations; in other words, that none else are likely to have occurred, because none else can with any probability be referred to the agency of the Deity, the only known cause of miraculous interposition. We exclude then

1. *Those which are not even referred by the workers of them to Divine Agency.*

Such are the extraordinary works attributed by some to Zoroaster; and, again, to Pythagoras, Empedocles, Apollonius, and others of their School; which only claim to be the result of their superior wisdom, and were quite independent of a Supreme Being.[r] Such are the supposed effects of witchcraft or of magical charms, which profess to originate with Spirits and Demons; for, as these agents, supposing them to exist, did not make the world, there is every reason for thinking they cannot of themselves alter its arrangements.[s] And those, as in some accounts of

[r] See, in contrast, Gen. xl. 8; xli. 16; Dan. ii. 27—30, 47; Acts iii. 12—16; xiv. 11—18; a contrast sustained, as these passages show, for 1500 years.

[s] Sometimes charms are represented as having an inherent virtue, independent of invisible agents, as in the account given by Josephus of Eleazar's drawing out a devil through the nostrils of a patient by means of a ring, which contained in it a drug prescribed by Solomon. Josephus, Antiq. viii. 2, Sec. 5. See Acts viii. 19.

apparitions, which are silent respecting their origin, and are referred to God from the mere necessity of the case.

2. *Those which are unworthy of an All-wise Author.*

1. As, for example, the Miracles of Simon Magus, who pretended he could assume the appearance of a serpent, exhibit himself with two faces, and transform himself into whatever shape he pleased.[t] Such are most of the Miracles recorded in the apocryphal accounts of Christ;[u] *e.g.*, the sudden ceasing of all kinds of motion at His birth, birds stopping in the midst of their flight, men at table with their hands to their mouths, yet unable to eat, etc.; His changing, when a child, His playmates into kids, and animating clay figures of beasts and birds; the practice attributed to Him of appearing to His disciples sometimes as a youth, sometimes as an old man, sometimes as a child, sometimes large, sometimes less, sometimes so tall as to reach the Heavens; and the obeisance paid Him by the military standards when He was brought before Pilate. Of the same cast is the story of His picture presented by Nicodemus to Gamaliel, which, when pierced by the Jews, gave forth blood and water.

[t] Lavington, Enthusiasm of Meth. and Papists comp. Part iii. Sec. 43.
[u] Jones, On the Canon, Part iii.

2. Under this head of exception fall many of the Miracles related by the Fathers ;[v] *e.g.*, that of the consecrated bread changing into a live coal in the hands of a woman, who came to the Lord's supper after offering incense to an idol ; of the dove issuing from the body of Polycarp at his martyrdom ; of the petrifaction of a fowl dressed by a person under a vow of abstinence ; of the exorcism of the demoniac camel ; of the stones shedding tears at the barbarity of the persecutions ; of inundations rising up to the roofs of churches without entering the open doors ; and of pieces of gold, as fresh as from the mint, dropt from heaven into the laps of the Italian Monks.[1]

3. Of the same character are the Miracles of the Romish Breviary ;[2] as the prostration of wild beasts before the martyrs they were about to devour ; the miraculous uniting of two chains with which St. Peter had been at different times bound ; and the burial of Paul the Hermit by lions.

4. Such again are the Rabbinical Miracles, as that of the flies killed by lightning for settling on a rabbi's paper. And the Miracles ascribed by some to Mahomet, as that the trees went out to meet him, the stones saluted him, and a camel complained to him.[x]

---

[v] Middleton, Free Enquiry.

[1] [Vide, however, Essay ii., *infra*, n. 48—50, 54, 58, etc.]

[2] [Vide ibid.]

[x] The offensiveness of these, and many others above in-

The exorcism in the Book of Tobit must here be mentioned, in which the Evil Spirit who is in love with Sara is driven away by the smell of certain perfumes.[y]

5. Hence the Scripture accounts of Eve's temptation by the serpent; of the speaking of Balaam's ass; of Jonah and the whale; and of the devils sent into the herd of swine, are by themselves more or less improbable, being unequal in dignity to the rest. They are then supported by the system in which they are found, as being a few out of a multitude, and therefore but exceptions (and, as we suppose, but apparent exceptions) to the general rule. In some of them, too, a further purpose is discernible, which of itself reconciles us to the strangeness of their first appearance, and suggests the possibility of similar reasons, though unknown, being assigned in explanation of the rest. As the Miracle of the swine, the object of which may have been to prove to us the reality of demoniacal possessions.[z]

6. Miracles of mere power, even when connected with some ultimate object, are often improbable for

stanced, consists in attributing *moral* feelings to inanimate or irrational beings.

[y] [So the Protestant version.] It seems to have been a common notion that possessed persons were beloved by the Spirit possessing them. See Philostr. iv. 25. Gospel of the Infancy, xiv.—xvi., xxxiii. Justin Martyr, Apol. p. 113, Ed. Thirlb. We find nothing of this kind in the account of Scripture demoniacs

[z] Divine Legation, Book ix. Chap. v.

Antecedent Credibility of a Miracle.

the same general reason, viz., as unworthy of an All-wise Author. Such as that ascribed to Zoroaster,[a] of suffering melted brass to be poured upon his breast without injury to himself. Unless indeed their immediate design be to exemplify the greatness of God, as in the descent of fire from heaven upon Elijah's sacrifice, and in Christ's walking on the sea,[b] which evidently possess a dignity fitting them to be works of the Supreme Being. The propriety indeed of the Christian Miracles, contrasted with the want of decorum observable in those elsewhere related, forms a most striking evidence of their divinity.

7. Here, too, ambiguous Miracles find a place, it being antecedently improbable that the Almighty should rest the credit of His Revelation upon events which but obscurely implied His immediate presence.

[a] Brucker, Vol. i. p. 147.

[b] Power over the elements conveyed the most striking proof of Christ's mission from the God of nature, who in the Old Testament is frequently characterized as ruling the sea, winds, etc. Psalm lxv. 7; lxxvii. 19; Job xxxviii. 11, etc. It is said, that a drawing of feet upon the water was the hieroglyphic for impossibility. Christ moreover designed, it appears, to make trial of His disciples' faith by this miracle. See Matt. xiv. 28—31; Mark vi. 52. We read of the power to "move mountains," but evidently as a proverbial expression. The transfiguration, if it need be mentioned, has a *doctrinal* sense, and seems besides to have been intended to lead the minds of the Apostles to the consideration of the Spiritual Kingdom. One of Satan's temptations was to induce our Lord to work a Miracle of mere power. Matt. iv. 6, 7. See Acts x. 38, for the general character of the Miracles.

8. And, for the same reason, those are in some measure improbable which are professed by different Religions; because from a Divine Agent may be expected distinct and peculiar specimens of divine agency. Hence the claims to supernatural power in the primitive Church are in general questionable,[8] as resting upon the exorcism of evil spirits, and the cure of diseases; works, not only less satisfactory than others, as evidence of a miraculous interposition, but suspicious, from the circumstance that they were exhibited also by Jews and Gentiles of the same age.[c] In the plagues of Egypt and Elijah's sacrifice, which seem to be of this class, there is a direct contest between two parties; and the object of the divine messenger is to show his own superiority in the very point in which his adversaries try their powers. Our Saviour's use of the clay in restoring sight has been accounted for on a similar principle, such external means being in repute among the Heathen in their pretended cures.

3. *Those which have no professed Object.*

1. Hence a suspicion is thrown on all miracles ascribed by the Apocryphal Gospels to Christ in His infancy; for, being prior to His preaching, they seem

[8] [Vide Essay ii. *infra*, n. 81, etc.]
[c] Middleton, Stillingfleet, Orig. Sacr. ii. 9, Sec. 1.

to attest no doctrine, and are but distantly connected with any object.

2. Those again on which an object seems to be forced. Hence many harmonizing in one plan arrest the attention more powerfully than a detached and solitary miracle, as converging to one point, and pressing upon our notice the end for which they are wrought. This remark, as far as it goes, is prejudicial to the miracle wrought (as it is said) in Hunneric's persecution, long after the real age of Miracles was past; when the Athanasian confessors are reported to have retained the power of speech after the loss of their tongues.

3. Those, too, must be viewed with suspicion which are disjoined from human instruments, and are made the vehicle of no message;[d] since, according to our foregoing view, Miracles are only then divested of their *à priori* improbability when furthering some great moral end, such as authenticating a divine communication. It is an objection then to those ascribed to relics generally, and in particular to those attributed to the tomb of the Abbé Paris, that they are left to tell their own story, and are but distantly connected with any object whatever. As it is, again, to many tales of apparitions, that they do not admit of a meaning, and consequently demand at most only an otiose assent, as Paley terms it. Hence there is a

[d] Farmer, On Miracles, Chap. v.

difficulty in the narrative contained in the first verses of John v.; because we cannot reduce the account of the descent of the Angel into the water to give it a healing power under any known arrangement of the divine economy. We receive it, then, on the general credit of the Revelation of which it forms part.[e]

4. For the same reason, *viz.*, the want of a declared object, a prejudice is excited when the professed worker is silent, or diffident as to his own power; since our general experience of Providence leads us to suppose that miraculous powers will not be committed to an individual who is not also prepared for his office by secret inspiration. This speaks strongly against the cures ascribed by Tacitus to Vespasian, and would be an objection to our crediting the prediction uttered by Caiaphas, if separated from its context, or prominently brought forward to rest an argument upon. It is in general a characteristic of the Scripture system, that Miracles and inspiration go together.[f]

5. With a view to specify the object distinctly, some have required that the Miracle should be wrought after the delivery of the message.[g] A message delivered an indefinite time after the Miracle, while it cannot

[e] The verse containing the account of the Angel is wanting in many MSS. of authority, and is marked as suspicious by Griesbach. The mineral spring of Bethesda is mentioned by Eusebius as celebrated even in his day.

[f] Douglas, Criterion. Warburton, Sermon on Resurrection.

[g] Fleetwood, Farmer, and others.

but excite attention from the general reputation of the messenger for an extraordinary gift, is not so expressly stamped with divine authority, as when it is ushered in by his claiming, and followed by his displaying, supernatural powers. For if a Miracle, once wrought, ever after sanctions the doctrines taught by the person exhibiting it, it must be attended by the gift of infallibility,—a sustained miracle, which is inconsistent with that frugality in the application of power which is observable in the general course of Providence.[h] On the other hand, when an unambiguous Miracle having been first distinctly announced, is wrought with the professed object of sanctioning a message from God, it conveys an irresistible evidence of its divine origin. Accident is thus excluded, and the final cause indissolubly connected with the supernatural event. I may remark that the Miracles of Scripture were generally wrought on this plan.[i] In conformity to which we find moreover that the Apostles, etc., could not work miracles when they pleased;[k] a circumstance more consistent with our

[h] The idea is accordingly discountenanced, Matt. vii. 22, 23; Heb. vi. 4—6; Gal. ii. 11—14.

[i] St. Mark ends his Gospel by saying, that the Apostles "went forth and preached everywhere, the Lord working with them, and *confirming the word by signs* FOLLOWING," chap. xvi. 20. See also Exodus iv. 29, 30; 1 Kings xiii. 2, 3; 2 Kings xx. 8—11; Acts xiv. 3, etc.

[k] *E.g.*, Acts xx. 22, 23; Phil. ii. 27; 2 Tim. iv. 20. In the Book of Acts we have not a few instances of the Apostles

ideas of the Divine government, and connecting the extraordinary acts more clearly with specific objects, than if the supernatural gifts were unlimited and irrevocable.

6. Lastly, under this head I may notice professed miracles which, as those attributed to Apollonius, may be separated from a narrative without detriment to it. The prodigies of Livy, for instance, form no part in the action of the history, which is equally intelligible without them.[1] The miraculous events of the Pentateuch, on the contrary, or of the Gospels and Acts, though of course they may be rejected together with the rest of the narrative, can be rejected in no other way; since they form its substance and groundwork, and, like the figure of Phidias on

---

acting under the immediate direction of the Holy Spirit. The gift of tongues is an exception to the general remark, as we know it was abused; but this from its nature was, when once given, possessed as an ordinary talent, and needed no fresh divine influence for subsequent exercise of it. It may besides be viewed as a medium of conveying the message, as well as being the seal of its divinity, and as such needed not in every instance to be marked out as a supernatural gift. Miracles in Scripture are not done by wholesale, *i.e.*, indiscriminately and at once, without the particular will and act of the individual; the contrary was the case with the cures at the tomb of the Abbé Paris. Acts xix. 11, 12, perhaps forms an exception; but the Miracles there mentioned are expressly said to be *special*, and were intended to put particular honour on the Apostle; Cf. Luke vi. 19; viii. 46, which seem to illustrate John iii. 34. [But vide Essay ii., n. 83—85.]

[1] *E.g.*, he says, "ADJICIUNT *miracula huic pugnæ*," ii. 7.

Minerva's shield, cannot be erased without spoiling the entire composition.[m]

4. *Those which are exceptionable as regards their Object.*

1. If the professed object be trifling and unimportant; as in many related by the Fathers, *e.g.*, Tertullian's account of the vision of an Angel to prescribe to a female the exact length and measure of her veil, or the divine admonition which Cyprian professes to have received to mix water with wine in the Eucharist, in order to render it efficacious.[n] Among these would be reckoned the directions given to Moses relative to the furnishing of the Tabernacle, and other regulations of the ceremonial law, were not further and important objects thereby effected; such as, separating the Israelites from the surrounding nations, impressing upon them the doctrine of a particular Providence, prefiguring future events, etc.

[m] Whereas other extraordinary accounts are like the statue of the Goddess herself, which could readily be taken to pieces, and resolved into its constituent parts, the precious metal and the stone. For the Jewish Miracles, see Graves, On the Pentateuch, Part i. It has been observed that the *discourses* of Christ so constantly grow out of His *Miracles*, that we can hardly admit the former without admitting the latter also. But His *discourses* form His *character*, which is by no means an obvious or easy one to imagine, had it never existed.

[n] Middleton, Free Inquiry. [No question relative to the Eucharistic rite can be unimportant.]

2. Miracles wrought for the gratification of mere *curiosity* are referable to this head of objection. Hence the triumphant invitations which some of the Fathers make to their heathen opponents to attend their exorcisms excite an unpleasant feeling in the mind, as degrading a solemn spectacle into a mere popular exhibition.

3. Those, again, which have a *political or party object*, as the cures ascribed to Vespasian, or as those attributed to the tomb of the Abbé Paris, and the Eclectic prodigies, all which, viewed in their best light, tend to the mere aggrandizement of a particular Sect, and have little or no reference to the good of Mankind at large. It tells in favour of the Christian Miracles, that the Apostles, generally speaking, were not enabled to work them for their own personal convenience, to avoid danger, escape suffering, or save life. St. Paul's preservation from the effects of the viper's bite on the Isle of Melita is a solitary exception to this remark, no mention being made of his availing himself of this Miracle to convert the natives to the Christian faith.[o]

4. For a similar reason, those bear a less appearance of probability which are wrought for the conviction of individuals. I have already noticed the

[o] Rev. J. Blanco White, Against Catholicism, Let. 6. The Breviary Miracles form a striking contrast to the Christian in this point. [Not surely on the point of their benefiting the worker.]

contrary character of the Scripture Miracles in this respect; for instance, St. Paul's miraculous conversion did not end with itself, but was followed by momentous and inestimable consequences.[p] Again, Miracles attended the conversion of the Æthiopian Eunuch, Cornelius, and Sergius Paulus; but these were heads and firstfruits of different classes of men who were in time to be brought into the Church.[q]

5. Miracles with a bad or vicious object are laden with an extreme antecedent improbability; for they cannot at all be referred to the only known cause of supernatural power, the agency of God. Such are most of the fables concerning the heathen deities; not a few of the professed Miracles of the primitive Church, which are wrought to sanction doctrines opposed not only to Scriptural truth, but to the light of nature;[r] and some related in the Apocryphal Gospels, especially Christ's inflicting death upon a schoolmaster who threatened to strike Him, and on a boy who happened to run violently against Him.[s] Here must be noticed several passages in Scripture, in which a miraculous gift seems at first sight to be exercised to

[p] Acts xxvi. 16.

[q] Ibid. viii. 26, 39; x. 3, etc.; xiii. 12. These three classes are mentioned together in prophecy. Isa. lvi. 4—8.

[r] *E.g.*, to establish Monachism, etc. [Monachism is not unnatural, unless we are prepared to maintain that an unnatural state of life has the sanction of our Lord and St. Paul.]

[s] Jones, On the Canon, Part iii.

gratify revengeful feelings, and which are, therefore, received on the credit of the system.[t]

6. Unnecessary Miracles are improbable; as those wrought for an object attainable without an exertion, or with less exertion, of extraordinary power.[u] Of this kind, we contend, would be the writing of the Gospel on the skies, which some unbelievers have proposed as but an adequate attestation to a Revelation; for, supposing the recorded fact of their once occurring be sufficient for a rational conviction, a perpetual Miracle becomes superfluous.[v] Such, again, would be the preservation of the text of Scripture in its verbal correctness, which many have supposed necessary for its infallibility as a standard of Truth.

7. The same antecedent objection presses on Miracles wrought in attestation of truths already known. We do not, for instance, require a Miracle to convince

[t] Gen. ix. 24—27; Judges xvi. 28—30; 2 Kings ii. 24; 2 Chron. xxiv. 22.

[u] It does not follow, because all Miracles are equally *easy* to an Almighty Author, that all are equally *probable*; for, as has been often remarked, a frugality in the application of power is observable throughout His works.

[v] Dr. Graves observes, of the miraculous agency in the age of Moses and Joshua, that "God continued it *only so long as* was indispensably necessary to introduce and settle the Jewish nation in the land of their inheritance, and establish this dispensation so as to answer the purposes of the divine economy. After this, He gradually withdrew His supernatural assistance; He left the nation collectively and individually to act according to their own choice," etc.—**Lectures on the** Pentateuch, Part iii. Lecture **2.**

us the Sun shines, or that Vice is blameable. The Socinian scheme is in a great measure chargeable with bringing the Miracles of the Gospel under this censure: for it prunes away the Christian system till little is left for the Miracles to attest. On this ground an objection has been taken to the Miracle wrought in favour of the Athanasians in Hunneric's persecution, as above mentioned; inasmuch as it merely professes to authorize a comment on the sacred text, *i.e.*, to sanction a truth which is not new, unless Scripture be obscure.[x] Here, too, may be noticed Miracles wrought in evidence of doctrines already established; such as those of the Papists, who seem desirous of answering the unbeliever's demand for a perpetual Miracle. Popish Miracles, as has often been observed, occur in Popish countries, where they are least wanted; whereas, if real, they would be invaluable among Protestants.[4] Hence the primitive Miracles become suspicious, in proportion as we find Christianity established, not only from the increasing facility of fraud, but moreover from the apparent needlessness of the extraordinary display. And hence, admitting the Miracles of Christ and His followers, future Miracles with the same end are somewhat improbable. For enough have been wrought to attest

[x] See Maclaine's Note on the subject, Mosheim, Eccl. Hist. Cent. v. Part ii. Chap. v. [Vide Essay ii., n. 220, etc.]

[4] [This is answered *infra*, Essay ii., n. 97, etc.]

the doctrine; and attention, when once excited by supernatural means, may be kept alive by a standing Ministry, just as inspiration is supplied by human learning.

8. I proceed to notice inconsistency in the objects proposed, as creating a just prejudice against the validity of miraculous pretensions. This applies to the claims of the Romish Church, in which Miracles are wrought by hostile sects in support of discordant tenets.[y] It constitutes some objection to the bulk of the Miracles of the primitive Church, when viewed as a continuation of the original gift, that they differ so much in manner, design, and attendant circumstances, from those recorded in Scripture.[5] "We see," says Middleton (in the ages subsequent to the Christian era) "a dispensation of things ascribed to God, quite different from that which we meet with in the New Testament. For in those days the power of working Miracles was committed to none but the Apostles, and to a few of the most eminent of the other disciples, who were particularly commissioned to propagate the Gospel and preside in the Church of Christ. But, upon the pretended revival of the same powers in the following Ages, we find the administration of them committed, not to those who were intrusted with the government of the Church, not to the successors

[y] Douglas, Criterion, p. 105, Note (8vo. edit. 1807).
[5] [All this is answered *infra*, Essay ii., n. 96, 101.]

Antecedent Credibility of a Miracle. 43

of the Apostles, to the Bishops, the Martyrs, nor to the principal champions of the Christian cause; but to *boys*, to *women*, and, above all, *to private and obscure laymen*, not only of an inferior but sometimes also of a *bad character*."[z]

9. Hence, to avoid the charge of inconsistency in the respective objects of the Jewish and Christian Miracles, it is incumbent upon believers in them to show that the difference between the two systems is a difference in appearance only, and that Christ came not to destroy but to fulfil the Law. Here, as far as its antecedent appearance is concerned, the Miracle said to have occurred on Julian's attempt to rebuild the Jewish Temple is seen to great advantage. The object was great, the time critical, its consequences harmonize very happily with the economy of the Mosaic Dispensation, and the general spirit of the Prophetical

---

[z] Scripture sometimes attributes miraculous gifts to men of bad character; but we have no reason for supposing such could work miracles at pleasure (see Numb. xxii. 18; xxiii. 3, 8, 12, 20; xxiv. 10—13), or attest any doctrine but that which Christ and His Apostles taught; nor is our faith grounded upon their preaching. Moreover, their power may have been given them for some further purpose; for though to attest a divine message be the primary object of Miracles, it need not be the only object. "It would be highly ridiculous," says Mr. Penrose in his recent work on Miracles, "to erect a steam engine for the mere purpose of opening and shutting a valve; but the engine being erected is very wisely employed both for this and for many other purposes, which, comparatively speaking, are of very little significance." [This applies to ecclesiastical miracles.]

writings, and the fact itself has some correspondence with the prodigies which preceded the final destruction of Jerusalem.[a]

10. Again, Miracles which do not tend to the accomplishment of their proposed end are open to objection; and those which have not effected what they had in view. Hence some kind of argument might be derived against the Christian Miracles, were they not accompanied by a prediction of their temporary failure in effecting their object; or, to speak more correctly, were it not their proposed object gradually to spread the doctrines which they authenticate.[b] There is nothing, however, to break the force of this objection when directed against the Miracles ascribed to the Abbé Paris; since the Jansenist interest, instead of being advanced in consequence of them, soon after lost ground, and was ultimately ruined.[c]

11. These Miracles are also suspicious, as having been stopped by human authority; it being improbable that a Divine Agent should permit any such interference with His plan. The same objection applies to the professed gift of exorcising demoniacs in the primitive Church; which was gradually lost after the decree of the Council of Laodicea confined

[a] See Warburton's Julian.
[b] See Parables in Matt. xiii. 3, 24, 31, 33, 47; xxiv. 12; Acts xx. 29, 30; 2 Thess. ii. 3; 2 Tim. iii. 1—5, etc.
[c] Paley, Evidences, Part i. Prop. 2.

the exercise of it to such as were licensed by the Bishop.[d] And lastly, to the supernatural character of Prince Hohenlohe's cures, which were stopped at Bamberg by an order from authority, that "none should be wrought except in the presence of Magistrates and medical practitioners."[e]

These are the most obvious objections which may be fairly made to the antecedent probability of miraculous narratives. It will be observed, however, that none of them go so far as to deprive testimony for them of the privilege of being heard. Even where the nature of the facts related forbids us to refer the Miracle to divine agency, as when it is wrought to establish some immoral principle, still it is not more than extremely improbable and to be viewed with strong suspicion. Christians at least must acknowledge that the *à priori* view which Reason takes would in some cases lead to an erroneous conclusion. A Miracle, for instance, ascribed to an Evil Spirit is, prior to

[d] It had hitherto been in the hands of the meaner sort of the Christian laity. After that time, "few or none of the clergy, nor indeed of the laity, were any longer able to cast out devils; so that the old Christian exorcism or prayer for the energumens in the church began soon after to be omitted as useless." Whiston, in Middleton. [Vid. Essay ii., n. 59.]

[e] Bentham, Preuves Judiciaires, Liv. viii. Chap. x. [This fact requires testimony stronger than Bentham's. However, as to the Abbé Paris, the epigram is well known,

"De par le roi, defense à Dieu,
De faire miracles en ce lieu."]

the information of Scripture, improbable; and if it stood on its own merits would require very strong testimony to establish it, as being referred to an unknown cause. Yet, on the authority of Scripture, we admit the occasional interference of agents short of divine with the course of nature. This, however, only shows that these *à priori* tests are not decisive. Yet if we cannot always ascertain what Miracles are improbable, at least we can determine what are not so; moreover, it will still be true that the more objections lie against any professed Miracle, the greater suspicion justly attaches to it, and the less important is the fact, even if capable of proof.

On the other hand, even when the external appearance is altogether in favour of the Miracle, it must be recollected, nothing is thereby proved concerning the fact of its occurrence. We have done no more than recommend to notice the evidence, whatever it may be, which is offered in its behalf. Even, then, could Miracles be found with as strong an antecedent case as those of Scripture, still direct testimony must be produced to substantiate their claims on our belief. At the same time, since there are none such, a fair prepossession is indirectly created in favour of the latter, over and above their intrinsic claims on our attention.

Some few indeed of the Scripture Miracles are open to exception; and have accordingly been noticed in the course of the above remarks as by themselves improbable. These, however, are seldom such in more than one respect ; whereas the other Miracles which came before us were open to several or all of the specified objections at the same time. And, further, as they are but a few in the midst of an overpowering majority pointing consistently to one grand object, they must not be torn from their moral context, but, on the credit of the rest, they must be considered but apparent exceptions to the rule. It is obvious that a large system must consist of various parts of unequal utility and excellence ; and to expect each particular occurrence to be complete in itself, is as unreasonable as to require the parts of some complicated machine, separately taken, to be all equally finished and fit for display.[f]

Let these remarks suffice on the question of the antecedent probability or improbability of a miraculous

[f] In thus refusing to admit the existence of *real* exceptions to the general rule, in spite of *appearances*, we are not exposing ourselves to that charge of excessive systematizing which may justly be brought against those who, with Hume, reject the very notion of a Miracle, as implying an interruption of physical regularity. For the Revelation which we admit, on the authority of the general system of Miracles, imparts such accurate and extended information concerning the attributes of God, over and about the partial and imperfect view of them which the world affords, as precludes the supposition of *any* work of His being evil or useless. Whereas there is no *voice* in the mere analogy of nature which expressly denies the possibility of real exceptions to its general course.

narrative. Enough, it may be hoped, has been said to separate the Miracles of Scripture from those elsewhere related, and to invest them with an importance exciting in an unprejudiced mind a just interest in their behalf, and a candid attention to the historical testimony on which they rest; inasmuch as they are ascribed to an adequate cause, recommended by an intrinsic dignity, and connected with an important object, while all others are more or less unaccountable, unmeaning, extravagant, and useless. And thus, *viz.*, on the ground of this utter dissimilarity between the Miracles of Scripture and those reported elsewhere, we are enabled to account for the incredulity with which believers in Revelation listen to any extraordinary account at the present day; and which sometimes is urged against them as inconsistent with their assent to the former. It is because they admit the Scripture Miracles. Belief in these has pre-occupied their minds, and created a fair presumption against those of a different class;—the prospect of a recurrence of supernatural agency being in some measure discountenanced by the Revelation already given; and again, the weakness and insipidity, the want of system and connexion, the deficiency in the evidence, and the transient repute of marvellous stories ever since, creating a strong and just prejudice against those similar accounts which now from time to time are noised abroad.

Section III.

ON THE CRITERION OF A MIRACLE, CONSIDERED AS A DIVINE INTERPOSITION.

IT has sometimes been asked, whether Miracles are a sufficient evidence of the interposition of the Deity? under the idea that other causes, besides divine agency, might be assigned for their production. This is obviously the reverse objection to that I have as yet considered, which was founded on the assumption that they could be referred to no known cause whatever. After showing, then, that the Scripture Miracles may be ascribed to the Supreme Being, I proceed to show that they cannot reasonably be ascribed to those other causes which have been sometimes assigned for them, for instance, to unknown laws of nature, or to the secret agency of Spirits.

1. Now it is evidently unphilosophical to attribute them to the power of invisible Beings, short of God; because, independently of Scripture (the truth of which, of course, must not be assumed in this question), we have no evidence of the existence of such

beings. Nature attests, indeed, the being of a God, but not of a race of intelligent creatures between Him and Man. In assigning a Miracle, therefore, to the influence of Spirits, an hypothetical cause is introduced merely to remove a difficulty. And even did analogy lead us to admit their possible existence, yet it would tend rather to disprove than to prove their power over the visible creation. They may be confined to their own province, and though superior to Man, still may be unable to do many things which he can effect ; just as Man in turn is superior to birds and fishes, without having, in consequence, the power of flying or of inhabiting the water.[g]

Still it may be necessary to show that on our own principles we are not open to any charge of inconsistency. That is, it has been questioned, whether, in admitting the existence and power of Spirits on the authority of Revelation, we are not in danger of invalidating the evidence upon which that authority rests. For the cogency of the argument from Miracles depends on the assumption, that interruptions in the course of nature must ultimately proceed from God ; which is not true, if they may be effected by other beings without His sanction. And it must be conceded that, explicit as Scripture is in considering Miracles as signs of divine agency, it still does seem

[g] Campbell, On Miracles, Part ii. Sec. 3. Farmer, Ch. ii. Sec. 1.

to give created Spirits some power of working them; and even, in its most literal sense, intimates the possibility of their working them in opposition to the true doctrine.[h] With a view of meeting this difficulty, some writers have attempted to make a distinction between great and small, many and few Miracles; and have thus inadvertently destroyed the intelligibility of any, as the *criterion* of a divine interposition.[i] Others, by referring to the nature of the doctrine attested, in order to determine the author of the Miracle, have exposed themselves to the plausible charge of adducing, first, the Miracle to attest the divinity of the doctrine, and then, the doctrine to prove the divinity of the Miracle.[k] Others, on the contrary,

[h] Deut. xiii. 1—3; Matt. xxiv. 24; 2 Thess. ii. 9—11.

[i] More or less, Sherlock, Clarke, Locke, and others.

[k] Prideaux, Clarke, Chandler, etc., seem hardly to have guarded sufficiently against the charge here noticed. There is an appearance of doing honour to the Christian doctrines in representing them as *intrinsically* credible, which leads many into supporting opinions which, carried to their full extent (as they were by Middleton), supersede the need of Miracles altogether. It must be recollected, too, that they who are allowed to praise have the privilege of finding fault, and may reject, according to their *à priori* notions, as well as receive. Doubtless the divinity of a clearly immoral doctrine could not be evidenced by Miracles; for our belief in the moral attributes of God is much stronger than our conviction of the negative proposition, that none but He can interfere with the system of nature. But there is always the danger of extending this admission beyond its proper limits, of supposing ourselves adequate judges of the *tendency* of doctrines, and because unassisted Reason informs us what is moral and immoral

have thought themselves obliged to deny the power of Spirits altogether, and to explain away the Scripture accounts of demoniacal possessions, and the narrative of our Lord's Temptation.[1] Without, however, having recourse to any of these dangerous modes of answering the objection, it may be sufficient to reply, that since, agreeably to the antecedent sentiment of reason, God has adopted Miracles as the seal of a divine message, we believe He will never suffer them to be so counterfeited as to deceive the humble inquirer. Thus the information given by Scripture in nowise undoes the original conclusions of Reason; for it anticipates the objection which itself furnishes, and by revealing the express intention of God in miracu-

in our own case, of attempting to decide on the abstract morality of actions; for many have rejected the miraculous narrative of the Pentateuch, from an unfounded and an unwarrantable opinion, that the means employed in settling the Jews in Canaan were in themselves immoral. These remarks are in nowise inconsistent with using (as was done in a former section) our actual knowledge of God's attributes, obtained from a survey of nature and human affairs, in determining the probability of certain professed Miracles having proceeded from Him. It is one thing to infer from the experience of life, another to imagine the character of God from the gratuitous conceptions of our own minds. From experience we gain but general and imperfect ideas of wisdom, goodness, etc., enough (that is) to bear witness to a Revelation when given, not enough to supersede it. On the contrary, our speculations concerning the Divine Attributes and designs, professing, as they do, to decide on the truth of revealed doctrines, in fact go to supersede the necessity of a Revelation altogether.

[1] Especially Farmer.

lous displays, guarantees to us that He will allow no interference of created power to embarrass the proof thence resulting, of His special interposition.[m] It is unnecessary to say more on this subject; and questions concerning the existence, nature, and limits of spiritual agency will find their place when Christians are engaged in settling among themselves the doctrines of Scripture. We take it, therefore, for granted, as an obvious and almost undeniable principle, that real Miracles, *i.e.*, interruptions in the course of nature, cannot reasonably be referred to any power but divine, because it is natural to refer an alteration in the system to its original author, and because Reason does not inform us of any other being but God exterior to nature; and lastly, because in the particular case of the Scripture Miracles, the workers of them confirm our previous judgment by expressly attributing them to Him.

2. A more subtle question remains, respecting the possible existence of causes in nature, to us unknown, by the supposed operation of which the apparent anomalies may be reconciled to the ordinary laws of the system. It has already been admitted that some difficulty will at times attend the discrimination of miraculous from merely uncommon events; and it must be borne in mind that in this, as in all questions

[m] Fleetwood, On Miracles, Disc. ii. p. 201. Van Mildert's Boyle Lectures, Serm. xxi.

from which demonstration is excluded, it is impossible, from the nature of the case, absolutely to disprove any, even the wildest, hypothesis which may be framed. It may freely be granted, moreover, that some of the Scripture Miracles, if they stood alone, might reasonably be referred to natural principles of which we were ignorant, or resolved into some happy combination of accidental circumstances. For our purpose, it is quite sufficient if there be a considerable number which no sober judgment would attempt to deprive of their supernatural character by any supposition of our ignorance of natural laws, or of exaggeration in the narrative. Raising the dead and giving sight to the blind by a word, feeding a multitude with the casual provisions which one individual among them had with him, healing persons at a distance, and walking on the water, are facts, even separately taken, far beyond the conceivable effects of artifice or accident; and much more so when they meet together in one and the same history. And here Hume's argument from general experience is in point, which at least proves that the ordinary powers of nature are unequal to the production of works of this kind. It becomes, then, a balance of opposite probabilities, whether gratuitously to suppose a multitude of perfectly unknown causes, and these, moreover, meeting in one and the same history, or to have recourse to one, and that a known power, then miraculously exerted for an extraordinary and worthy object. We may safely say no sound reasoner will hesitate on which alternative to decide. While, then, a fair proportion of the Scripture Miracles are indisputably deserving of their name, but a weak objection can be derived from the case of the few which, owing to accidental circumstances, bear at the present day less decisive marks of supernatural agency. For, be it remembered (and it is a strong confirmatory proof that the Jewish and Christian Miracles are really what they profess to be) that though the miraculous character of some of them is more doubtful in one age than in another, yet the progress of Science has made no approximation to a general explication of them on natural principles. While discoveries in Optics and Chemistry have accounted for a host of apparent miracles, they hardly touch upon those of the Jewish and Christian systems. Here is no phantasmagoria to be detected, no analysis or synthesis of substances, ignitions, explosions, and other customary resources of the juggler's art.[n] But, as before, we shall best be able to estimate their character in this respect by contrasting them with other occurrences which have sometimes been considered miraculous. Thus, too, a second line of difference will be drawn between them and the mass of rival prodigies, whether religious or otherwise, to which they are often compared.

[n] See Farmer, Ch. i. Sec. 3.

A Miracle, then, as far as it is an evidence of Divine interposition, being an ascertained anomaly in an established system, or an event without assignable physical cause, those facts, of course, have no title to the name—

1. *Which may be referred to misstatement in the testimony.*

1. Such are many of the prodigies of the Heathen Mythology and History, which have been satisfactorily traced to an exaggeration of natural events. For instance, the fables of the Cyclops, Centaurs, of the annual transformation of a Scythian nation into wolves, as related by Herodotus, etc. Or natural facts allegorized, as in the fable of Scylla and Charybdis. Or where the fact may be explained by supplying a probable omission; as we should account for a story of a man sailing in the air by supposing a balloon described.[o]

2. Or where the Miracle is but verbal, as the poetical prodigy of thunder without clouds, which is little better than a play upon words; for, supposing it to occur, it would not be called thunder. Or as when Herodotus speaks of wool growing on trees; for, even were it in substance the same as wool, it could not be called so without a contradiction in terms.

[o] Bentham, Preuves Judiciaires, Liv. viii. Ch. x.

3. Or where the Miracle is one simply of degree, for then exaggeration is more easily conceivable;—thus many supposed visions may have been but natural dreams.

4. Or where it depends on the combination of a multitude of distinct circumstances, each of which is necessary for the proof of its supernatural character, and where, as in fine experiments, a small mistake is of vast consequence. As those which depend on a coincidence of time, which it is difficult for any person to have ascertained. For instance, the exclamation which Apollonius is said to have uttered concerning the assassination of Domitian at the time of its taking place; and, again, the alleged fact of his appearing at Puteoli on the same morning in which he was tried at Rome. Such, too, in some degree, is the professed revelation made to St. Basil, who is said to have been miraculously informed of the death of the Emperor Julian at the very moment that it took place.[p] Here we may instance many stories of apparitions; as the popular one concerning the appearance of a man to the club which he used to frequent at the moment after his death, who was afterwards discovered to have escaped from his nurses in a fit of delirium shortly before it took place, and actually to have joined his friends. We may add the case related to M. Bonnet, of a woman who pretended to

[p] Middleton, Free Inquiry.

know what was passing at a given time at any part of the globe, and who was detected by the simple expedient of accurately marking the time, and comparing her account with the fact.q In the same class must be reckoned not a few of the answers of the Heathen Oracles, if it be worth while to allude to them; as that which informed Crœsus of his occupation at a certain time agreed upon. In the Gospel, the nobleman's son begins to amend at the very time that Christ speaks the word; but this circumstance does not constitute, it merely increases the Miracle. The argument from Prophecy is, in this point of view, somewhat deficient in simplicity and clearness, as implying the decision of many previous questions: such, for instance, as to the existence of the professed prediction before the event, the interval between the prediction and its accomplishment, the completeness of its accomplishment, etc. Hence Prophecy affords a more learned and less popular proof of Divine interposition than physical Miracles, and, except in cases where it contributes a very strong evidence, is commonly of inferior cogency.

2. *Those which, from suspicious circumstances attending them, may not unfairly be referred to an unknown cause.*

   1. As those which take place in departments of

   q Bentham, Preuves Judiciaires, Liv. viii. Ch. x.

Criterion of a Miracle. 59

nature little understood; for instance, Miracles of Electricity.—Again, an assemblage of Miracles confined to one line of extraordinary exertion in some measure suggests the idea of a cause short of divine. For while their repetition looks like the profession, their similarity argues a want, of power. This remark is disadvantageous to the Miracles of the primitive Church, which consisted almost entirely of exorcisms and cures;[6] to the Pythagorean, which were principally Miracles of sagacity; and, again, to those occurring at the tomb of the Abbé Paris, which were limited to cures, and cures, too, of particular diseases. While the Miracles of Scripture are frugally dispensed as regards their object and seasons, they are carefully varied in their nature; like the work of One who is not wasteful of His riches, yet can be munificent when occasion calls for it.

2. Here we may notice tentative Miracles, as Paley terms them; that is, where out of many trials only some succeed; for inequality of success seems to imply accident, in other words, the combination of unknown physical causes. Such are the cures of scrofula by the King's touch, and those effected in the Heathen Temples;[r] and, again, those at the tomb of the Abbé Paris, there being but eight or nine well-authenticated cures out of the multitude of trials that

[6] [Vide, however, *infra*, Essay ii., n. 82, etc.]
[r] Stillingfleet, Orig. Sacr. Book ii. Ch. x. Sec. 9.

were made.[s] One of the peculiarities of the cures ascribed to Christ is their invariable success.[t]

3. Here, for a second reason, diffidence in the agent casts suspicion on the reality of professed Miracles; for at least we have the sanction of his own opinion for supposing them to be the effect of accident or unknown causes.

4. Temporary Miracles also, as many of the Jansenist and other extraordinary cures,[u] may be similarly accounted for; for, if ordinary causes can undo, it is not improbable they may be able originally to effect. The restoration of Lazarus and the others was a restoration to their former condition, which was mortal; their subsequent dissolution, then, in the course of nature, does not interfere with the completeness of the previous Miracle.

5. The Jansenist cures are also unsatisfactory, as being gradual, and, for the same reason, the professed liquefaction of St. Januarius's blood; a progressive effect being a characteristic, as it seems, of the operations of nature. Hence those Miracles are most perspicuous which are wrought at the word of command; as those of Christ and His Apostles. For this as well as other reasons, incomplete Miracles, as imperfect

[s] Douglas, Criterion, p. 133.

[t] Ibid. p. 260, cites the following texts: Matt. iv. 23, 24; viii. 16; ix. 35; xii. 15; xiv. 12; Luke iv. 40; vi. 19.

[u] Douglas, Criterion, p. 190. Middleton, Free Inquiry, iv. Sec. 3.

cures, are no evidence of supernatural agency; and here, again, we have to instance the cures effected at the tomb of the Abbé Paris.

6. Again, the use of means is suspicious; for a Miracle may almost be defined to be an event without means. Hence, however miraculous the production of ice might appear to the Siamese, considered abstractedly, they would hardly so account it in an actual experiment, when they saw the preparation of nitre, etc., which in that climate must have been used for the purpose. In the case of the Steam-vessel or the Balloon, which, it has been sometimes said, would appear miraculous to persons unacquainted with Science, the chemical and mechanical apparatus employed could not fail to rouse suspicion in intelligent minds. Hence professed Miracles are open to suspicion, if confined to one spot; as were the Jansenist cures. For they thereby became connected with a necessary condition, which is all we understand by a means: for instance, such may often be imputed to a confederacy, which (as is evident) can from its nature seldom shift the scene of action. "The Cock-lane ghost could only knock and scratch in one place."[v] The Apostles, on the contrary, are represented as dispersed about, and working Miracles in various parts of the world.[x] These remarks are, of course, inappli-

[v] Hey's Lectures, Book i. Ch. xvi. Sec. 10.
[x] Douglas, Criterion, p. 337.

cable in a case where the apparent means are known to be inadequate, and are not constantly used ; as our Lord's occasional application of clay to the eyes, which, while it proves that He did not need such instrumentality, conveys also an intimation that all the efficacy of means is derived from His appointment.

3. *Those which may be referred to the supposed operation of a cause known to exist.*

1. Professed Miracles of knowledge or mental ability are often unsatisfactory for this reason ; being in many cases referable to the ordinary powers of the intellect. Of this kind is the boasted elegance of the style of the Koran, alleged by Mahomet in evidence of his divine mission. Hence most of the Miracles of Apollonius, consisting, as they do, in knowing the thoughts of others, and predicting the common events of life, are no criterion of a supernatural gift ; it being only under certain circumstances that such power can clearly be discriminated from the natural exercise of acuteness and sagacity. Accordingly, though a knowledge of the hearts of men is claimed by Christ, it seems to be claimed rather with a view to prove to Christians the doctrine of His Divine Nature than to attest to the world His authority as a messenger from God. Again, St. Paul's prediction of shipwreck on his voyage to Rome was intended to prevent it ; and so was the prediction of Agabus

concerning the same Apostle's approaching perils at Jerusalem.[y]

2. For a second reason, then, the argument from Prophecy is a less simple and striking proof of divine agency than a display of Miracles; it being impossible, in all cases, to show that the things foretold were certainly beyond the ordinary faculties of the mind to have discovered. Yet when this is shown, Prophecy is one of the most powerful of conceivable evidences; strict foreknowledge being a faculty not only above the powers, but even above the comprehension of the human mind.

3. And much more fairly may apparent Miracles be attributed to the supposed operation of an existing physical cause, when they are parallel to its known effects; as chemical, meteorological, etc., phenomena. For though the cause may not, perhaps, appear in the particular case, yet it is known to have acted in others similar to it. For this reason, no stress can be laid on accounts of luminous crosses in the air, human shadows in the clouds, appearances of men and horses on hills, and spectres when they are speechless, as is commonly the case, ordinary causes being assignable in all of these; or, again, on the pretended liquefaction of the blood of St. Januarius, or on the exorcism of demoniacs, which is the most frequent Miracle in the Primitive Church.

[y] Acts xxi. 10—14; xxvii. 10, 21.

4. The remark applies, moreover, to cases of healing, so far as they are not instantaneous, complete, etc.: conditions which exclude the supposition of natural means being employed, and which are strictly fulfilled in the Gospel narrative.

5. Again, some cures are known as possible effects of an excited imagination; particularly when the disease arises from obstruction and other disorders of the blood and spirits, as the cures which took place at the tomb of the Abbé Paris.[z]

6. We should be required to add those cases of healing in Scripture where the faith of the petitioners was a necessary condition of the cure, were not these comparatively few, and some of them such as no imagination could have effected (for instance, the restoration of sight), and some wrought on persons absent; and were not faith often required, not of the patient, but of the relative or friend who brought him to be healed.[a]

7. The force of imagination may also be alleged to account for the supposed visions and voices which some enthusiasts have believed they saw and heard; for instance, the trances of Montanus and his fol-

---

[z] Douglas, Criterion, p. 172.

[a] Mark x. 51, 52; Matt. viii. 5—13. See Douglas, Criterion, p. 258. "Where persons petitioned themselves for a cure, a declaration of their faith was often required, that none might be encouraged to try experiments out of curiosity, in a manner which would have been very indecent, and have tended to many bad consequences." Doddridge on Acts ix. 34.

lowers, the visions related by some of the Fathers, and those of the Romish saints;[7] lastly, Mahomet's pretended night-journey to heaven: all which, granting the sincerity of the reporters, may not unreasonably be referred to the effects of disease or of an excited imagination.

8. Such, it is obvious, might be some of the Scripture Miracles; for instance, the various appearances of Angels to individuals, the vision of St. Paul when he was transported to the third heaven, etc., which accordingly were wrought, as Scripture professes, for purposes distinct from that of evidencing the doctrine, viz., in order to become the medium of a revelation, or to confirm faith, etc. In other cases, however, the supposition of imagination is excluded by the vision having been witnessed by more than one person, as the Transfiguration; or by its correspondence with distinct visions seen by others, as in the circumstances which attended the conversion of Cornelius; or by its connection with a permanent Miracle, as the appearance of Christ to St. Paul in his conversion, is connected with his blindness in consequence, which remained three days.[b]

9. Much more inconclusive are those which are ac-

[7] [The visions of Catholic saints were granted to them, as is said in the next sentence about Scripture visions, "for purposes distinct from that of evidencing the doctrine."]

[b] Paley's Evidences, Part i. Prop. 2.

tually attended by a physical cause known or suspected to be adequate to their production. Some of those who were cured at the tomb of the Abbé Paris were at the time making use of the usual remedies; the person whose inflamed eye was relieved was, during his attendance at the sepulchre, under the care of an eminent oculist; another was cured of a lameness in the knee by the mere effort to kneel at the tomb.[c] Arnobius challenges the Heathens to produce one of the pretended miracles of their gods performed without the application of some prescription.[d]

10. Again, Hilarion's cures of wounds, as mentioned by Jerome, were accompanied by the application of consecrated oil.[e] The Apostles indeed made use of oil in some of their cures,[f] but they more frequently healed without a medium of any kind. A similar objection might be urged against the narrative of Hezekiah's recovery from sickness, both on account of the application of the figs, and the slowness of the cure, were it anywhere stated to have been miraculous.[g] Again, the dividing of the Red Sea, accompanied as it was by a strong east wind, would not have been clearly miraculous, had it not been effected at the word of Moses.

[c] Douglas, Criterion, pp. 143, 184, Note.
[d] Stillingfleet, Book ii. Ch. x. Sec. 9.
[e] Middleton, Free Inquiry, iv. Sec. 2.
[f] Mark vi. 13.
[g] 2 Kings xx. 4--7.

11. Much suspicion, too, is (as some think) cast upon the miraculous nature of the fire, etc., which put a stop to Julian's attempt to rebuild the Temple at Jerusalem, by the possibility of referring it to the operation of chemical causes.

12. Lastly, answers to prayer, however providential, are not miraculous; for in granting them, God acts by means of, not out of, His usual system, making the ordinary course of things subservient to a gracious purpose. Such events, then, instead of evidencing the Divine approbation to a certain cause, must be proved from the goodness of the cause to be what they are interpreted to be. Yet by supposed answers to prayer, appeals to Heaven, pretended judgments, etc., enthusiasts in most ages have wished to sanction their claims to divine inspiration. By similar means the pretensions of the Romish hierarchy have been supported.[8]

Here we close our remarks on the criterion of a Miracle; which, it has been seen, is no one definite peculiarity, applicable to all cases, but the combined force of a number of varying circumstances determining our judgment in each particular instance. It might even be said, that a determinate criterion is almost inconceivable. For when once settled, it might

[8] [But not ultimately founded and rested upon them, as has been the way with enthusiasts.]

appear, as was above remarked, to be merely the physical antecedent of the extraordinary fact; while, on the other hand, from the direction thus given to the ingenuity of impostors, it would soon itself need a criterion to distinguish it from its imitations. Certain it is, that the great variety of circumstances under which the Christian Miracles were wrought, furnishes an evidence for their divine origin, in addition to that derived from their publicity, clearness, number, instantaneous production, and completeness.

The exorcism of demoniacs, however, has already been noticed as being, perhaps, in every case deficient in the proof of its miraculous nature. Accordingly, this class of Miracles seems not to have been intended as a primary evidence of a divine mission, but to be addressed to those who already admitted the existence of evil spirits, in proof of the power of Christ and His followers over them.[h] To us, then, it is rather a doctrine than an evidence, manifesting our Lord's power, as other doctrines instance His mercy.

With regard to the argument from Prophecy, which some have been disposed to abandon on account of the number of conditions necessary for the proof of its supernatural character, it should be remembered,

[h] See Div. Leg. Book ix. Ch. v. Hence the exercise of this gift seems almost to have been confined to Palestine. At Philippi St. Paul casts out a spirit of divination in self-defence (Acts xvi. 16—18). In the transaction related Acts xix. 11—17, Jews are principally concerned.

Criterion of a Miracle.

that inability to fix the exact boundary of natural sagacity is no objection to such prophecies as are undeniably beyond it; and that the mere inconclusiveness of some of those in Scripture, as proofs of Divine Prescience, has no positive force against others contained in it, which furnishes a full, lasting, and, in many cases, growing evidence of its inspiration.[1]

[1] Some unbelievers have urged the irrelevancy of St. Matthew's citations from the Old Testament Prophecies in illustration of the events of Christ's life, *e.g.* ch. ii. 15. It must be recollected, however, that what is evidence in one age is often not so in another. That certain of the texts adduced by the Evangelist furnish at the present day no proof of Divine Prescience, is very true; but unless some kind of argument could have been drawn from them at the time the Gospel was written, from traditional interpretations of their sense, we can scarcely account for St. Matthew's introducing them. The question is, has there been a loss of what was evidence formerly, (as is often the case,) or did St. Matthew bring forward as a prophetical evidence what was manifestly not so, as if to hurt the effect of those other passages, as ch. xxvii. 35, which have every appearance of being real predictions? It has been observed, that Prophecy in general must be obscure, in order that the events spoken of may not be understood before their accomplishment.

Section IV.

ON THE DIRECT EVIDENCE FOR THE CHRISTIAN MIRACLES.

IMPORTANT as are the inquiries which I have hitherto prosecuted, it is obvious that they do not lead to any positive conclusion, whether certain miraculous accounts are true or not. However necessary a direct anomaly in the course of nature may be to rouse attention, and an important final cause to excite interest and reverence, still the quality of the testimony on which the accounts rest can alone determine our belief in them. The preliminary points, however, have been principally dwelt upon, because objections founded on them form the strong ground of unbelievers, who seem in some degree to allow the strength of the direct evidence for the Scripture Miracles. Again, an examination of the direct evidence is less necessary here, because, though antecedent questions have not been neglected by Christian writers,[k] yet the evidence

---

[k] Especially by Vince, in his valuable Treatise on the Christian Miracles ; and Hey, in his Lectures.

Evidence for the Christian Miracles. 71

itself, as might be expected, has chiefly engaged their attention.[1] Without entering, then, into a minute consideration of the facts and arguments on which the credibility of the Sacred History rests, I proceed to contrast its evidence generally with that produced for other miraculous narratives; and thus to complete a comparison which has been already instituted, as regards the antecedent probability and the criterion of Miracles.

For the present, then, I forego the advantage which the Scripture Miracles have gained in the preceding Sections over all professed facts of a similar nature. In reality, indeed, the very same evidence which would suffice to prove the former, might be inadequate when offered in behalf of those of the Eclectic School or the Romish Church. For the Miracles of Scripture, and no other, are unexceptionable, and worthy of a Divine Agent; and Bishop Butler has clearly shown, that, in a practical question, as the divinity of a professed Revelation must be considered, even the weakest reasons are decisive when not counteracted by any opposite arguments.[m] Whatever

---

[1] As of Paley, Lyttelton, Leslie, etc.

[m] The only fair objection that can be made to this statement is, that it is antecedently improbable that the Almighty should work Miracles with a view to general conviction, without furnishing strong evidence that they really occurred. This was noticed above, when the antecedent probability of Miracles was discussed. That it is unsatisfactory to decide on scanty

evidence, then, is offered for them is entirely available to the proof of their actual occurrence; whereas evidence for the truth of other similar accounts, supposing it to exist, would be first employed in overcoming the objections which attach to them all from their very character, circumstances, or object. If, however, it can be shown that the Miracles of Scripture as far surpass all others in their direct evidence, as they excel them in their *à priori* probability, a much stronger case will be made out in their favour, and an additional line of distinction drawn between them and others.

The credibility of testimony arises from the belief we entertain of the character and competency of the witnesses; and this is true, not only in the case of Miracles, but when facts of any kind are examined into. It is obvious that we should be induced to distrust the most natural and plausible statement when made by a person whom we suspected of a wish to deceive, or of relating facts which he had no sufficient means of knowing. Or if we credited his narrative, we should do so, not from dependence on the reporter, but from its intrinsic likelihood, or from circumstantial evidence. In the case of ordinary facts, therefore, we think it needless, as indeed it would be endless, to inquire rigidly into the credibility of the

evidence is no objection, as in other most important practical questions we are constantly obliged to make up our minds and determine our course of action on insufficient evidence.

testimony by which they are conveyed to us, because they in a manner speak for themselves. When, however, the information is unexpected, or extraordinary, or improbable, our only means of determining its truth is by considering the credit due to the witnesses; and then, of course, we exercise that right of scrutiny which we before indeed possessed, but did not think it worth while to claim. A Miracle, then, calls for no distinct species of testimony from that offered for other events, but for a testimony strong in proportion to the improbability of the particular fact attested; and it is as impossible to draw any line, or to determine how much is required, as to define the quantity and quality of evidence necessary to prove the occurrence of an earthquake, or the appearance of any meteoric phenomenon. Everything depends on those attendant circumstances, of which I have already spoken,—the object of the Miracle, the occasion, manner, and human agent employed. If, for instance, a Miracle were said to be wrought for an immoral object, then of course the fact would rest on the credibility of the testimony alone, and would challenge the most rigid examination. Again, if the object be highly interesting to us, as that professed by the Scripture Miracles, we shall naturally be careful in our inquiry, from an anxious fear of being biassed. But in any case the testimony cannot turn out to be more than that of competent and honest men; and an inquiry must not be prosecuted under the idea of finding something beyond this, but to obtain proofs of this.

And since the existence of competency and honesty may be established in various ways, it follows that the credibility of a given story may be proved by distinct considerations, each of which, separately taken, might be sufficient for the purpose. It is obvious, moreover, as indeed is implied by the very nature of moral evidence, that the proof of its credibility may be weaker or stronger, and yet in both cases be a proof; and hence, that no limit can be put to the conceivable accumulation of evidence in its behalf. Provided, then, the existing evidence be sufficient to produce a rational conviction, it is nothing to the purpose to urge, as has sometimes been alleged against the Scripture Miracles, that the extraordinary facts might have been proved by different or more overpowering evidence. It has been said, for instance, that no testimony can fairly be trusted which has not passed the ordeal of a legal examination. Yet, calculated as that mode of examination undoubtedly is to elicit truth, surely truth may be elicited by other ways also. Independent and circumstantial writers may confirm a fact as satisfactorily as witnesses in Court. They may be questioned and cross-questioned, and, moreover, brought up for re-examination in any succeeding age; whereas, however great may be the talents and experience of the men who conduct the legal investigation, yet when they have once closed it, and given in their verdict, we believe upon their credit, and we have no means of examining for ourselves. To say, however, that this kind of evidence might have been added to the other, in the case of the Christian Miracles,[n] is merely to assert that the proof of the credibility of Scripture might have been stronger than it is; which I have already allowed it might have been, without assignable limit.

The credibility, then, of Testimony depending on the evidence of honesty and competency in those who give it, it is prejudicial, first, to their character for honesty—

1. If desire of gain, power, or other temporal advantage may be imputed to them. This would detract materially from the authority of Philostratus, even supposing him to have been in a situation for ascertaining the truth of his own narrative, as he professes to write his account of Apollonius at the instance of his patroness, the Empress Julia, who is known to have favoured the Eclectic cause. Again, the account of the Miracle performed on the door-

[n] Some of our Saviour's Miracles, however, *were* subjected to judicial examination. (See John v. and ix.) In v. 16, the measures of the Pharisees are described by the technical word ἐδίωκον.

keeper at the cathedral at Saragossa, on which Hume insists, rests principally upon the credit of the Canons, whose interest was concerned in its establishment. This remark, indeed, obviously applies to the Romish Miracles generally.[9] The Christian Miracles, on the contrary, were attested by the Apostles, not only without the prospect of assignable worldly advantage, but with the certainty and after the experience of actual suffering.

2. When there is room for suspecting party spirit or rivalry, as in the miraculous biographies of the Eclectic philosophers; in those of Loyola and other saints of the rival orders in the Romish Church; and in the present Mahometan accounts of the Miracles of Mahomet, which, not to mention other objections to them, are composed with an evident design of rivalling those of Christ.[o]

3. Again, a tale once told may be persisted in from shame of retracting, after the motives which first gave rise to it have ceased to act, even at the risk of suffering. This remark cannot apply to the case of the Apostles, until some reason is assigned for their getting up their miraculous story in the first instance. If necessary, however, it could be brought with force against any argument drawn from the perseverance of

---

[9] [The Miracles of Catholic Saints as little benefited their workers as the Miracles of the Apostles.]

[o] See Professor Lee's Persian Tracts, pp. 446, 447.

the witnesses for the cures professedly wrought by Vespasian, "postquam nullum mendacio pretium;" for, as they did not suffer for persisting in their story, had they retracted, they would have gratuitously confessed their own want of principle.

4. A previous character for falsehood is almost fatal to the credibility of a witness of an extraordinary narrative; for instance, the notorious insincerity and frauds of the Church of Rome in other things are in themselves enough to throw a strong suspicion on its testimony to its own Miracles.[10] The primitive Church is in some degree open to a charge of a similar nature.[p] Or an intimacy with suspicious characters; for instance, Prince Hohenlohe's connection with the Romish Church, and that of Philostratus with the Eclectics, since both the Eclectic and Romish Schools have countenanced the practice of what are called pious frauds.[p]

5. Inconsistencies or prevarications in the testimony, marks of unfairness, exaggeration, suppression of particulars, etc. Of all these, Philostratus stands convicted, whose memoir forms a remarkable contrast

[10] [There *have* been frauds among Catholics, and for gain, as among Protestants, whether churchmen or dissenters, or among antiquarians, or transcribers of MSS., or picture-dealers, or horse-dealers; for the "Net gathers of every kind;" but that does not prove the Church to be fraudulent, unless geological or chemical frauds are slurs upon the character of the British Association.]

[p] Hey, Lectures, book i. ch. xii. sec. 15.

to the artless and candid narratives of the Evangelists. The Books of the New Testament, containing as they do separate accounts of the same transactions, admit of a minute cross-examination, which terminates so decidedly in favour of their fidelity, as to recommend them highly on the score of honesty, even independently of the known sufferings of the writers.

6. Lastly, objection may be taken to witnesses who have the opportunity of being dishonest; as those who write at a distance from the time and place of the professed Miracle, or without mentioning particulars, etc. But on these points I shall speak immediately in a different connection.

Secondly, witnesses must be not only honest, but competent also; that is, such as have ascertained the facts which they attest, or who report after examination. Here then I notice—

1. Deficiency of examination implied in the circumstances of the case. As when it is first published in an age or country remote from the professed time and scene of action; for in that case room is given to suspect failure of memory, imperfect information, etc., whereas to write in the presence of those who know the circumstances of the transactions is an appeal which increases the force of the testimony by associating them in it. Accounts, however, whether miraculous or otherwise, possess very little intrinsic authority, when written so far from the time or place

of the transactions recorded, as the biographies of Pythagoras, Apollonius, Gregory Thaumaturgus, Mahomet, Loyola, or Xavier.q The opposite circumstances of the Christian Testimony have often been pointed out. Here we may particularly notice the providential dispersion of the Jews over the Roman Empire before the age of Christ; by which means the Apostles' testimony was given in heathen countries, as well as in Palestine, in the face of those who had both the will and the power to contradict it, if incorrect.

While the testimony of contemporaries is necessary to guarantee the truth of ordinary history, Miracles require the testimony of eye-witnesses. For ordinary events are believed in part from their being natural, but testimony being the main support of a miraculous narrative, must in that case be the best of its kind. Again, we may require the testimony to be circumstantial in reference to dates, places, persons, etc.; for the absence of these seems to imply an imperfect knowledge, and at least gives less opportunity of inquiry to those who wish to ascertain its fidelity.r

Miracles which are not lasting do not admit of adequate examination; as visions, extraordinary voices, etc. The cure of diseases, on the other hand, is a

---

q Paley, Evidences, Part i. Prop. 2.

r The vagueness of the accounts of miraculous interpositions related by the Fathers is pointed out by Middleton. (Free Inquiry, ii. p. 22.) [*Vide infra*, Essay ii., n. 137, 138.]

permanent evidence of a divine interposition; particularly such cures of bodily imperfections as are undeniably miraculous in their nature, as well as permanent; to these, then, our Lord especially appeals in evidence of His divine mission.[s] Lastly, statements are unsatisfactory in which the miracle is described as wrought before a very *few;* for room is allowed for suspecting mistake, or an understanding between the witnesses. Or, on the other hand, those wrought *in a confused crowd;* such are many standing miracles of the Romanists, which are exhibited with the accompaniment of imposing pageants, or on a stage, or at a distance, or in the midst of candles and incense.[11] Our Saviour, on the contrary, bids the lepers He had cleansed *show* themselves to the Priests, and make the customary offering as a *memorial* of their cures.[t] And when He appeared to the Apostles after His Resurrection, He allowed them to examine His hands and feet.[u] Those of the Scripture Miracles which were wrought before few, or in a crowd, were permanent; as cures,[v] and the raising of Jairus's daughter; or were of so vast a nature, that a crowd could not prevent the wit-

---

[s] Matt. xi. 5.

[11] [Candles and incense are commonly used in the daytime; and our Lord wrought many of His miracles in a throng which was pressing upon Him.]

[t] Luke v. 14; xvii. 14.

[u] Luke xxiv. 39, 40.

[v] Mark viii. 22—26.

nesses from ascertaining the fact, as the standing still of the Sun at the word of Joshua.

2. Deficiency of examination implied in the character, etc., of the witnesses: (1) for instance, if there be any suspicion of their derangement, or if there be an evident defect in those bodily or mental faculties which are necessary for examining the Miracle, as when the intellect or senses are impaired. Number in the witnesses refutes charges of this nature; for it is not conceivable that many should be deranged or mistaken at once, and in the same way.

(2) Enthusiasm, ignorance, and habitual credulity, are defects which no number of witnesses removes. The Jansenist Miracles took place in the most ignorant and superstitious district of Paris.[x] Alexander Pseudomantis practised his arts among the Paphlagonians, a barbarous people. Popish Miracles and the juggles of the Heathen Priests have been most successful in times of ignorance.[12]

Yet, while we reasonably object to gross ignorance or besotted credulity in witnesses for a miraculous story, we must guard against the opposite extreme of requiring the testimony of men of science and general knowledge. Men of philosophical minds are often

[x] The Faubourg St. Marcel. Less.

[12] [Might not the same insinuations be thrown out against the miracles of Elisha? On the other hand, was the age of St. Ambrose and St. Augustine ignorant? or that of St. Philip Neri?]

too fond of inquiring into the causes and mutual dependence of events, of arranging, theorizing, and refining, to be accurate and straightforward in their account of extraordinary occurrences. Instead of giving a plain statement of facts, they are insensibly led to correct the evidence of their senses with a view to account for the strange phenomenon; as Chinese painters, who, instead of drawing in perspective, give lights and shadows their supposed meaning, and depict the prospect as they think it should be, not as it is.[y] As Miracles differ from other events only when considered relatively to a general system, it is obvious that the same persons are competent to attest miraculous facts who are suitable witnesses of corresponding natural ones. If a peasant's testimony be admitted to the phenomenon of meteoric stones, he may evidence the fact of an unusual and unaccountable darkness. A physician's certificate is not needed to assure us of the illness of a friend; nor is it necessary for attesting the simple fact that he has instantaneously recovered. It is important to bear this in mind, for some writers argue as if there were something intrinsically defective in the testimony given by ignorant persons to miraculous occurrences.[z] To say that unlearned persons are

[y] It is well known, that those persons are accounted the best transcribers of MSS. who are ignorant of the language transcribed; the habit of *correcting* being almost involuntary in men of letters.

[z] Hume, On Miracles, Part ii. Reason 1.

not judges of the fact of a miraculous event, is only so far true as all testimony is fallible and liable to be distorted by predjudice. Every one, not only superstitious persons, is apt to interpret facts in his own way; if the superstitious see too many prodigies, men of science may see too few. The facility with which the Japanese ascribed the ascent of a balloon, which they witnessed at St. Petersburgh, to the powers of magic, (a circumstance which has been sometimes urged against the admission of unlearned testimony,[a]) is only the conduct of theorists accounting for a novel phenomenon on the principles of their own system.

It may be said, that ignorance prevents a witness from discriminating between natural and supernatural events, and thus weakens the authority of his judgment concerning the miraculous nature of a fact. It is true; but if the fact be recorded, we may judge for ourselves on that point. Yet it may be safely said, that not even before persons in the lowest state of ignorance could any great variety of professed Miracles be displayed without their distinguishing rightly, on the whole, between the effects of nature and those of a power exterior to it; though in particular instances they doubtless might be mistaken. Much more would this be the case with the lower ranks of a civilized people. Practical intelligence is insensibly diffused from class to class; if the upper ranks are educated,

[a] Bentham, Preuves Judiciaires, Liv. viii. Ch. ii.

numbers besides them, without any formal and systematic knowledge, almost instinctively discriminate between natural and supernatural events. Here science has little advantage over common sense; a peasant is quite as certain that a resurrection from the dead is miraculous as the most able physiologist.[b]

The original witnesses of our Saviour's Miracles were very far from a dull or ignorant race. The inhabitants of a maritime and border country, as Galilee was, engaged, moreover, in commerce, composed of natives of various countries, and, therefore, from the nature of the case, acquainted with more than one language, have necessarily their intellects sharpened and their minds considerably enlarged, and are of all men least disposed to acquiesce in marvellous tales.[c] Such a people must have examined before they suffered themselves to be excited in the degree which the Evangelists describe.[d]

[b] It has been observed, that more suitable witnesses could not be selected of the fact of a miraculous draught of fishes than the fishermen of the lake wherein it took place.

[c] See Less, Opuscul.

[d] If, on the other hand, we would see with how unmoved an unconcern men receive accounts of miracles, when they believe them to be events of every-day occurrence, we may turn to the conduct of the African Christians in the Age of Austin, whom that Father in vain endeavoured to interest in miraculous stories of relics, etc., by formal accounts and certificates of the cures wrought by them. (See Middleton, p. 138.) The stir, then, which the miracles of Christ made in Galilee implies, that they were not received with an indolent belief. It must be noticed, moreover, in opposition to the statement of some

But even supposing those among them who were in consequence convinced of the divine mission of Christ, were of a more superstitious turn of mind than the rest, still this is not sufficient to account for their conviction. For superstition, while it might facilitate the bare admission of miraculous events, would at the same time weaken their practical influence. Miracles ceasing to be accounted strange, would cease to be striking also. Whereas the conviction wrought in the minds of these men was no bare and indolent assent to facts which they might have thought antecedently probable or not improbable, but a conversion in principles and mode of life, and a consequent sacrifice of all that nature holds dear, to which none would submit except after the fullest examination of the authority enjoining it. If additional evidence be required, appeal may be made to the multitude of Gentiles in Greece and Asia, in whose principles and mode of living belief in the Miracles made a change even more striking and complete than was effected in the case of the Jews. In a word, then, the conversion which Christ and His Apostles effected invalidates the charge of blind credulity in the witnesses; the practical nature of the belief wrought in them proving that it was founded on an examination of the Miracles.

unbelievers, that great numbers of the Jews were converted (Acts ii. 41; iv. 4; v. 13, 14; vi. 7; ix. 35; xv. 5; xxi. 20). On this subject, see Jenkin, On the Christian Religion, Vol. ii. Ch. xxxii.

(3) Again, it weakens the authority of the witnesses, if their belief can be shown to have been promoted by the influence of superiors; for then they virtually cease to be themselves witnesses, and report the facts on the authority (as it were) of their patrons. It is observable, that the national conversions of the Middle Ages generally began with the princes, and descended to their subjects; those of the Apostolic Age obviously proceeded in the reverse order.[e]

(4) It is almost fatal to the validity of the testimony, if the miracle which is attested coincides with a previous system, or supports a cause already embraced by the witnesses. Men are always ready to believe what flatters their own opinions, and of all prepossessions those of Religion are the strongest. There is so much in the principle of all Religion that is true and good, so much conformable to the best feelings of our nature, which perceives itself to be weak and guilty, and looks out for an unseen and superior being for guidance and support; and the particular worship in which each individual is brought up is so familiarized to him by habit, so endeared to his affections by the associations of place and the recollections of past years, so connected too with the ordinary transactions and most interesting events of life, that even should that form be irrational and degrading, still it will in most cases preserve a strong influence over his mind, and dispose

[e] Mosheim, Eccl. Hist. Cent. vi. viii. ix.

him to credit upon slight examination any arguments adduced in its defence. Hence an account of Miracles in confirmation of their own Religion will always be favourably received by men whose creed has already led them to expect such interpositions of superior beings. This consideration invalidates at once the testimony commonly offered for Pagan and Popish Miracles, and in no small degree that for the Miracles of the primitive Church.[13] The professed cures of Vespasian were performed in honour of Serapis in the midst of his worshippers; and the people of Saragossa, who attested the Miracle wrought in the case of the door-keeper of the Cathedral, had previous faith in the virtues of holy oil.[f]

Here the evidence for the Scripture Miracles is unique. In other cases the previous system has sup-

[13] [Vide Essay ii. n. 36—45. Ecclesiastical Miracles are mainly the rewards of faith; not, strictly speaking, evidence.]

[f] It has been noticed as a suspicious circumstance in the testimony to the reported miracle wrought in the case of the Confessors in the persecution of the Arian Hunneric, that Victor Vitensis, one of the principal witnesses, though writing in Africa, where it professedly took place, and where the individuals thus distinguished were then living, yet refers only to one of them, who was then living at the Athanasian Court at Constantinople, and held in particular honour by Zeno and the Empress.—" If any one doubt the fact, let him go to Constantinople." See the whole evidence in Milner's Church History, Cent. v. Ch. xi.; who, however, strongly defends the miracle. Gibbon pretends to do the same, with a view to provide a rival to the Gospel Miracles.

ported the Miracles, but here the Miracles introduced and upheld the system. The Christian Miracles in particular[g] were received on their own merits; and the admission of them became the turning-point in the creed and life of the witnesses, which thenceforth took a new and altogether different direction. But, moreover, as if their own belief in them were not enough, the Apostles went out of their way to debar any one from the Christian Church who did not believe them as well as themselves.[h] Not content that men should be converted on any ground, they fearlessly challenged refutation, by excluding from their fellowship of suffering any who did not formally assent, as a necessary condition of admittance and a first article of faith, to one of the most stupendous of all the miracles, their Master's Resurrection from the dead;—a procedure this, which at once evinces their own unqualified conviction of the fact, and associates, too, all their converts with them as believers in a miracle contemporary with themselves. Nor is this all; a religious creed necessarily prejudices the mind against admitting the miracles of hostile sects, in the very same proportion in which it leads it to acquiesce in such as support its own dogmas.[i] The Christian Miracles, then, have the strongest of conceivable attestations,

[g] Not to mention those of Moses and Elijah.
[h] Campbell, On Miracles, Part ii. Sec. 1.
[i] Ibid. Part i. Sec. 4.

in the conversion of many who at first were prejudiced against them, and in the extorted confession of enemies, who by the embarrassment which the admission occasioned them, at least showed that they had not made it till after a full and accurate investigation of the extraordinary facts.

(5) It has been sometimes objected, that the minds of the first converts might be wrought upon by the doctrine of a future state which the Apostles preached, and be thus persuaded to admit the miracles without a rigorous examination.[k] But, as Paley well replies, evidence of the truth of the promise would still be necessary; especially as men rather demand than dispense with proof when some great and unexpected good is reported to them. Yet it is more than doubtful whether the promise of a future life would excite this interest; for the desire of immortality, though a natural, is no permanent or powerful feeling, and furnishes no principle of action. Most men, even in a Christian country, are too well satisfied with this world to look forward to another with any great and settled anxiety. Supposing immortality to be a good, it is one too distant to warm or influence them. Much less are they disposed to sacrifice present comfort, and strip themselves of former opinions and habits, for the mere contingency of future bliss. The hope of another life, grateful as it is under affliction, will not

[k] Gibbon, particularly Ch. xv.

induce a man to rush into affliction for the sake of it. The inconvenience of a severe complaint is not outbalanced by the pleasure of a remedy. On the other hand, though we know that gratuitous declarations of coming judgments and divine wrath may for a time frighten weak minds, they will neither have effect upon strong ones, nor produce a permanent and consistent effect upon any. Persons who are thus wrought upon in the present day believe the denunciations because they are in Scripture, not Christianity because Scripture contains them. The authority of Revealed Religion is taken for granted both by the preacher and his hearers. On the whole, then, it seems inconceivable that the promise or threat of a future life should have supplied the place of previous belief in Christianity, or have led the witnesses to admit the Miracles on a slight examination.

(6) Lastly, love of the marvellous, of novelty, etc., may be mentioned as a principle influencing the mind to acquiesce in professed miracles without full examination. Yet such feelings are more adapted to exaggerate and circulate a story than to invent it. We can trace their influence very clearly in the instances of Apollonius and the Abbé Paris, both of whom had excited attention by their eccentricities, before they gained reputation for extraordinary power.[1] Such

---

[1] See the Author's memoir of Apollonius.—Of the Abbé, Mosheim says, "Diem vix obierat, voluntariis cruciatibus et

principles, moreover, are not in general practical, and have little power to sustain the mind under continued opposition and suffering.[m]

These are some of the obvious points which will come into consideration in deciding upon the authority of testimony offered for miracles; and they enable us at once to discriminate the Christian story from all others which have been set up against it. With a view of simplifying the argument, the evidence for the Jewish miracles has been left out of the question;[n] because, though strong and satisfactory, it is not at the present day so directly conclusive as that on which

poenis exhaustus, mirabilis iste homo, quum immensa hominum multitudo ad ejus corpus conflueret; quorum alii pedes ejus osculabantur, alii partem capillorum abscindebant, quam sancti loco pignoris ad mala quævis averruncanda servarent, alii libros et lintea quæ attulerant, cadaveri admovebant quod virtute quadam divina plenum esse putabant. Et statim vis illa mirifica, quâ omne, quod in terrâ hâc reliquit, præditum esse fertur, apparebat," etc. Inquisit. in verit. Miraculor. F. de Paris, Sec. 1.

[m] Paley, Evidences, Part i. Prop. 2.

[n] The truth of the Mosaic narrative is proved from the genuineness of the Pentateuch, as written to contemporaries and eye-witnesses of the miracles; from the predictions contained in the Pentateuch; from the very existence of the Jewish system (Sumner's Records); and from the declarations of the New Testament writers. The miracles of Elijah and Elisha are proved to us by the authority of the Books in which they are related, and by means of the New Testament.

the Christian rest. Nor is it necessary, I conceive, to bring evidence for more than a fair proportion of the Miracles; supposing, that is, those which remain unproved are shown to be similar to them, and indissolubly connected with the same system. It may be even said, that if the single fact of the Resurrection be established, quite enough will have been proved for believing all the Miracles of Scripture.

Of course, however, the argument becomes far stronger when it is shown that there *is* evidence for the great bulk of the miracles, though not equally strong for some as for others; and that the Jewish, sanctioned as they are by the New Testament, may also be established on distinct and peculiar grounds. Nor let it be forgotten, that the Christian story itself is supported, over and above the evidence that might fairly be required for it, by several bodies of testimony quite independent of each other.[o] By separate pro-

---

[o] The fact of the Christian miracles may be proved, first, by the sufferings and consistent story of the original witnesses; secondly, from the actual conversion of large bodies of men in the age in which they are said to have been wrought; thirdly, from the institution, at the time, of a day commemorative of the Resurrection, which has been observed ever since; fourthly, by collateral considerations, such as the tacit assent given to the miracles by the adversaries of Christianity, the Eclectic imitations of them, and the pretensions to miraculous power in the primitive Church. These are distinct arguments; no one of them absolutely presupposes the genuineness of the Scripture narrative, though the force of the whole is much increased when it is proved.

cesses of reasoning it may be shown, that if Christianity was established without miracles, it was, to say the least, an altogether singular and unique event in the history of mankind; and the extreme improbability of so many distinct and striking peculiarities uniting, as it were, by chance in one and the same case, raises the proof of its divine origin to a moral certainty. In short, it is only by being made unnatural that the Christian narrative can be deprived of a supernatural character; and we may safely affirm that the strongest evidence we possess for the most certain facts of other history, is weak compared to that on which we believe that the first preachers of the Gospel were gifted with miraculous powers.

And thus a case is established so strong, that even were there an antecedent improbability in the facts attested, in most judgments it would be sufficient to overcome it. On the contrary, we have already shown their intrinsic character to be exactly such as our previous knowledge of the attributes and government of the Almighty would lead us to expect in works ascribed to Him. Their grandeur, beauty, and consistency; the clear and unequivocal marks they bear of superhuman agency; the importance and desirableness of the object they propose to effect, are in correspondence with the variety and force of the evidence itself.

Such, then, is the contrast they present to all other professed miracles, from those of Apollonius downwards—which have been shown, more or less, to be improbable from the circumstances of the case, inconclusive when considered as marks of divine interference, and quite destitute of good evidence for their having really occurred.

Lastly, it must be observed, that the proof derived from interruptions in the course of nature, though a principal, is yet but one out of many proofs on which the cause of Revealed Religion rests; and that even supposing (for the sake of argument) it were altogether inconclusive at the present day, still the other evidences,[p] as they are called, would be fully equal to prove to us the divine origin of Christianity.

[p] Such as the system of doctrine, marks of design, gradual disclosure of unknown truths, etc., connecting together the whole Bible as the work of one mind :—Prophecy :—the character of Christ :— the morality of the Gospel :—the wisdom of its doctrines, displaying at once knowledge of the human heart, and skill in engaging its affections, etc.

ESSAY II.

THE MIRACLES OF EARLY ECCLESIASTICAL

HISTORY,

COMPARED WITH THOSE OF SCRIPTURE,

AS REGARDS

THEIR NATURE, CREDIBILITY, AND EVIDENCE.

ON ECCLESIASTICAL MIRACLES.

Chapter I.

INTRODUCTION.

1. SACRED History is distinguished from Profane by the nature of the facts which enter into its composition, and which are not always such as occur in the ordinary course of things, but are extraordinary and divine. Miracles are its characteristic, whether it be viewed as biblical or ecclesiastical: as the history of a reign or dynasty more or less approximates to biography, as the history of a wandering tribe passes into romance or poetry, as a constitutional history borders on a philosophical dissertation, so the history of Religion is necessarily of a theological cast, and is occupied with the supernatural. It is a record of "the kingdom of heaven," a manifestation of the Hand of God; and, "the temple of God being opened," and "the ark of His testament," there are "lightnings and voices," the momentary yet re-

curring tokens of that conflict between good and evil, which is waging in the world of spirits from age to age. This supernatural agency, as far as it is really revealed to us, is from its very nature the most important of the characteristics of sacred history, and the mere rumour of its manifestation excites interest in consequence of the certainty of its existence. But since the miraculous statements which are presented to us are often not mere rumours or surmises, but in fact essential to the narrative, it is plain that to treat any such series of events, (for instance, the history of the Jews, or of the rise of Christianity, or of the Catholic Church,) without taking them into account, is to profess to write the annals of a reign, yet to be silent about the monarch,—to overlook, as it were, his personal character and professed principles, his indirect influence and immediate acts.

2. Among the subjects, then, which the history of the early centuries of Christianity brings before us, and which are apt more or less to startle those who with modern ideas commence the study of Church History generally, (such as the monastic rule, the honour paid to celibacy, and the belief in the power of the keys,) it seems right to bestow attention in the first place on the supernatural narratives which occur in the course of it, and of which various specimens will be found in any portion of it which a reader takes in hand. It will naturally suggest itself to him

to form some judgment upon them, and a perplexity, perhaps a painful perplexity, may ensue from the difficulty of doing so. This being the case, it is inconsiderate and almost wanton to bring such subjects before him, without making at least the attempt to assist him in disposing of them. Accordingly, the following remarks have been written in discharge of a sort of duty which a work of Ecclesiastical History involves,[1]—not indeed without a deep sense of the arduousness of such an essay, or of the incompleteness and other great defects of its execution, but at the same time, as the writer is bound to add, without any apology at all for discussing in his own way a subject which demands discussion, and which, if any other, is an open question in the English Church, and has only during the last century been viewed in a light which he believes to be both false in itself, and dangerous altogether to Revealed Religion.

3. It may be advisable to state in the commencement the conclusions to which the remarks which follow will be found to tend; they are such as these:—that Ecclesiastical Miracles, that is, Miracles posterior to the Apostolic age, are on the whole different in object, character, and evidence, from those of Scripture on the whole, so that the one series or family ought never to be confounded with the other;

[1] [The occasion of this Essay was the publication of a portion of Fleury's Ecclesiastical History in English.]

yet that the former are not therefore at once to be rejected; that there was no Age of Miracles, after which miracles ceased; that there have been at all times true miracles and false miracles, true accounts and false accounts; that no authoritative guide is supplied to us for drawing the line between the two; that some of the miracles reported were true miracles; that we cannot be certain how many were not true; and that under these circumstances the decision in particular cases is left to each individual, according to his opportunities of judging.

Chapter II.

ON THE ANTECEDENT PROBABILITY OF THE ECCLESIASTICAL MIRACLES.

4. A FACT is properly called "improbable," only when it has some quality or circumstance attached to it which operates to the disadvantage of evidence adduced in its behalf. We can scarcely avoid forming an opinion for or against any statement which meets us; we feel well-disposed towards some accounts or reports, averse from others, sometimes on no reason whatever beyond our accidental frame of mind at the moment, sometimes because the facts averred flatter or thwart our wishes, coincide or interfere with the view of things familiar to us, please or startle our imagination, or on other grounds equally vague and untrustworthy. Such anticipations about facts are as little blameable as the fancies which spontaneously rise in the mind about a person's stature and appearance before seeing him; and, like such fancies, they are dissipated at once when the real state of the case is in any way ascertained. They

are simply notional; and form no presumption in reason, for or against the facts, or the evidence of the facts, to which they relate.

5. An antecedent improbability, then, in certain facts, to be really such, must avail to prejudice the evidence which is offered in their behalf, and must be of a nature to diminish or destroy its force. Thus it is improbable, in the highest degree, that our friend should have done an act of fraud or injustice; and improbable again, but in a slight degree, that our next-door neighbour should have been highly promoted, or that he should have died suddenly. We do not acquiesce in any evidence whatever that comes to hand even for the latter occurrence, and in none but the very best for the former. Again, there is a general improbability attaching to the notion that the members of certain sects or of certain political parties should commit themselves to this or that cast of opinions, or line of conduct; and, on the other hand, though there is no general improbability that individuals of the poorest class should make large fortunes, yet a strong probability may lie against certain given persons of that class in particular.

6. Now it may be asserted that there is no presumption whatever against miracles generally in the ages after the Apostles, though there may be and is a certain antecedent improbability in this or that particular miracle.

the Ecclesiastical Miracles. 103

There is no presumption against Ecclesiastical Miracles generally, because inspiration has stood the brunt of any such antecedent objection, whatever it be worth, by its own supernatural histories, and in establishing their certainty in fact, has disproved their impossibility in the abstract. If miracles are antecedently improbable, it is either from want of a cause to which they may be referred, or of experience of similar events in other times and places. What neither has been before, nor can be attributed to an existing cause, is not to be expected, or is improbable. But Ecclesiastical Miracles are occurrences not without a parallel; for they follow upon Apostolic Miracles. and they are referable to the Author of the Apostolic as an All-sufficient Cause. Whatever be the regularity and stability of nature, interference with it can be, because it has been; there is One who both has power over His own work, and who before now has not been unwilling to exercise it. In this point of view, then, Ecclesiastical Miracles are more advantageously circumstanced than those of Scripture.

7. What has happened once, may happen again; the force of the presumption against Miracles lies in the opinion entertained of the inviolability of nature, to which the Creator seems to "have given a law which shall not be broken." When once that law is shown to be but general, not necessary, and (if the word may be used) when its *prestige* is once destroyed,

there is nothing to shock the imagination in a miraculous interference twice or thrice, as well as once. What never has yet happened is improbable in a sense quite distinct from that in which a thing is improbable which has before now happened; the improbability of the latter class of facts may be greater or less, it may be very great; but whatever the strength of the improbability, it is different in kind from the improbability attaching to such as admit of being called impossible by those who reject them.

8. It may be urged in reply, that the precedent of Scripture is no special recommendation of Ecclesiastical Miracles; for the abstract argument against miracles, as such, has little or no force, as soon as the mere doctrine of a Creator and Supreme Governor is admitted, and even prior to any reference to inspired history; that there is no question among religious men of the existence of a Cause *adequate* to the production of miracles anywhere or at any period; the question rather is whether He *will* work them; whether the *Ecclesiastical* Miracles themselves, being what and when they were, are probable, not whether there is a general presumption against them all simply *as miracles;* on the other hand, that while the Scripture Miracles avail little as a precedent for subsequent miracles, *as miracles*, for no precedent is wanted, they do actually tend to discredit them, *as being subsequent*, for from the nature of the case irregularities can be

but rarely allowed in any system. It is at first sight not to be expected that the Author of nature should interrupt His own harmonious order at all, though He is powerful to do so ; and therefore the fact of His having done so once makes it only less probable that He will do so again. Moreover, if any recurrence of miraculous action is to be anticipated, it is the recurrence of a similar action, not a manifestation of power, ever so different from it ; whereas the miracles of the ages subsequent to the Apostles are on the whole so very unlike those of which we read in Scripture, in their object, circumstances, nature, and evidence, as even to be disproved by the very contrast. This is what may be objected.

9. Now as far as this representation involves the discussion of the special character and circumstances of the Ecclesiastical Miracles, it will come under consideration in the next Chapter ; here we are only engaged with the abstract question, whether the fact that miracles have once occurred, and that under certain circumstances and with certain characteristics, does or does not prejudice a proof, when offered, of their having occurred again, and that under other circumstances and with other characteristics.

10. On this point many writers have expressed opinions which it is difficult to justify. Thus Bishop Warburton, in the course of some excellent remarks on the Christian miracles, is led to propose a cer-

tain test of true miracles, founded on their professed *object*, and suggests that this will furnish us with means of drawing the line of supernatural agency in the early Church. " If [the *final cause*]," he says, " be so *important* as to make the miracle *necessary to the ends of the dispensation*, this is all that can be reasonably required to entitle it to our belief ; " so far he is vindicating the Apostolic Miracles, and his reasoning is unexceptionable ; but he adds in a note, " Here, by the way, let me observe, that what is now said gives that *criterion* which Dr. Middleton and his opponents, in a late controversy concerning miracles, demanded of one another, and which yet both parties, for some reasons or other, declined to give ; namely, some certain mark to enable men to distinguish, for all the purposes of religion, between true and certain miracles, and those which were false or doubtful."[a] He begins by saying that miracles which subserve a certain object deserve our consideration, he ends by saying that those which do not subserve it do not deserve our consideration, and he makes himself the judge whether they subserve it or not.

11. Bishop Douglas, too, after observing that the miracles of the second and third centuries have a character less clearly supernatural and an evidence less cogent than those of the New Testament, and that the fourth and fifth are " ages of credulity and

[a] Div. Leg. ix. 5.

superstition," and the miracles which belong to them are "wild and ridiculous," proceeds to lay down a *decisive criterion* between true miracles and their counterfeits, and this criterion he considers to be the gift of inspiration in their professed workers. "Though it may be a matter more of curiosity than of use, to endeavour to determine the exact time when miraculous powers were withdrawn from the Church, yet *I think that it may be determined with some degree of exactness.* The various opinions of learned Protestants, who have extended them at all after the Apostles, show how much they have been at a loss with regard to this, which has been urged by Papists with an air of triumph, as if, Protestants not being able to agree when the age of miracles was closed, this were an argument of its not being closed as yet. If there be anything in this objection, though perhaps there is not, *I think I have it in my power to obviate it,* by fixing upon a period, beyond which we may be *certain* that miraculous powers did not subsist." Then he refers to his argument in favour of the New Testament miracles, that "what we know of the attributes of the Deity, and of the usual methods of His government, *inclines us to believe* that miracles will never be performed by the agency and instrumentality of men, but when these men are set apart and chosen by God to be His ambassadors, as it were, to the world, to deliver some message or to preach some doctrine as a law from heaven; and in this case their being vested with a power of working miracles is the best credential of the divinity of their mission." So far, as Warburton, this author keeps within bounds; but next he proceeds, as Warburton also, to extend his argument from a defence of what is true to a test of what is false. "If we set out with this as a *principle*, then shall we easily determine when it was that miracles ceased to be performed by Christians; for we shall be led to conclude that the age of Christian miracles must have ceased with the age of Christian inspiration. So long as Heaven thought proper to set apart any particular set of men to be the authorized preachers of the new religion revealed to mankind, so long, may we rest satisfied, miraculous powers were continued. But whenever this purpose was answered, and inspiration ceased to be any longer necessary, by the complete publication of the Gospel, then would the miraculous powers, *whose end was to prove the truth of inspiration*, be *of course* withdrawn."[b]

12. Here he determines *à priori* in the most positive manner the "end" or object of miracles in the designs of Providence. That it is very natural and quite consistent with humility to form antecedent notions of what is likely and what not likely, as in other matters, so as regards the Divine dealings with us, has been implied above; but it is neither reverent

[b] Pp. 239—241, Edit. 4.

nor philosophical in a writer to "think he has it in his power" to dispense with good evidence in behalf of what professes to be a work of God, by means of a summary criterion of his own framing. His very mode of speech, as well as his procedure, reminds us of Hume, who in like manner, when engaged in invalidating the evidence for all miracles whatever, observes that "nothing is so convenient as a *decisive* argument," (such as Archbishop Tillotson's against the Real Presence,) "which must at least silence the most arrogant bigotry and superstition, and free us from their impertinent solicitations," and then "*flatters himself that he has discovered* an argument of a like nature, which, if just, will, with the wise and learned, be an everlasting check to all kinds of superstitious delusion, and, consequently, will be useful as long as the world endures."

13. It is observable that in another place Douglas had said, that "though we may be certain that God will never reverse the course of nature but for important ends, (the course of nature being the plan of government laid down by Himself,) Infinite Wisdom may see ends highly worthy of a miraculous interposition, the importance of *which may lie hid from our shallow comprehension.* Were, therefore, the miracles, about the credibility of which we now dispute, events brought about by invisible agency, though our being able to discover an important end served by a

miracle would be no weak additional motive to our believing it; yet our *not* being able to discover any such end *could be no motive to induce us to reject it*, if the testimony produced to confirm it be unexceptionable."[c] The author is here speaking of the miracles of the Old and New Testaments, which he believes; and, like a religious man, he feels, contrariwise to Hume, that it is not "convenient," but dangerous, to allow of an antecedent test, which, for what he knows, and before he is aware, may be applied in disproof of one or other instance of those gracious manifestations. But it is far otherwise when he comes to speak of Ecclesiastical Miracles, which he begins with disbelieving without much regard to their evidence, and is engaged, not in examining or confuting, but in burdening with some test or criterion which may avail, in Hume's words, "to silence bigotry and superstition, and to free us from their impertinent solicitations." He acts towards the miracles of the Church, as Hume towards the miracles of Scripture.

14. And surely with less reason than Hume, from a consideration already suggested; because, in being a believer in the miracles of Scripture, he deprives himself of that strong antecedent ground against all miracles whatever, both Scriptural and Ecclesiastical, on which Hume took his stand. Allowing, as he is obliged to allow, that the ecclesiastical miracles are

[c] Page 217.

possible, because the Scripture miracles are true, he rejects ecclesiastical miracles as not subserving the object which he arbitrarily assigns for miracles under the Gospel, while he protects the miracles of Scripture by the cautious proviso, that "Infinite Wisdom may see ends" for an interposition, "the importance of which may lie hid from our shallow comprehension." Yet it is a fairer argument against miraculous agency in a particular instance, before it is known in any case to have been employed, that its object is apparently unimportant, than after such agency has once been manifested. What has been introduced for greater ends may, when once introduced, be made subservient to secondary ones. Parallel cases are of daily occurrence in matters of this world; and if it is allowable, as it is generally understood to be, to argue from final causes in behalf of the being of a God—that is, to apply the analogy of a human framer and work to the relation subsisting between the physical world and a Creator—surely it is allowable also to illustrate the course of Divine Providence and Governance by the methods and procedures of human agents. Now, nothing is more common in scientific and social arrangements than that works begun for one purpose should, in the course of operation, be made subservient, as a matter of course, to lesser ones. A mechanical contrivance or a political organization is continued for secondary objects, when the primary has been attained; and thus miracles begun either for Warburton's object or Douglas's may be continued for others, "the importance of which," in the language of the latter, "may lie hid from our shallow comprehension."

15. Hume judges of professedly Divine acts by *experience;* Bishops Warburton and Douglas by the *probable objects* which a Divine Agent must pursue. Both parties draw extravagant conclusions, and that unphilosophically; but surely we know much less of the designs and purposes of Divine Providence, on which Warburton and Douglas insist, than we know of that physical course of things on which Hume takes his stand. Facts actually come before us; the All-wise Mind is hidden from us. We have a right to form anticipations about facts; we may not, except very reverently and humbly, attempt to trace, and we dare not prescribe, the rules on which Providence conducts the government of the world. The Apostle warns us, "Who hath known the mind of the Lord? and who hath been His counsellor?" And surely, a fresh or additional object in the course of Providence presents a less startling difficulty to the mind than an interposition in the laws of nature. If we conquer our indisposition towards the news of such an interposition by reflecting on the Sovereignty of the Creator, let us not be religious by halves, let us submit our imaginations to the full idea of that inscrutable

the Ecclesiastical Miracles.

Sovereignty, nor presume to confine it within bounds narrower than are prescribed by His own attributes.

16. This, then, is the proper answer to the objection urged against the post-apostolic miracles, on the ground that the first occurrence of miracles does in itself discredit their recurrence, and that the miracles subsequent to those of Scripture differ, in fact, from the Scripture miracles in their objects and circumstances. The ordinary Providence of God is conducted upon a *system ;* and as even the act of creation is now contemplated by some philosophers as possibly subject to law, so it is more probable than not that there is also a law of supernatural manifestations. And thus the occurrence of miracles is rather a presumption for than against their recurrence; such events being not isolated acts, but the indications of the presence of an agency. And again, since every system consists of parts varying in importance and value, so also as regards a dispensation of miracles, "God hath set every one of them in the body as it hath pleased Him;" and even "those members which seem to be more feeble" and less "comely" are "necessary," and are sustained by their fellowship with the more honourable.

17. It may be added that Scripture, as in Mark xvi. 17, 18, certainly does give a *primâ facie* countenance to the idea that miracles are a privilege accorded to true believers, and that where is faith, there will

be the manifested signs of its invisible Author. Hence it was the opinion of Grotius,[d] who is here quoted from his connection with English Theology, and of Barrow, Dodwell, and others, that miracles are at least to be expected as attendants on the labours of Missionaries. Now this Scripture intimation, whether fainter or stronger, does, as far as it goes, add to the presumption in favour of the miracles of ecclesiastical history, by authoritatively assigning them a place in the scheme of Christianity. But this subject, as well as others touched upon in this Chapter, will more distinctly come into review in those which follow.

[d] On Mark xvi. 17, Grotius avows his belief in the continuance of a miraculous agency down to this day. He illustrates that text from St. Justin, St. Irenæus, Origen, Tertullian, Minucius Felix, and Lactantius, as regards the power of exorcism, and refers to the acts of Victor of Cilicia in the Martyrology of Ado, and to the history of Sabinus, Bishop of Canusium, in Greg. Turon., for instances of miraculous protection against poison. As to missions, he asserts that the presence of miraculous agency is even a test whether the doctrine preached is Christ's. " Si quis etiam nunc gentibus Christi ignaris, (illis enim proprie miracula inserviunt, 1 Cor. xiv. 22), ita ut ipse annunciari voluit, annunciat, promissionis vim duraturam arbitror. Sunt enim ἀμεταμέλητα τοῦ θεοῦ δῶρα. Sed nos, cujus rei culpa est in nostra ignaviâ aut diffidentiâ, id solemus in Deum rejicere." Elsewhere he professes his belief in the miracle wrought upon the Confessors under Hunneric, who spoke after their tongues were cut out; and in the ordeals of hot iron in the middle ages (De Verit. i. 17); and in the miracles wrought at the tombs of the Martyrs. Ibid. iii. 7, fin. Vide also De Antichr. p. 502, col. 2.

Chapter III.

ON THE INTERNAL CHARACTER OF THE ECCLESIASTICAL MIRACLES.

18. THE miracles wrought in times subsequent to the Apostles are of a very different character, viewed as a whole, from those of Scripture viewed as a whole; so much so, that some writers have not scrupled to say that, if they really took place, they must be considered as forming another dispensation;[e] and at least they are in some sense supplementary to the Apostolic. This will be evident both on a survey of some of them, and by referring to the language used by the Fathers of the Church concerning them.

I.

19. The Scripture miracles are for the most part evidence of a Divine Revelation, and that for the sake of those who have not yet been instructed in it, and in order to the instruction of multitudes: but the

[e] Vide Middleton's Inquiry, p. 24. et alib. Campbell on Miracles, p. 121.

miracles which follow have sometimes no discoverable or direct object, or but a slight object ; they happen for the sake of individuals, and of those who are already Christians, or for purposes already effected, as far as we can judge, by the miracles of Scripture. The Scripture miracles are wrought by persons consciously exercising under Divine guidance a power committed to them for definite ends, professing to be immediate messengers from heaven, and to be evidencing their mission by their miracles : whereas Ecclesiastical miracles are not so much wrought as displayed, being effected by Divine Power without any visible media of operation at all, or by inanimate or material media, as relics and shrines, or by instruments who did not know at the time what they were effecting, or, if they were hoping and praying for such supernatural blessing, at least did not know when they were to be used as instruments, when not. The miracles of Scripture are, as a whole, grave, simple, and majestic : those of Ecclesiastical History often partake of what may not unfitly be called a romantic character, and of that wildness and inequality which enters into the notion of romance. The miracles of Scripture are undeniably beyond nature : those of Ecclesiastical History are often scarcely more than extraordinary accidents or coincidences, or events which seem to betray exaggerations or errors in the statement. The miracles of Scripture are definite and whole transactions, drawn out and carried through from first to last, with beginning and ending, clear, complete, and compact in the narrative, separated from extraneous matter, and consigned to authentic statements : whereas the Ecclesiastical, for the most part, are not contained in any authoritative form or original document ; at best they need to be extracted from merely historical works, and often are only floating rumours, popular traditions, vague, various, inconsistent in detail, tales which only *happen* to have survived, or which in the course of years obtained a permanent place in local usages or in particular rites or on certain spots, recorded at a distance from the time and country when and where they profess to have occurred, and brought into shape only by the juxta-position and comparison of distinct informations. Moreover, in Ecclesiastical History true and false miracles are mixed : whereas in Scripture inspiration has selected the true to the exclusion of all others.

2.

20. The peculiarity of these miracles, as far as their nature and character are concerned, which is the subject immediately before us at present, will be best understood by an enumeration of some of them, taken almost at random, in the order in which they occur in the authors who report them.

The Life of St. Gregory of Neocæsarea in Pontus

(A.D. 250), is written by his namesake of Nyssa, who lived about 120 years after him, and who, being a native and inhabitant of the same country, wrote from the traditions extant in it. He is called Thaumaturgus, from the miraculous gift ascribed to him, and it is not unimportant to observe that he was the original Apostle of the heathen among whom he was placed. He found at first but seventeen Christians in his diocese, and he was the instrument of converting the whole population both of town and country. St. Basil (A.D. 370), whose see was in the neighbourhood, states this circumstance, and adds, "Great is the admiration which still attends on him among the people of that country, and his memory resides in the Churches new and ever fresh, impaired by no length of time. And therefore no usage, no word, no mystic rite of any sort, have they added to the Church beyond those which he left. Hence many of their observances seem imperfect, on account of the ancient manner in which they are conducted. For his successors in the government of the Churches did not endure the introduction of anything which has been brought into use since his date."[f]

21. St. Gregory of Nyssa tells us that, when he was first coming into his heathen and idolatrous diocese, being overtaken by night and rain, he was obliged, with his companions, to seek refuge in a

[f] De Spir. S. 74.

the Ecclesiastical Miracles. 119

temple which was famous for its oracles. On entering he invoked the name of Christ, and made the sign of the cross, and continued till morning in prayer and psalmody, as was his custom. He then went forward, but was pursued by the Priest of the temple, who threatened to bring him before the magistrates, as having driven the evil spirit from the building, who was unable to return. Gregory tore off a small portion of the book he had with him, and wrote on it the words, "Satan, enter." The Priest, on returning, finding that the permission took effect as well as the former prohibition, came to him a second time, and asked to be instructed about that God who had such power over the demons. Gregory unfolded to him the mystery of the Incarnation; and the pagan, stumbling at it, asked to see a miracle. Nyssen, who has spoken all along as relating the popular account, now says that he has to relate what is "of all the most incredible." A stone of great size lay before them; the Priest asked that it might be made to move by Gregory's faith, and Gregory wrought the miracle. This was followed by the Priest's conversion, but not as an isolated event; for, on his entry into the city, all the inhabitants went out to meet him, and enough were converted on the first day by his preaching to form a church. In no long time he was in a condition to call upon his flock to build a place of worship, the first public Christian edifice on record; which remained to Nyssen's time, in spite of the serious earthquakes which had visited the city.

22. St. Gregory's fame extended into the neighbouring districts, and secular causes were brought for his determination. Among those who came to him were two brothers, who had come into their father's large property, and litigated about the possession of a lake which formed part of it. When his efforts to accommodate their difference failed, and the disputants, being strong in adherents and dependants, were even proceeding to decide the matter by force of arms, Gregory the day before the engagement betook himself to the lake, and passed the night there in prayer. The lake was dried up, and in Nyssen's time its bed was covered with woods, pasture and corn land, and dwellings. Another miracle is attributed to him of a similar character. A large and violent stream, which was fed by the mountains of Armenia, from time to time broke through the mounds which were erected along its course in the flat country, and flooded the whole plain. The inhabitants, who were heathen, having heard the fame of Gregory's miracles, made application to him for relief. He journeyed on foot to the place, and stationed himself at the very opening which the stream had made in the mound. Then invoking Christ, he took his staff, and fixed it in the mud; and then returned home. The staff budded, grew, and became a tree, and the stream never passed

it henceforth : since it was planted by Gregory at the very time when the mound had burst, and was appealed to by the inhabitants,[g] who were converted in consequence, and was still living in Nyssen's time, it became a sort of monument of the miracle. On one of his journeys two Jews attempted to deceive him ; the one lay down as if dead, and the other pretended to lament him, and asked alms of Gregory for a shroud. Gregory threw his garment upon him, and walked on. His companion called on him to rise, but found him really dead. One day when he was preaching, a boy cried out that some one else was standing by Gregory, and speaking instead of him ; at the end of the discourse Gregory observed to the bystanders that the boy was possessed, and taking off the covering which was on his own shoulders, breathed on it, and cast it on the youth, who forthwith showed all the usual symptoms of demoniacs. He then put his hand on him, and his agitation ceased, and his delusion with it.

23. Now, concerning these and similar accounts, it is obvious to remark, on the one hand, that the alleged miracles were wrought in order to the conversion of idolaters ; on the other hand, when we read of stones changing their places, rivers restrained, and

[g] Μεχρὶ τοῦ νῦν τοῖς ἐπιχωρίοις θέαμα γίνεται τό φυτὸν καὶ διήγημα. . . ὄνομα δὲ μεχρὶ τοῦ νῦν ἐστι τῷ δενδρῷ ἡ βακτηρία, μνημόσυνον τῆς Γρηγορίου χάριτος καὶ δυναμεως, τοῖς ἐγχωρίοις ἐν πάντι τῷ χρόνῳ σωζόμενον. T. ii. pp. 991, 992.

lakes dried up, and, at the same time, of buildings remaining in spite of earthquakes, we are reminded, as in the case of the Scripture miracle upon the cities of the plain, that a volcanic country is in question, in which such phenomena are to a great extent coincident with the course of nature. It may be added, that the biographer not only is frequent in the phrases "it is said," "it is still reported," but he assigns as a reason for not relating more of St. Gregory's miracles, that he may be taxing the belief of his readers more than is fitting, and he throughout writes in a tone of apology as well as of panegyric.

24. Next, let us turn to St. Athanasius's biographical notice of St. Antony, who began the solitary life A.D. 270. Athanasius knew him personally, and writes whatever he was able to learn from himself; for "I followed him," he says, "no small time, and poured water upon his hands;" and he adds, that "everywhere he has had an anxious regard to truth." The following are some of the supernatural or extraordinary portions of his narrative. He relates that the enemy of souls appeared to Antony, first like a woman, then like a black child, when he confessed himself to be the spirit of lewdness, and to have been vanquished by the young hermit. Afterwards, when he was passing the night in the tombs, he was attacked by evil spirits, and so severely stricken that he lay speechless till a friend found him next

day.[h] When he was on his first journey into the desert, a large plate of silver lay in his way; he soliloquized thus, "Whence this in the desert? This is no beaten path, no track of travellers; it is too large to be dropped without being missed; or if dropped, it would have been sought after and found, for there is no one else to take it. This is a snare of the devil; thou shalt not, O devil, hinder thus my earnest purpose; unto perdition be it with thee!" As he spoke, the plate vanished. He exhorted his friends not to fear the evil spirits: "They conjure up phantoms to terrify cowards; but sign yourselves with the cross, and go forth in confidence." "Once there appeared to me," he says, on another occasion, "a spirit very tall, with a great show, and presumed to say, 'I am the Power of God,' and 'I am Providence; what favour shall I do thee?' But I the rather spit upon him, naming the Christ, and essayed to strike him, and I think I did; and straightway this great personage vanished with all his spirits at Christ's name. Once he came, the crafty one, when I was fasting, and as a Monk, with the appearance of loaves, and bade me eat: 'Eat, and

---

[h] Eusebius relates of one Natalis, a Confessor of the end of the second century, that he fell into the heresy of Theodotus, a sort of Unitarianism, and was warned by our Lord in visions. On neglecting these, he was severely scourged by angels all through the night. Hist. v. 28. Vide Hieron. adv. Rufin. p. 414.

have over thy many pains; thou too art a man, and art like to be sick;' I, perceiving his craft, rose up to pray. He could not bear it, but vanished through the door, like smoke. Listen to another thing, and that securely and fearlessly; and trust me, for I lie not. One time some one knocked at my door in the monastery; I went out, and saw a person tall and high. 'Who art thou?' says I; he answers, 'I am Satan.' Then I asked, 'Why art thou here?' He says, 'Why do the Monks, and all other Christians, so unjustly blame me? Why do they curse me hourly?' 'Why troublest thou them?' I rejoin. He, 'I trouble them not; they harass themselves; I have become weak. I have no place left, no weapon, no city. Christians are now everywhere; at last even the desert is filled with Monks. Let them attend to themselves, and not curse me, when they should not.' Then I said to him, admiring the grace of the Lord, 'A true word against thy will, who art ever a liar, and never speakest truth; for Christ hath come and made thee weak, and overthrown thee and stripped thee.' At the Saviour's name he vanished; it burned him, and he could not bear it."

25. Once, when travelling to some brethren across the desert, water failed them; they sat down in despair, and let the camel wander. Antony knelt down and spread out his hands in prayer, when a spring of water burst from the place where he was praying. A

person came to him, who was afflicted with madness or epilepsy, and begged his prayers; he prayed for him, and then said, "Go, and be healed." The man refusing to go, Antony said, "If thou remainest here, thou canst not be healed; but go to Egypt, and thy cure shall be wrought in thee." He believed, went, and was cured as soon as he got sight of Egypt. At another time he was made aware that two brothers were overtaken in the desert by want of water; that one was dead, and the other dying; he sent two Monks, who buried the one and restored the other. Once, on entering a vessel, he complained of a most loathsome stench; the boatmen said that there was fish in it, but without satisfying Antony, when suddenly a cry was heard from a youth on board, who was possessed by a spirit. Antony used the name of our Lord, and the sick person was restored. St. Athanasius relates a similar instance of Antony's power, which took place in his presence. When the old man left Alexandria, whither he had gone to assist the Church against the Arians, Athanasius accompanied him as far as the gate. A woman cried after him, "Stop, thou man of God; my daughter is miserably troubled by a spirit." Athanasius besought him too, and he turned round. The girl, in a fit, lay on the ground; but on Antony praying, and naming the name of Christ, she rose restored. It should be observed, that Alexandria was at this time still in a great measure a heathen city. Athanasius says that, while Antony was there, as many became Christians in a few days as were commonly converted in the course of the year. This fact is important, not only as showing us the purpose which his miracles answered, but as informing us by implication that pretensions such as Antony's were not of every day's occurrence then, but arrested attention and curiosity at the time.

26. We have a similar proof of the comparative rareness of such miraculous power in St. Jerome's Life of Hilarion. When the latter visited Sicily, one of his disciples, who was seeking him, heard in Greece from a Jew that "a Prophet of the Christians had appeared in Sicily, and was doing so many miracles and signs, that men thought him one of the old Saints." Hilarion was the first solitary in Palestine, and a disciple of St. Antony. St. Jerome enumerates various miracles which were wrought by him, such as his giving sight to a woman who had been ten years blind, restoring a paralytic, procuring rain by his prayers, healing the bites of serpents with consecrated oil, curing a dropsy, curbing the violence of the sea upon a shore, exorcising the possessed, and among these a camel which had killed many persons in its fury. When he was solemnly buried, ten months after his death, his Monk's dress was quite whole upon him, and his body was entire as if he had been alive, and sent forth a most exquisite fragrance.

27. Sulpicius gives us an account of his master St. Martin's miracles, which encountered much incredulity when he first published it. "I am shocked to say what I lately heard," says his friend to him in his Dialogues; "but an unhappy man has asserted that you tell many lies in your book." As St. Martin was the Apostle of Gaul, the purpose effected by his miracles is equally clear and sufficient, as in the instance of Thaumaturgus; and they are even more extraordinary and startling than his. Sulpicius in his Dialogues solemnly appeals to our Lord that he has stated nothing but what he saw himself, or knew, if not on St. Martin's own word, at least on sure testimony. He also appeals to living witnesses. The following are instances taken from the first of his two works.

28. Before Martin was a Bishop, while he was near St. Hilary at Poictiers, a certain Catechumen, who lived in his monastery, died of a fever, in Martin's absence, without baptism. On his return, the Saint went by himself into the cell where the body lay, threw himself upon it, prayed, and then raising himself with his eyes fixed on it, patiently waited his restoration, which took place before the end of two hours. The man, thus miraculously brought to life, lived many years, and was known to Sulpicius, though not till after the miracle. At the same period of his life he also restored a servant in a family, who had

hung himself, and in the same way. Near Tours, which was his See, a certain spot was commonly considered to be the tomb of Martyrs, and former Bishops had placed an altar there. No name or time was known, and Martin found reason to suspect that the tradition was unfounded. For a while he remained undecided, as being afraid of encouraging either superstition or irreverence; at length he went to the tomb, and prayed to Christ to be told who was buried there, and what his character. On this a dismal shade appeared, who, on being commanded to speak, confessed that he was a robber who had been executed for his crimes, and was in punishment. Martin's attendants heard the voice, but saw nothing. Once, when he was on a journey, he saw at a distance a heathen funeral procession, and mistook it for some idolatrous ceremonial, the country people of Gaul being in the practice of carrying their gods about their fields. He made the sign of the cross, and bade them stop and set down the body; this they were constrained to do. When he discovered their real business, he suffered them to proceed At another time, on his giving orders for cutting down a pine to which idolatrous honour was paid, a heathen said, " If thou hast confidence in thy God, let us hew the tree, and do thou receive it as it falls; if thy Lord is with thee, thou wilt escape harm." Martin accepted the condition, and when the tree was falling upon him, made the sign of the cross; the tree reeled round and fell on the other side. This miracle converted the vast multitude who were spectators of it.[i] About the same time, when he had set on fire a heathen temple, the flames spread to a house which joined it. Martin mounted on to the roof of the building that was in peril, and by his presence warned off the fire, and obliged it to confine itself to the work intended for it. At Paris a leper was stationed at the gate of the city; Martin went up and kissed and blessed him, and his leprosy disappeared.

29. St. Augustine, again, enumerates at the end of his *De Civitate Dei*, certain miracles which he himself had witnessed, or had on good authority, such as these. An actor of the town of Curulis was cured of the paralysis in the act of baptism; this Augustine knew, on what he considered the best authority. A person known to Augustine, who had received earth from the Holy Sepulchre, asked him and another Bishop to place it in some oratory for the profit of worshippers. They did so, and a country youth, who was paralytic, hearing of it, asked to be carried to the spot. After praying there, he found himself recovered, and walked home. By the relics of St. Stephen one man was

[i] Sulpicius adds, "Et vere ante Martinum pauci admodum, imo pæne nulli, in illis regionibus Christi nomen receperant: quod adeò virtutibus illius exemploque convaluit, ut jam ibi nullus locus sit, qui non aut ecclesiis frequentissimis aut monasteriis sit repletus." V. Mart. 10.

cured of a fistula, another of the stone, another of the gout; a child who had been crushed to death by a wheel was restored to life; also a nun, by means of a garment which had been taken to his shrine and thrown over her corpse; and another female by the same means; and another by the oil used at the shrine; and a dead infant who was brought to it. In less than two years even the formal statements given in of miracles wrought at St. Stephen's shrine at Hippo were almost seventy.

3.

30. These miracles are recorded by writers of the fourth century, though they belong, in one case wholly, in another partially, to the history of the third. When we turn to earlier writers, we find similar assertions of the presence of a miraculous agency in the Church, and its manifestations have the same general character. Exorcisms, cures, visions, are the chief miracles of the fourth century; and they are equally so of the second and third, so that the former have a natural claim to be considered the continuation of the latter. But there are these very important differences between the two,—that the accounts in the fourth century are much more in detail than those of the second and third, which are commonly vague and general; and next, that in the second and third those kinds of miraculous operations which are the most

decisive proofs of a supernatural presence are but sparingly or scarcely mentioned.

31. Middleton's enumeration of these primitive miracles, which on the whole may be considered to be correct, is as follows: "The power of raising the dead, of healing the sick, of casting out devils, of prophesying, of seeing visions, of discovering the secrets of men, of expounding the Scriptures, of speaking with tongues."[k] Of these the only two which are in their nature distinctly miraculous are the first and last; and for both of these we depend mainly on the testimony of St Irenæus, who lived immediately after the Apostolical Fathers, that is, close upon the period when even modern writers are disposed to allow that miracles were wrought in the Church. Douglas observes, "If we except the testimonies of Papias and Irenæus, who speak of raising the dead, . . . I can find no instances of miracles mentioned by the Fathers before the fourth century, as what were performed by Christians in their times, but the cures of diseases, particularly the cures of demoniacs, by exorcising them; which last indeed seems to be their favourite standing miracle, and the only one which I find (after having turned over their writings carefully, and with a view to this point,) they challenged their adversaries to come and see them perform."[1]

32. It must be observed, however, that though

[k] Page 72.   Page 232.

certain occurrences are in their character more miraculous than others, yet that a miracle of *degree* may, in the particular case, be quite as clearly beyond the ordinary course of nature. Imagination can cure the sick in certain cases, in certain cases it cannot ; and we shall have a very imperfect view of the alleged miracles of the second and third centuries, if, instead of patiently contemplating the instances recorded, in their circumstances and details, we content ourselves with their abstract character, and suffer a definition to stand in place of examination. Thus if we take St. Cyprian's description of the demoniacs, in which he is far from solitary,[m] we shall find that while it is quite open to accuse him and others of misstatement, we cannot accept his description as it stands, without acknowledging that the conflict between the powers of heaven and the evil spirit was then visibly proceeding as in the time of Christ and His Apostles. " O would you listen to them," he says to the heathen Demetrian, "and see them, when they are adjured and tormented by us with spiritual lashes, hurled with words of torture out of bodies they have possessed, when shrieking and groaning at a human voice, and beneath a power divine laid under lash and stripe, they

---

[m] For ancient testimonies to the power of exorcism, vid. Middleton, pp. 80—90. Douglas's Criterion, p. 232, Note 1. Farmer, On Miracles, pp. 241, 242. Whitby's Preface to Epp. § 10.

confess the judgment to come. You will find that we are entreated of them whom you entreat, feared by them whom you fear, and whom you adore. Surely thus, at least, will you be brought to confusion in these your errors, when you behold and hear your gods at once, upon our questioning, betraying what they are, and unable, even in your presence, to conceal their tricks and deceptions."[n] Again, " You may see them by our voice, and through the operation of the unseen Majesty, lashed with stripes, and scorched with fire; stretched out under the increase of their multiplying penalty, shrieking, groaning, entreating, confessing from whence they came, and when they depart, even in the hearing of their own worshippers; and either leaping out suddenly, or gradually vanishing, as faith in the sufferer aids, or grace in the curer conspires."[o] Passages equally strong might be cited from writers of the same period.

33. And there are other occurrences of a distinctly miraculous character in the earlier centuries, which come under none of Middleton's or Douglas's classes, but which ought not to be overlooked. For instance, a fragrance issued from St. Polycarp when burning at the stake, and on his being pierced with a sword a dove flew out. Narcissus, Bishop of Jerusalem, about the end of the second century, when oil failed for the

[n] Treat. viii. 8. Oxford tr.
[o] Treat. ii. 4. Oxford tr.

lamps on the vigil of Easter, sent persons to draw water instead ; which, on his praying over it, was changed into oil. Eusebius, who relates this miracle, says that small quantities of the oil were preserved even to his time. St. Cyprian speaks of a person who had lapsed in persecution, attempting to communicate ; when on opening the arca, or receptacle in which the consecrated Bread was reserved, fire burst out from it and prevented her. Another, on attending at church with the same purpose, found that he had received from the priest nothing but a cinder.

34. Lastly, in this review of the miracles belonging to the early Church, it will be right to include certain isolated ones which have an historical character, and are accordingly more celebrated than the rest. Such is the miracle of the thundering Legion, that is, of the rain accorded to the prayers of Christian soldiers in the army of Marcus Antoninus, when they were perishing by thirst ; the appearance of a Cross in the sky to Constantine's army, with the inscription, " In hoc signo vinces ; " the sudden death of Arius, close upon his proposed re-admission into the Church, at the prayers of Alexander of Constantinople ; the discovery of the Cross, the multiplication of its wood, and the miracles wrought by it ; the fire bursting forth from the foundations of the Jewish temple, which hindered its rebuilding ; the restoration of the blind man on the discovery of the relics of St. Gervasius and St.

the Ecclesiastical Miracles.

Protasius; and the power of speech granted to the African confessors who had lost their tongues in the Vandal persecution.p These and other such shall be considered separately, before I conclude.

35. Imperfect as is this survey of the miracles ascribed to the ages later than the Apostolic, it is quite sufficient for the purpose for which it has been made; viz., to show that those miracles are on the whole very different in their character and attendant circumstances from the Gospel miracles, which certainly are very far from preparing us for them, or rather at first sight indispose us for their reception.q

4

36. And in the next place this important circumstance must be considered, which is as clear as it is decisive, that the Fathers speak of miracles as having in one sense ceased with the Apostolic period;—that is to say, whereas they sometimes speak of miracles as

---

p For other ancient testimonies to the ecclesiastical miracles, vid. Dodwell. Dissert. in Irenæum. ii. 41—60. Middleton's Inquiry, pp. 2—19. Brook's Defens. Miracl. Eccl. pp. 16—22. Mr. Isaac Taylor's Anc. Christ. part 7.

q On the difference between the miracles of Scripture and of Ecclesiastical History, vid. Douglas's Crit. pp. 221—237. Paley's Evidences, Part i. Prop. 2. Middl. pp. 21—26, 91—96, etc. Bishop Blomfield's Sermons, note on p. 82. Dodwell attempts to draw a line between the Ante-Nicene and the later miracles, in favour of the former (Dissert. in Iren. ii. 62—66), as regards testimony, nature, instrument, and object.

existing in their own times, still they say also that *Apostolic* miracles, or miracles *like* the Apostles', whether in their object, cogency, impressiveness, or character, were no longer of occurrence in the Church; an interpretation which they themselves in some passages give to their own testimony. "Argue not," says St. Chrysostom, "because miracles do not happen now, that they did not happen then. . . . In those times they were profitable, and now they are not." He proceeds to say that, in spite of this difference, the mode of conviction was substantially the same. "We persuade not by philosophical reasonings, but from Divine Scripture, and we recommend what we say by the miracles then done. And then, too, they persuaded not by miracles only, but by discussion." And presently he adds, "The more evident and constraining are the things which happen, the less room there is for faith."[r] And again in another passage, "Why are there not those now who raise the dead and perform cures? I will not say why not; rather, why are there not those now who despise the present life? why serve we God for hire? When, however, nature was weak, when faith had to be planted, then there were many such; but now He wills not that we should hang on these miracles, but be ready for death."[s]

37. In like manner St. Augustine introduces his

[r] Hom. in 1 Cor. vi. 2 and 3.
[s] Hom. 8, in Col. § 5.

catalogue of contemporary miracles, which has been partly given above, by stating and allowing the objection that miracles were not then as they had been. "Why, say they, do not these miracles take place now, which, as you preach to us, took place once? I might answer that they were necessary before the world believed, that it might believe."[t] He then goes on to say that miracles were wrought in his time, only they were not so public and well-attested as the miracles of the Gospel.

38. St. Ambrose, on the discovery of the bodies of the two Martyrs, uses the language of surprise; which is quite in accordance with the feelings which the miracles of Antony and Hilarion seem to have roused in Alexandria and in Sicily. "You know, you yourselves saw, that many were cleansed from evil spirits; very many, on touching with their hands the garment of the Saints, were delivered from the infirmities which oppressed them. The *miracles of the old time* are come *again*, when by the advent of the Lord Jesus a fuller grace was shed upon the earth." Under a similar feeling[u] he speaks of the two corpses, which happened to be of large size, as "miræ magnitudinis, ut prisca ætas ferebat."[v]

---

[t] De Civ. Dei, xxii. 8, § 1.

[u] Ep. i. 22, § 9. The same feeling of reverence for times past must be taken partly to account for the expressions ἴχνη and ὑπολέλειπται in Origen, Eusebius, etc., below note a.

[v] Ibid. § 2.

39. And Isidore of Pelusium, after observing that in the Apostles holiness of life and power of miracles went together, adds, "Now, too, if the life of teachers rivalled the Apostolic bearing, perhaps miracles would take place; though if they did not, such life would suffice for the enlightening of those who beheld it."[x]

40. The doctrine, thus witnessed by the great writers of the end of the fourth century, is supported by as clear a testimony two centuries before and two centuries after. Pope Gregory, at the end of the sixth, in commenting on the text, "And these signs shall follow those that believe," says, "Is it so, my brethren, that, because ye do not these signs, ye do not believe? On the contrary, they were necessary in the beginning of the Church: for, that faith might grow, it required miracles to cherish it withal; just as when we plant shrubs, we water them till they seem to thrive in the ground, and as soon as they are well rooted we cease our irrigation. This is what Paul teaches, 'Tongues are a sign, not for those who believe, but for those who believe not;' and there is something yet to be said of these signs and powers of a more recondite nature. For Holy Church doth spiritually every day, what she then did through the Apostles, corporally. For when the Priests by the grace of exorcism lay hands on believers, and forbid evil spirits to

[x] Ep. iv 80.

inhabit their minds, what do they but cast out devils? And any believers soever who henceforth abandon the secular words of the old life, and utter holy mysteries, and rehearse, as best they can, the praise and power of their Maker, what do they but speak with new tongues? Moreover, while by their good exhortations they remove evil from the hearts of others, they are taking up serpents, etc.; . . . which miracles are the greater, because they are the more spiritual: the greater, because they are the means of raising, not bodies, but souls; these signs, then, dearest brethren, by God's aid, ye do if ye will."[y] And St. Clement of Alexandria, at the end of the second century: "If it was imputed to Abraham for righteousness on his believing, and we are the seed of Abraham, we too must believe by hearing. For Israelites we are, who are obedient, not through signs,[z] but through hearing."[a]

[y] In Evang. ii. 29.

[z] Strom. ii. 6, p. 444. So Mr. Osburn, (Errors Apost. Fathers, p. 12,) and I think rightly. The Bishop of Lincoln, however, observes, "I find *only one* passage in the writings of Clement which has any bearing on the question of the existence of miraculous powers in the Church;" and proceeds to refer to the Extracts from the writings of Theodotus. Kaye's Clement, p. 468. The Bishop argues, in his work upon Tertullian, that miracles had then ceased, from a passage in the De Pudicitiâ, in which, after saying that the Apostles had spiritual powers peculiar to themselves, Tertullian adds, "Nam et mortuos suscitaverunt, quod Deus solus; et debiles redintegraverunt, quod nemo nisi Christus; immo et plagas inflixerunt, quod voluit Christus." c. 21.

[a] The following passages will be found to testify to the same

5.

41. What the distinctions are between the Apostolic and the later miracles, which allow of the Fathers saying in a true sense that miracles ceased with the first age, has in many ways appeared from what has already come before us. For instance, it has appeared that the Ecclesiastical Miracles were but locally known, or were done in private; or were so like occurrences which are not miraculous as to give rise to

general fact, that the special miraculous powers possessed by the Apostles did not continue in the Church after them. Eusebius says that, according to St. Irenæus, instances of miraculous powers, ἐν ἐκκλησίαις τισὶν ὑπολέλειπτο, Hist. v. 7. ἴχνη, of the miracles still remain, says Origen contra Cels. i. 2, fin. ἴχνη, καί τινά γε μείζονα. *Ibid.* ii. 8. ἴχνη παρ ὀλίγοις. *Ibid.* vii. 8, fin. In two of these passages the gift is connected with holiness of life, a doctrine which Dodwell denies to have existed till the middle ages, Dissert. in Iren. ii. 64, though he is aware of these passages. οὐδὲ ἴχνος ὑπολέλειπται, Chrysost. de Sacerd. iv. 3, fin. οἱ δὲ νῦν πάντες ὁμοῦ cannot do as much as St. Paul's handkerchiefs. *Ibid.* iv. 6. He implies that the dead were not raised in his day. "If God saw that the raising of the dead would profit the living, He would not have omitted it." De Lazar. iv. 3. "Where is the Holy Spirit now? a man may ask; for then it was appropriate to speak of Him, when miracles took place, and the dead were raised, and all lepers were cleansed; but now," etc. De Sanct. Pent. i. 3. He adds that now we have the sanctifying gifts instead. So, again, "The Apostles indeed enjoyed the grace of God in abundance; but if *we* were bid raise the dead, or open the eyes of the blind, or cleanse lepers, or straighten the lame, or cast out devils, and heal the like disorders," etc. Ad Demetr. i. 8. "When the knowledge of Him as yet was doubt and perplexity, at the time or afterwards, as to their real character; or they were so unlike the Scripture Miracles, so strange and startling in their nature and circumstances, as to need support and sanction rather themselves than to supply it to Christianity; or they were difficult from their drift, or their instruments or agents, or the doctrine connected with them. In a word, they are not primarily and directly evidence of Revelation, though they may become so accidentally,

---

not spread abroad, then miracles used to take place; but now there is no need of that teaching, the facts themselves proclaiming and manifesting the Lord." In Psalm cxlii. 5. Vid. also Inscript. Act. ii. 3. Speaking of the miracles in the wilderness, he says, "In our case also, when we came out of error, many wonders were displayed; but after that they stopped, when religion was planted everywhere. And if subsequently they happened [to the Jews], they were few and scattered, as when the sun stood, etc., and this too has appeared in our case;" and then he goes on to mention the "fiery eruption at the temple," etc., in Matth. Hom. iv. 1. And ibid. Hom. xxxii. 7, after mentioning the Apostolic miracles of cleansing lepers, exorcising spirits, and raising the dead, he says, "This is the greatest proof of your nobleness and love, to believe God without pledges; for this is one reason, among others, why God ceased miracles. . . Seek not miracles, then, but health of soul." And then he contrasts with visible miracles the "greater" ones of beneficence, self-command, etc., to the end of the Homily. And in Joan. "Now, too, there are those who seek and say, Why are there not miracles now? If thou art faithful as behoveth, and love Christ as thou shouldest, miracles thou needest not." Hom. xxiv. 1. Elsewhere, after speaking of the gift of the Spirit dwelling in us, he adds, "Not that we may raise the dead, nor cleanse lepers, but that or to certain persons, or in the way of confirmation. That they are not the direct evidence of revealed truth, is fully granted by St. Augustine in the following striking passage from one of his works against the Donatists :—

42. "Let him prove that we must hold to the Church in Africa only, to the loss of the nations, or again that we must restore and complete it in all nations from Africa ; and prove it, not by saying 'It is true, because I say it,' or 'because my associate says it,' or

---

we show forth the greatest miracle of all, charity," in Rom. Hom. viii. 7. After quoting the text, "We are changed into the same image from glory to glory," he adds, "This was shown more manifestly when the gifts of miracles were in operation ; but even now it is not difficult to discern it when a man has believing eyes," etc., in 2 Cor. Hom. vii. 5. In like manner, St. Augustine, after mentioning the Apostolic miracles, "Sanati languidi, mundati leprosi, incessus claudis, cæcis visus, surdis auditus est redditus," and the changing of water into wine, the multiplication of the loaves, etc., continues, "Cur, inquis, ista modò non fiunt ? quia non moverent, nisi mira essent : at si solita essent, mira non essent." De Util. cred. 16. He adds, in his Retractations, "Hoc dixi, quia non tanta, nec omnia modo, non quia nulla fiunt etiam modo." Again, "Cum Ecclesia Catholica per totum orbem diffusa atque fundata sit, nec miracula illa in nostra tempora durare permissa sunt, ne animus semper visibilia quæreret," etc. De Ver. Rel. 25. He adds, in his Retractations, "Non sic accipiendum est quod dixi, ut nunc in Christi nomine fieri miracula nulla credantur. Nam ego ipse, quando istum ipsum librum scripsi, ad Mediolanensium corpora Martyrum in eâdem civitate cæcum illuminatum fuisse jam noveram," etc. Vid. also Pope Greg. Mor. xxvii. 18.

'my associates,' or 'these our Bishops,' 'Clerks,' or 'people;' or 'it is true because Donatus, or Pontius, or any one else, did these or those marvellous acts,' or 'because men pray at the shrines of our dead brethren, and are heard,' or 'because this or that happens there,' or 'because this brother of ours,' or 'that our sister,' 'saw such and such a vision when he was awake,' or 'dreamed such and such a vision when he was asleep.' Put away what are either the fictions of men who lie, or the wonders of spirits who deceive. For either what is reported is not true, or, if among heretics wonders happen, we have still greater cause for caution, inasmuch as our Lord, after declaring that certain deceivers were to be, who should work some miracles, and deceive thereby, were it possible, even the elect, added an earnest charge, in the words, 'Behold, I have told you before.' Whence also the Apostle warns us that 'the Spirit speaketh expressly, in the latter times some shall depart from the faith, giving heed to seducing spirits, and doctrines of devils.' Moreover, if any one is heard who prays at the shrines of heretics, what he receives, whether good or bad, is consequent not upon the merit of the place, but upon the merit of his own earnest desire. For 'the Spirit of the Lord,' as it is written, 'hath filled the whole world,' and 'the ear of His zeal heareth all things.' And many are heard by God in anger; of whom saith the Apostle. 'God gave them up to the desires of their own hearts.' And to many God in favour gives not what they wish, that He may give what is profitable. . . . Read we not that some were heard by the Lord God Himself in the high places of Judah, which high places notwithstanding were so displeasing to Him, that the kings who overthrew them not were blamed, and those who overthrew them were praised? Thus it appears that the state of heart of the suppliant is of more avail than the place of supplicating.

43. "Concerning deceitful visions, they should read what Scripture says, that 'Satan himself transforms himself into an angel of light,' and that 'dreams have deceived many.' And they should listen, too, to what the Pagans relate, as regards their temples and gods, of wonders either in deed or vision; and yet 'the gods of the heathen are but devils, but it is the Lord that made the heavens.' Therefore many are heard and in many ways, not only Catholic Christians, but Pagans and Jews and heretics, involved in various errors and superstitions; but they are heard either by seducing spirits, (who do nothing, however, but by God's permission, judging in a sublime and ineffable way what is to be bestowed upon each;) or by God Himself, whether for the punishment of their wickedness, or for the solace of their misery, or as a warning to them to seek eternal salvation. But salvation itself and life eternal no one attains, unless he hath Christ the Head. Nor can any one have Christ the Head, who is not in

His body, which is the Church; which, as the Head Himself, we are bound to discern in holy canonical Scripture, not to seek in the various rumours of men, and opinions, and acts, and sayings, and sights.

44. "Let no one therefore object such facts who is prepared to answer me; for I too am far from claiming credit for my position, that the communion of Donatus is not the Church of Christ, on the ground that certain bishops in it are convicted, in records ecclesiastical, and municipal, and judicial, of burning the sacred books, . . . or that the Circumcelliones have committed so much evil, or that some of them cast themselves down precipices, or throw themselves into the fire, . . . or that at their sepulchres herds of strollers, men and women, in a state of drunkenness and abandonment, bury themselves in wine day and night, or pollute themselves with deeds of profligacy. Let all this be considered merely as their chaff, without prejudice to the Church, if they themselves are really holding to the Church. But whether this be so, let them prove only from canonical Scripture; just as we do not claim to be recognized as in the Church of Christ, because the body to which we hold has been graced by Optatus of Milevis or Ambrose of Milan, or other innumerable Bishops of our communion, or because it is set forth in the Councils of our colleagues, or because through the whole world in holy places, which are frequented by our communion, so

great marvels take place, whether answers to prayer, or cures; so that the bodies of Martyrs, which had lain concealed so many years, (as they may hear from many if they do but ask,) were revealed to Ambrose, and in presence of those bodies a man long blind and perfectly well known to the citizens of Milan recovered his eyes and sight; or because one man has seen a vision, or because another has been taken up in spirit, and heard either that he should not join, or that he should leave, the party of Donatus. All such things which happen in the Catholic Church, are to be approved because they are in the Catholic Church; not she manifested to be Catholic, because these things happen in her."[b]

6.

45. So far St. Augustine; it being granted, however, that the object of Ecclesiastical Miracles is not, strictly speaking, that of evidencing Christianity, still they may have other uses, known or unknown, besides that of being the argumentative basis of revealed truth; and therefore it does not at once destroy the credibility of such miraculous narratives, vouched to us on good authority, that they have no assignable object, or an object different from those which are specified in Scripture, as was observed in the foregoing Chapter.

[b] De Unit. Eccl. 49, 50.

the Ecclesiastical Miracles.

46. Here we are immediately considering the *internal character* of the miracles later than the Apostolic period: and what real prejudice ought to attach to them from the dissimilarity or even contrariety of many of them to the Scripture Miracles will be best ascertained by betaking ourselves to the argument from Analogy, and attempting to measure these occurrences by such rules and suggestions as the works of God, brought before us whether in the visible creation or in Scripture, may be found to supply. And first of the natural world as it meets our senses:—

47. "All the works of the Lord are exceeding good," says the son of Sirach; "a man need not to say, What is this? Wherefore is that? for He hath made all things for their uses." Yet an exuberance and variety, a seeming profusion and disorder, a neglect of severe exactness in the prosecution of its objects, and of delicate adjustment in the details of its system, are characteristics of the world both physical and moral, and characteristics of Scripture also; but still the Wise Man assures us, that the purposes of the Creator are not forgotten by Him, or missed because they are hidden, or the work faulty because it is subordinate or incomplete. All things are not equally good in themselves, because they are diverse, yet everything is good in its place. "All the works of the Lord are good, and He will give every needful thing in

due season. So that a man cannot say, This is worse than that; for in time they shall all be well approved."[c] To persons who have not commonly the opportunity of witnessing for themselves this great variety of the Divine works, there is something very strange and startling,—it may even be said, unsettling—in the first view of nature as it is. To take, for instance, the case of animal nature, let us consider the effect produced upon the mind on seeing for the first time the many tribes of the animal world, as we find them brought together for the purposes of science or exhibition in our own country. We are accustomed, indeed, to see wild beasts more or less from our youth, or at least to read of them; but even with this partial preparation, many persons will be moved in a very singular way on going for the first time, or after some interval, to a menagerie. They have been accustomed insensibly to identify the wonder-working Hand of God with the specimens of its exercise which they see about them; the forms of tame and domestic animals, which are necessary for us, and which surround us, are familiar to them, and they learn to take these as a sort of rule on which to frame their ideas of the animated works of the Creator generally. When an eye thus habituated to certain forms, colours, motions, and habits in the inferior animals, is suddenly brought into the full assemblage of those mysterious beings,

[c] Ecclus. xxxix. 16—35

with which it has pleased Almighty Wisdom to people the earth, a sort of dizziness comes over it, from the impossibility of our reducing all at once the multitude of new ideas poured in upon us to the centre of view habitual to us; the mind loses its balance, and it is not too much to say, that in some cases it even falls into a sort of scepticism. Nature seems to be too powerful and various, or at least too strange, to be the work of God, according to that Image which our imbecility has set up within us for the Infinite and Eternal, and as we have framed to ourselves our contracted notions of His attributes and acts; and if we do not submit ourselves in awe to His great mysteriousness, and chasten our hearts and keep silence, we shall be in danger of losing our belief in His presence and providence altogether.

48. We have hitherto known enough of Him for our personal guidance, but we have not understood that only thus much has been the extent of our knowledge of Him. Religion we know to be a grave and solemn subject, and some few vague ideas of greatness, sublimity, and majesty, have constituted for us our whole image of Him whom the Seraphim adore. And then we are suddenly brought into the vast family of His works, hardly one of which is a specimen of those particular and human ideas with which we have identified the Ineffable. First, the endless number of wild animals, their independence of man,

and uselessness to him ; then their exhaustless variety ; then their strangeness in shape, colour, size, motions, and countenance; not to enlarge on the still more mysterious phenomena of their natural propensities and passions ; all these things throng upon us, and are in danger of overpowering us, tempting us to view the Physical Cause of all as disconnected from the Moral, and that, from the impression borne in upon us, that nothing we see in this vast assemblage is *religious* in our sense of the word "religious." We see full evidence there of an Author,—of power, wisdom, goodness ; but not of a Principle or Agent correlative to our religious ideas. But without pushing this remark to an extreme point, or dwelling on it further than our present purpose requires, let two qualities of the works of nature be observed before leaving the subject, which (whatever explanation is to be given of them, and certainly some explanation is not beyond even our limited powers) are at first sight very perplexing. One is that principle of *deformity*, whether hideousness or mere homeliness, which exists in the animal word; and the other (if the word may be used with due soberness) is the *ludicrous ;*—that is, judging of things, as we are here judging of them, by their impression upon our minds.

49. It is obvious to apply what has been said to the case of the miracles of the Church, as compared with those in Scripture. Scripture is to us a garden

of Eden, and its creations are beautiful as well as "very good;" but when we pass from the Apostolic to the following ages, it is as if we left the choicest valleys of the earth, the quietest and most harmonious scenery, and the most cultivated soil, for the luxuriant wildernesses of Africa or Asia, the natural home or kingdom of brute nature, uninfluenced by man. Or rather, it is a great injustice to the times of the Church, to represent the contrast as so vast a one; and Adam might much more justly have been startled at the various forms of life which were brought before him to be named, than we may rationally presume to decide that certain alleged miracles in the Church are not really such, on the ground that they are unlike those to which our eyes have been accustomed in Scripture. There is far greater difference between the appearance of a horse or an eagle and a monkey, or a lion and a mouse, as they meet our eye, than between even the most august of the Divine manifestations in Scripture and the meanest and most fanciful of those legends which we are accustomed without further examination to cast aside. Such contrary properties, or rather such impressions of them on our minds, may be the necessary consequence of Divine Agency moving on a system, and not by isolated acts; or the necessary consequence of its deigning to work with or through the eccentricities, the weaknesses, nay, the wilfulness, of the human mind. As, then, birds are different from beasts, as tropical plants differ from the productions of the north, as one scene is severely beautiful, and another rich or romantic, as the excellence of colours is incommensurate with excellence of form, as pleasures of sight have nothing in common with pleasures of scent, except that they are pleasures; so also in the case of those works and productions which are above or beside the ordinary course of nature, in spite of their variety, "to every thing there is a season, and a time to every purpose under the heaven," and " He hath made every thing beautiful in His time." And, as one description of miracles may be necessary for evidence, viz., such as are at once majestic and undeniable, so for those other and manifold objects which the economy of the Gospel kingdom may involve, a more hidden and intricate path, a more complex exhibition, a more exuberant method, a more versatile rule, may be essential; and it may be as shallow a philosophy to reject them merely because they are not such as we should have expected from God's hand, or as we find in Scripture, as to judge of universal nature by the standard of our own home, or again, with the ancient heretics, to refuse to admit that the Creator of the physical world is also the Father of our Lord Jesus Christ.

50. Nay, it may even be urged that the variety of nature is antecedently a reason for expecting variety in a supernatural agency, if such be introduced; or,

the Ecclesiastical Miracles.

again, (as has been already observed,) if such agency is conducted on a system, it must even necessarily involve diversity and inequality in its separate parts; and, granting it was intended to continue after the Apostolic age, the want of uniformity between the miracles first wrought and those which followed, as far as it is found, might have been almost foretold without the gift of prophecy in that age, or at least may be fully vindicated in this,—nay, even the inferiority of the Ecclesiastical Miracles to the Apostolic; for, if Divine Wisdom had determined, as is not difficult to believe, that the wonderful works which illuminate the history of the first days of the Church should be the best and highest, what was left to subsequent times, by the very terms of the proposition, but miracles which are but second best, which must necessarily have belonged to some other and independent system if they too were the best, and which admit of belonging to the same system for the very reason that they are not the best?

7.

51. So much, then, on the general correspondence between the works of nature, on the one hand, and the Miracles of sacred history, whether Biblical or Ecclesiastical, viewed as one whole, on the other. And while the physical system bears such an analogy to the supernatural system, viewed in its Biblical and

Ecclesiastical portions together, as forms a strong argument in defence of the supernatural, it is, on the other hand, so far unlike the Biblical portion of that supernatural, when that portion is taken by itself, as to protect the portion not Biblical from objections drawn from any differences observable between it and the portion which is Biblical. If it be true that the Ecclesiastical Miracles are in some sense an innovation upon the idea of the Divine Economy, as impressed upon us by the Miracles of Scripture, it is at least equally true that the Scripture Miracles also innovate upon the impressions which are made upon us by the order and the laws of the natural world; and as we reconcile our imagination, nevertheless, to such deviation from the course of nature in the Economy of Revelation, so surely we may bear without impatience or perplexity that the subsequent history of Revelation should in turn diverge from the path in which it originally commenced.[d]

[d] This is Middleton's ground in the following passage, with which should be compared the passages from Hume in the text: "The present question concerning the reality of the miraculous powers of the primitive Church depends on the joint credibility of the facts, pretended to have been produced by those powers, and of the witnesses who attest them. If either part be infirm, their credit must sink in proportion; and if the facts especially be incredible, must *of course* fall to the ground, *because* no force of testimony can alter the nature of things. The credibility of facts lies open to the trial of our reason and senses, but the credibility of witnesses depends on

the Ecclesiastical Miracles.

52. Hume argues against miracles generally, "Though the Being to whom the miracle is ascribed be, in this case, Almighty, it does not, upon that account, become a whit more probable; since it is impossible for us to know the attributes or actions of such a Being, otherwise than from the experience which we have of His productions in the usual course

a variety of principles wholly concealed from us; and though in many cases it may reasonably be presumed, yet in none can it certainly be known. For it is common with men, out of crafty and selfish views, to dissemble and deceive; or out of weakness and credulity to embrace and defend with zeal what the craft of others had imposed upon them; but plain facts cannot delude us—cannot speak any other language, or give any other information but what flows from nature and truth. The testimony, therefore, of facts, as it is offered to our senses in this wonderful fabric and constitution of worldly things, may properly be called the *testimony of God Himself,* as it carries with it the surest instruction in all cases, and to all nations, which in the ordinary course of His providence He has thought fit to appoint for the guidance of human life." Pp. ix. x.

Again, "Our first care should be to inform ourselves of the proper nature and condition of those miraculous powers, . . . as they are represented to us in the history of the Gospel; for till we have learned from those sacred records what they really were, for what purposes granted, and in what manner exerted by the Apostles and first possessors of them, we cannot form a proper judgment on those evidences which are brought either to confirm or confute their continuance in the Church, and must dispute consequently at random, as chance or prejudice may prompt us, about things unknown to us." P. xi.

Again, "The whole which the wit of man can possibly discover either of the ways or will of the Creator, must be acquired . . not by imagining vainly within ourselves what may be proper or improper for Him to do, but by looking abroad and contemof nature."[e] And elsewhere he says, "The Deity is known to us only by His productions. . . . As the universe shows wisdom and goodness, we infer wisdom and goodness. As it shows a particular degree of these perfections, we infer a particular degree of them, precisely adapted to the effect which we examine. But further attributes, or further degrees of the same attributes, we can never be authorized to infer or suppose, by any rules of just reasoning."[f] And in a note he adds, "In general, it may, I think, be established as a maxim, that where any cause is known only by its particular effects, it must be impossible to infer any new effects from that cause. . . . To say that the new effects proceed only from a continuation of the same energy, which is already known from the first effects, will not remove the difficulty. For even granting this to be the case, (which can seldom be supposed,) the very continuation and exertion of a like energy, (for it is impossible it can be absolutely the same,) I say, this exertion of a like energy, in a different period of space and time, is a very arbitrary supposition, and what there cannot possibly be any traces of in the

plating *what He has actually* done; and attending seriously to that revelation which He made of Himself from the beginning, and placed continually before our eyes, in the wonderful works and beautiful fabric of this visible world." P. xxii.

[e] Essay on Miracles, Part ii. circ. fin.
[f] Essay on Providence.

the Ecclesiastical Miracles.

effects, from which all our knowledge of the cause is originally derived. Let the inferred cause be exactly proportioned, as it should be, to the known effect; and it is impossible that it can possess any qualities, from which new or different effects can be inferred."

53. This is not the place to analyze a paradox which is sufficiently refuted by the common sense of a religious mind; but the point which concerns us to consider is, whether persons who, not merely question, but prejudge the Ecclesiastical Miracles on the ground of their want of resemblance, whatever that be, to those contained in Scripture,—as if the Almighty could not do in the Christian Church anything but what He had already done at the time of its foundation, or under the Mosaic Covenant,—whether such reasoners are not siding with the sceptic who in the above passages denies that the First Cause can act supernaturally at all, because in nature He can but act naturally, and whether it is not a happy inconsistency by which they continue to believe the Scripture record, while they reject the records of the Church.

54. Indeed, it would not be difficult to show that the miracles of Scripture are a far greater innovation upon the economy of nature than the miracles of the Church upon the economy of Scripture. There is nothing, for instance, in nature at all to parallel and mitigate the wonderful history of the assemblage of

all animals in the Ark, or the multiplication of an artificially prepared substance, such as bread. Walking on the sea, or the resurrection of the dead, is a plain reversal of its laws. On the other hand, the narrative of the combats of St. Antony with evil spirits is a development rather than a contradiction of Revelation ; viz., as illustrating such texts as speak of Satan being cast out by prayer and fasting. To be shocked then at the miracles of Ecclesiastical History, or to ridicule them for their strangeness, is no part of a scriptural philosophy.

55. Nor can the argument from *à priori* ideas of propriety be made available against Ecclesiastical Miracles with more safety than the argument from experience. This method of refutation, as well as the other, (to use the common phrase,) proves too much. Those who have condemned the miracles of the Church by such a rule, have before now included in their condemnation the very notion of a miracle altogether, as the creation of barbarous and unphilosophical minds, who knew nothing of the beautiful order of nature, and as unworthy to be introduced into our contemplation of the providences of Divine Wisdom. A miracle has been considered to argue a defect in the system of moral governance, as if it were a correction or improvement of what is in itself imperfect or faulty, like a patch of new cloth upon an old garment. The Platonists of old were influenced by something like this

feeling, as if none but low and sordid persons would either attempt or credit miracles truly such, and none but quacks and impostors would profess them. The only true miracles, in the conception of such a school, are miracles of knowledge;—words or deeds which are the result of a greater insight into, or foresight of, the course of nature, and are proofs of a liberal education and a cultivated and reflective mind.[g] It is easy to see how a habit of this sort may grow upon scientific men, especially at this day, unless they are on their guard against it. There is so much beauty, majesty, and harmony in the order of nature, so much to fill, satisfy, and tranquillize the mind, that by those who are accustomed to the contemplation, the notion of an infringement of it will at length be viewed as a sort of profanation, and as even shocking, as the mere dream of ignorance, the wild and atrocious absurdity

[g] Hence the charge against the Christians of magic, or γοητεία. Tertull. Apol. 23. Origen in Cels. i. 38, ii. 9. Arnob. contr. Gent. i. Euseb. Dem. Ev. iii. 5 and 6, pp. 112, 130. August. Serm. xliii. 4, contr. Faust. xii. 45, Ep. cxxxviii. fin. Julian calls St. Paul the greatest of rogues and conjurors, τὸν πάντας πανταχοῦ τοὺς πώποτε γόητας καὶ ἀπατεῶνας ὑπερβαλλόμενον Παῦλον. Ap. Cyr. iii. p. 100. Apollonius professed a knowledge of nature as the secret of his miracles. Vid. Philostr. Vit. Ap. v. 12. Also Quæst. ad Orthod. 24, where Apollonius is said to have done his miracles κατὰ τὴν ἐπιστήμην τῶν φυσικῶν δυνάμεων, not κατὰ τὴν θείαν αὐθεντίαν. Philostratus illustrates this when he seems to doubt whether the young woman was really dead, whom Apollonius raised, iv. 45. [Vid. Kortholt. de Vit. et Mor. Christ. c. 3, 4.]

of superstition and enthusiasm, (if it is right to use such language even in order to describe the thoughts of others,) and as if analogous, to take another and less serious subject, to some gross solecism, or indecorum, or wanton violation of social usages or feelings. We should be very sure, if we resolve on rejecting the Ecclesiastical Miracles, that our reasons are better than that false zeal for our Master's honour, which such philosophers express for the honour of the Creator, and which reminds us of the exclamation, " Be it far from Thee, Lord: this shall not be unto Thee!" as uttered by one who heard for the first time that doctrine which to the world is foolishness.

8.

56. The question has hitherto been argued on the admission, that a distinct line can be drawn in point of character and circumstances between the Miracles of Scripture and those of Church History; but this is by no means the case. It is true, indeed, that the Miracles of Scripture, viewed as a whole, recommend themselves to our reason, and claim our veneration, beyond all others, by a peculiar dignity and beauty; but still it is only as a whole that they make this impression upon us. Some of them, on the contrary, fall short of the attributes which attach to them in general, nay, are inferior in these respects to certain ecclesiastical miracles, and are received only on the

credit of the system, of which they form part. Again, specimens are not wanting in the history of the Church, of miracles as awful in their character and as momentous in their effects, as those which are recorded in Scripture. The fire interrupting the rebuilding of the Jewish temple, and the death of Arius, are instances, in Ecclesiastical History, of such solemn events. On the other hand, difficult facts in the Scripture history are such as these:—the serpent in Eden, the Ark, Jacob's vision for the multiplication of his sheep, the speaking of Balaam's ass, the axe swimming at Elisha's word, the miracle on the swine, and various instances of prayers or prophecies, in which, as in that of Noah's blessing and curse, words which seem the result of private feeling are expressly or virtually ascribed to a Divine suggestion.

57. And thus, it would seem, there exists in matter of fact that very connection and intermixture between ecclesiastical and Scripture miracles, which, according to the analogy suggested in a former page, the richness and variety of physical nature rendered probable. Scripture history, far from being broadly separated from ecclesiastical, does in part countenance what is strange in the miraculous narratives of the latter, by affording patterns and precedents for them itself. It begins a series which has, indeed, its higher specimens and its lower, but which still proceeds in the way of a series, with a progress and continuation, without any

sudden breaks and changes, or even any exact law of variation according to the succession of periods. As in the natural world the animal and vegetable kingdoms imperceptibly melt into each other, so are there mutual affinities and correspondences between the two families of miracles as found in inspired and uninspired history, which show that, whatever may be their separate peculiarities, yet as far as concerns their internal characteristics, they admit of being parts of one system.

58. For instance, there is not a more startling, yet a more ordinary gift in the history of the first ages of the Church than the power of exorcism; while at the same time it is open to much suspicion, both from the comparative facility of imposture and the intrinsic strangeness of the doctrine it inculcates. Yet, here Scripture has anticipated the Church in all respects, even going the length of testifying to the diabolical possession of brutes, which appears so extravagant when introduced, as instanced above, into the life of Hilarion by St. Jerome. Again, that relics should be the instruments of exorcism is an aggravation of a doctrine already difficult; yet we read in Scripture, " And God wrought special miracles by the hands of Paul, so that from his body were brought unto the sick handkerchiefs or aprons, and the diseases departed from them, and the evil spirits went out of them."[h]

[h] Acts xix. 11, 12.

Similar precedents for a supernatural presence in things inanimate are found in the miracles wrought by the touch of our Saviour's garments, not to insist on what is told us about St. Peter's shadow. Again, we have to take into account the resurrection of the corpse which touched Elisha's bones, a work of Divine Power, which, whether considered in its appalling greatness, the absence of apparent object, and the means through which it was accomplished, we should think incredible, with the now prevailing notions of miraculous agency, were we not familiar with it. Elijah's mantle is another instance of a relic endued with miraculous power. Again, the multiplication of the wood of the Cross (the *fact* of which is not here determined, but must depend on the testimony and other evidence producible) is but parallel to Elisha's multiplication of the oil, and of the bread and barley, and to our Lord's multiplication of the loaves and fishes. Again, the account of the consecrated host becoming a cinder in unworthy hands is not so strange as the very first miracle wrought by Moses, the first evidential miracle recorded in Scripture, when his rod became a serpent, and then a rod again; nor stranger than our Lord's first miracle, when water was turned into wine. When the tree was falling upon St. Martin, he is said to have caused it to whirl round and fall elsewhere by the sign of the Cross; is this more startling than

Elisha's causing the iron axe-head to swim by throwing a stick into the water?

59. It is objected by Middleton, that after the decree of the Council of Laodicea, restricting exorcism to such as were licensed by the Bishop, the practice died away;[1] this, indeed, implies a very remarkable committal or almost abandonment of a Divine gift, supposing it such, to the discretion of its human instruments; but how does it imply more than we read of in the Apostolic history of the Corinthian Christians, who had so absolute a possession of their supernatural powers that they could use them disorderly, or pervert them to personal ends? The miracles in Ecclesiastical History are often wrought without human instruments, or by instruments but partially apprehensive that they are such; but did not the rushing mighty wind, at Pentecost, come down "suddenly" and unexpectedly? and were not the Apostles forthwith carried away by it, not in any true sense *using* the gift, but compelled to speak as the Spirit gave them utterance? It is objected that ecclesiastical miracles are not so distinct and unequivocal as to have a claim to be accounted true, but admit of being plausibly attributed to fraud, collusion, or misstatement in narrators; yet, in like manner, St. Matthew tells us that the Jews persisted in maintaining that the disciples had stolen away

[1] Inquiry, pp. 95, 96.

our Lord's Body, and He did not show Himself, when risen, to the Jews; and various other objections, to which it is painful to do more than allude, have been made to other parts of the sacred narrative. It is objected that St. Gregory's, St. Martin's, or St. Hilarion's miracles were not believed when first formally published to the world by Nyssen, Sulpicius, and St. Jerome; but it must be recollected that Gibbon observes scoffingly, that "the contemporaries of Moses and Joshua beheld with careless indifference the most amazing miracles," that even an Apostle, who had attended our Lord through His ministry, did not believe his brethren's report of His resurrection, and that St. Paul's supernatural power of punishing offenders was doubted at Corinth by the very parties who had seen his miracles and had been his converts. That alleged miracles, then, should admit of doubt, or be what is called "suspicious," is not at all inconsistent with their title to be considered the immediate operation of Divine Power.

60. It is observable also, that this intercommunion of miracles, if the expression may be used, which exists between the respective supernatural agencies contained in Scripture and in Church history, is seen also in the separate portions of Scripture history. The miracles of Scripture may be distributed into the Mosaic, the Prophetical, and the Evangelical; of which

the first are mainly of a judicial and retributive character, and wrought on a large field; the last are miracles of mercy; and the intermediate are more or less of a romantic or poetical cast. Yet, among the Mosaic we find the changing of the rod into a serpent, and the sweetening of the water by a branch, which belong rather to the second period; and among the Christian are the deaths of Ananias and Sapphira, which resemble the awful acts of the first; while Philip's transportation by the Spirit, and the ship's sudden arrival at the shore, might be ranked among those of the second.

9.

61. And moreover this circumstance is worth considering, that a sort of analogy exists between the Ecclesiastical and Evangelical histories, and the Prophetical and Mosaic. The Prophetical and Ecclesiastical are, each in its place, a sort of supplement to the supernatural manifestations with which the respective Dispensations open, and present to us a similar internal character. And, whereas there was an interval between the age of Moses and the revival of miraculous power in the Prophets, though extraordinary providences were never wholly suspended, so the Ecclesiastical gift is restricted in its operation in the first centuries compared with the exuberant exercise recorded of it in the fourth and fifth; and as the

the Ecclesiastical Miracles. 167

Prophetical miracles in a great measure belong to the schools of Elijah and Elisha, so the Ecclesiastical have a special connection with the ascetics and solitaries, and the orders of families of which they were patriarchs, with St. Antony, St. Martin, and St. Benedict, and other great confessors or reformers, who are the antitypes of the Prophets. Moreover, much might be said concerning the romantic character of the Prophetical miracles. Those of Elisha in particular are related, not as if parts of the history, but rather as his " Acta ;" as illustrations indeed of that double portion of power gained for him by Elijah's prayer, and perhaps with some typical reference to the times of the Gospel, but still with a profusion and variety very like the luxuriance which offends us in the miraculous narratives of ecclesiastical authors. Elisha begins by parting Jordan with Elijah's mantle ; then he curses the children, and bears destroy forty-two of them ; then he supplies the kings of Judah, Israel, and Edom with water in the wilderness, and gives them victory over Moab ; then he multiplies the oil ; then he raises the Shunammite's son ; then he renders the poisonous pottage harmless by casting meal into it ; then he multiplies the bread and barley ; then he directs Naaman to a cure of his leprosy ; then he reads Gehazi's heart, follows him throughout his act of covetousness, and inflicts on him Naaman's leprosy ; then he makes the iron swim ; then he reveals to the king of Israel the counsels of Syria, and casts an illusion before the eyes of his army; then he prophesies plenty in the siege; then he foretells Hazael's future course. These wonderful acts are strung together as the direct and formal subjects of the chapters in which they occur : they have no continuity ; they carry on no action or course of Providence. At length Elisha falls sick, and, on the king's visiting him, promises him a series of victories over the Syrians ; then he dies and is buried, and by accident a corpse is thrown into his grave; and "when the man was let down, and touched the bones of Elisha, he revived, and stood up on his feet."[k] Surely it is not too much to say, that after this inspired precedent there is little in ecclesiastical legends of a nature to offend as regards their matter; their credibility turning first on whether they are to be expected at all, and next whether they are avouched on sufficient evidence.

62. Or take again the history of Samson ; what a mysterious wildness and eccentricity is impressed upon it, upon the miracles which occur in it, and upon its highly favoured though wayward subject ! " At this juncture," says a recent writer, speaking of the low estate of the chosen people when Samson was born, " the most extraordinary of the Jewish heroes appeared ; a man of prodigious physical power, which

[k] 2 Kings xiii. 21.

he displayed, not in any vigorous and consistent plan of defence against the enemy, but in the wildest feats of personal daring. It was his amusement to plunge headlong into peril, from which he extricated himself by his individual strength. Samson never appears at the head of an army, his campaigns are conducted in his own single person. As in those of the Grecian Hercules and the Arabian Antar, a kind of comic vein runs through the early adventures of the stout-hearted warrior, in which love of women, of riddles, and of slaying Philistines out of mere wantonness, vie for the mastery. Yet his life began with marvel, and ended in the deepest tragedy."[1] The tone of this extract cannot be defended; yet what else has the writer done towards the inspired narrative, but invest it in those showy human colours which legendary writers from infirmity, and enemies from malice, have thrown over the miracles of the Church? There is certainly an aspect of romance in which Samson may be viewed, though he was withal the instrument of a Divine Presence; and so again there may have been a divinity in the acts and fortunes, and a spiritual perfection in the lives, of the ancient Catholic hermits and missionaries, in spite of whatever is wild, uncouth, and extravagant in their personal demeanour and conduct, or rather in the record of them. Once more; the books of Daniel and Esther are very different in com-

Milman's History of the Jews, vol. i. p. 204.

position and style from the earlier portions of the sacred volume, and present a view of the miraculous dealings of the Almighty with His Church, very much resembling what we disparage in ecclesiastical legends, or again in the historical portions of the so-called Apocrypha, as if poetical or dramatic.

63. The two Economies then, the Prophetical and the Ecclesiastical, thus resembling each other in their character as well as their position in their two Covenants respectively, should any one urge, as was stated in a former place,[m] that the Ecclesiastical Miracles virtually form a new dispensation, we need not deny it *in the sense* in which the Prophetical Miracles are distinct from the Mosaic; that is, not as if the Law was in any respect or in any part repealed by the Prophetical Schools, but that they, as well as other works of God, had a character of their own, and, as in other things, so in their miracles, were a new exhibition of that Supernatural Presence which overshadowed Israel from first to last. And it may be added, that, as a gradual revelation of Gospel truth accompanied the miracles of the Prophets, so to those who admit the Catholic doctrines as enunciated in the Creed, and commented on by the Fathers, the subsequent expansion and variation of supernatural agency in the Church, instead of suggesting difficulties, will seem to be in correspondence, as they are

[m] Supra, p. 115.

the Ecclesiastical Miracles.

contemporaneous, with the developments and additions in dogmatic statements which have occurred between the Apostolic and the present age, and which are but a result and an evidence of spiritual life.

10.

64. Nor, lastly, is it any real argument against admitting the Ecclesiastical Miracles on the whole, or against admitting certain of them, that certain others are rejected on all hands as fictitious or pretended. It happens as a matter of course, on many accounts, that where miracles are really wrought, miracles will also be attempted, or simulated, or imitated, or fabled; and such counterfeits become, not a disproof, but a proof of the existence of their prototypes, just as hypocrisy and extravagant profession are an argument for, and not against, the reality of virtue.[n] It is doubtless the tendency of religious minds to imagine mysteries and wonders where there are none; and much more, where causes of awe really exist, will they unintentionally misstate, exaggerate, and embellish, when they set themselves to relate what they have witnessed or have heard.[o] A fact is not disproved because the testimony is confused or insufficient; it is only unproved. And further, the imagination, as is well known, is a fruitful cause of apparent

[n] Douglas' Crit. p. 19.
Camp. Miracl. p. 122.   Jenkins' Christ. Rel. vol. ii. p. 455.

miracles;[p] and hence, wherever there are works wrought which absolutely surpass the powers of nature, there are likely to be others which surpass its ordinary action. It would be no cause for surprise if, as the destruction of Sodom is said to have arisen from volcanic influence, so in the multitude of cures which the Apostles effected some were solely attributable to natural, but unusual, effects of faith. And if Providence sometimes makes use of natural principles even when miracles seem intended as evidence of His immediate presence, much more is He likely to intermingle the ordinary and the extraordinary, when His object is not to prove a revelation, to accredit a messenger, or to certify a doctrine, but to confirm or encourage the faithful, or to rouse the attention of unbelievers. And it will be impossible to draw the line between the two; and the possibility of explaining some of them on natural principles will unjustly prejudice the mind against accounts of those which cannot be so explained.

65. Moreover, as Scripture expressly shows us, wherever there is miraculous power, there will be curious and interested bystanders who would fain "purchase the gift of God" for their own aggrandisement, and "cast out devils in the Name of Jesus," and who counterfeit what they have not really to exhibit, and gain credit and followers among the ignorant and

[p] Le Moyne Miracl. pp. 486, 502. Douglas' Crit. p. 93, etc.

perverse. The impostures, then, of various kinds which from the first hour abounded in the Church [q] prove as little against the truth of her miracles as against the canonicity of her Scriptures. Yet here too pretensions on the part of worthless men will be sure to scandalize inquirers, and the more so if, as is not unlikely, such pretenders manage to ally themselves with the Saints, and have an historical position in the fight which is made for the integrity or purity of the faith; yet, St. Paul was not less an Apostle, nor have Confessors and Doctors been less his successors, because "as they have gone to prayer" a spirit of Python has borne witness to them as "the servants of the most high God," and the teachers of "the way of salvation."

66. Nor is it any fair argument against Ecclesiastical miracles, that for the most part they have a legendary air, while the miracles contained in Scripture are on the contrary so soberly, so gravely, so exactly stated; unless indeed it is an absurdity to contemplate a gift of miracles without an attendant gift of inspiration to record them. Were it not that the Evangelists were divinely guided, doubtless we should have in Scripture that confused mass of truth and fiction together, which the Apocryphal Gospels exhibit, and to which St. Luke seems to allude. I repeat, the character of facts is not changed because they are incor-

---

[q] Vid. Acts viii. 9; xvi. 17; xix. 13. Vid. Lucian. Peregr. etc. ap. Middlet. Inqu. p. 23.

rectly reported ; distance of time and place only does injury to the record of them. The Scripture miracles were in themselves what they are to us now, at the very time that the world was associating them with the prodigies of Jewish strollers, heathen magicians and astrologers, and idolatrous rites ; they would have been thus associated to this day, had not inspiration interposed ; yet, in spite of this, they would have been deserving our serious attention as now, so far as we were able to separate the truth from the falsehood. And such is the state in which Ecclesiastical miracles actually do come to us, because inspiration was not continued ; they are dimly seen in twilight and amid shadows ;—let us not, then, quarrel with them on account of a characteristic which is but the necessary consequence of external circumstances.

Chapter IV.

ON THE STATE OF THE ARGUMENT IN BEHALF OF THE ECCLESIASTICAL MIRACLES.

67. VARIOUS able writers, Leslie, Paley, and Douglas, have laid down certain tests or criteria of matters of fact, which may serve as guarantees that the miracles really took place which are recorded in Scripture. They consider these criteria to be of so rigid a nature that an alleged event which satisfies them must necessarily have occurred, and that, as their argument seems to imply, however great its antecedent improbability. Thus they reply to objections such as Hume's drawn from the uniformity of nature; not meeting them directly, but rather superseding the necessity of considering them; for what is proved to be true, need not be proved to be possible. Hume scruples not to use "miracle" and "impossibility" as convertible terms;[r] Leslie before him,

[r] "What have we to oppose to such a cloud of witnesses but the absolute *impossibility* or *miraculous nature* of the events which they relate?" (Essay on Miracles.)

and Douglas after him, seem to answer, "Would you believe a miracle if you *saw* it? Now we are prepared to offer evidence, if not as strong, still as convincing, as ocular demonstration." Thus they escape from the abstract argument by a controversial method of a singularly practical, and as it may be called, English character.

68. It would be well if such writers stopped here, but it was hardly to be expected. Disputants are always exposed to the temptation of being over-candid towards objections which they think they have outrun; they admit as facts or truths what they have shown to be irrelevant as arguments. Thus, even were there nothing of a kindred tone of mind in Hume, who has assailed the Scripture miracles, and in some of our friends who have defended them, it might have been anticipated that the consciousness of possessing an irresistible weapon in the contest would have led us to treat the arguments of our opponents with a dangerous generosity. But, unhappily, there is much in Protestant habits of thought actually to dispose our writers to defer to a rationalistic principle of reasoning, the force of which they have managed to evade in the particular case. Hence, though they are earnest in their protest against Hume's summary rejection of all miraculous histories whatever, they make admissions, which only do not directly tell against the principal Scripture miracles, and do tell against all others.

They tacitly grant that the antecedent improbability of miracles is at least so great that it can only be overcome by the strongest and most overpowering evidence; that second-best evidence does not even tend to prove them; that they are absolutely incredible up to the very moment that all doubt is decisively set at rest; that there can be no degrees of proof, no incipient and accumulating arguments to recommend them; that no relentings of mind or suspense of judgment is justifiable, as various fainter evidences are found to conspire in their favour; that they may be scorned as fictions, if they are not to be venerated as truths.

69. It looks like a mere truism to say that a fact is not disproved, because it is not proved; ten thousand occurrences are ever passing, which leave no record behind them, and do not cease to have been because they are forgotten. Yet Bishop Douglas, in his defence of the New Testament Miracles in answer to Hume, certainly assumes that no miracle is true which has not been proved so, or that it is safe to treat all miracles as false which are not recommended by evidence as strong as that which is adducible for the Miracles of Scripture.

70. In estimating statements of fact, it is usual to allow that various occurrences may be all true, which rest upon very different degrees of evidence. It does not prove that this passage of history is false and the

fabrication of impostors, because that passage is attested more distinctly and fully. Writers, however, like Douglas, are constantly reminding us that we *need* not receive the Ecclesiastical miracles, *though* we receive those of the New Testament. But the question is not whether we *need* not, but whether we *ought* not to receive the former, as well as the latter; and if it really is the case that we ought not, surely this must be in consequence of some positive reasons, not of a mere inferiority in the evidence. It is plain, then, that such reasoners, though they deny that an *à priori* ground can be maintained in fact against the miracles of Scripture, still at least agree with Hume in thinking such a ground does exist, and that it is conclusive against ecclesiastical miracles even antecedent to the evidence.

71. In the title of his Dissertation, Douglas promises us "a criterion by which the *true* miracles recorded in the New Testament are distinguished from the *spurious* miracles of the Pagans and Papists;" yet, when he proceeds to state in the body of the work the real object to which he addresses himself, we find that it relates quite as much to the *evidence* for either class of miracles as to the fact itself of their occurrence. He says, that whereas "the accounts which have been published to the world of miracles in general," are concerned with events which are supernatural either in themselves or under their circumstances, while the

latter class can be explained on natural principles, the former "*may*, from the *insufficiency* of the evidence produced in support of them, be *justly suspected* to have never happened."[s] But how does *insufficiency* in the evidence create a positive prejudice against an alleged fact? How can things depend on our knowledge of them? This writer must mean that evidence of an inferior kind is insufficient to overcome a certain *pre-existing objection* which attaches to the very notion of these miracles; otherwise even slight evidence is sufficient to influence our minds, as Bishop Butler would tell us, so far as it is positive, and evidence of this defective kind may constitute the very trial of our obedience.

72. Douglas continues: "I flatter myself, that the evidence produced in their support,"—in support of the miracles of "Pagans and Papists,"—"will appear to be so very defective and insufficient, as *justly to warrant* our rejecting them as idle tales that never happened, and *the inventions of bold and interested deceivers*."[t] There are many reasons to warrant our disbelieving alleged facts, and ascribing them to imposture; for instance, if the evidence is contradictory, or attended by suspicious circumstances; if the witnesses are of bad character, or strong inducements to fraud exist; but it is difficult to see how its mere

[s] Page 25.
[t] Page 26.

insufficiency or *defectiveness* is a justification of so decided a step. The direct effect of evidence is to create a presumption, according to its strength, in favour of the fact attested; it does not appear how it can create a presumption the other way. The real explanation of this mode of writing certainly must be, that the writer takes it for granted that all miraculous accounts are already in a manner self-condemned, as being miraculous, *till* they are proved; and that evidence offered for them, which does not amount to a proof, is but involved in that existing prejudice. There is no medium then; the testimony must either prevail or be scouted; it is certainly a fraud, if it is not an overpowering demonstration.

73. But the author in question scarcely leaves us in doubt of his meaning, when he avails himself of the following maxim of Dr. Middleton's: "I have already observed," he says, "that the testimony supporting [miracles] must be free from every suspicion of fraud and imposture. And the reason is this: the history of miracles (to make use of the words of an author whose authority you will think of some weight) is of a kind totally different from that of common events; the one *to be suspected always of course without the strongest evidence* to confirm it; the other to be admitted of course without as strong reason to suspect it. So that, wherever the evidence urged for miracles *leaves grounds* for a suspicion of fraud and imposition,

the very suspicion furnishes *sufficient reasons* for disbelieving them. And what I shall offer under this head will make it evident, that those miracles which the Protestant Christian thinks himself at liberty to reject have always been so *insufficiently* attested as to *leave full scope* for fraud and imposition."[u] That is, we may ascribe a story to fraud, whenever it is not absolutely impossible so to ascribe it; we may summarily reject and vilify all evidence *up to* such evidence as is a moral demonstration, though to such we must immediately yield, because we cannot help it; and this as a matter " of course." All this surely implies the existence of some deep latent prejudice in the writer's mind against miraculous occurrences, considered in themselves; else it is not a reasonable mode of arguing.

74. The Bishop continues in the same strain to "lay down a few general rules by which we may try those pretended miracles, one and all, wherever they occur, and which may set forth *the grounds on which we sus-*

[u] How much more cautious is Jortin! " Though miracles," he says, " *may* be wrought in secret, and cannot be disproved only because they were seen by few, yet they *often* afford motives for suspicion, and a wise inquirer would perhaps *suspend* his assent in such cases, and pass *no judgment* about them." (Eccl. History, Works, vol. ii. p. 3, ed. 1810.) Again, " As far as the subsequent miracles mentioned by Christian writers fall short of the distinguishing characters belonging to the works of Christ and His Apostles, *so far* they must fail of giving us *the **same** full persuasion and satisfaction.*" (P. 20.)

pect them false." [v] And then, " by way of illustration," he selects three, telling us that we suspect them false, or " we *may* suspect them false," when the existing accounts of miracles were not published till long after the time when, or not at the place where, they are said to have occurred ; or, at least, if it seems probable that they were suffered to get into circulation without examination at the time and place. Here of course he does but act up to Middleton's bold principle which he has adopted ; he considers himself at liberty to bid defiance and offer resistance to all evidence, till he is fairly subdued by it, till it is impossible to doubt, and no merit to believe; while he would never reject or impute fraud to a record of ordinary events, merely because it was published in a foreign country, or a hundred years after the events in question, however he might justly consider such circumstances to weaken the force of the evidence.

75. In a subsequent page of his work he speaks still more pointedly : " When the reporters of miracles," he says, " content themselves with general assertions and vague claims to a miraculous power, without ever attempting to corroborate them by descending to particular facts, and leave us strangely in the dark as to the persons by whom, the witnesses before whom, and the objects upon whom these miraculous powers are said to be exercised, omitting every circumstance

[v] Page 27.

necessary to be related by them before any inquiry can be made into the truth of the pretension; when miracles, I say, are reported in this *unsatisfactory* manner, (and instances of miracles reported on the spot by contemporary writers, in such a manner, might be mentioned,) in this case it would be *the height of credulity* to pay *any* regard to them in a distant age, because no regard could possibly be paid to them in their own."[x] Yet it does not appear how this "unsatisfactory manner" in the report can touch the events reported; if they took place, they were before and quite independent of the evidence at present existing for them, be it greater or less; our knowledge or ignorance does not create or annihilate facts.

76. Now these passages from Bishop Douglas have been drawn out, not simply with a view of criticising him, but in order to direct attention to the fact which he illustrates, viz., that our feeling towards the Ecclesisatical Miracles turns much less on the evidence producible for them, than on our view concerning their antecedent probability. If we think such interpositions of Providence likely or not unlikely, there is quite enough evidence existing to convince us that they really do occur; if we think them as unlikely as they appear to Douglas, Middleton, and others, then even evidence as great as that which is producible for the miracles of Scripture would not be too much,

[x] Page 50.

nay, perhaps not enough, to conquer an inveterate, deep-rooted, and (as it may be called) ethical incredulity.

77. It shall here be assumed that this incredulity is a fault; and it is the result of a state of mind which has been prevalent among us for some generations, and from which we are now but slowly extricating ourselves. We have been accustomed to believe that Christianity is little more than a creed or doctrine, introduced into the world once for all, and then left to itself, after the manner of human institutions, and under the same ordinary governance with them, stored indeed with hopes and fears for the future, and containing certain general promises of aid for this life, but unattended by any special Divine Presence or any immediately supernatural gift. To minds habituated to such a view of Revealed Religion, the miracles of ecclesiastical history must needs be a shock, and almost an outrage, disturbing their feelings and unsettling their most elementary notions and thoroughly received opinions. They are eager to find defects in the evidence, or appearances of fraud in the witnesses, as a relief to their perplexity, and as an excuse for rejecting, as if on the score of reason, what their heart and imagination have rejected already. Or they are too firmly persuaded of the absurdity, as they consider it, which such pretensions on the part of the Church involve, to be moved by them at all; and they content

themselves with coldly demanding to know points which cannot now be known, or to be satisfied about difficulties which never will be cleared up, before they can be asked to take interest in statements which they consider so unreasonable. And certainly they are both philosophical and religious in thus acting, granting that the Lord of all is present with Christians only in the way of nature, as with His creatures all over the earth. On the other hand, if we believe that Christians are under an extraordinary Dispensation, such as Judaism was, and that the Church is a supernatural ordinance, we shall in mere consistency be disposed to treat even the report of miraculous occurrences with seriousness, from our faith in a Present Power adequate to their production. Nay, if we only go so far as to realize what Christianity is, when considered merely as a creed, and what stupendous overpowering facts are involved in the doctrine of a Divine Incarnation, we shall feel that no miracle can be great after it, nothing strange or marvellous, nothing beyond expectation.

2.

78. All this applies to the view we shall take of the nature of the facts which are laid before us, as well as of the character of the evidence. If we disbelieve the divinity of the Church, then we shall do our best to deny that the facts attested are miraculous, even

admitting them to be true. "Though our not knowing on whom, or by whom, or before whom, the miracles recorded by the Fathers of the second and third centuries were wrought," says Douglas, "should be allowed not to destroy their credit (though this is a concession which very few will make . . .), yet the facts appealed to are of so *ambiguous* a kind, that, granting they did happen, it will remain to be decided, by a consideration of the circumstances attending the performance of them, whether there was any miracle in the case or no." [y] Certainly it is a rule of philosophy to refer effects, if possible, to known causes, rather than to imagine a cause for the occasion ; and, on the other hand, to be suspicious of alleged facts for which no cause can be assigned, or which are unaccountable. If, then, there is nothing in the Church more than in any other society of men, it is natural to attribute the miracles alleged to have been wrought in it to natural causes, where that is possible, and to disparage the evidence where it is not so. But if the Church be possessed of supernatural powers, it is not unnatural to refer to these the facts reported, and to feel the same disposition to heighten their marvellousness as otherwise is felt to explain it away. Thus our view of the evidence will practically be decided by our views of theology. There are two providential systems in operation among us, the visible and the invisible, in-

[y] Page 228.

tersecting, as it were, each other, and having a certain territory in common; and in many cases we do not know the exact boundaries of each, as again we do not know the minute details of those facts which are ascribed by their reporters to a miraculous agency. For instance, faith may sometimes be a natural cause of recovery from sickness, sometimes a miraculous instrument; the application of oil may be a mere expedient of medical art, or parallel to the application of water in Baptism. The Martyrs have before now found redhot iron, on its second application, even grateful to their seared limbs; on the other hand, cases of a similar kind are said to have occurred where religion was not in question, and where a divine interposition cannot be conjectured. Sudden storms and as sudden calms on the lake of Gennesareth might be of common occurrence; yet the particular circumstances under which the waters were quieted at our Lord's word may have been sufficient to convince beholders that it was a miracle. The Red Sea may have been ordinarily exposed to the influence of the East Wind, and nevertheless the separation of its waters, as described in the Book of Exodus, may have required a supernatural influence. In these and numberless other instances men will systematize facts in their own way, according to their knowledge, opinions, and wishes, as they are used to do in all matters which come before them; and they will refer them to causes which they see or believe, in spite of their being referable to other causes about which they are ignorant or sceptical.

79. When, then, controversialists go through the existing accounts of ecclesiastical miracles, and explain one after another on the hypothesis of natural causes; when they resolve a professed vision into a dream, a possession into epilepsy or madness, a prophecy into a sagacious conjecture, a recovery into the force of imagination, they are but expressing their own disbelief in the Grace committed to the Church; and of course they are consistent in denying its outward triumphs, when they have no true apprehension of its inward power. Those, on the other hand, who realize that the bodies of the Saints were in their lifetime the Temples of the Holiest, and are hereafter to rise again, will feel no offence at the report of miracles wrought through them; nor ought those who believe in the existence of evil spirits to have any difficulty at the notion of demoniacal possession and exorcism. And it may be taken as a general truth, that where there is an admission of Catholic doctrines, there no prejudice will exist against the Ecclesiastical Miracles; while those who disbelieve the existence among us of the hidden Power, will eagerly avail themselves of every plea for explaining away its open manifestations. All that can be objected here is, that miracles which admit of this double reference to causes natural and super-

natural, taken by themselves and in the first instance, are not evidence of Revealed Religion; but I have nowhere maintained that they are. Yet, though not part of the philosophical basis of Christianity, they may be evidence still to those who admit the Divine Presence in the Church, and in proportion as they realize it; they may be evidence in combination with more explicit miracles, or when viewed all together in their cumulative force; they may confirm or remind of the Apostolic miracles; they may startle, they may spread an indefinite awe over certain transactions or doctrines; they may in various ways subserve the probation of individuals to whom they are addressed, more fully than occurrences of a more marked character. The mere circumstance that they do not carry their own explanation with them is no argument against them, unless we would surrender the most sacred and awful events of our religion to the unbeliever.[z] As the admission of a Creator is necessary for the argumentative force of the miracles of Moses or St. Paul, so does the doctrine of a Divine Presence in the Church supply what is ambiguous in the miracles of St. Gregory Thaumaturgus or St. Martin.

[z] Μετὰ ταῦτα προσωποποιεῖ Ἰουδαῖον αὐτῷ διαλεγόμενον τῷ Ἰησοῦ καὶ ἐλέγχοντα αὐτὸν . . ὡς πλασαμένον αὐτοῦ τὴν ἐκ παρθένου γένεσιν . . . . φησὶ δὲ αὐτὴν καὶ ὑπὸ τοῦ γήμαντος, τέκτονος τὴν τέχνην ὄντος, ἐξεῶσθαι, ἐλεγχθεῖσαν ὡς μεμοιχευμένην· εἶτα λέγει, ὡς ἐκβληθεῖσα ὑπὸ τοῦ ἀνδρὸς, καὶ πλανωμένη ἀτίμως σκότιον ἐγέννησε τὸν Ἰησοῦν. Orig. contr. Cels. i. 28.

3.

80. The course of these remarks has now sufficiently shown that in drawing out the argument in behalf of ecclesiastical miracles, the main point to which attention must be paid is the proof of their antecedent probability.[a] If that is established, the task is nearly accomplished. If the miracles alleged are in harmony with the course of Divine Providence in the world, and with the analogy of faith as contained in Scripture, if it is possible to account for them, if they are referable to a known cause or system, and especially if it can be shown that they are recognized, promised, or predicted in Scripture, very little positive evidence is necessary to induce us to listen to them or even accept them, if not one by one, at least viewed as a collective body. In that case they are but the natural effects of supernatural agency, and Middleton's canon, which Douglas,

---

[a] " Men will be inclined to determine this controverted question according to their preconceived notions and their accustomed way of thinking ; for there appears to be a sort of fatality in opinions of this kind, which, when once taken up, are seldom laid down." (Jortin, ibid. p. 24.) Yet he says elsewhere of Theophilus, an Arian missionary, " I blame not Tillemont for rejecting all these miracles, which seem to have been rumours raised and spread to serve a party ; but the true reason of his disbelief is, that they were Arian miracles ; and if they had been reported concerning Athanasius, all difficulties would have been smoothed over and accounted of small moment." (P. 219.) As if a miracle wrought by Athanasius was not more likely than miracles wrought by an Arian, though a missionary.

for the Ecclesiastical Miracles.

as above quoted, adopts to their disadvantage, becomes their protection. Then "the history of miracles," instead of being "suspected always of course, without the strongest evidence to confirm it," is at first sight almost "to be admitted of course, without a strong reason to suspect it;" such suspicions as attach to it arising from our actual experience of fraud, not from difficulties in its subject matter. If "the tabernacle of God is with men, and He will dwell with them;" if the Church is "the kingdom of heaven;" if our Lord is with His disciples "alway, even unto the end of the world;" if He promised His Holy Spirit to be to them what He Himself was when visibly present, and if miracles were one special token of His Presence when on earth; if moreover miracles are expressly mentioned as tokens of the promised Comforter; if St. Paul speaks of "mighty signs and wonders by the power of the Spirit of God," and of his "speech and preaching" being "in demonstration of the Spirit and of power," and of "diversities of gifts but the same Spirit," and of "healing," "working of miracles," and "prophecy," as among His gifts; surely we have no cause to be surprised at hearing supernatural events reported in any age, and though we may freely exercise our best powers of inquiry and judgment on such and such reports, as they come before us, yet this is very different from hearing them with prejudice, and examining them with contempt or insult.

81. This Essay, indeed, is not the place for doctrinal discussions: there is one text, however, to which attention may be drawn, without deviating into theology, in consequence of what may be called its historical character, which on other accounts also makes it more to our purpose,—our Lord's charge to His disciples at the end of St. Mark's Gospel. It might in truth have been anticipated that, among the promises with which He animated His desponding disciples when He was leaving them, some mention would be made of those supernatural powers which had been the most ready proof of His own divinity, and the most awful of the endowments with which during His ministry He had invested them. Nor does He disappoint the expectation; for in the passage alluded to He distinctly announces a continuation of these pledges of His favour, and that without fixing the term of it. At the very time apparently when He said to them, "Lo, I am with you alway, even unto the end of the world," He also made two announcements, one for this life, the other for the life to come. "He that believeth and is baptized shall be saved," was for the future; and the present promise, which concerns us here, ran thus: "These signs shall follow them that believe; In My Name shall they cast out devils; they shall speak with new tongues; they shall take up serpents; and if they drink any deadly thing, it shall not hurt them; they shall lay hands on the sick, and they

shall recover." Now let us see what presumption is created or suggested by this passage in behalf of the miraculous passages of Ecclesiastical History as we have received them.

82. First, let it be observed, five gifts are here mentioned as specimens of our Lord's bequest to His disciples on His departure : exorcism, speaking with new tongues, handling serpents, drinking poison without harm, and healing the sick. When our Lord first sent out the Apostles to preach during His ministry, He had specified four : "Heal the sick, cleanse the lepers, raise the dead, cast out devils." Comparing these two passages together, we find that two gifts are common to both of them, and thereby stand out as the most characteristic and prominent constituents of the supernatural endowment. It is observable, again, that these two gifts, of which there is this repeated mention, are not so wonderful or so decisively miraculous as those of which mention only occurs in one of the two texts. The power of exorcism and of healing is committed by our Lord to the Apostles, both when He first calls them, and when He is leaving them ; but they are promised the gift of tongues only on their second mission, and that of raising the dead only on the first. This does not prove that they could not raise the dead when our Lord had left them ; indeed, we know in matter of fact that they had, and that they exercised, the power; but it is natural to suppose that a stress is laid on what is

mentioned twice, and to form thence some idea, in consequence, of the predominant character of their miraculous endowment, when it was actually brought into exercise. In accordance with this anticipation, whatever it is worth in itself, St. Matthew heads his report of our Lord's charge to His Apostles on their first mission with mention of these very two gifts, and these only: "And when He had called unto Him His twelve Disciples, He gave them power *against unclean spirits, to cast them out,* and *to heal all manner of sickness and all manner of disease.*" And in like manner when the Seventy are sent, these two gifts, and these only, are specified by St. Luke as imparted to them; our Lord saying to them, "Heal the sick," and they answering, "Lord, even the devils are subject unto us through Thy Name."

83. Further, when we turn to the history of the Book of Acts we find the general tenor of the Apostles' miracles to be just such as these passages in the Gospels would lead us to expect; that is, were a Jew or heathen of the day, who had a fair opportunity of witnessing their miracles, to be asked what those miracles consisted in, the general impression left by them on his mind, and the best account which he could give of them would be, that they were the healing the sick and casting out devils. We have indeed instances recorded of their raising the dead, but only two in the whole book, those of Tabitha and Eutychus; and of these

the latter was almost a private act, and wrought expressly for the comfort of the brethren, not for the conviction of unbelievers ; and though the former was the means of converting many in the neighbourhood, yet it was wrought at Joppa, among a number of " widows" and "saints," not in Jerusalem, where the jealous eyes of enemies would have been directed upon it. In the same book there are three instances of the gift of tongues, at Pentecost, in Cornelius's house, and at Ephesus on the confirmation of St. John's disciples. There is one instance of protection from the bite of serpents, that of St. Paul at Melita. There is no instance of cleansing leprosy, or of drinking poison without harm. With this frugality in the display of their highest gifts is singularly contrasted the bountifulness of the Apostles in exercising their powers of healing and exorcising. "They brought forth the *sick* into the streets, and laid them on beds and couches, that *at the least the shadow of Peter* passing by might overshadow some of them. There came also a *multitude* out of the cities *round about* unto Jerusalem, bringing *sick* folks, and *them that were vexed with unclean spirits;* and they were *healed every one.*" Again, when St. Philip went down to Samaria, and "the people with one accord gave heed unto those things which Philip spake, hearing and seeing the miracles which he did," what were the particular gifts which he exercised ? the inspired writer continues, " For *unclean spirits*, crying with loud voice, came out of *many* that were possessed with them; and many taken with *palsies*, and that were *lame*, were healed. And there was great joy in that city." Again, we read of St. Paul, in a later part of the same book, as has been already quoted in another connection, that "from his body were brought unto the sick handkerchiefs or aprons, and the *diseases* departed from them, and the *evil spirits* went out of them."[b]

84. If there is one other characteristic gift in the Book of Acts in addition to these, it is the gift of visions and divine intimations. And, as if to make up for our Lord's silence concerning it in the Gospel of St. Mark, St. Peter opens the sacred history of the Acts with a reference to the Prophet Joel's promise of the time, when "their sons and their daughters should prophesy, and their young men should see visions, and their old men should dream dreams;" an announcement of which the narrative which follows abundantly records the fulfilment. St. Stephen sees our Lord before his martyrdom; the Angel directs St. Philip to go towards Gaza, and the Holy Spirit Himself bids him join himself to the Ethiopian's chariot; St. Paul is converted by a vision of our Lord; St. Peter has the vision of the clean and unclean beasts, and Cornelius is addressed by an Angel; Angels release first the Apostles, then St. Peter from prison; "a vision appeared to Paul in the night, there stood a man of Macedonia;" at Corinth Christ

[b] Acts v. 15, 16; viii. 6—8; xix. 12.

"spake to Paul in the night by a vision, Be not afraid;" Agabus and St. Philip's four daughters prophesy; in prison "the Lord stood by Paul, and said, Be of good cheer;" on board ship an Angel stood by him, saying, "Fear not, Paul, thou must be brought before Cæsar."[c]

85. Such is the general character of the miracles of the Book of Acts; and next let it be observed, such is the character of our Lord's miracles also, as they would strike the bulk of spectators. He raises indeed the dead three times, He feeds the multitude in the desert, He cleanses the leprosy, He gives sight to the blind, on various but still definite occasions; but how different is the language used by the Evangelists when His powers of healing and exorcising are spoken of! We read of "a great *multitude* of people out of all Judea and Jerusalem, and from the sea coast of Tyre and Sidon, which came to hear Him and to be healed of their *diseases;* and they that were *vexed with unclean spirits;* and they were healed. And the *whole* multitude sought to *touch* Him; for there went *virtue out of Him*, and healed them *all*." Again, "*Whithersoever He entered*, into villages, or cities, or country, they *laid the sick in the streets*, and besought Him that they might touch if it were but the corner of His garment; and *as many as touched Him were made whole*." Again, "They brought unto Him *all sick people* that were taken with divers *diseases* and *torments*, and

[c] Acts vii. 56; viii. 26, 29; ix. 3—6; x. 3, 10, etc.

those that were possessed with devils, and those that were *lunatic,* and those that had the *palsy;* and He healed them."[d] It may be added that of other miraculous occurrences in the Gospels none are more frequent than visions and voices, from the Angel which appeared to Zacharias to the vision of Angels seen by the women after our Lord's resurrection; as is obvious without proof.

86. It appears, then, that the two special powers which were characteristic, as of our Lord's miraculous working, so also of His Apostles after Him, were exorcism and healing; and moreover that these were in matter of fact the two gifts especially promised to the Apostles above other gifts. It appears, also, that if one other gift must be selected from the Gospels and Book of Acts as of greater prominence than the rest it will be the gift of visions; so that cures, exorcisms, and visions are on the whole the three distinguishing specimens of Divine Power, by which our Lord authenticated to the world the Religion He bestowed upon it. Now it has already been observed[2] that these are the very three especially claimed by the Primitive Church; while, as to the more stupendous miracles of raising the dead, giving sight to the blind, cleansing lepers, and the like, of these certainly she affords instances also, but very rarely, as if after the

[d] Luke vi. 17—19; Mark vi. 56; Matt. iv. 24.
[2] [N. 30, *supra.*]

manner of Scripture. This surely is a remarkable coincidence; and is the rather to be dwelt upon, because those who consider the vagueness of the language with which the ecclesiastical miracles are attested, as a proof that they were merely the fabrication of fraud or credulity, have to explain how it was that, while the parties accused were exercising their powers of imagination or imposture, they did not embellish their pages with similar vague statements of miracles of a more awful character, even from the mere love of variety, instead of confining themselves to those which in appearance at least were shared with them by Jews and heathen.

87. Nor can it reasonably be urged that their acquaintance with Scripture suggested to them in this matter an imitation of the Divine procedure as there recorded; because Scripture does not on the face of it impress upon the reader the fact which has been here pointed out. The actual course of the *events* which Scripture relates is one thing, and the course of the *narrative* is another; for the sacred writers do not state events with that relative prominence in which they severally occurred in fact. Inspiration has interfered to select and bring into the foreground the most cogent instances of Divine interposition, and has identified them by a number of distinct details; on the other hand, it has covered up from us the "many other signs" which "Jesus did in the presence of His disciples," "the which, if they should be written every

one, even the world itself," as St. John speaks, "could not contain the books that should be written." And doubtless there are doctrinal reasons also for this circumstance, if we had means of ascertaining them. But so it is, that the *primâ facie* appearance of the Gospel Miracles does not so correspond to that of the Ecclesiastical Miracles, as probably it would have corresponded, had St. John, for instance, given us a description of the second and third centuries, instead of St. Justin and Origen, or had Sulpicius described the Miracles of the Apostles at Jerusalem or Ephesus.

4.

88. And now, if this representation has any truth in it, if our Lord, in the passage of St. Mark in question, promised five gifts to His disciples, two of which were those of exorcism and healing; if these same two, distinguished in other places of the Gospels above the rest, are the prominent external signs of power in the history both of our Lord and of His Apostles; if these particular Miracles are the special instruments of the conversion of whole multitudes; if on account of the cures and exorcisms wrought by the twelve Apostles " believers were the more added to the Lord, multitudes both of men and women;" if on St. Philip's casting out devils, and curing palsy and lameness, " the people with one accord gave heed," and " there was great joy in that city;" if when an evil spirit had con-

fessed, "Jesus I know, and Paul I know, but who are ye?" "fear fell on them all," and "the Name of the Lord Jesus was magnified," and "the word of God grew mightily and prevailed;" what is to be said of those modern Apologists for Christianity who do their best to prove that these phenomena have nothing necessarily miraculous in them at all? So much is evident at once, that had they been the persons encountered by these miracles of the Apostles, had they been the Samaritans to whom St. Philip came, or the Ephesians who were addressed by St. Paul, they would have thought it their duty to have felt neither "much joy" with the one, nor "fear" with the other; and that, if Samaritans and Ephesians had acted on the modern view of what is rational and what is evidence, what sound judgment and what credulity, Christianity would not have made way and prospered, but we all should have been heathen at this day.

89. Bishop Douglas, for instance, observes, that the circumstance that the Fathers allow that "cures of diseases, particularly of demoniacs by exorcising them," "were exercised by pagans with the assistance of their demons and gods," and admit that "there were exorcists among the Jews and Gentiles, who by the use of certain forms of words, used as charms, and by the practice of certain rites, cast out devils, as well as the Christian exorcists," that this circumstance "some may think puts these feats of jugglers and impostors

upon the same footing of credibility with the works ascribed to Christians"[e]:—why not with the works ascribed to Apostles? Again he urges, that "the cures ascribed to the prayers of Christians, to the imposition of their hands, etc., in those early times, *might, for aught we know*, be really brought about in a *natural* way, and be accounted for in the same way in which we have accounted for those ascribed to the Abbé Paris, and those attributed by the superstitious Papists to the intercession of the Saints":—perhaps the acute unbelievers of Corinth or Ephesus by a parallel argument justified their rejection of St. Paul. At Ephesus, when the demoniac leapt on the Jewish exorcists, "and overcame them, and prevailed against them, so that they fled out of that house naked and wounded," " fear" in consequence "fell on all the Jews and Greeks also dwelling at Ephesus;" but the Bishop would have taught them that "a few grimaces, wild gestures, disordered agitations, and blasphemous exclamations, suited to the character of the supposed infernal inhabitants, constitute all we know of their disease; and consequently, as *all* these symptoms are *ambiguous*, and may be assumed at pleasure by an impostor, a collusion between the exorcist and the person exorcised will account for the whole transaction, and every one who would avoid the character of being superstitiously credulous will naturally account for it in

[e] Page 233—236.

for the Ecclesiastical Miracles. 203

this manner, rather than by supposing that any supernatural cause intervened."[f] Such is this author's judgment of one of the two exhibitions of miraculous power with which our Saviour specially and singularly gifted His Apostles, and by which they, in matter of fact, converted the world. The question is not, whether in *particular cases* its apparent exercise may not be suspicious and inconclusive, for Douglas is speaking against the gift as such; so that a heathen of Ephesus would have been justified on his principles in demanding of St. Paul to see a man raised from the dead, before he believed in Christ. And such was the nature of the demand made by Autolycus upon St. Theophilus at the end of the second century, and Middleton and Gibbon justify it, and seem moreover to consider the mere silence of Theophilus to be a proof that such a miracle was utterly unknown in his days, as if resurrections abounded in the Acts.[g]

90. Again, St. Peter cured Æneas of the palsy, "and all that dwelt at Lydda and Saron saw him, and turned to the Lord;" but the Bishop would have

[f] Page 146. Douglas is speaking here primarily of the Church of Rome; afterwards he apparently refers to the passage when speaking of the Primitive Church, p. 236.

[g] Defecere etiam mortuorum excitationes. Certe Autolyco roganti ut vel unum ostenderet qui fuisset è mortuis revocatus, ita respondit Theophilus quasi vel unum demonstrare minime potuerit. Dodw. in Iren. Dissert. ii. 44. Jortin is more cautious. "It is probable," he says, "from his [Theophilus's] silence, that he had heard of no instance of such a miracle in

advised them to wait till they had seen Tabitha raised; because "palsies, it is well known, arise from obstructions of the spirits that circulate in the nerves, so that their influx into the muscles is impeded, or from obstructions of the arterious blood. Nothing more, therefore, was required here than to remove that obstruction."[h]

91. We read in Scripture of the sudden cure of the dropsy; but the Bishop observes, "That enthusiasm should warm its votaries to a holy madness, and excite the wildest transports and agitations throughout their whole frame, is an effect which, in a country so fruitful of this production as is ours (though enthusiasm be the product of *every* soil and of *every* religion), must be consistent with the experience of many."[i] Then he adds, speaking of some particular cases: "As one of the curative indications of a dropsy is an evacuation of the water by perspiration, and as the medicines administered by the physician aim to produce this effect, . . . what could be more

---

his days; probable, I say, but not certain; because, though he had heard of it, he might possibly have thought it to no purpose to tell his friend that there were Christians who *affirmed* such things, and he might suspect that Autolycus *would not have admitted the testimony* of persons with whom he had no acquaintance, and for whom he had little regard." Eccl. Hist. (Works, vol. ii. p. 92, ed. 1810). Vid. the striking statement of Origen. contr. Cels. i. 46. Greg. Nyss. tom. ii. p. 1009.

[h] Page 82.   [i] Page 104.

for the Ecclesiastical Miracles. 205

likely to excite such copious perspiration than the enthusiastic transport with which they prayed, and the convulsive struggles which shook their whole frame?"[k]

92. Peter's wife's mother was raised from her fever at once, so as even to be able to "minister" to the holy company; but Bishop Douglas would have suggested to the Pharisees that, had there been more raising of the dead, more restoring of sight to the blind, such cures might have been dispensed with, because, where minds are "heated and inflamed, and every faculty of their souls burning with the raptures of devout joy and enthusiastic confidence," it is "far from being impossible ... that in some cases a change might be wrought on the habit of the body;"[l] for "in this case the nervous system is strongly acted upon, and fresh and violent motions are communicated to the fluids;"[m] and "such agitations necessarily suppose that the velocity of the fluids" is "greatly accelerated;"[n] and "gouts, palsies, *fevers* of all kinds, and even ruptures, have been thus cured."[o] It certainly does not appear why a class of miracles which was, in matter of fact, the principal means of the conversion of the world in the age of the Apostles, should, when professed in the second and third centu-

[k] Page 107.
[l] Page 102.
[m] Page 106.
[n] Ibid.
[o] Page 101.

ries, be put aside by our Apologists on the excuse that "powers were not appealed to, less ambiguous in their nature," nor "other works performed, which admit of no solution from natural causes, and were incapable of being the effects of fraud and collusion."[p]

93. This being the language of so respectable a writer as Bishop Douglas, the following sentiments from Middleton cannot surprise us. Of miracles of healing he says: "In truth, this particular claim of curing diseases miraculously affords great room for . . . delusion and a wide field for the exercise of *craft*. Every man's experience has taught him that diseases thought fatal and desperate are oft surprisingly healed of themselves, by some secret and sudden effort of nature impenetrable to the skill of man; but to ascribe this presently to a miracle, as weak and superstitious minds are apt to do, to the prayers of the living or the intercessions of the dead, is what neither sound reason nor true religion will justify."[q] Of exorcisms: that certain circumstances "concerning the speeches and confessions of the devils, their answering to all questions, owning themselves to be wicked spirits, etc., . . . may not improbably be accounted for, either by the disordered state of the patient, answering wildly and at random to any questions proposed, or by the *arts of imposture and contrivance* between the parties concerned in the

[p] Page 236. [q] Page 79.

act."[r] And of visions: "To declare freely what I think, whatever ground there might be in those primitive ages either to reject or to allow the authority of those visions, yet, from all the accounts of them that remain to us in these days, there seems to be the greatest reason to suspect that they were *all contrived, or authorized at least, by the leading men of the Church.*"[s]

94. Such, then, is the opinion of Christian Apologists concerning the nature of those miracles to which our Lord mainly entrusted the cause of His sacred truth; for, however great the differences may be between the Scripture and Ecclesiastical miracles, viewed as a whole, so far is certain, that the actual and immediate instruments by which the world was convinced of the Gospel were those which these writers distinctly discredit as of an ambiguous and suspicious character. And, if it be asked whether, after all, such miracles are not suspicious, whatever be the consequence of admitting it, I answer, that they are suspicious to read of, but not to see. The particular circumstances of an exorcism, which no narrative can convey, might bring home to the mind a conviction that it was a divine work, quite sufficient for conversion; and much more a number of such awful exhibitions. Generalized statements and abstract arguments are poor representations of fact;

[r] Page 82.   [s] Page 109.

but, as they are used to serve the purpose of those who would disparage Saints, it is necessary to show that they can be turned by unbelievers as plausibly, though as sophistically, against Apostles.

5.

95. To proceed. The same words of our Saviour which have introduced these remarks in defence of the nature of the ecclesiastical gifts will suggest an explanation of certain difficulties in the mode of their exercise. Christ says, first, "He that believeth shall be saved;" and then, "These signs shall follow them that believe." Here it is obvious to remark, that the power of working miracles is not promised in these words to the *preachers* of the Gospel merely, but to the *converts*.[t] It is not said, "Preach the Gospel to

[t] "Nec enim prædicantes illa secutura signa pollicetur, sed credentes; nec eos qui jam antea credidissent, sed qui essent postea deinde credituri. Responditque eventus accuratissimè; conversis enim, non conversoribus, gratias illas donatas esse constat de quibus legimus in primis Ecclesiarum conversionibus." Dodw. in Iren. Dissert. ii. 28. This is so fully taken for granted by St. Bernard, that he thinks it necessary to answer the objection why "credentes" did not work miracles in his day: "Quis enim ea, quæ in præsenti loco scripta sunt, signa videtur habere credulitatis, sine quâ nemo poterit salvari? quoniam qui non crediderit condemnabitur, et sine fide impossibile est placere Deo." Serm. i. de Ascens. 2. He answers to the question as St. Gregory does in the passage quoted, *supra*, n. 40, making the miracles now wrought by the faithful to be moral ones. Kuinoel says: "Per τοὺς πιστεύοντας *non omnes* Christi sectatores intelligendi sunt, nam non

for the Ecclesiastical Miracles.

every creature, and these signs shall follow your preaching," but "these signs shall follow them that believe," the same persons to whom salvation is promised in the verse preceding.[u] And further, whereas final salvation is there represented as a personal gift, the gift of miracles is not granted here to "*him* that believeth," but to "*them* that believe." And the

omnes Christiani ejusmodi miracula patrabant, qualia hoc loco describuntur, sed agit Christus hoc loco ut locis parallelis, Luc. 24, 48. John 20, 19, *cum legatis suis*, atque adeo significantur imprimis Apostoli, et præter eos alii tunc temporis præsentes, qui haud dubiè è numero septuaginta discipulorum erant. Vid. Luc. 24, 33, coll. Luc. 10, 1 ; 9, 17, Etiam infra v. 20, disertè commemorantur ἐκεῖνοι, illi Christi discipuli, quibus ea dixit, quæ hoc loco leguntur, et ad hos σημεῖα referuntur. Monuit præterea Storrius articulum τοῦs sæpe *certos, quosdam*, non omnes universos significare. Vid. Luc. 18, 15. Coll. Marc. 10, 13. Matt. 21, 34. 36. 27, 62. 28, 12. Insignivit autem, ut opinor, Christus discipulos suos, futuros religionis suæ doctores, tunc temporis præsentes, voce τοῖs πιστεύσασι, quoniam paulo ante eorum incredulitatem vituperarat : " in loc. This is such strange reasoning, that it is the best argument for showing how futile the attempt is to wrest our Lord's words from their plain meaning. The elder school of Protestants was more candid. " Non omnibus omnia," says Grotius, " ita tamen ut cuilibet, ut oportet, credenti, aliqua tunc data sit admirabilis facultas, quæ se non semper quidem, sed datâ occasione, explicaret."

[u] Sulpicius almost grounds his defence of St. Martin's miracles on the antecedent force of this text. He says of those who deny them, " Nec Martino in hac parte detrahitur, sed fidei Evangelii derogatur. Nam cùm Dominus ipse testatus sit istiusmodi opera, quæ Martinus implevit, ab omnibus fidelibus esse facienda, qui Martinum non credit ista fecisse, non credit Christum ista dixisse." Dial. i. 18.

particular word used, which the Authorized Version translates "follow," suggests or encourages the notion that the miracles promised were to *attend upon* or to be *collateral with* their faith, as general indications and tokens;[v] not indeed that they were to be the result of every act of faith and in every person, but that on the whole, where men were united together by faith in the name of Christ, there miracles would also be wrought by Him who was "in the midst of them." Thus the gift was rather in the Church than of the Church.

96. An important text already quoted teaches us the same thing: "I will pour out My Spirit upon all flesh; and your sons and your daughters shall prophesy, your old men shall dream dreams, your young men shall see visions: and also upon the servants and upon the handmaids in those days will I pour out My Spirit." The young, the old, the bond and the free, all flesh, all conditions of men, were to be the recipients of the miraculous illuminations of the Gospel. The event exactly accomplished the prediction. In the very opening of the New Dispensation, not only Zacharias the Priest, but Mary the young

[v] Σημεῖα ταῦτα παρακολουθήσει. "Stephanus in Thes. hæc citat ex Dioscoride in præf. lib. 6. τὰ παρακολουθοῦντα σημεῖα ἑκάστῳ τῶν φαρμάκων." Raphel. Annot. in loc. Vid. ibid. in Luc. i. 3. In the last words of the Gospel, where the "signs following" are wrought by the *Apostles*, and in *confirmation*, the word is ἐπακολουθούντων.

maiden, Elizabeth the matron, Anna the widow of fourscore and four years, and just and aged Simeon, were inspired to bear witness to it. Again, in the Book of Acts, while Peter was preaching to Cornelius, "the Holy Ghost fell on *all* them which heard the word." At Ephesus, when St. Paul had laid his hands on John's disciples, the Holy Ghost came on them, "and all the men were about twelve." Moreover, we hear of St. Philip's "four daughters, virgins, which did prophesy." And the disorders of the Church of Corinth plainly show that the miraculous gifts were not confined to one or two principal persons of high station or spiritual attainments, but were "dispersed abroad" with a bountiful hand over all the faithful. The same inference may be drawn from St. Peter's direction, "As every man hath received the gift, even so minister the same one to another, as good stewards of the manifold grace of God." Such, then, is the Scripture account of the bestowal of the miraculous powers in the Apostolic age; and, I repeat, it serves to remove certain misapprehensions and objections which have been made to their exhibition as instanced in the times that follow.

97. For instance, there seems a fallacy in the mode in which a phrase is used, which often occurs in the controversy. It has been contended that there is no "standing gift of miracles" in the Church; and then it is concluded that *therefore* no manifestation of

Divine Power takes place in it, but those rare and solemn interpositions which we have reason to think actually occur even in heathen countries. "The position which I affirm," says Middleton, "is that, after the days of the Apostles, no *standing power* of miracles was continued *to* the Church, to which they might perpetually appeal for the conviction of unbelievers. Yet all my antagonists treat my argument as if it absolutely rejected *everything* of a miraculous kind, whether wrought within the Church by the agency of men, or on any other occasion by the immediate hand of God."[x] Now, there is an ambiguity in the words "standing power," according as we take it to mean a capacity committed *to* particular persons and exercised *by* them, or a Divine Agency generally operating *in* the Church and *among* Christians, as its Almighty Author wills. Middleton denies the standing power in its former sense; but in our Lord's promise, as well as in St. Paul's description of the presence of the Holy Spirit in the Church, the latter is the prominent idea. Middleton speaks, just after the passage above quoted, of "the Church *having* no standing power of *working*" miracles, and elsewhere of a "standing power of *working* miracles, as *exerted openly* in the Church, *for* the conviction of unbelievers."[y] Again, he speaks of the "opinion that after

[x] Vindic. p. 32, as quoted by Douglas, p. 224.
[y] Inquiry, p. 9.

for the Ecclesiastical Miracles. 213

the days of the Apostles there resided still in the primitive Church, through several successive ages, a divine and extraordinary *power of working miracles*, which was frequently and openly *exerted*, in confirmation of the truth of the Gospel, and for the conviction of unbelievers."[z] In like manner Douglas says of Middleton that "his Free Inquiry is not, whether any miracles were performed after the times of the Apostles, but whether, after that period, *miraculous powers subsisted* in the Church ; not whether God interposed at all, but whether He interposed by making use of men as His instruments."[a] Here he makes "the subsistence of miraculous powers" equivalent with "the instrumentality of men in their operation ;" meaning by the latter the conscious exercise of them by inspired persons in proof of a divine mission, as a former passage of his work shows.[b] The present Bishop of Lincoln (Kaye) takes the same view of the controversy, observing that Middleton's object "was to prove that, after the Apostolic age, no *standing power* of working miracles existed in the Church, that there was *no regular succession* of favoured *individuals* upon whom God conferred supernatural powers, *which they could exercise* for the benefit of the Church of Christ, whenever their *judgment*, guided by the in-

---

[z] Introd. Disc. init. ; but in Pref. p. xxxii. he speaks more to the purpose.

[a] Page 224.   [b] Page 216.

fluence of the Holy Spirit, told them that it was expedient so to do."[c] Certainly, if this is what Middleton set about to do, he had not a difficult task before him.

98. Yet Lord Barrington, before Middleton, had implied that the question lay between the same two issues. "There cannot be much doubt," he says, "of these gifts lasting as much longer as the oldest of those lived to whom St. John imparted them. . . . Irenæus, speaking of the prophetic gifts, mentions the gift of tongues and the discernment of spirits. And that these did not last longer seems to have been the case in fact, since Irenæus, who died about the year 190, in a very old age, speaks of his having *seen* these gifts, but says nothing of *his own* having them."[d] That is, Barrington makes no medium between a definite transmission of the gift from Christian to Christian by imposition of hands or similar formal act, such as would involve Irenæus's own possession of it, and on the other hand its having utterly failed. Irenæus saw the gift, he had it not, therefore it was failing in his time; else he would have had it.

99. What ecclesiastical history rather inculcates is the doctrine of an abiding presence of Divinity such as dwelt upon the Ark, showing itself as it would, and when it would, and without fixed rules; which

[c] Kaye's Tertull. p. 104.
[d] Vol. i. pp. 221, 222, ed. 1828.

for the Ecclesiastical Miracles.

was seated primarily in the body of Christians, and manifested itself sometimes in persons, sometimes in places, as the case might be, in saintly men, or in "babes and sucklings," or in the very stones of the Temple; which for a while was latent, and then became manifest again; which to some persons, places, or generations was an evidence, and to others was not.[e] The ideas of "regular succession," conscious "exercise" of power, objects deliberately contemplated, discretionary use of a gift, and the like, are quite foreign to a theory of miraculous agency of this kind; yet, at the same time, it cannot surely be denied that in one sense such an appointment may

[e] Dodwell has a theory (which agrees with what is said in the text, except that he applies it only to the first ages) that miracles abounded or became scarce according to the need, the conversion of the nations being the chief object. "Promisit Dominus majora editurum, qui in illum postea crediderit, miracula quam quæ ipse Dominus ediderit. Quod ego facile moderandum esse concessero, ut et de certis Evangelii propagandi temporibus promissio illa fuerit intelligenda. . . Sed nec ita adimpleta est quin superesset adhuc satis amplus locus futuris postea conversionibus, futurisque adeo miraculis. . . Trajano Imperante novas Evangelii propagandi causâ susceptas expeditiones memorat Eusebius, et quidem id novâ Dei comitante gratiâ atque συνεργείᾳ. . . Ortis jam sub Hadriano Hæreticis, . . factum est ut miracula infidelium hæreticorum causâ præstanda fuerint etiam et ipsa frequentiora. . . A Marci temporibus deficere cœperunt, . . cùm nullas aut raras admodum per ea sæcula expeditiones obirent Christiani ad gentes ex professo convertendas ; . . satis tamen liberalem adhuc fuisse Deum multa ostendunt," etc., etc. Dissert. in Iren. ii. 28—45, etc.

rightly be called a "standing power," and that it is very much more than such rare "interpositions of Providence," and such "miracles of invisible agency," as the above writers seem to consider the only alternative to the admission of a discretionary, and conscious, and transmitted gift.

100. The Ark was a standing instrument of miraculous operation, yet it did not send forth its virtue at all times, nor at the will of man. What was the nature of its mysterious powers we learn from the beginning of the First Book of Samuel; where we read of it first as stationed in the tabernacle, and of the Almighty speaking from it to the child Samuel; next it is captured in battle by the Philistines; but next, when it is set up in the house of Dagon, the idol, without visible cause, falls down before it, and its worshippers are smitten. Next, the cattle which are yoked to it are constrained against their natural instinct to carry it back to Israel. And then the men of Bethshemeth are smitten for looking into it. Was there, or was there not, then, a standing power of miracles in the Jewish Church? There was not, in the sense in which Middleton understands the phrase; there was no "regular succession" of "individuals" who exercised supernatural gifts with a divinely enlightened discretion; even the Prophets were not such a body; yet the Divine Presence consisted in much more than an occasional and extraordinary visitation or intervention

in the course of events. That such too should be the nature of the Presence in the Christian Church is at least quite consistent with the tenor of the new Testament; and is almost implied when, in the text which has given rise to these remarks, our Lord bestows its miraculous manifestations upon the body at large. The supernatural glory might abide, and yet be manifold, variable, uncertain, inscrutable, uncontrollable, like the natural atmosphere; dispensing gleams, shadows, traces of Almighty Power, but giving no such clear and perfect vision of it as one might gaze upon and record distinctly in its details for controversial purposes. Thus we are told, " The wind bloweth where it listeth;" "a little while, and ye shall not see Me: and again, a little while, and ye shall see Me;" "their eyes were holden," and "they knew Him, and He vanished;" "suddenly there came a sound from heaven;" when they had prayed, the place was shaken where they were assembled together; "all these worketh that One and the selfsame Spirit, dividing to every man severally as He will." At one time our Lord connects the gift with special holiness, as when He says that certain exorcisms require " prayer and fasting;" at another He allows it to the reprobate, as when He says that those whom He never knew will in the last day appeal to the wonderful works they did in His Name. At one time St. Paul, in evidence of his divine mission, says, " Truly the signs of an

Apostle were wrought among you;" at another he seems to ascribe the power to an imposture: "Though an Angel from heaven preach any other Gospel unto you, let him be accursed."

6.

101. Another difficulty which the text in question enables us to meet is the indiscriminate bestowal of the miraculous gift, as we read of it in ecclesiastical history. Its being in the Church, not of the Church, implies this apparent disorder and want of method in its manifestations, as has been already observed. Yet Middleton objects, speaking of the Fathers, " None of these venerable Saints have anywhere affirmed, that either they themselves, or the Apostolic Fathers before them, were endued with any power of working miracles, but declare only *in general*, that such powers *were actually subsisting* in their days and openly existed in the Church; that they had often seen the wonderful effects of them; and that everybody else might see the same, whenever they pleased; but as to the persons who wrought them, they leave us strangely in the dark; for instead of specifying names, conditions, and characters, their general style is, Such and such works are done among us or by us; by our people; by a few; by many; by our exorcists; by ignorant laymen, women, boys, and any simple Christian whatsoever."[f] That is, his objection

[f] Page 22.

for the Ecclesiastical Miracles. 219

is against the very idea of a gift, committed to the body of the Church, or abiding in the Church. Objectors are hard to please ; sometimes they imply dislike of the notion of the gift as delegated to a ministerial succession, and formally transmitted from individual to individual, and then, on the contrary, of its belonging to the Church itself without the intervention of rites of appropriation or definite recipients: what is this but saying that they will not entertain the notion of a continuance of miracles at all? As to Middleton's objection, it seems directed against the prophetic anticipation of the times of the Gospel made to the Jews, as quoted already, that " their sons and daughters should prophesy, their young men see visions, and their old men dream dreams," quite as much as against any seeming incongruities and anomalies which are found in the early Church.

102. Middleton's complaint, that the Fathers do not themselves profess a miraculous gift, is echoed by Gibbon. "It may seem somewhat remarkable," he says, "that Bernard of Clairvaux, who records so many miracles of his friend St. Malachi, never takes any notice of his own, which, in their turn, however, are carefully related by his companions and disciples. In the long series of ecclesiastical history, does there exist a single instance of a Saint asserting that he himself possessed the gift of miracles?"[g] The con-

[g] Ch. xv. note s.

cluding question concerns our present subject, though St. Bernard himself is far removed from the period of history on which we are engaged. I observe then, first, that it is not often that the *gift* of miracles is even ascribed to a Saint.[h] In many cases miracles are only ascribed to their tombs or relics ; or when miracles are ascribed to them when living, these are but single and occasional, not parts of a series. Moreover, they are commonly what Paley calls *tentative* miracles, or some out of many which have been attempted, and have been done accordingly without any previous confidence in their power to effect them. Moses and Elijah could predict the result ; but the miracles in question were scarcely more than experiments and trials, even though success had been granted them many times before.[i] Under these cir-

[h] "Hoc intercedit discrimen inter sanctos antiqui et Novi Testamenti, quòd Deus, intercessione Sanctorum V. T., miracula operari dignatus est sæpius in vitâ, et rarius post obitum eorum ; et quoad Sanctos N. T. sæpius post obitum et rarius in vitâ ipsorum ; cùm Sancti V. T. utpote a Deo ipso canonizati, miraculis post obitum non indigerent ; sancti autem N. T. ab Ecclesiâ canonizandi, miraculis post obitum indigeant . . . Cùm nulla [S. Joannes B.] in vitâ miracula fecisset, putavit Herodes eum post suam in Christo resurrectionem miracula fuisse editurum, ' Ait pueris suis, Hic est Joannes Baptista, etc., et ideo virtutes operantur in eo.'" Bened. xiv. de Canon. Sanct. iv. 1. § 26.

[i] The present Bishop of London argues from Origen's expression, οὓς ὁ θεὸς βούλεται, (Contr. Cels. ii. 33), "that the attempts, which no doubt were made to effect miraculous cures, were not always successful ;" vid. Athan. Vit. Ant. 56

cumstances, how could the individual men who wrought them appeal to them themselves? It was not till afterwards, when their friends and disciples could calmly look back upon their life, and review the various actions and providences which occurred in the course of it, that they would be able to put together the scattered tokens of Divine favour, none or few of which might in themselves be a certain evidence of a miraculous power. As well might we expect men in their lifetime to be called Saints, as workers of miracles. But this is not all; the objection serves to suggest a very observable distinction, which holds good between the conduct of those whose miracles are designed to be evidence of the truth of religion, and that of others though similarly gifted. The Apostles, for instance, did their miracles openly, because these were intended to be instruments of conversion; but when the supernatural Power took up its abode in the Church, and manifested itself as it would, and not for definite objects which it signified at the time of its manifestation, it could not but seem to imply some personal privilege, when operating in an individual, who would in consequence be as little inclined to proclaim it aloud as to make a boast of his graces.

where this very thing is confessed: then he continues: "and *if so*, we may *safely infer* that where they *did* succeed, they were to be ascribed to the *ordinary* means of healing under the Divine blessing." Bishop Blomfield's Sermons, p. 434. I cannot follow his Lordship in calling this inference a safe one.

7.

103. The same peculiarity in the gift will also account for that deficiency in the evidence, and other unsatisfactory circumstances of a like nature, which have already been spoken of. Since the Divine manifestation was arbitrary, the testimony would necessarily be casual. What else could be expected in the case of occurrences of which there was no notice beforehand, and often no trace after, and where we are obliged to be contented with such witnesses as happened to be present, or, if they cannot be found, with the mere report which has circulated from them? and when perhaps, as was noticed in the last paragraph, the principal parties felt it to be wrong to court publicity, after our Lord's pattern, and perhaps shrank from examination? "There is no man," said His brethren to Him, "that doeth anything in secret, and he himself seeketh to be known openly; if Thou do these things, show Thyself to the world." In our Lord's own case there was a time for concealment and a time for display; and, as it was a time for evidence when miracles were wrought by the Apostles, so afterwards there was a time for other objects and other uses, when miracles were wrought through the Church; and as our Lord's miracles were true, though the Jews complained that He "made them so long to doubt," so it is no disproof of the miracles of the Church, that those who do not wish them true have

for the Ecclesiastical Miracles.

8.

104. One more remark is in point. Middleton, in the extract above quoted, finds fault with the Fathers for "declaring only in *general*" that miracles continued, that they had seen them themselves, and that any one else might see them who would, while they made no attempt to specify the names, conditions, and characters of the persons working them. Yet surely this is but natural, if such miracles were as frequent as ecclesiastical history represents. Instead of its being an objection to them, it is just the state of things which must necessarily follow, supposing they were such and so wrought as is described. When we are speaking of what is obvious, and allowed on all hands, we do not go about to prove it. We only argue when there is doubt; we only consult documents, and weigh evidence, and draw out proofs, when we are not eye-witnesses. If the Fathers had seen miracles of healing or exorcisms not unfrequently, and were writing to others who had seen the like, they would use the confident yet vague language which we actually find in their accounts. The state of the testimony is but in keeping with the alleged facts.

105. For instance, St. Justin speaks of the Incarna-

tion as having taken place "for the sake of believers, and for the overthrow of evil spirits;" and "*you may know this now,*" he continues, "*from what passes before your eyes;* for many demoniacs all over the world, and in your own metropolis, whom none other exorcists, conjurers, or sorcerers have cured, these have many of our Christians cured, adjuring by the Name of Christ, and still do cure." Again: "With us even hitherto are prophetical gifts, *from which* you Jews ought to gather that what formerly belonged to your race is transferred to us;" and soon after, quoting the passage from the prophet Joel, he adds, "and with us *may be seen* females and males with gifts from the Spirit of God." And St. Irenæus: "In His Name His true disciples, receiving the grace from Himself, work for the benefit of other men, as each has received the gift from Him. For some cast out devils certainly and truly, so that oftentimes the cleansed persons themselves become believers, and join the Church. Others have foreknowledge of things future, visions, and prophetical announcements. Others by imposition of hands heal the sick, and restore them to health. Moreover, as I have said, before now even the dead have been restored to life, and have continued with us for many years. *Indeed, it is not possible to tell the number* of gifts which the Church throughout the world has received from God in the Name of Christ Jesus, who was crucified under Pontius Pilate, and exercises day by day for the benefit of the nations, neither seducing nor taking money of any." Shortly before he observes, that the heretics could not raise the dead, " as our Lord did, and the Apostles by prayer ; and in the brotherhood *frequently* for some necessary object, (the whole Church in the place asking it with much fasting and supplication,) the spirit of the dead has returned, and the man has been granted to the prayers of the Saints." And again, he speaks of his " *hearing* many brothers in the Church who had prophetical gifts, and spoke by the Spirit in all tongues, and brought to light the hidden things of men for a profitable purpose, and related the mysteries of God." And in like manner Tertullian : " *Place some possessed person before your tribunals ;* any Christian shall command that spirit to speak, who shall as surely confess himself to be a devil with truth, as elsewhere he will call himself a god with falsehood. . . . What work can be clearer ? . . . there will be no room for suspicion ; you would say that it is magic, or some other deceit, if your eyes and ears allowed you, for what is there to urge against that which is proved by its naked sincerity ?" Again Origen speaks of persons healing, " with no invocation over those who need a cure, but that of the God of all and the Name of Jesus, with some narrative concerning Him. By these," he adds, " we, too, *have seen many* set free from severe complaints, and loss of mind, and madness, and numberless other such evils, which neither men nor devils had cured."[k]

106. This is the very language which we are accustomed to use, when facts are so notorious that the *onus dubitandi* may fairly be thrown upon those who question them. All that can be said is, that the facts are not notorious *to us;* certainly not, but the Fathers wrote for contemporaries, not for the eighteenth or nineteenth century, not for modern notions and theories, for distant countries, for a degenerate people and a disunited Church. They did not foresee that evidence would become a science, that doubt would be thought a merit, and disbelief a privilege; that it would be in favour and condescension to them if they were credited, and in charity that they were accounted honest. They did not feel that man was so self-sufficient, and so happy in his prospects for the future, that he might reasonably sit at home closing his ears to all reports of Divine interpositions till they were actually brought before his eyes, and faith was superseded by sense; they did not so disparage the Spouse of Christ

[k] Justin, Apol. ii. 6. Tryph. 82, 88. Iren. Hær. ii. 32, § 4, 31, § 2, v. 6, § 1. Tertull. Apol. 23. Origen, contr. Cels. iii. 24. Vid. also Justin, Apol. 1, 40. Tryph. 30, 39, 76, and 85. Tertull. Apol. 37, 43. Scorp. 1. Test. Anim. 3 Ad. Scap. 4. Minuc. F. 27. Theoph. ad Autol. ii. 8. Origen, contr. Cels. i. 46, 67, ii. 33, iii. 36. Cyprian, Ep. 76, fin. ad. Magn. circa fin. vid. supr. n. 32. [Vid. also note and passages in Murdoch's Mosheim, t. i. p. 128.]

as to imagine that she could be accounted by professing Christians a school of error, and a workshop of fraud and imposture. They wrote with the confidence that they were Christians, and that those to whom they transmitted the Gospel would not call them the ministers of Antichrist.

Chapter V.

ON THE EVIDENCE FOR PARTICULAR ALLEGED MIRACLES.

107. IT does not strictly fall within the scope of this Essay to pronounce upon the truth or falsehood of this or that miraculous narrative as it occurs in Ecclesiastical History; but only to furnish such general considerations as may be useful in forming a decision in particular cases. Yet considering the painful perplexity which many feel when left entirely to their own judgments in important matters, it may be allowable to go a step further, and without ruling open questions this way or that, to throw off the abstract and unreal character which attends a course of reasoning, by setting down the evidence for and against certain miracles as we meet with them. Moreover, so much has been said in the foregoing pages in behalf of the Ecclesiastical Miracles, antecedently considered, that it may be hastily inferred that all miraculous relations and reports should be admitted unhesitatingly and indiscriminately, without any attempt at separating truth from falsehood, or suspense

of judgment, or variation in the reliance placed in them one with another, or reserve or measure in the open acknowledgment of them. And such an examination of particular instances, as is proposed, may give opportunity to one or two additional remarks of a general character for which no place has hitherto been found.

108. An inquirer, then, should not enter upon the subject of the miracles reported or alleged in ecclesiastical history, without being prepared for fiction and exaggeration in the narrative, to an indefinite extent. This cannot be insisted on too often; nothing but the gift of inspiration could have hindered it. Nay, he must not expect that more than a few can be exhibited with evidence of so cogent and complete a character as to demand his acceptance; while a great number of them, as far as the evidence goes, are neither certainly true nor certainly false, but have very various degrees of probability viewed one with another; all of them recommended to his devout attention by the circumstance that others of the same family have been proved to be true, and all prejudiced by his knowledge that so many others on the contrary are certainly not true. It will be his wisdom, then, not to reject or scorn accounts of miracles, where there is a fair chance of their being true; but to allow himself to be in suspense, to raise his mind to Him of whom they may possibly be telling to "stand in awe,

and sin not," and to ask for light,—yet to do no more; not boldly to put forward what, if it be from God, yet has not been put forward by Him. What He does in secret, we must think over in secret; what He has " openly showed in the sight of the heathen," we must publish abroad, " crying aloud, and sparing not." An alleged miracle is not untrue because it is unproved; nor is it excluded from our faith because it is not admitted into our controversy. Some are for our conviction, and these we are to " confess with the mouth" as well as "believe with the heart;" others are for our comfort and encouragement, and these we are to " keep, and ponder them in our heart," without urging them upon unwilling ears.

109. No one should be surprised at the admission that few of the Ecclesiastical Miracles are attended with an evidence sufficient to subdue our reason, because few of the Scripture Miracles are furnished with such an evidence. When a fact comes recommended to us by arguments which do not admit of an answer, when plain and great difficulties are in the way of denying it, and none, or none of comparative importance, in the way of admitting it, it may be said to subdue our reason. Thus Apologists for Christianity challenge unbelievers to produce an hypothesis sufficient to account for its doctrines, its rise, and its success, short of its truth; thus Lord Lyttelton analyses the possible motives and principles of the human

Alleged Miracles.

mind, in order to show that St. Paul's conversion admits of but one explanation, viz., that it was supernatural; thus writers on Prophecy appeal to its fulfilment, which they say can be accounted for by referring it to a Divine inspiration, and in no other way. Leslie, Paley, and others have employed themselves on similar arguments in defence of Revealed Religion. I am not saying how far arguments of a bold, decisive, and apparently demonstrative character, however great their value, are always the deepest and most satisfactory; but they are those which in this day are the most popular; they are those, the absence of which is made an objection to the Ecclesiastical Miracles. It is right then to remind those who consider this objection as fatal to these miracles, that the Miracles of Scripture are for the most part exposed to the same. If the miracles of Church History cannot be defended by the arguments of Leslie, Lyttelton, Paley, or Douglas, how many of the Scripture miracles satisfy their conditions? Some infidel authors advise us to accept no miracles which would not have a verdict in their favour in a court of justice; that is, they employ against Scripture a weapon which Protestants would confine to attacks upon the Church; as if moral and religious questions required legal proofs, and evidence were the test of truth.

110. It is true that the Scripture miracles were, for the most part, evidence of a Divine Revelation at the

time when they were wrought; but they are not so at this day. Only a few of them fulfil this purpose now; and the rest are sustained and authenticated by these few.[1] The many never have been evidence except to those who saw them, and have but held the place of doctrine ever since; like the truths revealed to us about the unseen world, which are matters of faith, not means of conviction. They have no existence, as it were, out of the record in which they are found; they are not found as facts in the world, influencing its course, and proving their reality by their power, but as sacred truths taught us by inspiration. Such are the greater number of our Lord's miracles viewed individually; we believe His restoration of the widow's son, or His changing water into wine, as we believe His transfiguration, on the word of His Evangelists. We believe the miracles of Elisha, because our Lord has Himself recognised the book containing the record of them. The great arguments by which unbelievers are silenced do not reach as far as these particular instances. As was just now noticed, one of the most cogent proofs of the miracles of Christ and His Apostles is drawn from their effects; it being inconceivable that a rival power to Cæsar should have started out of so obscure and ignorant a spot as Galilee, and have prevailed, without some such extraordinary and divine gifts: yet this argument, it will be

[1] Vid. *supr.* Essay i. pp. 9, 55, 91, 92; also pp. 187, 207.

Alleged Miracles. 233

observed, proves nothing about the miracles *one by one* as reported in the Gospels, but only that the Christian *story* was miraculous, or that miracles attended it. Paley's argument goes little beyond proving the fact of the Resurrection, or, at most, that there were certain sensible miracles wrought by our Lord, such as cures, to which St. Peter alludes in his speech to Cornelius, yet without specifying what. Again, Douglas considers that " we may suspect miracles to be false," the account of which was not published at the time or place of their alleged occurrence, or if so published, yet without careful attention being called to them ; yet St. Mark is said to have written at Rome, St. Luke in Rome or Greece, and St. John at Ephesus ; and the earliest of the Evangelists wrote some years after the events recorded, while the latest did not write for sixty years ; and, moreover, true though it be that attention was called to Christianity from the first, yet it is true also that it did not succeed at the spot where it arose, but principally at a distance from it. Once more, Leslie almost confines his tests to the Mosaic miracles, or rather to certain of them ; and though he is unwilling to exclude those of the Gospel from the benefit of his argument, yet it is not easy to see how he brings them under it at all.

111. On the whole, then, it will be found that the greater part of the Miracles of Revelation are as little evidence for Revelation at this day, as the Miracles

of the Church are now evidence for the Church. In both cases the number of those which carry with them their own proof now, and are believed for their own sake, is small; and these furnish the grounds on which we receive the rest. The difference between the two cases is this:—that, since an authentic document has been provided for the miracles by which Revealed Religion was introduced, which are thus connected together into one whole, we know here exactly what miracles are to be received on warrant of those which are already proved; but since the Church has never catalogued her miracles, those which are known to be such do but create an indefinite presumption in favour of others, but cannot be taken in proof of any in particular.

112. On the other hand, that fables have ever been in circulation, some vague and isolated, others attached to particular spots or to particular persons, is too notorious to need dwelling on: it is more to the purpose to observe that the fact of such pretences has ever been acknowledged even by those who have been believers or reporters of miraculous occurrences. We have seen above[m] that one of St. Martin's first miracles in his episcopate, as recorded by Sulpicius, was the detection of a pretended Saint and Martyr, whose tomb had been an object of veneration to the ignorant people. And in the very beginning of Christianity St. Luke, in speaking of the "many" who had "taken in hand to set forth in

[m] N. 28

Alleged Miracles.

order a declaration of those things which are most surely believed among us," seems to allude to the Apocryphal Gospels,[n] which ascribe a number of trifling as well as fictitious miracles to our Lord. And when St. Paul cautions the Thessalonians against being "soon shaken in mind or troubled, by spirit or by letter, as from himself, as that the day of Christ was at hand," he testifies both to the fact that spurious writings were then ascribed to him, and that they contained professedly supernatural matter.

113. What is confessed by Apostles and Evangelists in the first century, and by Martyrologists in the fourth, would naturally happen both in the interval and afterwards. Hence Pope Gelasius, while warning the faithful against several Apocryphal works, mentions among them the Acts of St. George, the Martyr under Dioclesian, which had been so interpolated by the Arians, that to this day, though he is the patron of England, and in Chapters of the Garter is commemorated with honours which even Apostles do not gain from us, nothing whatever is known for certain of his life, sufferings, or miracles.[o] Again, we are told by St. John Damascene, and in the Revelations of St. Bridget and St. Mathildis, that the Em-

---

[n] Jones, On the Canon, part i. ch. 2, has collected the ancient and modern authorities in proof that St. Luke was alluding to the Apocryphal writings. Wolf denies it, Cur. Phil. in loc.

[o] Baron, Annal. 290. 35. Martyrol. Apr. 23.

peror Trajan was delivered from the place of punishment at the prayers of St. Gregory the First; but Baronius says, concerning this and similar stories, "Away with idle tales; silence once for all on empty fables; be they buried in eternal silence. We excuse those who, accounting true what they received as fact, committed it to writing; praise to their zeal, who, when they found it asserted, discussed in scholastic fashion how it might be; but more praise to them who, scenting the falsehood, detected the error."[p] Melchior Canus, again, a Dominican and a Divine of Trent, uses the same language even of St. Gregory's Dialogues and the Ecclesiastical History of Bede. "They are most eminent persons," he says, "but still men; they relate certain miracles as commonly reported and believed, which critics, especially of this age, will consider uncertain. Indeed, I should like those histories better, if their authors had joined more care in selection to severity in judgment;"[q] though he adds that far more was to be retained in their works than was to be rejected. He does not, however, speak even in these measured terms of the Speculum Exemplorum, and the Aurea Legenda of Jacobus de Voragine; the former of which, he says, contains "monsters of miracles rather than truths;" and the latter is the production of "an iron mouth, a leaden heart, and an

[p] Emunctis naribus odorati. Annal. 604. 49.
[q] Loc. Theol. xi. 6.

Alleged Miracles.

intellect without exactness or discretion." Avowals such as these from the first century to the sixteenth, from inspired writers to the schools of St. Dominic and the Oratory, may serve to prepare us for fictitious miracles in ecclesiastical history in no small measure, and to show us at the same time that such fictions are no fair prejudice to others which possess the characters of truth.[r] And in like manner, if it be necessary, exceptions might be taken to certain of the miracles recorded by Palladius in his Lausiac, and by Theodoret in his Religious History, and by the unknown collector of the miracles of St. Stephen, which a late writer has brought forward with the hope of thereby

[r] The illustration of this subject might be pursued without limit. Tillemont quotes from a writer of the thirteenth century the broad maxim : " Quand la raison se trouve contraire à l'usage, il faut que l'usage cede à la raison ; " and proceeds to quote Papebrok as saying that we cannot too often repeat this excellent rule, "à ceux qui trouvent mauvais qu'on accuse de fausseté diverses choses qui se sont introduites dans l'Eglise par l'ignorance de l'histoire." vol. vii. p. 640. The Bollandists say, " Nimiâ profecto simplicitate peccant qui scandalizantur quoties audiunt aliquid ex jam olim creditis, et juxta Breviarii præscriptum hodiedum recitandis, in disputationem adduci." Dissert. Bolland. tom. ii. p. 140. Vid. also Alban Butler's Saints, Introd. Disc. p. xlvii., etc., ed. 1833. Bauer's Theolog. tom. i. art. ii. p. 487, and works there referred to. Benedict. XIV. de Canon. Sanct. iv. p. l. c. 5, etc. Farmer, On Miracles, p. 320 ; also the passages from various authors quoted in Geddes' Tracts, vol. iii. pp. 115,—118, ed. 1730 ; who also furnishes, though not in a good spirit, a number of specimens of the sort of miracles which such authors condemn.

involving all the supernatural histories of antiquity in a general suspicion and contempt. That Palladius has put in writing a report of a hyena's asking pardon of a solitary for killing sheep, and of a female turned by magic into a mare, or that one of the Clergy of Uzalis speaks of a serpent that was seen in the sky, will appear no reason, except to vexed and heated minds, for accusing the holy Ambrose of imposture, or the keen, practised, and experienced intellect of Augustine of abject credulity.[s]

114. Nor is there anything strange or startling in this mixture of fable with truth, as appeared from what was said on the subject in a former page. It as little derogates from the supernatural gift residing in the Church that miracles should have been fabricated or exaggerated, as it prejudices her holiness that within her pale good men are mixed with bad.

[s] "Ambrose occupies a high position among the Fathers; and there was a vigour and dignity in his character, as well as a vivid intelligence, which must command respect; but in proportion as we assign praise to the man individually, we condemn the system which could so far vitiate a noble mind, and impel one so lofty in temper to act a part which heathen philosophers would utterly have abhorred. . . . Under the Nicene system, Bishops in the great cities could stand up in crowded churches, without shame, and with uplifted hands appeal to Almighty God in attestation of that, as a miracle, which themselves had brought about by trickery, bribes, and secret instructions." Ancient Christ. part vii. pp. 270, 271. "He [Augustine] was the dupe of his own credulity, not the machinator of fraud." P. 318.

Alleged Miracles.

Fiction and pretence follow truth as its shadows; the Church is at all times in the midst of corruption, because she is in the midst of the world, and is framed out of human hearts; and as the elect are fewer than the reprobate, and hard to find amid the chaff, so false miracles at once exceed and conceal and prejudice those which are genuine. Nor would the difficulty be overcome, even if we took on ourselves to reject all the Ecclesiastical Miracles altogether; for the fictions which startle us must in fairness be viewed as connected, not only with the Church and her more authentic histories, but with Christianity, as such. Superstition is a corruption of Christianity, not merely of the Church; and if it discredits the divine origin of the Church, it discredits the divine origin of Christianity also. Those who talk even most loudly of the corruptions of the fourth and fifth centuries, seem, when closely questioned, still to admit that Christianity was not extinct, but overlaid by corruptions. If, then, the Church herself, and her miracles *in toto,* are to be included in that corruption, then of course the corruption was only deeper and broader, than if she is to be accounted as in herself a portion of Apostolic Christianity; and if such greater corruption does not compromise the divinity of Christianity, so the lesser surely does not compromise the real power and gifts of the Church. On both sides fanaticism, imposture, and superstition are admitted as existing in the history of miracles; and on neither side must these evil agents be held to throw suspicion on particular miracles which have no direct or probable connection with them.

And now, after these preliminary considerations, let us proceed to inquire into the evidence and character of several of the miracles in particular, which we meet with in the first centuries of Christianity.

Section I.

THE THUNDERING LEGION.

115. CLAUDIUS APOLLINARIS, Bishop of Hierapolis, addressed an Apology for Christianity to the Emperor Marcus, about A.D. 176. It is lost but reference to it, as it would appear, or at least to one of his works, is made by Eusebius,[r] in which Apollinaris bore witness to a remarkable answer to prayer received a year or two before by the Christian soldiers of that very Emperor's army in the celebrated war with the Quadri. Tertullian, writing about A.D. 200, and also in a public Apology, urges the same fact upon the Proconsul of Africa whom he is addressing.

116. The words of Eusebius, introductory of the evidence of Apollinaris and Tertullian, are these: " It is said that when Marcus Aurelius Cæsar was forming his troops in order of battle against the Germans and Sarmatians, he was reduced to extremities by a failure of water. Meanwhile the soldiers in the so-

[r] Hist. v. 5.

called Melitene[s] legion, which for its faith remains to this day, knelt down upon the ground, as we are accustomed to do in prayer, and betook themselves to supplication. And whereas this sight was strange to the enemy, another still more strange happened immediately,—thunderbolts, which caused the enemy's flight and overthrow; and upon the army to which the men were attached, who had called upon God, a rain, which restored it entirely when it was all but perishing by thirst." He adds, that this account was given by heathens as well as by Christians, though they did not allow that the prayers of Christians were concerned in the event. Then he quotes Apollinaris for the fact that in consequence the legion received from the Emperor the name of "Thundering." Again, Tertullian speaks of " the letters of Marcus Aurelius, an Emperor of great character, in which he testifies to the quenching of that German thirst by the shower gained by the prayers of soldiers who happened to be Christians."[t] He adds that, "while the Emperor did not openly remove the legal punishment from persons of that description, yet he did in fact dispense with it by placing a penalty, and that a more fearful one, on their accusers." And in his Ad Scapulam: "Marcus Aurelius in the German expedition obtained showers

[s] On the question of this Melitine or Melitene legion, vid. Vales. in loc. Euseb.
[t] Apol. c. 5.

in that thirst by the prayers offered up to God by Christian soldiers."[u] The statement, then, as given by two writers, one writing at the very time, the other about twenty years later, is this : that the soldiers in or of one of the Roman legions, gained by their prayers a seasonable storm of rain and thunder and lightning, when the army was perishing by thirst, and was surrounded by an enemy; and they add two evidences of it—Apollinaris, that the legion in which these soldiers were found was thenceforth called the Thundering Legion ; and Tertullian, that the Emperor in consequence passed an edict in favour of the Christians.

117. Here we are only concerned with the *fact*, not with its alleged *evidences;* and this is worth noticing, for it so happens that the fact is true, but the evidences, *as* evidences, are not true ; that is, there is just enough incorrectness in the statement to hinder their availing as evidences. This, I say, is worth noticing, because it may serve in other cases to make us cautious of rejecting facts stated by the Fathers because we discredit (rightly or wrongly is not the question) the grounds on which they rest them. Did we know no other evidence than what Apollinaris and Tertullian allege for the sudden relief of the Roman legions in Germany, we should have rejected the fact when we had invalidated the evidence; but this, as

[u] Ad Scap. c. 4.

the event shows, would have been a hasty proceeding. Sometimes facts are so notorious that proof is *ex abundanti;* and sometimes writers like those in question hurt a good cause by not leaving it to itself.

118. Now, as to the corroborative statement made by Apollinaris, writers of great authority assume that he, or other early writers, speak as if a legion in the Roman army was composed *wholly* of Christians.[v] Yet even Eusebius does but speak of "the soldiers in the Melitene legion," which is an ambiguous form of expression; while Tertullian uses the phrase, "Christianorum *forte* militum precationibus," "Christianorum militum orationibus," no mention being made of a legion at all, and the word "forte" strongly opposing the idea that the Christians formed an entire body of troops. As to Apollinaris, he, it is true, stated in his lost work, that in consequence of the miracle a legion was called "Thundering"; but we may not assume that he said more than that the Christians who prayed were *in* the legion, since there is nothing strange in the idea of a whole body obtaining a name from the good deed of some of them, nor strange, again, considering that bodies of troops were drawn, then as now, from particular places, and were open to various local or other influences, that Christians should have been numerous enough in one particular

[v] Vales. in Euseb. Hist. v. 5. Moyle's Posthumous Works, Vol. ii. p. 82. Jablonski's Opusc. Tom. iv. p. 9.

legion to give a character to it. This difficulty, however, being disposed of, a more important objection remains; there was indeed a Thundering Legion, as Apollinaris says, but then it was as old as the time of Trajan, nay, of Augustus.[x] This circumstance, of course, is fatal to his argument. Moyle, upon this, observes that "Apollinaris, the first broacher of the miracle, was grossly mistaken, to say no worse;"[y] but, though it was a mistake, it surely is not grosser than if a country clergyman at this day were to commit a blunder in speaking of the Queen's regiments serving

[x] Moyle's Posthumous Works, Vol. ii. p. 90, and Scaliger and Valesius before him. Baronius accounts for the fact by supposing that the Christian soldiers were in all parts of the army, and after this were incorporated into the existing Thundering Legion. "Par est credere, ipsum eosdem ob tam egregium atque mirandum facinus Fulminantium nomine nobilitasse, ac eosdem simul ejusdem nominis legioni pariter aggregasse." Ann. 176, 20; vid. also Witsius, Diatrib. 46. Mr. King, too, observes that Xiphilin is the only author who "absolutely affirms the soldiers of the Melitenian Legion to be all Christians." Ap. Moyle, p. 116; vid. also Milman, Christ. Vol. ii. p. 190. Moyle answers that King is the first person who has interpreted Eusebius, etc., otherwise, p. 212. Lardner, Testim. Vol. ii. Ch. 15; and Mosheim, ant. Constant. Sec 2. Ch. 17, side with Moyle. Mosheim connects "forte" with "precationibus impetrato." [Lumper, t. 7, p. 510 note, says that "forte" is African Latin for "fortuito;" he seems to agree with Mosheim in the construction. He gives a list of authors who have treated of the occurrence, p. 515.]

[y] He retracts and throws the blame on Eusebius, p. 221, almost denying that Apollinaris made the statement imputed to him. So does Neander, Church Hist., Vol. i. 1, 2.

in India or Canada. In spite of our advantages from the present diffusion of knowledge, certainly our parish priests do not know much more of the constitution or history of the British army than the Bishop of Hierapolis of the military establishments of Rome.

119. Tertullian, on the other hand, tells us that the Emperor, in a formal document, acknowledged the miracle as obtained by the prayers of the Christians, and favoured the whole body in consequence; not, indeed, repealing the laws against them, but putting a heavier punishment on informers against them than on themselves. And it would appear that the Emperor did issue a rescript in their favour in an earlier period of his reign, which Eusebius has preserved,[z] to the effect that "the parties accused of Christianity shall be pardoned, though it be proved against them, and the informer shall undergo the penalty instead;" and in the reign of Commodus, the son of Marcus, a Pagan actually had his legs broken, and was put to death, for bringing an accusation against a Christian.[a] And, further, that the Em-

[z] Moyle denies the genuineness of this Rescript, and Dodwell suspects it. Dissert. Cypr. xi. 34, fin. Moyle adds, p. 337, that G. Vossius wrote a Dissertation to prove it a forgery. Pagi and Valesius maintain it; so does Jablonski, l. c., assigning it with Pagi to the ninth year of Antoninus, while Valesius assigns it to the first.

[a] Jablonski, ibid. p. 18. Moyle suspects the story, yet without strong grounds, p. 249. It is found in Eusebius.

peror, about the time of the German war, showed a leaning towards "foreign rites," which might easily be mistaken by the Christians to include or even to imply Christianity, is made clear by one of the authors to whom reference has just been made at the foot of the page.[b] Moreover, that the Emperor recognized the miracle is very certain, as will appear directly; but, all this being undeniable, still there is no evidence for the very point on which the force of Tertullian's proof depends, viz., that his act of grace towards the Christians was in *consequence* of his belief in the miracle, and his belief that they were the cause of it.[c] So far from it, he was in a course of persecution against the Church, both before and after its date. How severely that persecution raged a few years afterwards, the well-known epistle of the Churches of Gaul informs us;[d] though its force must at least have been suspended as regards Asia Minor, otherwise Apollinaris, writing at the time, could not

[b] Jablonski, ibid. Moyle, with a different purpose, gives instances of the Emperor's leaning towards Chaldeans, magicians, etc., p. 235; vid. also p. 356.

[c] Moyle maintains, p. 244, that Tertullian does not assert this connection of Antoninus's acknowledgment of the miracle with his edict, nor any other ancient writer.

[d] Witsius, to evade the difficulty, maintains that the persecution was the consequence of a riot, and the hostility of local governors, Diatrib. c. 66. King maintains the same, ap. Moyle, p. 309. Eusebius certainly speaks of it as ἐξ ἐπιθέσεως τῶν δήμων. Hist. v. procem.

have fancied that the Emperor had recognized the miracle as the result of Christian prayer.

120. Dismissing, however, these two statements, which, though they cannot be maintained as they stand, still are not necessary conditions of the alleged miracle, and which admit, as we have seen, of a very ready explanation, we have, nevertheless, the following decisive evidence in proof of the occurrence of some extraordinary and providential storm, when the Roman army was in very critical circumstances in the course of the German war.

121. Eusebius observes that even the Pagans confessed the miracle, though they did not allow that it was attributable to the prayers of the Christians; and what is left of antiquity sufficiently confirms his statement. Indeed, so certain was the fact, that nothing was left to the Pagans but to record it and to account for it. They accounted for it by referring it to their own divinities; they recorded it on medals and on monuments. Dio Cassius calls it a "wonderful and providential" preservation, and attributes it to an Egyptian magician, of the name of Arnuphis, who invoked "Mercury, who is in the air, and other spirits." Julius Capitolinus attributes it to the Emperor's prayers. Themistius, who says the same, adds that he had seen a picture, "in the middle of which the Emperor was praying in the line of battle, and his soldiers were catching the rain in their hel-

mets, and quenching their thirst with the draught thus providentially granted." Moreover, the memorial of it is sculptured on the celebrated Antonine column at Rome, where is a figure of Jupiter Pluvius scattering lightning and rain, the enemy and their horses lying prostrate, and the Romans, sword in hand, rushing on them. A medal, too, is or was extant, of the very year of the occurrence, with the head of Antoninus crowned with laurel on one side, and a figure of Mercury on the reverse.

122. The very fact of this event being recorded with such formality on the column of Antoninus, is of itself a sufficient proof of its importance; but perhaps the reader will be more impressed by the pagan Dio's description of it, which runs as follows: "When the Barbarians would not give them battle, in hopes of their perishing by heat and thirst, since they had so surrounded them that they had no possible means of getting water, and when they were in the utmost distress from sickness, wounds, sun, and thirst, and could neither fight, nor retreat, but remained in order of battle and at their posts in this parched condition, suddenly clouds gathered, and a copious rain fell, not without the mercy of God. And when it first began to fall, the Romans, raising their mouths towards heaven, received it upon them; next, turning up their shields and helmets, they drank largely out of them, and gave to their horses. And when the Barbarians

charged them, they drank as they fought; and numbers of them were wounded, and drank out of their helmets water and blood mixed. And while they were thus incurring heavy loss from the assault of the enemy, because most of them were engaged in drinking, a violent hail-storm and much lightning were discharged upon the enemy. And thus water and fire might be seen in the same place falling from heaven, that some might drink refreshment, and others be burned to death; for the fire did not touch the Romans, or if so, it was at once extinguished; nor did the wet help the Barbarians, but burned like oil; so that, drenched with rain, they still needed moisture, and they wounded their own selves, that blood might put out the fire."[e] This of course is rhetorically written, but men do not write rhetorically without a cause, and the effort of the composition shows the marvellousness of the occurrence.

123. We are sure, then, of the providential deliverance of the army, as Eusebius and the others state it. And that there were Christians in the army we may be quite sure, from what we gather from the general history of the times, [f]even independently of what these

[e] This is translated from Baronius; but it agrees with the original in all important points, though not always literal. Dion. Hist. lxxi. p. 805. Vid. also Themist. Orat. 15.

[f] Moyle indeed contends "that there were few or none at all in the army," and observes, "Considering the passive principles of the age, I would as soon believe my Lord Marl-

writers state. And further, we may be sure also, even before we have definite authority for the fact, that they offered up prayers for deliverance.

124. Under these circumstances I do not see what remains to be proved. Here is an army in extreme jeopardy, with Christians in it; the enemy is destroyed and they are delivered. And Apollinaris, Tertullian, and Eusebius, attest[g] that these Christians

borough had a whole regiment of Quakers in his army as that Antoninus had a whole legion of Christians in his." pp. 84, 85. He argues from the testimonies of the early Fathers, of Celsus, etc., and from the oaths and other idolatrous acts to which soldiers were obliged to submit, adding, "that it was impossible for a Christian to serve in them unless it were by the help of Occasional Conformity. At least in such a case the prayers of such mock Christians would hardly work wonders." p. 87. This is an objection which, if valid, strikes deeper than any of those which I have noticed in the text. Mr. Milman observes of the alleged apparition of the Cross to Constantine, "This irreconcilable incongruity between the symbol of universal peace and the horrors of war, in my judgment, is conclusive against the miraculous or supernatural character of the transaction." Hist. of Christ, Vol. ii. p. 354. He adds, "This was the first advance to the military Christianity of the middle ages." He refers in a note to Mosheim for similar sentiments, "for which," he says, "I will readily encounter the charge of Quakerism." He then refers to the Empress Helena's turning the nails of the Cross into a helmet and bits for Constantine's war-horse. "True or false," he observes, "this story is characteristic of the Christian sentiment then prevalent." [Vid. also Lupus, Opp. t. xi. p. 94, etc. Pusey on Tertullian, p. 184. Gibbon, Miscellan. Works, p. 759, ed. 1837.]

[g] Moyle indeed maintains that the Christians in general did not believe it to be a miracle: he argues from the silence of

in the army prayed, and that the deliverance was felt at the time to be an answer to their prayers; what remains but to accept their statement? We, who are Christians as well as they, can feel no hesitation on the score that pagan writers attribute the occurrence to another cause, to magic or to false gods. Surely we may accept the evidence of the latter to the fact, without taking their hypothetical explanation of it. And we may give our own explanation to it for our own edification, in accordance with what we believe to be divine truth, without being obliged to go on to use it in argument for the conversion of unbelievers. It may be a miracle, though not one of evidence, but of confirmation, encouragement, mercy, for the sake of Christians.

125. Nor does it concern us much to answer the objection that there is nothing strictly miraculous in such an occurrence, because sudden thunder-clouds after drought are not unfrequent; for in addition to other answers which have been made to such a remark in other parts of this Essay, I would answer, Grant me such miracles ordinarily in the early Church, and I will ask no other; grant that upon prayer benefits are vouchsafed, deliverances are effected, unhoped-for

St. Theophilus, St. Clement, Origen, St. Cyprian, Arnobius, and Lactantius, p. 277. W. Lowth, however, refers to a passage in St. Cyprian, ad Demetrian. Routh, t. i. p. 153. It really seems unreasonable to demand that every Father should write about everything.

success obtained, sickness cured, tempests laid, pestilences put to flight, famines remedied, judgments inflicted, and there will be no need of inquiring into the causes, whether supernatural or natural, to which they are to be referred.[h] They may or they may not, in this or that case, follow or surpass the laws of nature, and they may surpass them plainly or doubtfully, but the common sense of mankind will call them miraculous; for by a miracle, whatever be its formal definition, is popularly meant an event which impresses upon the mind the immediate presence of the Moral Governor of the world. He may sometimes act through nature, sometimes beyond or against it, but those who admit the fact of such interferences will have little difficulty in admitting also their strictly miraculous character, if the circumstances of the case require it, and those who deny miracles to the early Church will be equally strenuous against allowing her the grace of such intimate influence (if we may so speak upon the course of Divine Providence, as

[h] Moyle is obliged to allow so much as this, saying of the defeat of the Philistines by a storm on Samuel's prayers, "This fact, though it cannot properly, in the strict and genuine sense of the word, be called a miracle, yet well deserves a place in the lower form of miracles, because it was *preternatural*, and not performed by the ordinary concurrence of second causes, but by the immediate hand of God." p. 286. Vid. Benedict. xiv. de Can. Sanct. iv. part i. 11, who instances the hail-stones in Joshua's battle as "præter naturam." Vid infr. n. 143. 193.

is here in question, even though it be not miraculous.

126. On the whole then we may conclude that the facts of this memorable occurrence are as the early Christian writers state them; that Christian soldiers did ask, and did receive, in a great distress, rain for their own supply, and lightning against their enemies; whether through miracle or not we cannot say for certain, but more probably not through miracle in the philosophical sense of the word. All we know, and all we need know is, that "He made darkness His secret place, His pavilion round about Him, with dark water and thick clouds to cover Him; the Lord thundered out of heaven, and the Highest gave His thunder; hail-stones and coals of fire. He sent out His arrows, and scattered them; He sent forth lightnings, and destroyed them."

Section II.

THE CHANGE OF WATER INTO OIL AT THE PRAYER OF ST. NARCISSUS OF JERUSALEM.

127. NARCISSUS, Bishop of Jerusalem, when oil failed for the lamps on the vigil of Easter, sent the persons who had the care of them to the neighbouring well for water. When they brought it, he prayed over it, and it was changed into oil.[i] Narcissus was made Bishop about A.D. 180, at the age of eighty-four; he was at a Council on the question of Easter 195, and lived through some years of the third century, dying at the extraordinary age of a hundred and sixteen, or more.

128. It is favourable to the truth of this account, that the instrument of the miracle was an aged, and, as also was the case, a very holy man. It may be added that he was born in the first century, before St. John's death, and was in some sense an Apostolical Father, as Jortin observes.

129. But there are certain remarkable circumstances connected with him, which, as persons regard them,

[i] Euseb. Hist. vi. 9.

will be viewed in contrary lights, as making the miracle more or as less probable. Eusebius informs us that Narcissus was for some years the victim of a malignant calumny. Three men, disliking his strictness and the discipline he exercised, accused him of some great crime, with an imprecation on themselves if they spoke falsely; the first that he might perish by fire, the second that he might be smitten with disease, and the third that he might lose his eyesight. Narcissus fled from his Church, and lived many years in the wild parts of the country, as a solitary. At length the first of his three accusers was burned in his house, with all his family; the second was covered from head to foot with the disease which he had named; and the third confessed his crime, but, overcome with shame and remorse, lost his eyes by weeping. Narcissus was restored, and died in possession of his see.

130. Now it may be said that the extraordinary nature of this history only increases the improbability of the miracle. It reads like a made story; there is a completeness about it; and there is an extravagance in the notion of the loss of sight by weeping. Yet the same thing happened to St. Francis. "His eyes," says Butler, "seemed two fountains of tears, which were almost continually falling from them, insomuch that at length he almost lost his sight." He was scared with red-hot iron from the ear to the eye-brow,

of Water into Oil.

with the hope of saving it. In his last illness "he scarce allowed himself any intermission from prayer, and would not check his tears, though the physician thought it necessary for the preservation of his sight; which he entirely lost upon his death-bed."[k] However, even though we allow that the history in question is embellished, still the general outline may remain, that Narcissus was unjustly accused and by a wonderful providence vindicated. In this point of view it surely adds to the probability of the miracle before us, that it is attributed to a man, not only so close upon Apostolic times and persons, so holy, so aged, but in addition so strangely tried, so strangely righted. It removes the abruptness and marvellousness of what at first sight looks like "naked history," as Paley calls it, or what we commonly understand by a legend. Such a man may well be accounted "worthy for whom Christ should do this." And if the foregoing circumstances are true, not only in outline, but in detail, then still greater probability is added to the miracle.

131. Jortin objects that "the change of water into oil to supply the church lamps has the air of a miracle performed upon an occasion rather too slender."[l] But Dodwell[m] had already observed that the mystical idea connected with the sacred lights gives a meaning to

[k] Lives of the Saints, Oct. 4.   [l] Dissert. in Iren. ii. 49.
[m] Vol. ii. p. 103.

it, and particularly at that season; and Eusebius tells us that the people were much troubled[n] at their failure.

132. Jortin also observes that "in the time of Augustus a fountain of oil burst out at Rome, and flowed for a whole day. In natural history there are accounts of greasy and bituminous springs, when something like oil has floated on the water. Pliny, and Hardouin in his notes, mention many such fountains, 'qui explent olei vicem,' and 'quorum aquâ lucernæ ardeant.'" This circumstance perhaps adds probability to the miracle, both as lessening its violence, (if the word may be used,) as the accompanying history of the Bishop's trials lessens it in another way, and because in matter of fact Almighty Wisdom seems, as appears from Scripture, not unfrequently to work miracles beyond, rather than against nature.

133. Eusebius notices pointedly that it was the *tradition* of the Church of Jerusalem.[o] It should be recollected, however, that the tradition had but a narrow interval to pass from Narcissus to Eusebius,—not above fifty or sixty years, as the latter was born about A.D. 264.

134. On the whole then there seems sufficient ground to justify us in accepting this narrative as in truth an instance of our Lord's gracious presence

---

[n] Δεινῆς ἀθυμίας διαλαβούσης τὸ πᾶν πλῆθος.

[o] Ὡς ἐκ παραδόσεως τῶν κατὰ διαδοχὴν ἀδελφῶν.

with His Church, though the evidence is not so definite or minute as to enable us to *realize* the miracle. This is a remark which is often in point; belief, in any true sense of the word, requires a certain familiarity or intimacy of the mind with the thing believed. Till it is in some way brought home to us and made our own, we cannot properly say we believe it, even when our reason receives it. This occurs constantly as regards matters of opinion and doctrine. Take any characteristic point of detail in the religious views of a person whom we revere and follow on the whole ; do we believe this particular doctrine or opinion of his, or do we not? We do not like to pledge ourselves to it, yet we shrink from saying that it is not true, and we defend it when we hear it attacked. We have *no doubt* about it, yet we cannot bring ourselves to say positively that we *believe* it, because belief implies an habitual presence and abidance of the matter believed in our thoughts, and a familiar acquaintance with the ideas it involves, which we cannot profess in the instance in question. Here we see the use of reading and studying the Gospels in order to true belief in our Lord ; and, again, of acting upon His words, in order to true belief in them [3] This being considered, I do not see that we can be said actually to *believe* in a miracle like that now in question, of which so little is known in detail, and

[3] [Vid. Essay towards a Grammar of Assent, Ch. iv. § 2.]

which is so little personally interesting to us; but we cannot be said to disbelieve it, there being sufficient grounds for conviction in the sense in which we believe the greater part of the accounts of general history.

Section III.

THE MIRACLE WROUGHT ON THE COURSE OF THE RIVER LYCUS BY ST. GREGORY THAUMATURGUS.

135. DOUGLAS, in his great earnestness to prove that no real miracles were wrought by the Fathers and Saints of the second and third centuries, tells us that the miracles of St. Gregory Thaumaturgus, some of which have been detailed above, " are justly rejected as inventions of a later age, and can be believed by those only who can admit the miracles ascribed to Apollonius, or those reported so long after his death to Ignatius. Gregory of Nyssa," the biographer of Thaumaturgus, " according to Dr. Cave's character of him, was apt to be too credulous. No wonder, therefore, he gave too much credit to old women's tales, as the anecdotes of the Wonder-worker must be allowed to be, when related, as we learn from St. Basil, by his aged grandmother Macrina."[p] This is not respectful either to St. Macrina or to St. Gregory Thaumaturgus, to say nothing of his treat-

[p] Page 327, note.

ment of St. Gregory Nyssen; plainly, it can mean nothing else but that St. Gregory did no miracles, and that it is weak, nay, even heathenish, to believe he did. Otherwise thinks a very careful and learned writer, not a member of our Church, and his statement may fitly be placed in contrast with the opinion of one who was a Bishop in it. "His history," says Lardner, speaking of Thaumaturgus, "as delivered by authors of the fourth and following centuries, particularly by Nyssen, it is to be feared, has in it somewhat of fiction; but there can be no reasonable doubt made but he was very successful in making converts to Christianity in the country of Pontus about the middle of the third century; and that, beside his natural and acquired abilities, he was favoured with extraordinary gifts of the Spirit, and wrought miracles of surprising power. The plain and express testimonies of Basil and others, at no great distance of time or place from Gregory, must be reckoned sufficient grounds of credit with regard to these things. Theodoret, mentioning Gregory, and his brother, and Firmilian, and Helenus, all together, ascribes miracles to none but him alone. They were all Bishops of the first rank; nevertheless Gregory had a distinction even among them. It is the same thing in Jerome's letter to Magnus; there are mentioned Hippolytus, Julius Africanus, Dionysius of Alexandria, and many others, of great note and eminence for learning and piety. But Theodore, afterwards called Gregory, is the only one who is called a man of Apostolical signs and wonders."q

136. These remarks of Lardner should be kept in mind by those who would examine the miracles attributed to St. Gregory. For it is obvious to reflect, that if we once believe that he did work miracles, it is the height of improbability that in the course of a century all of these should be forgotten, and a set of pretended miracles substituted in their place, and that among a people who are noted for a particular attachment to their old customs, and especially to the rites and usages introduced by St. Gregory. "The people of Neocæsarea," says Lardner, "retained for a long while remarkable impressions of religion; and they had an affection for the primitive simplicity, very rare and uncommon, almost singular, at that time, when innovations came into the Church apace."r And if reasons can be given for believing one of the miracles, a favourable hearing will be gained for the rest, which belong to one family with it, and are conveyed to us through the same channels. All are of the romantic kind, all come to us on tradition committed to writing by St. Gregory Nyssen. That is, we shall have reason for believing his narrative in its substance, for still there is nothing to prevent misstatement in its detail. Against this, indeed, inspiration alone could secure us.

q Credib. ii. 42, § 5.   r Vid. also above, n. 20.

137. This absence of a perfection which only attaches to inspired documents, has often been made an objection to receiving the miracles which ecclesiastical history records.[s] But there is another peculiarity about its existing materials, which applies in particular to Nyssen's Life of Thaumaturgus. That Life does not answer the purpose for which critics and controversialists require it at this day; it is very unsatisfactory as an attestation of miracles, and would not read well in a process of canonization. For in truth the author did not set himself to attest them at all; he wrote a sacred panegyrical discourse, and from the nature of the composition he left out names, dates, places, particulars, all of them necessary indeed for critical proof, had he been engaged in furnishing evidence. But, on the contrary, he was only an encomiast of a departed Saint; and why not, if he found it fitting for his people? He even omits particulars which he certainly knew well, and every one else; as the name of Gregory's see, and of the Em-

"The miracles of Christ and His Apostles have not escaped the adulterations of monkery; and if this were sufficient to discredit truth, there is not a fact in civil history that would stand its ground. As to those who expect a certain innate virtue in it, of force to extrude all heterogeneous mixture, they expect a quality in truth which was never yet found in it, nor, I fear, ever will. Nay, the more notorious a fact of this kind is, that is to say, the more eye-witnesses there are of it, the more subject it is to undesigned depravation," etc. Warburton, Julian, § 2, n. 3, p. 96, ed. 1750.

peror under whose persecution he fled from it; why then need we be suspicious of other omissions, as if they necessarily reflected on the general authenticity of his narrative? why may he not put off a secular style and manner, when he is treating a religious subject? Why is he to be compelled to turn the Church into a court of law, and to introduce a prosaic phraseology into the hymns, the anthems, and the lessons of the Euchology? He wrote for the faithful and devout, and he had a right to do so.

138. Dr. Lardner, a calm and impartial critic, as we have seen, here loses himself. He seems to forget that a Bishop may, if he pleases, write homilies and panegyrics, and read martyrologies, and that inspired Scripture itself is not over-careful in dating, locating, and naming the sacred persons and sacred things which it introduces. Would not then St. Gregory's simple answer to such criticism as the following be, that he did not write for Dr. Lardner? That candid writer seems to forget this, when he makes the following additional remarks on his Oration:—" It is plain it is a panegyric, not a history. Nyssen is so intent upon the marvellous, that he has scarce any regard to common things; he relates distinctly the mysterious faith which Gregory received one night from John the Evangelist, but he despatches in a very few words the instructions which Gregory received from Origen, though he was five years under his tuition, and had before him excellent

materials to enlarge upon concerning that part of our Bishop's history. Then he takes little or no notice of circumstances of time and place, or the names of persons; these he omits as things of no moment. Indeed, he has been so good as to inform us of Gregory's native city and country, and that he studied some time, as he says, at Alexandria; but he does not let us know where Gregory was acquainted with Origen, whether at Alexandria or at Cæsarea. He does not inform us of the Temple where Gregory lodged and silenced the demon; neither where it stood, nor to what god it was dedicated. He has not so much as once mentioned the name of the Priest who was converted in so extraordinary a manner; nor has he mentioned the name of any one of the many persons, subjects of Gregory's miraculous works." "Possibly it will be said," he continues, "that it was contrary to the rules of rhetoric to be more particular in an oration. If that be so, and all that Nyssen aimed at was to entertain his hearers or readers with a fine piece of oratory, we must consider it as such; but then, though it may afford us some good entertainment, it will hardly be a ground for much faith; for a story to be amusing is one thing, to be credible is another." But is there no refuge from the rostrum on the one hand, and the witness-box on the other? Must a style be either rhetorical or controversial? May it not be ecclesiastical? However, Lardner grants that the miracle wrought upon the Lycus is at least particularized by the name of the river; and as some may think that it even approaches to fulfil Leslie's celebrated criterion of a miracle, a few words shall be given to it here.

139. Leslie's tests of the truth of a miracle are these: that it should be sensible; public; verified by some monument and observance; and that set up at the very time when it was wrought. Now St. Gregory is said by his biographer, as we have seen above,[t] to have restrained a mountain-stream within its mounds, which had been accustomed to flood the plain country into which it descended. He tells us the place, as well as the river, and the mountains from which it flowed; he describes its impetuosity as recurring, according as it was swollen by the waters from the mountains, and its ravages as very serious. But he adds, that, after Gregory had visited the spot and prayed, the calamity was stopped once for all, though the stream descended with fury as before, and came up to the very place which St. Gregory had marked as its limit. He specifies this place by referring his readers to a monument standing upon it, and that from the time of the miracle, and moreover, a monument which in its history involves an additional miracle. He says that the Saint took his staff, and fixed it at the opening of the mound which the current had forced; that the staff grew into a tree, and that the

waters swept it, but never passed it, and that it remained to his own day, being known by the people of the country as "the staff." Moreover, it may be said there was an observance, as well as a monument, which dates from the time of the miracle; for surely the conversion of the people benefited, upon their receipt of the benefit, is, in its results, of the nature of a standing observance, and well fitted to preserve and continue the knowledge of the supernatural act. And further, as some immediate extraordinary occurrence is necessary to enable us to account for so extraordinary an event as the conversion of a whole people, but the success of St. Gregory's restraint upon the stream could not be known till after an interval, or rather only in a course of years, some probability is thereby added to the idea that in the manner or circumstances of his action itself there was something impressive and convincing, and such the miracle wrought upon the staff would have been in an eminent way.

140. Further, Nyssen not only lived too near the times to allow of a spurious tradition fastening itself on the history, whether of the tree or of the people, but he was a native and inhabitant of that part of Asia Minor, and his family before him. His grandmother, Macrina, was brought up at Neocæsarea, Gregory's see, by his immediate disciples. Should the account be false, it will be somewhat of a parallel to suppose a person, at this day, in high ecclesiastical

station, born and educated and writing in the Isle of Man, and assuring us that Bishop Wilson once laid a storm in behalf of the fishermen, and that a lighthouse was built at the time, and still remains, in commemoration of the event; and writers, moreover, of this day, in England, Scotland, and Ireland, confirming the testimony, by incidentally observing, without allusion to the particular story, that Bishop Wilson had the gift of miracles. We should say it was impossible that such evidence could be offered in behalf of a fiction now; and why not say the same of a similar case then? "But a fiction was possible then," it may be argued, "because the age was more superstitious than now." I answer, "And so was a miracle possible, because Christendom was more Catholic and Apostolic."

141. Of course, an objection may be raised, on the score of the miracle not being of such a kind as to preclude the possibility of our referring it to physical causes, in a country where earthquakes were not uncommon. But miracles of degree, which admit abstractedly and hypothetically of being explained by the joint operation of nature and of exaggeration in the informant, are among the most common in Scripture, and may nevertheless be cogent and convincing in the particular case, as has been already observed. No east wind could raise the waters of the Red Sea, as Scripture describes them to be raised at the time of the Exodus; no supposition of earth-

quake or other physical disturbance will suffice to deprive Nyssen's narrative, as it stands, of its miraculous character. Nor may we take on ourselves to mutilate or deface either it or the Book of Exodus, or any other professed statement of fact, without first assigning reasons for our proceeding.

Section IV.

APPEARANCE OF THE CROSS IN THE SKY TO CONSTANTINE.

142. WHEN Constantine was on his march to Rome to attack Maxentius, at a time when he was as yet undecided about the truth of Christianity, a luminous Cross is said to have appeared in the sky at mid-day, in sight of himself and his army, with the inscription, "In this conquer."[a] His victory and his conversion followed. The date of these transactions is A.D. 311 and 312.

143. Now, here the fact reported is plainly miraculous. No known physical cause could have formed a sentence of Greek or Latin in the air. It has

---

Philostorgius, Nicephorus, and Zonaras say that the inscription was in Latin. Eusebius gives the impression that it was in Greek. So says the Emperor Leo expressly; vid. Grets. de Cruc. tom. ii. p. 37, who, mentioning this difference of statement, *ibid.*, also determines against Brentius that the apparition was that of the Cross with the monogram of χρ, and not merely of the monogram. Rivetus too contends for the monogram only. Cath. Orth. ii. 19, p. 168.

sometimes been supposed, indeed, that letters were not really exhibited, but only some emblem, such as a crown, which denoted conquest;[v] and that then what remains of the phenomenon may be resolved into meteoric effects. But since any extraordinary appearance at such a juncture, whatever be its physical cause, or whether it have one or no, is undeniably the result of an immediate Divine superintendence, it is not easy to see what is gained by an hypothesis of this nature. If in matter of fact our Lord was then really addressing Constantine, it seems trifling to make it a grave point to prove that He did so in this way, and not in that. In such a case nature either would be made to minister, or would be no impediment, to His Will; and His Will to address Constantine is sufficient surely by itself to account for a contravention or suspension of the laws of nature, and to overcome the presumption which *primâ facie* lies against the miracle. That He *should* address Constantine intelligibly is a miracle already. And surely to sway and overrule the physical system towards a moral object, is a miracle only different in degree from an interference with it for such an object. For this is to impose on nature a constraint *beyond and above itself*, i.e. a *supernatural* constraint; and if it is subordinate to moral laws, why should it not sometimes give way to them? In short, does the case

[v] Fabric. Dissert. de Cruce 10.

to Constantine.

ever stand thus, if it may be reverently said that the Almighty *would* address man, *unless* nature stood in the way? Does He fetter Himself with its laws, who, even in the days of His flesh, did but submit to them, in order in the event to dispense with them? Such explanations, then, either imply that the inviolability of creation is more sacred than a Purpose of the Creator, or they tamper with historical evidence for an insufficient end. To mutilate the evidence is to incur all the difficulty of denying it, with none of the gain. So this question may be passed over.

144. In the next place the *à priori* aspect of the reported miracle, if it is so to be called,[x] is in its favour. The approaching conversion of the Roman empire, in the person of its head, was as great an event as any in Christian history. Constantine's submission of his power to the Church has been a pattern for all Christian monarchs since, and the commencement of her state establishment to this day; and, on the other hand, the fortunes of the Roman empire are in prophecy apparently connected with her in a very intimate manner, which we are not yet able fully to comprehend. If any event might be said to call for

[x] "Confudit Danæus apparitiones Crucis cum miraculis Crucis; etsi enim apparitiones Crucis possunt miracula appellari, Bellarminus tamen apparitiones a miraculis distinxit, miracula vocans ea, quæ per Crucem supra naturæ vim et ordinem patrata sunt." Gretzer de Cruce, iv. 12, p. 253, ed. 1734.

a miracle, it was this; whether to signalize it or to bring it about. Thus it was that the fate of Babylon was written on the wall of the banqueting hall; also portents in the sky preceded the final destruction of Jerusalem, and are predicted in Scripture as forerunners of the last day. Moreover our Lord's prophecy of "the Sign of the Son of Man in heaven"[y] was anciently understood of the Cross. And, further, the sign of the cross was at the time, and had been from the beginning, a received symbol and instrument of Christian devotion, and cannot be ascribed to a then rising superstition. Tertullian speaks of it as an ordinary rite for sanctifying all the ordinary events of the day; it was used in exorcisms; and, what is still more to the point, it is regarded by St. Justin, Tertullian, and Minucius as impressed with a providential meaning upon natural forms and human works, as well as introduced by divine authority into the types of the Old Testament.

One would be inclined then to receive the wonderful event in question on very slight evidence, if that evidence were good as far as it went; and now let us see what, and of what kind, is producible in its behalf. It is on the whole sufficient, yet not without its difficulties.

[y] On the sign of the Son of Man being understood of the Cross by the Fathers, vid. G. Voss. Thes. Theolog. xvi. 9, Cornel. a Lapid. in loc. Matt. and Maldonat. in loc.

145. In the panegyrical oration delivered immediately upon the victory, the speaker, who is a Pagan, asks, "What God, what Divine Presence encouraged thee, that when nearly all thy companions in arms and commanders not only had secret misgivings but had open fears of *the omen*, yet against the counsels of men, against the warnings of the diviners, thou didst by thyself perceive that the time of delivering the city was come?"[z] Now here an omen is mentioned of a public nature, which dismayed the heathen priests and soldiers; it is remarkable too that *what* it was is not mentioned. All this would be sufficiently accounted for, if it was the sign of the Cross which they had seen; a spectacle of all others of bad augury with the hierarchy of the pagan city.[a] And in corroboration of this interpretation, Eusebius, in his own account of the miracle, tells us that on sight of the apparition Constantine, who was still fluctuating between Christianity and Paganism, was at first much distressed from a doubt what it portended.

146. Next, about the year 314 or 315, that is, three years after the event, Constantine erected his tri-

[z] Baron. Ann. 312, 14.

[a] Julian is said to have found a cross upon the entrails of a victim he was offering in sacrifice; the sight φρικήν παρέσχε καὶ ἀγωνίαν. Naz. Orat. iv. 54. He upbraids the Christians with their worship of the wood of the Cross, and signing it upon their foreheads and sculpturing it upon their dwellings. Cyril contr. Julian, p. 194.

umphal arch at Rome, which still remains, with an inscription testifying that he had gained the victory "*instinctu divinitatis*, mentis magnitudine."[b]

147. Further, before[c] 314, Lactantius or Cæcilius, as we determine the author, published his De Mortibus Persecutorum; in which he asserts, not in a rhetorical tone or in the form of panegyric, but in the grave style of history, that Constantine, in consequence of a dream, caused the initial letter of the word Christ to be inscribed on the shields of his soldiers, and that he thereby gained the victory. "Constantine," he says, "was admonished in sleep to mark the heavenly sign of God on the shields, and so to engage the enemy. He did as he was bidden, and marks the name of Christ on the shields, by the letter χ drawn across them, with the top circumflexed. Armed with this sign, his troops take up arms. The enemy marches to meet them without their imperial Commander, and passes over the bridge," etc.[d] Here is no mention of an *apparition*, but still the author speaks of the "*heavenly* sign."

148. On the 1st of March, 321, Nazarius, a pagan

[b] Burton, however, tells us that "the words *instinctu divinitatis* are supposed to have been added afterwards, as the marble is there rather sunk in, and the holes for the bronze letters are confused." Rome, p. 215. Yet the inscription reads oddly without them.

[c] *i.e.* Before the first breach between Constantine and Licinius. Vid. Gibbon, Ch. xx. note 40.

[d] De M. P. § 44.

orator of celebrity, pronounced, apparently at Rome, and not in Constantine's presence, a panegyrical oration upon the Emperor. In this he speaks of the assistance which the latter had received against Maxentius in the following terms:—" Thou didst fight, O Emperor, by compulsion; but it was thy best claim upon victory, that thou didst not seek it. Peace was denied to him for whom victory was destined. . . . In short, it is the talk of all the Gallic provinces, that hosts were seen, who bore on them the character of divine messengers. And though heavenly things use not to come to sight of man, in that the simple and uncompounded substance of their subtle nature escapes his heavy and dim perception, yet those, thy auxiliaries, bore to be seen and to be heard; and when they had testified to thy high merit, they fled from the contagion of mortal eyes. And what accounts are given of that vision, of the vigour of their frames, the size of their limbs, the eagerness of their zeal! Their flashing bosses shot an awful radiance, and their heavenly arms burned with a fearful light; such did they come, that they might be understood to be thine. And thus they spoke, thus they were heard to say, 'We seek Constantine; we go to aid Constantine.' Even divine natures have their boastings, and heavenly natures are touched by ambition. Warriors who had glided down from heaven, warriors who were divinely sent, even they did glory that they were marching with thee. Their leader, I suppose, was thy father Constantius," etc.[e]

149. It is impossible to doubt from these contemporaneous witnesses, witnesses more exactly contemporaneous than are commonly producible, that some remarkable portent appeared, or was generally believed in, when Constantine was in anticipation of his engagement with Maxentius, and about the time that he first professed Christianity. After all allowances for the rhetoric of Nazarius, his story surely must have had some foundation; by it he is virtually doing homage to a religion which he disowns, though he adroitly converts it to the service of Paganism, by recurring to the old heathen prodigies, such as the appearance of Castor and Pollux, and seeking to authenticate them by the recent apparition. Even if the Cross appeared, he could not be expected to mention it; he could not have done more than he has done. The same may be said for the still earlier orator, who is obliged to allude to the Emperor's Christianity, while he is complimenting him on having rightly interpreted what his friends thought an omen of evil. Lactantius, though he adds nothing to the evidence of the apparition in the sky,[f] testifies to the

[e] Ap. Baron. Ann. 312. 11.

[f] Socrates, Philostorgius, Gelasius, Nicephorus, say that the Cross was in the sky. Sozomen first speaks of it as seen in a dream, and then, on the authority of Eusebius, describes the apparition in the sky. Rufinus also gives both accounts.

general idea of some wonderful occurrence having attended the conversion of the Emperor. He testifies also to a fact which from its boldness requires accounting for, Constantine's marking the symbol of the Cross upon the arms of his soldiers.

150. Nor is this the only indication of some extraordinary influence then exerted upon the Emperor's mind. Not to dwell on the words already quoted from his arch, which make no express mention of the Cross, we find him even going so far as to form a new military standard, and that is the Labarum, or Standard of the Cross. And on his entering Rome in triumph, he forthwith erected a statue of himself with a Cross in his hand, and an inscription to the effect that " with that saving sign " he had delivered the city from a tyrant. But the most remarkable evidence in point is a medal, extant in the last century, which bears the figure of the Labarum with the very words, " In this sign thou shalt conquer."[g] Thus his assaults upon Paganism and the supernatural explanation of them go together; one and the same auspicious omen is repeated, whether in ensigns, medals, or monuments. And indeed, if we may dare to judge of the course of

---

[g] So says Gibbon, referring to the Abbé du Voisin and a Jesuit, the Père de Grainville. Such a medal is not described in Baronius, Gretser, or Lipsius. Fabricius says, "Nullus extat nummus, nullum vetus monumentum, quo crux, in cœlo a Constantino visa, diserte confirmatur." Script. Græc. lib. v. c. 40. (t. 6. p. 706, ed. Harles.)

Providence in this instance by its general laws, it is scarcely possible to think that no divine direction was given to such an instrument of its purposes on so great an occasion. In junctures of such awful moment, nay, in far inferior ones, men are not left alone, but strange impressions come over them, without which they would not have nerve for bold deeds. It was an act surely of no ordinary courage in Constantine to introduce the Labarum into the Roman armies to the virtual disparagement of those standards which had carried them to victory through so many fights, whether we regard the feelings of his soldiers or the misgivings of his own mind.

151. From this strictly contemporaneous testimony little or no part of which can be called ecclesiastical, we seem to gather thus much, that an omen happened to Constantine and his army, which most men thought bad, but which he trusted;—there was some appearance in the heavens visible to all;—some vision granted to himself;—and a Cross,—but where seen does not appear, whether in his dream, or as part of the visible appearance, and in connection with the omen spoken of; we are but able to discern it in its reflection,— upon the shields, helmets, and standards of his forces, and in his public commemorations of his victory.

152. Thus rests the evidence of the miracle in Constantine's lifetime; after his death Eusebius gives the Emperor's own account of it, which certainly does in

a remarkable way explain those acts of his which we have been recounting, and combine the scattered rumours which accompanied them. Eusebius declares on the word of Constantine, who confirmed it with an oath, that Constantine on his march saw, together with his whole army, a luminous Cross in the sky above the mid-day sun, with the inscription, " In this conquer ; " and that in the ensuing night he had a dream, in which our Lord appeared with the Cross, and directed him to frame a standard like it as a means of victory in his contest with Maxentius. Such is the statement ascribed by Eusebius to Constantine; and it must be added that the historian had no leaning towards over-easiness of belief, as many passages of his history show.[h]

153. This then is the state of the argument in behalf of the miracle ; on the other hand, there are these two difficulties in the way of receiving it. First, Constantine's testimony, which alone is direct and trustworthy, is not given till many years after the event ; moreover, it is given with an oath and in private, though it concerns an occurrence of public

[h] *E.g.* He omits mention of the dove in the martyrdom of St. Polycarp, of the miracles of St. Gregory Thaumaturgus, etc. In such miracles as he does record, he is careful not to commit himself to an absolute assent to them, but commonly introduces qualifying phrases: And his answer to Hierocles is written in a very sober tone. Vid. Kestner. de Euseb. Auct. et Fid. § 56, 57.

notoriety; and it is not published in his lifetime, nor till twenty-six years after the time to which it refers.[i] And next, it is supported by no independent and by no ecclesiastical testimony. "The advocates for the vision," says Gibbon, "are unable to produce a single testimony from the Fathers of the fourth and fifth centuries, who in their voluminous writings repeatedly celebrate the triumph of the Church and of Constantine."[k] It is remarkable too that even Eusebius does not mention it in his History, but in his Life of Constantine, as if, instead of its being a public event, it were but a visitation or providence personal to the Emperor.

154. This, however, may be said in reply: It has already been shown that rumours of some or other extraordinary occurrence abounded from almost the time of the Gallic march;[l] Nazarius says that it was the talk of the whole of Gaul; and we see from his own account of it that it was mixed up with fiction, as such popular reports are sure to be. An army is not like

[i] This objection is urged by Gibbon, Ch. 20. Lardner, Credib. ii. 70. § 3. Hoornebeek ap. Noris. Hist. Donat. App. 8.

[k] Ch. xx. note 52:

[l] It is remarkable, however, as is observed by Gothofred. Diss. in Philostorg. i. 6, that Optatianus Porphyrius, in his Panegyric. ad Constant. written in the year 326, does not mention the apparition, except that he calls the Cross "cœleste signum." He wrote, however, from banishment, though the place is not known.

a neighbourhood, or a class of society; it is cut off from the world, it has no home, it acts as one man, it is of an incommunicative nature, or at least does not admit of questioning. The troops of Constantine saw the vision, and marched on ; they left behind them a vague testimony, which would fall misshapen and distorted on the very ears that heard it, which would soon be filled out with fictitious details because the true were not forthcoming, and which took a pagan form in a country of Pagans. It was not unnatural that under such circumstances Constantine should have been led formally to impart to Eusebius the fact as it really took place ; nor, considering the misstatements that abounded, and the apparent unbelief of intelligent Pagans,[m] that he should have confirmed his account of it with an oath. Nor is it wonderful that Eusebius should not appeal to living witnesses of it, an omission which Gibbon urges, as if an army, or the constituent parts of an army, had a residence and an address, and that at the distance of twenty-six years; or as if an ecclesiastic, a native of Palestine, must have had many acquaintances among the veterans of Gaul.[n] Nor is it any great difficulty that, in a work professedly panegyrical, and not historical, and written with

[m] Vid. Gelas. Conc. Nic. i. 4.

[n] Eusebius says that he *once* or *sometimes* happened to see the Labarum. ὃ δὴ καὶ ἡμᾶς ὀφθαλμοῖς ποτὲ συνέβη παραλαβεῖν. V. Const. i. 30.

much oratory of phrase and circumlocution, and continual vagueness and indeterminateness in statement,[o] the writer should not have mentioned the time and place of the miraculous occurrence.

155. It is a more serious difficulty that Eusebius's statement is not supported by other Fathers of his own and the following century; yet this is not so great as at first sight appears. It is not pretended that any of them contradicts or interferes with his account of the matter; and at the very time, there were no great ecclesiastical writers to speak one way or the other. The miracle is said to have taken place in 311 or 312; the only writer of note extant during the first fifty years of the century, besides Eusebius is Athanasius; and his writings are taken up with later transactions and a far different subject. Nor does there seem any special reason why later writers should mention it.[p] The real miracle was encompassed with even heathen fables; the classical or philosophical description contained in the panegyric of

[o] Vid. infr. n. 157. note t.

[p] Columbus, however, in Lactant. de Mort. Pers. 44, refers to St. Gregory Nazianzen's second invective against Julian, where he speaks of the Cross seen in the air when the works at the Temple were miraculously stopped, and observes that he certainly would have alluded to Constantine's Cross, had he known of it. Yet surely he would have been going out of his way to do so, considering it was but one portent out of many which he was recounting, and another Cross had been seen over Jerusalem in St. Cyril's time.

Nazarius had been almost coeval with its occurrence, and was not likely to prejudice the Church in its favour, and yet was, as far as we know, the only testimony by which it was conveyed to the Fathers of the fourth century. At least Gibbon himself grants that they were not acquainted with Eusebius's statement, and grants it for the very reason that they did not avail themselves of it. He confirms this opinion by the fact of St. Jerome's ignorance of the Life of Constantine, in which Eusebius reports the miracle, a work which he considers "was recovered by the diligence of those who translated or continued his Ecclesiastical History."[q] Nor does it appear why the Fathers of the Church should have mentioned the miracle, even had they known it. It was not a miracle especially addressed to them, or wrought for the uses of the Church at large. It was, first, a fitting rite of inauguration when Christianity was about to take its place among the powers to whom God has given rule over the earth; next, it was an encouragement and direction to Constantine himself and to the Christians who marched with him; but it neither seems to have been intended, nor to have operated, as a display of Divine power to the confusion of infidelity or error. In like manner, while the Fathers appeal to the fiery eruption at the Jewish Temple, because it was the means of a signal triumph over an enemy, on the other hand,

[q] Ibid. Ch. xx. note 52. [Vid. Danz. de Euseb. Cæsar. p. 71.]

they refer to the destruction of Jerusalem without mentioning the prodigies which attended it. The distinction is clear. First, the taking of Jerusalem and the conversion of Constantine were events of a past day; Julian's antichristian attempt was of their own day. Again, the portents in the sky and the luminous Cross did but concur with and, as it were, illustrate the march of events, which was evident to all men without them; but the fire which burst forth when Julian would rebuild the Temple, was in opposition to the apparent course of things, and arrested them and defeated them. It did a deed, whereas the luminous Cross did but herald one.

156. It may be added, that there is a beautiful harmony and contrast in the omens by which the overthrow of Judaism and Paganism were respectively preceded. The omens in the former instance were only evil, for the chosen people was falling away; but since the nations were to be brought into the Church who had hitherto been outcasts, the sign in the heavens in the latter case was the Cross itself, a terror indeed and dismay at first sight to the ignorant Pagan beholders, but their redemption and salvation under the awful compulsion of Him who suffered on it.

Section V.

THE DISCOVERY OF THE HOLY CROSS.

157.   IN the year after the Nicene Council, A.D. 326, St. Helena, mother of Constantine, and then nearly eighty years of age, went on a pilgrimage, as it was afterwards called, to the Holy Land, and especially to Jerusalem. Her purpose was to visit the scene of the wonderful events recorded in Scripture, and the spots consecrated by the presence of our Lord. Among other objects of her pious search was the Cross upon which He suffered. It was the custom of the Jews to bury the instruments of death with the corpses of the malefactors;[r] and, considering their eagerness to remove the bodies both of Christ and of His two companions before the approaching Feast, there seemed no reason to doubt that, after Joseph had begged His body of Pilate, and placed it in the neighbouring tomb, His Cross, and

[r] "Accedit consuetudo Judæorum quibus solemne instrumenta suppliciorum juxta cadavera sontium obruere." Gretser de S. Cruc. tom. I. i. 37, he refers to Baronius and Velser. S. Basnage agrees, Annal. 326. g. [Vid. also Aringhi Rom. Subterr. p. 98, ed. 1659.]

those of the two thieves, as well as their corpses, had hastily been thrown into the ground on the very place of crucifixion. But where that place was, at first sight, was not so easy to determine. The city had been destroyed, and its soil (it is said) ploughed up, in punishment of the very deeds, of which Helena was seeking to recover the memorial. Our Lord had suffered outside the walls; but the population, driven beyond Mounts Sion and Acra, which it had hitherto occupied, had overflowed toward the north, and, without as yet covering Calvary itself,[s] had obliterated the features of the immediate neighbourhood. And Hadrian, by erecting statues of the Pagan divinities over the sacred spots which were in question,[t] had driven away worshippers, and at length

[s] St Cyril says of Calvary, that "it was a garden before, and the tokens and traces thereof remain." Catech. xiv. 5.

[t] St. Jerome mentions Hadrian by name. Eusebius, in the vague way which he adopts on other occasions (as not writing a history but a panegyric, V. Const. i. 11), says, "Ungodly men formerly, or rather the whole race of demons by means of them." V. Const. iii. 26. In like manner he speaks of "tyrants of our days who essayed to fight against the God of all, and oppressed His Church," i. 12, meaning Dioclesian; "the Emperor who had first rank," i. 14, meaning the same; "tyrannical slavery," i. 26, *i.e.*, the sovereignty of Maxentius; vid. also i. 33, etc., "news came that some dreadful beast was attacking," etc. viz. Licinius. i. 49, "news came of no small disturbance having possessed the Churches," ii. 61, meaning the Arian controversy; "a man well approved by Constantine for the sobriety of faith," etc., meaning Hosius, ii. 63; "the ruling city of Bithynia," meaning Nicomedia, iii. 50, etc., etc.

effaced all general recollections of their respective localities. But what had destroyed the tradition about them with the many might reasonably be expected to be the means of preserving it with the few; nor did it seem difficult, even without such accidental advantage, to recover, with proper pains, at least the general position of the spot where so great and memorable a deed had been done. The Empress availed herself of the assistance of the most learned both of Christians and of Jews,[u] and she seems to have been animated by a hope, surely not presumptuous, that she was under a guidance greater than human.[v] At length there is said to have been a general agreement as to the place; it was covered, first with a vast quantity of earth, next with the Pagan edifices; the place of Crucifixion and Burial lay beneath. Helena gave the word, and the soldiers who attended her began to clear away both buildings and soil.

158. Hitherto the main outlines of the history are confirmed by Eusebius, though he speaks of Constantine, his Imperial Patron, instead of St. Helena, and only of the Holy Sepulchre, not of the Holy

[u] This consideration answers, as far as the present question is concerned, Professor Robinson's remark, that "the Fathers of the Church in Palestine, and their imitators the Monks, were themselves for the most part not natives of the country." Palestine, Vol. i. p. 373.

[v] Calvin, however, considers that St. Helena was urged by "stulta curiositas," or "ineptus religionis zelus." De Reliqu, p. 276.

Cross. And though Constantine seems, during the years 326, 327, to have remained in the parts of his Empire between Thessalonica, Sirmium, and Rome, yet under his direction or authority Helena doubtless acted. Eusebius attests the intention of Constantine to build a church over the Holy Sepulchre; its desecrated state; the huge mound and stone-work which covered it; the shrine of Venus which had been raised at the top; and then the demolition of the whole mass of heathenism at the Emperor's command, statues, altars, buildings, mound, and the earth which lay under it. He then continues thus: "And when another level appeared instead of the former, viz., the ground which lay below, then at length the solemn and all-holy memorial of the Saviour's Resurrection appeared beyond all hope; and thus the cave, a holy of holies, imaged the Saviour's revival, and, after being sunk in darkness, came to light again, and to those who came to the sight presented a manifest history of the wonders which had there been done, witnessing by facts more eloquently than by any voice the Resurrection of the Saviour."[x] Here Eusebius ends his narrative; he proceeds, indeed, to speak of the church which Constantine built upon the spot, but he says nothing of any discovery besides that of the Sepulchre itself. As to the Cross on which our Lord suffered, judging from the course of his narra-

[x] V. Const. iii. 28.

of the Cross. 291

tive, we should conclude, not only that it was not found, but that it was not even sought after, nay, according to his literal statements, that St. Helena did not come to Jerusalem, only to Mount Olivet and Bethlehem.ʸ

159. Yet, though he is silent himself, he has preserved Constantine's Letter to Macarius, Bishop of that see, on occasion of the proposed Martyry or Church of the Resurrection. This letter does not contain any express mention of the Cross; and yet, did we read it without knowing the fact of the historian's silence when writing in his own person, we certainly should have the impression that it is of the Cross that Constantine was speaking. He says that "the *token* of the Saviour's most holy *passion*" had been "buried under the earth for many years;" and he speaks of it as a discovery "surpassing all human *calculation* and all *amazement*," and again and again of the *miracle* which it involved or had effected.ᶻ

ʸ Dallæus objects that St. Cyril "nihil addit de Helenâ." Rel. Cult. Obj. v. 1. p. 709. Yet we shall see Professor Robinson's reluctant admission presently, note d. As to Eusebius, his object was to praise Constantine. In V. Const. iii. 41, he first speaks as if Constantine founded the Churches at Bethlehem and Mount Olivet, and then corrects himself. [It is remarkable, moreover, that the Bourdeaux Pilgrim, A. D. 333, vid. Wesseling Itinerarium, pp. 589—596, whose silence about the Cross is sometimes brought in corroboration, (vid. Gibbon, Hist. Ch. xxiii., note 63), is also silent about St. Helena's Church on Olivet, which no one doubts about; vid. Euseb. V. Const. iii. 42, 43.]

∴ Const. iii. 30. Mr. Taylor says, that "the phrases he

160. It is remarkable, too, that Eusebius also, though silent about the Cross, makes mention of miracles as attending the discovery of the Sepulchre, in a passage of his Commentary upon the Psalms. Treating of the words, "Dost Thou show wonders among the dead?" he says, "If any one will give his attention to the marvels which in our time have been performed at the Sepulchre and the Martyry of our Saviour, truly he will perceive how the prediction has been fulfilled in the event."[a] Yet, commenting on the 108th (109th) Psalm, he mentions the honours paid to "the Sepulchre of Him who was delivered over to the Cross and death," without saying a word of honours paid to the Cross itself. Eusebius died about A.D. 338, *i.e.* eleven years after St. Helena's visit to Jerusalem; and this is all the evidence which

---

[Eusebius] employs [*i.e.* in Constantine's Letter] clearly imply the invention of the Cross, although apart from other evidence they would leave us in the dark as to the facts." Anc. Christ. Part vii. p. 296. I should say the same; but it is not granted by the Centuriators (who say that St. Ambrose is the first to mention the discovery), nor by Dallæus, S. Basnage (who speaks of the "intoleranda Bellarmini sive inscitia sive audacia" in maintaining it, Annal. 326, 9), Hospinian, etc. The elder Protestants wish to put the "cultus reliquiarum" as late as possible; Mr. Taylor as early. Tillemont understands Constantine to speak of the Cross, but Zaccaria, Dissert. t. 1. v. 4. § 5, is disposed, at least for argument's sake, to give up the point.

[a] Psalm lxxxvii. 13. Thus Montfaucon, but Zaccaria strangely denies the allusion.

we have on the subject, whatever is its value, for about the first twenty years.

161. St. Cyril of Jerusalem is our next informant concerning the discovery of the Cross. He was one of the Clergy of the Church of Jerusalem, and delivered his Catechetical Lectures about A.D. 347, in the very Church of the Resurrection which by that time Constantine had built; and in the first year of his Episcopate, A.D. 351, he wrote his letter to Constantius concerning a luminous Cross which had just then appeared in the air over Jerusalem. As he died A.D. 386, and was a Priest and (as St. Jerome says) a young man in 347, he must have been in his boyhood at the time of St. Helena's visit; whether in Jerusalem is not known. In his Catechetical Lectures he speaks of the Holy Cross as discovered, though he does not mention the circumstances or the time of its discovery. Speaking of our Lord's crucifixion, he says, "Shouldest thou be disposed to deny it, the very place which all can see refutes thee, even this blessed Golgotha, in which, on account of Him who was crucified on it, we are now assembled; and further, the whole world is filled with the portions of the Wood of the Cross." Again, speaking of the witness borne in such manifold ways to Christ, he says, "The Holy Wood of the Cross is His witness, which is seen among us to this day, and by means of those who have in faith taken thereof, has from this place now

almost filled the whole world." Once more, speaking against the heretics who denied the reality of our Lord's passion, "Though I should now deny it, this Golgotha confutes me, near which we are now assembled ; the wood of the Cross confutes me, which has from hence been distributed piecemeal to all the world."[b] Considering then that we hear nothing of the Wood of the Cross in Ecclesiastical history before this date, and that this date follows close upon the discovery of the Holy Sepulchre, it does not need further proof, though St. Cyril said nothing else, that there is some connection between this alleged discovery of the Cross, and that of the Sepulchre. It does not need St. Cyril's express statement to that effect in his Letter to Constantius a few years later, as we there read it ; and it does not matter, even though that letter be spurious, as some Protestant critics, though without strong reason, contend.[c] His words are these : " In the time of thy father, the divinely favoured Constantine of blessed memory, the salutary

[b] Cat. iv. 10 ; x. 19 ; xiii. 4.

[c] The authenticity of this Epistle is denied from its omission in St. Jerome's list of his works, and its mention of the ὁμοούσιον ; e.g., by Dallæus, Rel. Cult. Obj. v. 1. p. 707. J. Basnage Hist. de l'Eglise, p. 3. xviii. 13. § 2. Mr. Taylor seems to grant it, Anc. Christ. Part vii. p. 292. The mention of the ὁμοούσιον would be decisive against it, did it not occur at the end, in a sort of doxology which will admit of being considered an addition. The question is discussed at length by Zaccaria, ibid. in answer to Oudinus.

Wood of the Cross was found in Jerusalem, divine grace granting the discovery of the hidden holy places to one who laudably pursued religious objects."

162. From the evidence of St. Cyril and the passages of Eusebius, we gain, then, as much as this; that the discovery of the Holy Cross was a received fact twenty years after St. Helena's search for the Holy Sepulchre ; that it was by that time notorious throughout the world, because portions of the Cross had been sent in all directions ; hence, that the professed discovery must have taken place some years before the end of the twenty years when St. Cyril mentions it, to allow of such a general publication and dispersion of it ; and that it must have been well known to Eusebius, who wrote his Life of Constantine A.D. 337, only ten years before St. Cyril's Lectures, whether he believed it or not ; further, that his silence about it did not necessarily proceed from disbelief, because he is silent about St. Helena's search after it, nay, as I have said above, even about her visiting Jerusalem, an historical fact which cannot be gainsaid,[d] and

---

[d] "Such is the account which Eusebius, the contemporary and eye-witness, gives of the Churches erected in Palestine by Helena and her son Constantine. Not a *word*, not a *hint*, by which the reader would be led to suppose that the mother of the Emperor had anything to do with the discovery of the Holy Sepulchre, or the building of a Church upon the spot. But . . . all the writers of the *following* century relate as with one voice that the mother of Constantine," etc. Robinson,

again, because, in his Comment on the Psalms, he speaks also of miracles wrought at the Sepulchre, of which nevertheless he says nothing at a later date, in his Life of Constantine; lastly, that Constantine recognized the discovery of the Cross at the very time, because, while the terms[e] he employs in his Letter to Macarius are more suitable to denote the Cross than the Sepulchre, the strong expressions of his amazement are also more suitable to the discovery of the former than of the latter, a discovery which, as we have seen, was certainly reported and generally believed a few years later.

163. I conceive, then, that the evidence already brought together is conclusive of the fact of the alleged discovery of the Cross about the time of St. Helena's visit to Jerusalem, and in connection with that visit. Eusebius's silence is of course a difficulty, and, as it would appear, cannot satisfactorily be accounted for.[f] Yet he is silent at other times about

---

Palestine, Vol. ii. p. 14. Yet this same writer says in the very next page, "Leaving out of view the obviously legendary portions of this story, it would seem *not improbable*, that Helena *was* the prime mover in searching for and discovering the sacred Sepulchre!"

[e] Γνώρισμα τοῦ πάθους, V. C. iii. 30; whereas Eusebius calls the Sepulchre τῆς ἀθανασίας μνῆμα, 26; τῆς ἀναστάσεως μαρτύριον, 28.

[f] "Notwithstanding the silence of Eusebius, there would seem to be hardly any fact of history better accredited than this alleged discovery of the True Cross." Rob[i]nson's Palest. Vol. ii. pp. 15, 16; vid. also, "However difficult," etc., p. 76.

of the Cross.

facts which he cannot be said to disbelieve.[g] We should also ask ourselves *what* it is that his silence is to be taken to prove; not that he had not *heard* of the alleged discovery, for that it was alleged is undeniable; it can only be taken to show that he did not *believe* in it.[h] Yet his statement elsewhere, that certain miracles occurred at the Sepulchre, while it suggests some further story which he does not relate, is favourable, as far as it goes, to his belief in the received one. Moreover, if the discovery was not really made, there was *imposture* in the proceeding;[i] an imputation upon the Church of Jerusalem, nay, in the event on the whole Christian world, so heavy, as

[g] He does not mention St. Antony, or Methodius of Tyre, or the Martyrdoms of Perpetua and Felicitas, etc., etc.

[h] Dallæus contends Eusebium *nescivisse* quod tacet. Rel. Cult. Obj. v. 1. p. 706. The Centuriators are vague, so is J. Basnage, Hist. de l'Egl. p. 3. xviii. 13. § 2. S. Basnage implies Eusebius's *knowledge* but *disbelief* of the story. Annal. 326. 9. Jortin says that Eusebius "*either* knew nothing *or* believed nothing of it." Eccles. Hist. Vol. ii. p. 223.

[i] S. Basnage considers it a pious fraud of St. Cyril's. Annal. 326. 9. Mr. Taylor prefers to impute it to Macarius to imagining "Cyril and his colleagues to have hatched the fraud coolly and at leisure twenty years afterwards." Anc. Christ. Part vii. p. 297. "Cyril of Jerusalem and Augustine are the two Fathers who may be believed to have been the *dupes* of, rather than the actors in, the frauds of their times. Ibid. p. 292. "It would perhaps not *be doing injustice* to the Bishop Macarius and his clergy," says Professor Robinson, "if we regard the whole as a *well-laid* and *successful* plan for restoring to Jerusalem its former consideration, and elevating his see to a higher degree of influence and dignity." p. 80.

to lead us to weigh well which is the more probable hypothesis of the two, so systematic and sustained a fraud, or the discovery of a relic, or in human language an antiquity, three hundred years old.

164. Now let it be observed that hitherto this passage of history has had nothing definitely miraculous in it. It does but relate to the discovery, by ordinary methods of inquiry, of an instrument of death used by Roman executioners three centuries before. And perhaps it is right to draw a line between the above testimony and the evidence which follows at a later date, and which is next to be considered, except so far as the later evidence happens to be confirmatory of the earlier. It would seem impossible that the original story should not receive a colour or an exaggeration [k] when taken up as a matter of popular belief, and that in countries far removed from the scene to which it belongs. While, then, we may be prepared for additions which will not compromise the original evidence, those additions, when we find them in subsequent writers, whether true or false, are exposed *primâ facie* to a suspicion which does not

[k] We have an instance of such exaggeration in the report of the Samaritan woman, "Come, see a man which told me *all* things that ever I did." If the men of her city had been instructed in Protestant divinity, they would have cross-examined her as to what she meant by *all*, and then said that there was evident inaccuracy, and grounds for suspicion, that they were not called upon to stir, that they were not obliged to believe her, etc., etc.

of the Cross. 299

attach to the particulars which we have hitherto been reviewing.

165. Now St. Ambrose, in his discourse upon the death of Theodosius, (A.D. 395,) and St. Chrysostom, in his Homilies upon St. John, (about A.D. 394,) speak of three Crosses, not one; and say that the True Cross was known by the title which Pilate fixed on it.

166. St. Paulinus, St. Sulpicius, and Theodoret, agreeing in the main in the additional circumstances related by St. Ambrose and St. Chrysostom, differ from them in assigning a miracle as the test by which our Lord's Cross was ascertained. Paulinus writes to Sulpicius, and the latter reports in his history, that it was distinguished from the other two by its restoration of a corpse to life. These two authors write about A.D. 400, Paulinus in Italy, Sulpicius in Gaul. Theodoret, who wrote his Church History, about A.D. 440, in Syria, speaks, not of a corpse restored to life, but of a sick woman restored to health.

167. Again, Rufinus, (about A.D. 400,) and Socrates and Sozomen, (both about A.D. 440,) say that the inscription was detached from the Cross, and that the female, who was the subject of the miracle, was only on the point of death. Moreover St. Ambrose, Rufinus, Theodoret, Socrates, and Sozomen speak of the nails as found at the same time. A further miracle is spoken of by Paulinus; that the portion of the Cross

kept at Jerusalem gave off fragments of itself without diminishing;[1] and he adds, that "it has imbibed this undecaying virtue and this unwasting solidity from the blood of that Flesh, which underwent death, yet saw not corruption."[m] This is mentioned here, as being one of the alleged miracles which followed upon the discovery of the Cross, though it has no connection with the discovery itself, which is our proper subject.

168. Such is the evidence arranged in order of time, in behalf of this most solemn and arresting occurrence,[n] which is kept in memory, even to this distant generation, in the Greek, Latin, and English Calendars on the 3rd of May and the 14th of September. It seems hardly safe absolutely to deny what is thus affirmed by the whole Church;[o] whether however

[1] Jortin, Eccles. Hist. (Works, Vol. ii. p. 222), translates Tillemont as believing this miracle, and as saying that "St. Paulinus relates a very *singular* thing," putting the words in italics, and prefacing his extract with observing that "the words of Tillemont are full of what the French call *unction*, and the English *canting*;" whereas in fact Tillemont at the least doubts Paulinus's account. Mem. Eccles. Vol. vii. p. 8.

[m] Ep. 31. fin.

[n] St. Jerome too says of St. Paula, A.D. 386, "Prostrataque ante Crucem, quasi pendentem Dominum cerneret, adorabat." Ep. 108. n. 9.

[o] "This history of the discovery of the Holy Cross," says W. Lowth in Socr. i. 17. ed. Read., "is not found in Eusebius. But Cyril, Bishop of Jerusalem, who lived in the same age, openly witnesses that the Wood of the Holy Cross was divinely shown to the Emperor Constantine; also in his Catechetical

miracles accompanied the discovery, must ever remain uncertain. That a sick, dying, or dead person was restored by means of the Cross, rests on the authority of Latins writing at the distance of seventy years after the discovery, and of Greek authors of forty years later still; not on any testimony given with particularity or at the time. Moreover, such an occurrence is inconsistent with the account, taken in the letter, of St. Ambrose and St. Chrysostom, who say that the True Cross was recognized by its title. On the other hand, whether there was one Cross or three,[p] some *mode* of recognizing it is implied in the very idea of recognition; and a miraculous recognition is perhaps the most natural and obvious hypothesis. Nay, the very fact that a beam of wood should be found undecayed after so long a continuance in the earth would in some cases be a miracle.[q] And per-

Lectures he speaks of its discovery, as of a thing known to all. Wherefore of the faith of this history we cannot doubt." Upon this Jortin asks, "What did this Protestant Divine of ours mean? Could he believe that the True Cross was found? or would he only say that a pretended one was discovered?" Ibid.

[p] S. Basnage urges, however, "vero non esse proximum, latronum cruces cum illa Christi, uno eodemque loco fuisse conditas;" Annal. 326. 9. *because* crosses were always buried with the bodies, *but* no bones were found with the Cross,—an assumption. There were too many bones surely in "the place of a skull," to discriminate, or to mention the fact.

[q] "Quæri et illud potest, num annis pænè trecentis in solo absque putredine cessante miraculo," etc. S. Basnag. Ann. 326. 9.

haps there are few imaginations, which are once able to surmount the shock of hearing that the very Cross on which our Lord suffered was really recovered, but will be little sensitive of difficulty in the additional statement, that miracles were wrought by means of it. It must not be forgotten too, that Eusebius himself, though silent about the Cross, alludes to the occurrence of miracles at the Sepulchre; and these of course become more credible, if we suppose some great object, such as the recognition of the Cross, to account for them.

169. An objection, however, has from time to time been urged with much earnestness by several writers, which, if substantiated, would altogether overthrow the history of the discovery of the Cross; viz., that Helena chose a wrong site for the Holy Sepulchre. This was Dr. Clarke's opinion, whose reasons were discussed and answered by a writer, it is believed Bishop Heber, in the *Quarterly Review* for March, 1813. It has lately been revived with some additional considerations by one or two controversialists, one of them at least with the view, not simply of disproving the fact, which is a point of secondary importance, but of fixing upon the Fathers and Church of the fourth century the imputation of deliberate imposture, and that for selfish ends. Indeed, a drift of this kind is the only intelligible explanation of the earnest-

ness which such writers manifest.[r] It might not seem to be worth any great exertion to construct a proof that the Holy Sepulchre was not found by St. Helena, if no conclusion is to follow but that we need not pay attention to the festivals of the Cross, or to the claims of particular pieces of wood professing to be fragments of it. Even admitting the True Cross was discovered, it would be still open to Protestants to treat it with neglect or disrespect, and they would doubtless exercise their right. The Cross on which Christ suffered would be in their eyes but a piece of wood ; or again, as they sometimes speak both of it and of the sign of it, it would be a something loathsome and hateful, bringing our Lord under the curse rather than sanctified by Him ; and that the more, because, like the Brazen Serpent, it had been the occasion of superstition and idolatry. When then writers set themselves to oppose passages of history such as that now before us, it is for a far bolder purpose than is directly implied in their opposition ; it is of course in order to depreciate or destroy the authority of the Church. It is an attempt to transfer the quarrel between her reli-

[r] The Quarterly Reviewer of December, 1841, professes to consider it only a question of "poetic statement," "fond reminiscences," "reverential feelings," "pleasing visions," and the like ; and contrasts with them "the stern voice of truth," etc., etc., whereas the simple question is whether we shall consider the Church of the fourth century very credulous or very profligate. Mr. Taylor is far more perspicacious.

gion and their own, from the province of opinion to the ground of matter of fact; nor can there be in itself a fairer procedure towards the Church, or one of which her children have less cause to complain, however they may be pained at the spirit in which it originates.

170. Nay, perhaps such controversialists are fairer to the Church than to themselves; and though undoubtedly, if they once prove their point, they will but gain the greater credit and the more decisive victory, by so frank a procedure, yet it is plain there is at first sight a very strong probability *against* their proving it. The chance is, that they have undertaken more than they can accomplish. For it stands to reason, which of two parties is the more likely to be right in a question of topographical fact, men who lived three hundred years after it and on the spot, or those who live at a distance of eighteen hundred, and at the Antipodes? Granting that the fourth century had very poor means of information, it does not appear why the nineteenth should have more ample. There are indeed branches of knowledge in which we have decidedly the advantage of the early Church. If it were a point of philology which was under review; or a question about the critical interpretation of the Hebrew text, or the etymological force or derivation of a Greek term; or a problem in physics, such as whether or not such and such an occurrence were beyond, or beside, or according to the

laws of nature, and properly miraculous; or if it required some subtle analysis, and could only be wrought out by a mathematical formula; or if, though a question of history, or chronology, or topography, it was disputed by writers of the fourth century one with another, so that we must oppose this great name or that, and choose a side; or if it was advanced by some one Father, and by him unsupported, and in himself of no great authority, then the attempt to contradict him would be plausible; but in such a matter and under such circumstances as the present, when Calvary is the spot and Eusebius the informant, when a very learned and not over-credulous writer, whose silence about the Cross is thought so ominous of his disbelief, reports and assents to the unanimous decision of the local Church in favour of the discovery of the Sepulchre, and is supported, not merely by the silent assent, but by the concurrence of the literature of his own century,[5] the presumption is very great, before going into

---

[5] The main *authority* for the present site of the Holy Sepulchre is Eusebius; and the *warrant* for its preservation or recovery is the Pagan Temple raised over it upon the destruction of the city by Hadrian, which became a lasting record of the spot. What is to be urged against Eusebius I know not; but it is urged against the argument from the Pagan Temple, first, that only St. Jerome, and not Eusebius, attributes its erection to Hadrian. But why is not St. Jerome, a learned Father, well acquainted with Palestine, and no friend at all (as Mr. Taylor allows) to the superstitions and pollutions of which in his time Jerusalem was the scene, why is he not a sufficient

the case, that such acute and ingenious persons, as now for the first and last time in their lives traverse Jerusalem with their measuring tape, are wrong, and those who were natives of the place fifteen hundred years ago are right. Of course such presumption constitutes no plea at all for declining to examine their arguments; it weighs nothing against an overwhelming proof, when they have brought it; but, to use the language of their school, when speaking of the miracles of the Church, unless the proof is overwhelm-

authority? whereas Eusebius (*after his manner*) does but say "ungodly men;" vid. supr. n. 157, note t. Next, it is objected that there was no *recognized tradition* of the spot, because St. Helena had to *search* for it, and to summon learned Jews and Christians to her assistance: but it does not follow, because there was no popular tradition, that therefore there was no historical and antiquarian knowledge of the fact, or, again, no means of recovering it, though forgotten. Further, it is urged that it was unlike Hadrian's character to insult the Christians, when he was but punishing the Jews. But, granting his general leniency towards the former, what Sulpicius says, Hist. Sacr. ii. 45, suggests the conjecture, that, from the circumstance of the Jewish Bishops not only being natives and inhabitants of the place, but practising *circumcision*, he confused them and their flocks and the objects of their veneration with the Jews. From these three considerations, (1) that St. Jerome is the first informant that Hadrian placed a Temple over the Sepulchre; (2) that there was no continuous public local tradition to that effect; and (3) that it is a deed unlike Hadrian, it is proposed to infer that a place was pitched upon at random as the site of the Sepulchre, and that, among all places in Jerusalem, a heathen temple. As to the actual Sepulchre found under the mound, that of course is the work of *fraud*.

ing we are not "obliged" to accept it; when there is but a balance of arguments, "we may suspect it" to be fallacious, and may pronounce it "unsatisfactory." It may be entered upon with a just prejudice, listened to with suspicion, criticized with fastidious precision, and rejected on the ground of counter-arguments in themselves of inferior cogency.

171. Let it carefully be observed that a point of evidence like this has nothing to do with the question of honesty or dishonesty in the parties who give it. Were Macarius or St. Cyril and the Clergy of Jerusalem the most covetous and unprincipled of hypocrites, why should this lead them to fix on a false site for our Lord's crucifixion and burial? Why should they not do their best to fix on the right one? why should they subject themselves to an additional chance of detection, and give to persons like their present impugners a gratuitous advantage, as if it were not enough to fabricate a Cross, but they must hazard a superfluous mistake in fabricating a Sepulchre? Were they then knaves and impostors of the deepest dye, this would be no reason for their omitting, nay, the strongest reason for their taking, all possible pains to find the very and true spot where our Lord suffered. And therefore the question returns to the issue on which it has already been put—which is the more *likely*, that inhabitants of Jerusalem in the fourth century, or of New York in the

nineteenth, should be able rightly to determine Calvary and the Holy Sepulchre.[t] I mean no disrespect to the traveller to whom I allude, which is not due to one who accuses the Church of Jerusalem of the fourth century of deliberate fraud. And I make a great distinction between a learned person like himself, who writes with gravity and temper, and the English writer who has made use of his statements in a work to which reference has been several times made at the foot of the page. Yet I do not see why

[t] As if to meet this presumption, Dr. Robinson and Mr. Taylor set themselves to prove incontrovertibly that St. Helena did fix the site of the Ascension on Mount Olivet wrongly; and if she was wrong in one case, she might be in another. And their proof is as follows: 1st, St. Luke in his Gospel says that our Lord led out His disciples as far as *Bethany*, therefore He ascended from Bethany (in spite of his saying in the Acts, that they returned from *Olivet*); 2nd, St. Luke says that from Mount Olivet to Jerusalem is a Sabbath-day's journey; but the Church of the Ascension is only half a mile from Jerusalem. It has been usual to say in answer (1) that Bethany was not only a village, but a district which extended over a portion of Olivet. Thus Bethany is considered by Lightfoot, Chorogr. in Matt. 37; ibid. 4; Chorogr. in Marc. 4; Hor. Hebr. in Luc. xxiv. 50. and in Act. Ap. i. 12. In a previous work he had thought otherwise, vid. Comment. in Act. Ap. on the ground that names of towns and names compounded with "Beth" never were extended to a district. He gets over this difficulty, in his later work, by saying that the town was called from the district, not the district from the town. The same explanation of "Bethany" is given by Beza, Grotius, Sanctius, and De Dieu in Poole's Synopsis. Again, Spanheim calls it "tractus montis Oliveti." Geogr. Sacr. part i. fin. (2) As to the alleged difficulty of the Sabbatical distance, it is not

of the Cross.

weak arguments should be treated with indulgence because they are directed against sacred persons and better times. In order to form a due estimate of them, we must now consider with some attention the site of Jerusalem.

172. Jerusalem in our Lord's time occupied four hills: Sion, on which was the city of David, or the upper city, on the south (A); on the north of it, Acra, the site of Jerusalem proper, or the lower city (B); to the east of Acra, Moriah, on which was the

---

really such, till critics are agreed *what* that distance is. "Iter Sabbaticum *octo stadia* excepit aut totum milliare." Lightfoot, Chorogr. in Matt. 40. Elsewhere he says, "Iter Sabbaticum ex septem et dimidio," in Luc. xxiv. 50, adding, that it was "bis mille cubitorum." Yet, Comment. in Act. i. 12. he says that, while the Sabbatical distance is nine stadia if the cubit is three feet, it is but four and a half if the cubit be a foot and a half; and that the latter is the true calculation. "What space is a Sabbatical journey?" says Drusius in Poole's Synopsis; "in the number two thousand most agree; but some say cubits, others paces, Jerome feet, Origen ells, which Origen's translator calls cubits." De Dieu (ibid.) with Lightfoot in Act. makes the cubit a foot and a half, or the Sabbatical journey about five stadia, which is the distance of Mount Olivet, according to Josephus, and the actual distance of the Church of the Ascension, from Jerusalem. Grotius considers it eight stadia. Reland quotes Origen for its being eight (Palæst. i. 52. fin.), but thinks this too much; and quotes Epiphanius for its being six, which according to him (vid. Wolf in Act. Ap. i. 12.) would make the Sabbatical journey a quarter of an hour's walk. It must be added that, if the Church of the Ascension is short of the Sabbatical distance (which, as we see, it is not proved to be), at all events Bethany is in excess of it.

Temple (C); and to the north of Moriah, Bezetha (D), on which lay the new city, containing the overflowings of the population, which were at that time very considerable. Denoting them by the four letters, A, B, C, and D, we shall have the nearest idea of their relative position by considering B and C on a line running from west to east; A under B, and D above C. The Church of the Holy Sepulchre is in the space between B and D, and the question, roughly stated, is whether the city wall which went across from B to D fell within or without its site.

173. The first and most ancient wall, which included A and C, Mounts Sion and Moriah, ran nearly in a straight line, on its north side, which alone it concerns us here to consider, from the north-west corner of Sion, where Herod afterwards built a tower called Hippicus, to the western portico of the Temple on Moriah. Accordingly the lower city (B) was exterior to it, or, if any part was included, it was whatever lay in the angle between Sion and Moriah, A and C. This wall is supposed to be as early as David's time; and in its northern line, which thus divided Sion and Acra (A and B), stood the gate Gennath, from which in process of time was drawn a second wall, across or around Acra, terminating in the tower Antonia, which stood at the north-west corner of the Temple, opposite Bezetha (D). After our Lord's death a third wall was drawn by Agrippa, which inclosed Bezetha also; but

of the Cross. 311

with this we are not concerned. At the time of His crucifixion the second wall was the limit of the city; and the question in controversy is whether that second wall went across Acra or outside it. Our Lord suffered and was buried outside the wall: now St. Helena's traditional site is nearly upon the descent of Acra on the north.[u] If, then, the wall traversed the hill, that site falls without the wall; if it inclosed the hill, within it.

174. The argument advanced by the learned writer in question for the latter of these alternatives is of the following kind: he admits that a straight line drawn from Gennath to Antonia would fall short of the Church of the Holy Sepulchre, but he observes truly that Josephus expressly says that the wall had a curvature in the interval between its extreme points. Next he draws attention to a certain pool called the pool of Hezekiah, which is situated only a little to the south-west of the Church of the Sepulchre, and which he remarks Hezekiah formed inside the city. If, then, the pool was within the wall, the Church must have been within the wall too; for the wall could not include the former and exclude the latter without making a short turn at their point of contact, which we have no warrant in supposing. Further,

[u] Clarke and Maundrell make it on the edge of Mount Moriah; but Dr. Robinson "directly on the ridge of Acra." Vol. i. p. 391.

unless we suffer the wall to extend beyond the alleged site of the Holy Sepulchre, we shall not allow room enough for the lower city, which in our Saviour's time was extensive and populous. And, lastly, there are certain circumstances in the ground which interfere with the supposition of a narrower circuit; and there are some large hewn stones far to the north, near the gate of Damascus, which, being masonry probably of an age long anterior to that of our Lord, cannot belong to the third, and therefore are probably a part of the second wall.

175. Now, of these arguments it is obvious that not much stress can be laid upon the last. The ground on which Jerusalem stands has gone through many alterations at various times: valleys have been filled up, summits have been levelled. If the surface was so much changed that Helena could not at once find the Holy Sepulchre, surely its changes are great enough to hinder a modern traveller from determining, by its present appearance, the course of the second wall. Nor does it follow, though the ruins at the Damascus gate are as early as the date of the Jewish Kings, as this writer implies, that therefore they belong to the second wall, for he does not prove that the second wall existed so early as that time, as will be noticed presently; and they may be remains of some other ancient work, even if it did.

176. Nor surely is it any great objection that the

lower city will be much straitened if we draw its boundary short of the present Holy Sepulchre; for Josephus expressly speaks of the scantiness of the limits of the city, and of the population exceeding them in consequence. The population covered the north side of the Temple Mount, and then crossing the deep trench which bounded it, overflowed upon the opposite hill Bezetha, where it formed two large suburbs, one or both of which were called the "New City,"[v] and both of which were external to the then walls. Mount Sion itself also contained ample room for a population, the original city of David being but a citadel upon it. And, for what appears, the eminence or ridge Ophel to the south of Moriah afforded additional accommodation.[x] But however this be,

[v] Josephus in one place speaks of "Bezetha *and* the new city;" Bell. Jud. ii. 19. § 4; at another of "ἡ κατωτέρω καινόπολις," v. 12. § 2. If this second suburb was to the west of Bezetha, it must occupy the north of the present Sepulchre; which would almost be a proof that the present Sepulchre was without the second wall.

[x] Sion seems to have been covered with streets and private houses, in spite of its public buildings. Josephus says that "the houses" on Sion and on Acra "*ended* in the ravine between them:" v. 4; and says that Sion was called "the Upper Agora," which implies a population. De Bell. Jud. v. 4. In the sacking of Sion, he speaks of small houses on it (δωμάτια), and lanes or alleys, στενωποί, ibid. vi. 8. § 5. Indeed, we might infer a population from the length of the hill, which was far beyond the needs of a citadel, palace, and public buildings. Manasseh, too, seems to have taken in a space beyond the city of David to the south; 2 Chron. xxxiii.

the simple question for us to consider is whether the *deduction* from the supposed larger area of the city which adherence to the present site of the Sepulchre requires, will materially lessen that area. I conceive

14. Bezetha seems to have been very thickly inhabited; Josephus speaks of the shops of mercers and braziers, the clothes-market, and the alleys running upon the city wall. De Bell. Jud. v. 7. fin. The lower city, too, was full of alleys or narrow lanes, as appears by the following chapter. The Tyropœum, or deep valley between Acra and Sion [and Acra and Moriah], was "ædificiis densa." Spanheim's Geograph. p. 49. The height of the houses, too, in such localities should be considered. At Rome a law was passed by Augustus, that houses should not be above seventy feet high. The poor inhabited them in floors. Vid. Gibbon, Ch. xxxi. [vid. also Merivale, Rom. Empire, Vol. 5. Ch. 40.] It is a question, too, whether a portion of the inhabitants did not live in the excavations under Sion and Moriah. The deeper caves were used for the purposes of concealment in the sack of the city by Titus. Lightfoot tells us, Chorogr. in Luc. 1. § 6, that both Iturea and Idumæa were remarkable for their caverns, and he even derives the name of the former from this circumstance. Strabo speaks of two caverned mountains, one of which would hold four thousand men; Lib. xvi. p. 1074. The cave of Zedekiah, according to a Rabbinical authority, whom Lightfoot quotes, held eighteen thousand. And according to William of Tyre there was a cave on the other side of Jordan, sixteen miles from Tiberias, with different stories in it. Vid. also Joseph. Antiqu. xv. 10. § 1. It is the Ecclesiastical tradition that a cave was the place of the Nativity; S. Justin Martyr notices it, and Origen says that in his day it was visited by pilgrims. However, Dr. Robinson brings this tradition specially as a sample of the spuriousness of traditions about sacred history in general, because a cave or grotto is introduced. Nothing, he says, is done without grottoes. As if, too, some traditions might not be true and some false; the latter imitations of the earlier.

not.ʸ If the area be too scanty for the population with this reservation, will it be sufficient without it? Sion, the greater part of Acra, and Moriah, within the walls, and Bezetha outside of them, remain; and if we suppose the wall which is in question, on starting from Gennath, first to run north, and then to curve round, when it came over against the site of the present Latin convent, very little of Acra will be lost. Dr. Robinson refers to a passage in Josephus, in which that historian speaks of a northern and a southern portion of the second wall, a mode of expression which requires some such change of direction to account for it.

177. Nor is it easy to see how the New City can be altogether excluded from the second wall, as we know it to have been, if the second wall is extended any great way beyond the present Holy Sepulchre; and if it is not extended, how any great increase of room will be obtained merely by including the Holy Sepulchre. Nor is it natural in Josephus to speak of the population overflowing across the trench of Moriah upon Bezetha, if it lay all along the west of the latter

ʸ The Quarterly Reviewer for December, 1841, says: "One argument appears to us absolutely insuperable. To exclude the Church of the Holy Sepulchre, the ancient city, that is, *the part between the western wall and* the hill of the Temple, must be narrowed to less than a quarter of a mile." This is an inexplicable statement. It assumes that the second wall always continued *at the same distance* from the Temple Mount which it had over against the Sepulchre.

hill already, and had thence extended itself upon Bezetha eastward. In short, if there be a difficulty in accommodating the population, it lies in this, that the hill of Acra, from Hippicus, on the north-west corner of Sion, to the east side of the Temple, is little more than the third of a mile across, as Dr. Robinson measures it.[z] No theory about the north wall of the city can dispose of this fact.[a]

178. Putting aside, then, considerations such as these, which might be useful to corroborate a proof, but have very little intrinsic force to create one, we come to the *main circumstance* on which the author's argu-

[z] Dr. Robinson says that "the *breadth* of the city is the same now as anciently," Vol. ii. p. 67; *i.e.*, to show that it could spare nothing in length; now he says elsewhere that the breadth from the brow of the valley of Hinnom near the Yaffa gate to the brink of the valley of Jehoshaphat is 1,020 yards; while the length, measured on his map, from Herod's Gate to the limit of the ancient city on the south, is 1,700 yards, or short of a mile. Therefore an area of a mile by ⅘ of a mile is *greater* than the site of the old city, and makes no allowance for the Temple, fort, etc., etc., yet even this is little more than half a square mile. Here then is a fixed limit agreed on by all who do not adopt the random hypothesis of Dr. Clarke, that the Hill of Evil Counsel is Sion. Might not an objection be made to the smallness of even such an area by those who do not consider how the population of fortified cities *packs?* Nothing seems known for certain about the *ordinary* population of Jerusalem. Mr. Greswell makes several calculations, Dissert. xxiii., which exceed what at first sight the space could seem possibly to admit.

[a] Such difficulties are of frequent occurrence in history; *e.g.*, Oxford in the middle ages is said to have had 30,000 students.

ment depends, and which certainly deserves a careful consideration,—viz., the position of the pool of Hezekiah. To judge from his plan, this pool nearly joins the Holy Sepulchre on the south-west; and was once even considered as attached to it, and was called from it. Now Hezekiah formed his pool or reservoir within the city; either, then, the Holy Sepulchre lay within the city also, or the wall ran between the pool and the Sepulchre.

179. Now, first I would observe that there is no absurdity in the latter supposition. Let us allow that it would involve a sharp bend in the second wall,[b] which is our author's objection to it; yet Josephus, as we have seen, expressly speaks of a northern and southern portion of the wall, which implies a change of direction somewhere; and even though a range be supposed for the wall beyond the present Sepulchre, it could not materially change its direction without considerable abruptness. Dr. Robinson observes that the wall could not exclude the Holy Sepulchre, unless it

[b] Mr. [Dr.] Milman has no difficulty in such a supposition; "the second wall," he says, "began at a gate in the old or inner one, called Gennath, the gate of the gardens; it intersected the lower city, and having struck northward for some distance, *turned* to the east, and joined the north-west corner of the town of Antonia." Hist. of Jews, Vol. iii. p. 16. And he even represents it on his plan of the city as turning at an acute angle. Dr. Robinson himself, as is said over-leaf, cannot escape a bend. When he has brought his supposed second wall near Bezetha, he speaks of its "*bending* southward to the corner of Antonia." Vol. i. p. 468.

" made an angle expressly in order to exclude" it; but let it be observed, the angle *must* be made anyhow in order to arrive at Antonia; nay, and such an angle he himself makes in his own conjectural description of it.

180. Again, it is obvious to remark that, supposing Calvary was a place used for the execution and burial of criminals, as is not unnatural to suppose, and as its name may be taken to mean, there was a reason why the second wall, whenever drawn, should avoid it. And we know that, wherever it was, it was close upon the wall, both from the Apostle's saying that it was " without the *gate*," and from the custom of the Jews fixing their places of execution outside their cities.[c]

181. But, next, dismissing this question, we come to this most important and remarkable circumstance, which will strike most readers even at first sight; viz., that the author under review, whose learning none can question, and whose zeal for Scripture all must honour, has fixed the site of Hezekiah's pool by *tradition*, and *tradition alone*. He says that Hezekiah "built

[c] Deut. xvii. 5; Luke iv. 29; also 2 Kings x. 8; vid. also Lev. xxiv. 14; Numb. xv. 35. Zorn. Opusc. Sacr. Vol. ii. p. 193, upon Heb. xiii. 12, refers to 1 Kings xxi. 13; Acts vii. 59. And for the like custom among the Romans, to Plaut. Mil. Act. ii. sc. 4; Tac. Ann. ii. 32; Hor. Epod. 5. 99. On the Jewish cemeteries as without the cities, vid. Lightfoot, Chorograph. in Matt. 100. However, they were far enough to be out of sight of the inhabitants. The cemeteries of the Levitical cities were two thousand cubits off. Ibid. Chorograph. in Marc. 8. § 8.

within the city a pool, apparently the same which now *exists under his name;*" and upon this traditionary determination of the pool of Hezekiah he proceeds to deny the faithfulness of the tradition concerning the site of the Holy Sepulchre. Yet it does not at all appear why the latter tradition is not as good as the former, especially since far greater pains have been taken to ascertain the site of the Sepulchre than that of the pool. Nor can it here be urged that springs of water are not of a nature to be formed at will; that they have a perpetuity and a possession of the soil which mounds, or walls, or sepulchres have not; that they are not of common occurrence in Jerusalem, and that there is no great choice of pools between which the tradition might err. This, indeed, would be an argument if the pool were any more than a reservoir; and that too, as Dr. Robinson himself observes, in part at least of modern workmanship; but as the case stands, of course it is quite inapplicable. Nor can he intend to make a distinction between Christian tradition and Jewish, as if the Jews were deserving of more consideration and credit than the interested clergy or the superstitious laity of the Christian Church. For he candidly admits that the destruction of Jerusalem by Hadrian involved the destruction of all their local recollections. "It may perhaps be asked," he says, "whether there does not exist a Jewish tradition, which would also be trustworthy? *not in respect to Jerusalem itself;* for the Jews for centuries could approach the Holy City only to weep over it."[d] By a law of Hadrian they were forbidden to approach within some miles of the city, and Constantine did but permit them to view it from the neighbouring hills.

182. It seems, then, that our author's argument against the alleged site of the Holy Sepulchre depends on a definite and single fact, and for that single fact he offers no proof whatever, except that very kind of proof, and that not so good in its kind as that on which the site of the Holy Sepulchre is at present received. He cannot tell how long the reservoir has been called Hezekiah's pool, though he does tell us that it used to be called by the Monks the Pool of the Sepulchre; while we know, on the other hand, that the Sepulchre was fixed in its present site as much as fifteen hundred years ago. He does not know under what circumstances the pool was determined to be Hezekiah's; whereas we do know that the site of the Sepulchre was settled after a public formal examination, and, as it is reported, with the united aid of learned Jews and Christians, and with a unanimous decision. Yet, if the real pool was within the wall, and the real Sepulchre without it, and if their professed sites are so close to each other that

[d] Vol. i. p. 376, note; **vid.** also p. 350; [vid. Lumper, P. H. t. 6. p. 660.]

both must have been without or both within (a point which itself, as we have seen, is not at all clear), he asserts that the tradition concerning the Sepulchre must be the false, and the tradition concerning the pool must be the true.[e]

183. To proceed: it will be observed that Dr. Robinson takes for granted another point, besides that of the existing pool being really Hezekiah's; viz., that Hezekiah's pool was within the *second* wall. Certainly it was within the city wall, as it ran in Hezekiah's time; but it is obvious to ask, why was it only within the *second* wall, and not within the

[e] Professor Robinson, after speaking of Hippicus, Antonia, and Hezekiah's pool, says: " We have then three points for determining the probable course of this wall" (the second); " we repaired *personally* to *each* of these *three points*," etc. Vol. ii. p. 67. Now of the first he does but say himself, "it early *occurred* to us that [the tower of David] was *very probably* a remnant of the tower of Hippicus," Vol. i. p. 455; " this *impression* was strengthened," etc.; of the second Lami says, "I have set down several places in the map, whose true situation is *not known;* as, for instance, the castle Antonia;" App. Bibl. p. 76, ed. 1723, London; though Dr. Robinson considers he has ascertained it. And what reliance is to be placed on the site of the pool we have seen in the text. In like manner Dr. Robinson can but say of Gennath "*apparently* near Hippicus," p. 411; " *doubtless* near Hippicus," p. 461. And of the second wall, "Josephus's description of the second wall is very short and *unsatisfactory*," p. 461. And he locates the Tyropœum differently from other writers. Yet on these private inferences from doubtful conjectures on probable assumptions from unsatisfactory testimony, the Catholic Church is to be convicted of fraud and folly.

first, which was drawn short of the second? Did the second wall exist as early as Hezekiah? But if Hezekiah's pool was within the first wall, and the existing pool is Hezekiah's, then Dr. Robinson will have proved too much; for he will have brought up the city of David all across the valley of the Tyropœum to the ridge of Acra on which the Holy Sepulchre stands, and within "less than a quarter of an English mile" of the north-west corner of the Temple.

184. It is necessary then for his argument that he should clearly show, not only that the pool really was Hezekiah's, but also that the second wall was built and bounded the city, in Hezekiah's time. On this point, however, he does but speak as follows; "Of the date of this erection," *i.e.* the second wall, "we are *nowhere informed;* but it must *probably* have been *older* than the time of Hezekiah, who built within the city a pool, *apparently* the same which now exists under his name."[f] That is, on the one hand, Hezekiah's pool was within the second wall, not within the first, because the second wall, not the first, was in Hezekiah's time the boundary of the city; and on the other hand, the second wall, not the first, was in Hezekiah's time the boundary of the city, because Hezekiah's pool is within, not the first wall, but the second. Such is the author's proof of the second fact

[f] Vol. ii. p. 67.

by which he shows that the Church of the Sepulchre was built upon a pretended site.

185. But it may be asked whether Scripture throws no light upon the position of the pool; for in this way perhaps the tradition respecting it may gain an authority which it has not in itself. No tradition certainly is tenable which contradicts Scripture; but many a tradition deserves attention or commands assent about which Scripture is silent, or to which it devotes but a few words or a passing allusion. Dr. Robinson is more rigorous on this point than I should be myself; "This is the point," he says, "to which I would particularly direct the reader's attention, that all Ecclesiastical tradition respecting the ancient places in and around Jerusalem and throughout Palestine *is of no value*" (and he prints the words in capitals,) "except so far as it is supported by circumstances known to us from the Scriptures or from other contemporary testimony."[g] It would seem, then, as if according to his deliberate principle, distinctly and formally avowed, some Scriptural argument ought to be forthcoming in favour of the traditionary settlement of the site of Hezekiah's pool;—what Scripture does say, may be told in a very few words.

186. In the Second Book of Chronicles we simply read as follows: "This same Hezekiah also stopped the upper water-course of Gihon, and brought it

[g] Vol. i, p. 374.

straight down to the *west side* of the city of David."[h] Now, what Gihon is, and where, is not here the question; Dr. Robinson has some very interesting remarks on the subject, on its concealment by Hezekiah, and on the subterraneous channels by which he fed the reservoirs in Jerusalem. All that here concerns us to observe in this passage are two distinct statements, each of them quite inconsistent with the tradition that the supposed pool of Hezekiah is really the work of that king. First, the inspired writer tells us above that Hezekiah brought the water to *the city of David*, and the pretended pool is *not* in that city; and next, that he brought it to the *west* side of the city, and the pool is on the *north* of it. What then can be said, but that this author's argument against the truth of the alleged site of the Holy Sepulchre is based, not only on a blind Jewish tradition, the like of which he elsewhere reprobates, but on a disregard of the sacred text which it is the special object of his work to exalt?

187. In conclusion, I will but draw attention to the light which this discussion has thrown upon the ex-

---

[h] 2 Chron. xxxii. 30. If it is necessary to appeal to authority, Calmet considers Hezekiah's pool to have been in the western quarter of the city of David, in 2 Paralip. xxxii. 30, and fed by Gihon, in 2 Esdr. ii. 14. So does Lightfoot, Chorograph. in Matt. 25, and in Joan. 5. §§ 2, 3. Reland places the fount of Gihon, from which it was fed, at the south-west. Palest. iii. p. 859.

treme improbability, which was noticed before entering into it, that the parties who aided St. Helena in her search should have placed the Sepulchre where we find it, unless it were the true site. If facts are as clear as Dr. Robinson would consider them, they were too clear for any one to miss them.[1] If the present pool of Hezekiah was then acknowledged to be such, close upon the present Sepulchre, is it credible that, with that intimate knowledge of the letter of the inspired writings which no one denies to their times, the clergy of Jerusalem should have fixed on a site for the Sepulchre which, according to Dr. Robinson, they would be confessing to be, not only within the lower city, but even within the city of David? Did the pool escape their eyes, or its title their ears, or the sacred text their memory, or the conclusion from

[1] Dr. Robinson begins by speaking of the "difficulty arising from the *present* location" of the Sepulchre "in the heart of the city," which "has been felt by *many pious minds.*" Yet what so natural, as Maundrell observes, as that the Sepulchre, when found, should attract the city round it? Again, why is it not a difficulty that Sion is now so deserted? Is not this extension, if not change, of site, what happens to all cities of any standing? Was Dr. Robinson sceptical about St. Giles's in the Fields when he came to London? Pope Gregory was perfectly aware of the change of site of the city. " Hoc quoque quod additur," he says, " Non relinquent in te lapidem super 'lapidem,' etiam ipsa jam ejusdem civitatis *transmigratio* testatur ; quia dum nunc in eo loco constructa est, ubi *extra portam* fuerat Dominus crucifixus, prior illa Jerusalem, ut dicitur, funditus est eversa." Hom. in Evang. 39. init.

these data their reason? Could it be that a pool, which Scripture says was within the walls, should be situated upon a place of execution which Scripture as surely places without them? And in like manner we might ask, were it worth while, if the stones near the Damascus gate wear an antique look now, were they not likely to tell their own story better, if they were on the spot then? and have traces of the old wall become fainter or stronger in the course of years? and had the disposition of the ground undergone more alteration then than now, or less, considering Hadrian rebuilt the city on the site on which he found it?[k] But it is needless to dwell on the improbability of an hypothesis which has been shown to be altogether gratuitous.

188. On the whole, then, I cannot doubt that the Holy Sepulchre was really discovered as Eusebius declares it to have been; and I am as little disposed to deny that the Cross was discovered also, as that the relics of St. Cuthbert or the coffin of Bishop Coverdale have been found here in England, in our own day.

[k] Those who deny that the Pagan Temple was built on the site of the Sepulchre, have to account for the utter oblivion to which, on their hypothesis, the place of our Lord's crucifixion was consigned; whereas the circumstances attendant on that profanation which the Temple occasioned will explain such partial ignorance concerning it as seems to have obtained among the Christians of Jerusalem.

Section VI.

THE DEATH OF ARIUS.

189. CONSTANTINE, being gained over by the Arian party, called Arius to Constantinople, with the intention of obliging Alexander, the Bishop of that see, to restore him to the communion of the Church. The old man, who was at that time ninety-seven years of age, betook himself with his people to prayer and fasting. He shut himself up in the church, and continued in supplication for several days and nights. The coming Sunday was appointed for the reception of Arius, and on the preceding day Alexander was summoned before Constantine, and commanded to comply with his wish. On his refusal the Emperor grew angry, and Alexander withdrew in silence to urge the cause of Catholic truth with greater earnestness in a more suitable Presence. He fell on his face before the altar, and he conjured Christ, the Lord of all and King of kings, to deliver the Church from the danger and disgrace which threatened it One of the persons attendant on him was Macarius, from whom St. Athanasius relates it.

Macarius followed his prayer as he spoke it, and it ran thus: "If Arius communicates to-morrow, then let Thy servant depart, and destroy not the righteous with the wicked. But if Thou sparest Thy Church, and I know Thou sparest it, have respect unto the words of the Eusebians, and give not Thine heritage unto ruin and reproach; and take Arius away, lest if he enter into the Church his heresy seem to enter with him, and henceforth religion be counted as irreligion."[1] This prayer is said to have been offered about three p.m. on the Saturday; that same evening Arius was in the great square of Constantine when he was suddenly seized with indisposition. On retiring, he was overtaken by what is commonly considered to be the fate of Judas, as described in the Book of Acts. The building where this event took place became a record of it to future times, and, as Socrates tells us, "rendered the manner of his death ever memorable, all passers-by pointing the finger at it."[m]

190. Now of this occurrence it is obvious to remark, first of all, that it is strictly of an historical character. It enters into the public transactions of the times, and is one of a chain of events which are linked together, and form a whole. It has a meaning, and gives a meaning to the course of action in which it is found. It is in no sense what Paley calls "naked history," and in this respect differs from certain other extraor-

[1] De Mort. Ar.   [m] Hist. i. 38.

The Death of Arius.

dinary occurrences, such, for instance, as are recorded in the lives of the Monks; nay, from certain miracles of Scripture, such as St. Paul's preservation from the viper, of which nothing comes, and still more the resurrection wrought by Elisha's bones. "It has been said," says Paley, "that if the prodigies of the Jewish history had been found only in fragments of Manetho or Berosus, we should have paid no regard to them; and I am willing to admit this. If we knew nothing of the facts but from the fragment; if we possessed no proof that these accounts have been credited and acted upon from times, probably, as ancient as the accounts themselves; if we had no visible effects connected with the history, no subsequent or collateral testimony to confirm it; under these circumstances I think that it would be undeserving of credit." He goes on to say that this is not the case as regards the introduction of Christianity; nor, as we may add, as regards the history of Arius.

191. Again, it must be observed that this is more strictly a miracle of the Church than many which occur within her pale and among her members; that is, it is done by the Church as the Church. Though it bears a tentative character, it is the result of a solemn intercession, a solemn anathema, of the Church. Miracles happened in the kingdom of Israel, where there was no Church; but here is a contest between an Emperor and a heresy on the one side,

and the Church on the other; the Church speaks through her constituted authorities, and the judgment which is inflicted on her enemy is an attestation to her divinity.

192. Further, it was done in the presence of hostile power, which was awed by it, and altered its line of action in consequence. Paley observes, when arguing for the miracles of the Gospel, "We lay out of the case those which come merely in affirmance of opinions already formed. It has long been observed that Popish miracles happen in Popish countries, that they make no converts. In the moral as in the natural world, it is change which requires a cause. Men are easily fortified in their old opinions, driven from them with great difficulty."[n] Now the event in question was a Catholic miracle in an Arian city, before an Arian court, amid a prevalent Arianism extending itself all through the East.

193. "But after all, was it a miracle? for if not, we are labouring at a proof of which nothing comes." The more immediate answer to this question has already been suggested several times. When a Bishop with his flock prays night and day against a heretic, and at length begs of God to take him away, and when he is suddenly taken away almost at the moment of his triumph, and that by a death awfully significant, from its likeness to one recorded in Scrip-

[n] Evidences, Part ii. Ch. i.

The Death of Arius. 331

ture, is it not trifling to ask whether such an occurrence comes up to the definition of a miracle? The question is not whether it is formally a miracle, but whether it is an event, the like of which persons who deny that miracles continue will consent that the Church should be considered still able to perform. If they are willing to allow to the Church such extraordinary protection, it is for them to draw the line, to the satisfaction of people in general, between these and strictly miraculous events; if, on the other hand, they deny their occurrence in the times of the Church, then there is sufficient reason for our appealing here to the history of Arius in proof of the affirmative. This is what suggests itself at first sight; however, that it was really miraculous, Gibbon surely is a sufficient voucher. "Those," he says, "who press the literal narrative of the death of Arius, must make their option between poison and miracle." Now, considering that this awful occurrence took place in an Arian city and court, and in the face of powerful and quick-sighted adversaries, who had every means and every interest to detect an act of such dreadful wickedness as Gibbon insinuates, surely, putting aside all higher considerations, there are insuperable difficulties in the theory of poison; while those who do not deny the moral governance of God, and the heretical and ungodly character of Arianism, will have no difficulty in referring the catastrophe to miracle.

194. One other question may be asked, though it is of a doctrinal nature, and therefore hardly needs to be considered here; whether so solemn a denunciation as that adopted by Alexander, and so positive a reference of the event which followed to that denunciation as a cause, are not modes of acting and judging uncongenial to the Christian religion. One passage there certainly is in the New Testament which at first sight seems in opposition to it. When James and John wished to be allowed to call down fire from heaven upon the Samaritans, as Elijah had done upon Ahaziah's messengers, Christ answered, " Ye know not what manner of spirit ye are of: for the Son of man is not come to destroy men's lives, but to save them." However, it is obvious to reply, first, that Elijah, in the passage in question, called down a miraculous punishment on the soldiers of Ahaziah mainly in his own defence; and it is observable that the Apostles asked leave to do the same, when the Samaritans had refused to receive their Lord and them ; whereas the great rule of the Gospel is to "avenge not ourselves, but rather give place unto wrath," as our Lord exemplified when " they went to another village." But whether there be any force in this distinction or not, certain it is that in the Acts, in which we surely have the principles of the Gospel drawn out into action, two precedents occur in justification of the conduct of St. Alexander, one given us by St. Peter

The Death of Arius.

and the other by St. Paul. St. Peter's denunciation of Ananias and Sapphira was followed by their instantaneous deaths; St. Paul's denunciation of Elymas, by his immediate blindness. These instances, moreover, suggest that our Lord's earthly ministry might probably be conducted on different laws from those which belonged to His risen power, when the Spirit had descended, and light was spread abroad; according to the text in which blasphemy against the Son of man and blasphemy against the Spirit are contrasted. Hence St. Paul calls Elymas, who was "seeking to *turn away* the deputy from the faith," an "*enemy* of all righteousness," and a "*perverter* of the right ways of the Lord;" and St. Peter still more expressly accuses Ananias and his wife of "lying against the Holy Ghost," and "tempting the Spirit of the Lord." It is obvious also to refer to St. Paul's imprecation on Alexander the copper-smith, that the Lord would reward him according to his works. Here St. Paul, who had the gift of inspiration, speaks of Alexander personally; but the Bishops of the Church did not venture so much as this; they did but contemplate her enemies *in* their opposition, *as* heretics or rebels, and dealt with them accordingly, without any direct reference to their real and absolute state in the sight of God.

Section VII.

THE FIERY ERUPTION ON JULIAN'S ATTEMPT TO REBUILD THE JEWISH TEMPLE.

195. BISHOP WARBURTON, as is well known, has written in defence of the miraculous character of the earthquake and fiery eruption which defeated the attempt of the Emperor Julian to rebuild the Jewish Temple. Though in many most important respects he shows his dissent from the view of the Ecclesiastical Miracles taken in these pages, yet the propositions which he lays down in the commencement of his work are precisely those which it has been here attempted to maintain; first, "that not all the miracles recorded in Church history are forgeries or delusions;" next, "that their evidence doth not stand on the same foot of credit with the miracles recorded in Gospel history." In drawing out the facts and the evidence of the miracle in question, I shall avail myself of the work of this learned and able writer, with which I agree in the main, though of course there is room for difference of opinion, both as regards the details of the one and the other, and as regards the view to be taken of them.

Fiery Eruption at the Temple.

196. In the year 363, Julian, in the course of his systematic hostilities against Christianity, determined to rebuild the Temple at Jerusalem. The undertaking was conducted on a magnificent scale, large sums being assigned out of the public revenue for its execution. Alypius, an intimate friend of Julian, was set over the work; the Jews aided him with a vast collection of materials and of workmen. Both sexes, all ranks, took part in the labour, entering upon the ruins, clearing away the rubbish, and laying bare the foundations.[o] What followed is attested by a number of authorities, who agree with each other in all substantial respects, though, as was to be expected, no single writer relates every one of the particulars. First, we have the contemporary testimony of the Pagan historian Ammianus Marcellinus, and we may add of Julian himself; then of St. Gregory Nazianzen,[p] St. Ambrose, and St. Chrysostom, who were more or less contemporaries; and of Rufinus, Socrates, Sozomen, and Theodoret, of the century following. They declare as follows. The work was interrupted by a violent whirlwind, says Theodoret, which scattered about vast quantities of lime, sand, and other loose materials collected for the building. A storm of thunder and

[o] It was quite an enthusiastic movement. We are told that the spades and pickaxes were of silver, and the rubbish was removed in mantles of silk and purple. Vid. Gibbon, Ch. xxiii.

[p] Orat. v. 4—7. The Oration was composed the very year of the miracle. [Vid. Fabric. Salutaris Lux. p. 124, Gothofr. in Philostorg. p. 296.]

lightning followed; fire fell, says Socrates; and the workmen's tools, the spades, the axes, and the saws, were melted down. Then came an earthquake, which threw up the stones of the old foundations of the Temple, says Socrates; filled up the excavation, says Theodoret, which had been made for the new foundations; and, as Rufinus adds, threw down the buildings in the neighbourhood, and especially the public porticoes, in which were numbers of the Jews who had been aiding the undertaking, and who were buried in the ruins. The workmen returned to their work; but from the recesses laid open by the earthquake, balls of fire burst out, says Ammianus; and that again and again, so often as they renewed the attempt. The fiery mass, says Rufinus, ranged up and down the street for hours; and St. Gregory, that when some fled to a neighbouring Church for safety, the fire met them at the door, and forced them back with the loss either of life or of their extremities. At length the commotion ceased; a calm succeeded; and, as St. Gregory adds, in the sky appeared a luminous Cross surrounded by a circle. Nay, upon the garments and upon the bodies of the persons present Crosses were impressed, says St. Gregory; which were luminous by night, says Rufinus; and at other times of a dark colour, says Theodoret; and would not wash out, adds Socrates. In consequence, the attempt was abandoned.

197. There is no reason for doubting any part of this narrative; however, enough will remain if we accept only the account given us by Ammianus, who, to use the words of Warburton, was "a contemporary writer, of noble extraction, a friend and admirer of Julian, and his companion in arms, a man of affairs, learned, candid, and impartial, a lover of truth, and the best historian of his times," and "a Pagan professed and declared." "Though Julian," says this writer, "with anxious anticipation of contingencies of every kind, was keenly engaged in the prosecution of the numberless arrangements incident to his [Persian] expedition, yet that no place might be without its share in his energy, and that the memory of his reign might continue in the greatness of his works, he thought of rebuilding at an extravagant expense the proud Temple once at Jerusalem, which after many conflicts and much bloodshed, in the siege under Vespasian first, and then Titus, was with difficulty taken; and he committed the accomplishment of this task to Alypius of Antioch, who had before that been Lieutenant of Britain. Alypius therefore set himself vigorously to the work, and was seconded by the governor of the province; when fearful balls of fire, breaking out near the foundations, continued their attacks, till the workmen, after repeated scorchings, could approach no more; and thus, the fierce element obstinately repelling them, he gave over his attempt."

198. Julian, too, seems awkwardly to allude to it in a fragment of a letter or oration, which Warburton has pointed out, and which is so curious an evidence of his defeat and its extraordinary circumstances that it may be fitly introduced in this place. He is encouraging the zeal of the Pagans for the honour of their divinities, and he says: "Let no one disbelieve the gods, from seeing and hearing that their statues and their temples have been insulted in some quarters. Let no one beguile us by his speeches, or unsettle us on the score of providence; for those who reproach us on this head, I mean the Prophets of the Jews, what will they say about their own Temple, which has been thrice overthrown, and is not even now rising?[q] This I have said with no wish to reproach them, inasmuch

---

[q] Fabricius and De la Bleterie consider the "three times" to include Julian's own attempt to rebuild; yet it is harsh, as Warburton observes, to call a hindrance in rebuilding an actual destruction of the building, though the hindrance was a destruction as far as it went. But Lardner and Warburton seem to mistake when they argue against Fabricius that ἐγειρομένου δὲ οὐδὲ νῦν means "not *raised again* to this day," whereas it must rather be construed "not *rising*" or "in *course of building.*" Warburton reckons the alterations and additions under Herod as by implication a destruction of the second temple; and as another hypothesis he suggests the profanation under Antiochus. Lardner thinks Julian spoke vaguely or rhetorically, or that he referred to the calamities which came upon Jerusalem in the time of Adrian. "Julien loin de conclure de ce qui étoit arrivé à Jerusalem la vérité de la religion Chrétienne, en inferoit que la revelation judaïque étoit fausse." De la Bleterie. Julian, v. p. 399.

as I myself, at so late a day, had in purpose to rebuild it for the honour of Him who was worshipped there. Here I have alluded to it, with the purpose of shewing that of human things nothing is imperishable, and that the Prophets who wrote as I have mentioned, raved, and were but the gossips of canting old women. Nothing, indeed, contradicts the notion of that God being great, but He is unfortunate in His Prophets and interpreters; I say that they did not take care to purify their souls by a course of education, nor to open their fast-closed eyes, nor to dissipate the darkness which lay on them. And, like men who see a great light through a mist, not clearly nor distinctly, and take it not for pure light, but for *fire*, and are blind to all things around about it, they cry out loudly, 'Shudder and fear; fire, flame, death, sword, lance,' expressing by many words that one destructive property of *fire*."[r] When it is considered that Julian was, as it were, defeated by the prophets of that very people he was aiding; that he desired to rebuild the Jewish Temple, and the Christians declared that he could not, for the Jewish Prophets themselves had made it impossible; we surely may believe, that

---

[r] Page 295. Ed. Spanh. Lardner contends that this letter from its tone must have been written *before* any attempt to rebuild the Temple; which indeed he considers Julian never to have put into execution. This is a paradox more in the style of Warburton, whom he is opposing, than of so sensible and sober a writer.

in the foregoing passage this was the thought which was passing in his mind, while the prophetic emblem of fire haunted him, which had been so recently exhibited in the catastrophe by which he had been baffled.

199. The fact then cannot be doubted;[s] it may be asked, however, whether the perpetual ruin of the Temple was actually predicted in the Prophets; and if not, what was the drift of this miracle, and how it was connected with the Church. It is connected with the Church and the Prophets by one circumstance, if by no other, and that a remarkable one; that before the actual attempt to rebuild, a Bishop of the Church had denounced it, prophesied its failure, and that

It is objected by Lardner that St. Jerome, Prudentius, and Orosius are silent about the miracle. Others have alleged the silence of St. Cyril of Jerusalem. But if, as a matter of course, good testimony is to be overborne because other good testimony is wanting, there will be few facts of history certain. Why should Ammianus be untrue because Jerome is silent? Sometimes the notoriety of a fact leads to its being passed over. Moyle is "unwilling to reject all [miracles since the days of the Apostles] without reserve, for the sake of a very remarkable one which happened at the rebuilding of the Temple," etc. Posth. Works, Vol. i. p. 101. He professes to be influenced by the testimony and the antecedent probability. Douglas speaks of Warburton's defence of it as "a work written with a solidity of argument which might always have been expected from the author, and with a spirit of candour which his enemies thought him incapable of." These admissions are very strong, considering the authors. Mosheim takes the same side. J. Basnage, Lardner, Hey, etc., take the contrary.

to Rebuild the Jewish Temple.

from the light thrown upon the subject by the Prophets of the Old Testament. "Cyril, Bishop of Jerusalem," says Socrates, "bearing in mind the words of the Prophet Daniel, which Christ had confirmed in the Holy Gospels, declared to many beforehand, that now the time was come, when stone should not remain upon stone for that Temple, but the Saviour's prophecy should be fulfilled."[t] St. Cyril seems to have argued that since our Lord prophesied the utter destruction of the Temple, and since that destruction was not yet fully accomplished, but only in course of accomplishment, for the old foundations at that time still remained, therefore Julian was reversing the Divine order of things, and building up when God was engaged in casting down, and in consequence was sure to fail. And as Julian probably understood Daniel's and our Lord's words in the same way, and did set himself deliberately and professedly to contravene them, viewed as fulfilled in the for-

[t] Hist. iii. 20. Lardner (Testimonies, Ch. 46. 3) says, that "it is very absurd for any Christians to talk in this manner. Christ's words had been fulfilled almost 300 years before;" and refers to Rufinus as giving the true account of St. Cyril's words, viz., that "it could not be that the Jews should be *able* to lay them stone upon stone;" but St. Cyril himself expressly says what Socrates reports of him, Catech. xv. 15: "Antichrist shall come *at a time when* there shall not be left one stone upon another in the Temple." This was written before Julian's attempt; and St. Chrysostom, after it, pronounces the prophecy of "not one stone upon another" not fulfilled even then. Hom. 75. in Matth.

tunes of the Temple, he was evidently placing himself in open hostility to Christ and His Prophet, and challenging Him to the encounter. No circumstances then could be more fitting for the interposition of a miracle in frustration of his undertaking.

200. The same conclusion may be argued from our Lord's words to the Samaritan woman. He does not indeed mention the Temple by name, but he must be considered to allude to it, when He says that men should not "*worship* at Jerusalem." They were indeed to worship there, as everywhere, but to worship without the Temple; and that because they were to worship "in spirit and in truth." A spiritual worship was incompatible with the Judaic services; so that when Christianity appeared the Temple was destroyed. Julian then, in building again the Temple, was doing what he could to falsify Christianity.

201. But, again, the Jewish Temple was confessedly the *centre* of the Jewish worship and polity; to rebuild the Temple, then, was to establish the Jews, *as Jews*, in their own land, an event which, if prophecy is sure, never is to be. "The building of [the Temple]," says Mr. Davison, "was directed for this reason, that God had given '*rest* to His people,' and henceforth would not suffer them to *wander* or be disturbed; so long as they enjoyed the privilege of being His people at all. 'Moreover, I will appoint a *place* for my people Israel, and will plant them, that they may *dwell* in a place

of their own, and *move no more.*' This promise of rest was connected with the Temple, for it was spoken when God confirmed and commanded the design of building it." He continues presently, " Their national estate was henceforth attached to this Temple. It fell with them; when they returned and became a people again, it rose also. . . Excepting around this Temple, they have never been able to settle themselves, as a people, nor find a public home for their nation or their religion. . . So that the long desolation of their Temple, and their lasting removal from the seat of it, are no inconsiderable proofs that their *polity and peculiar law* are come to an end in the purposes of Providence, and according to the intention of the Temple-appointment, as well as in the fact."[u] Julian then, in proposing to rebuild the Jewish Temple, aimed at the re-establishment of Judaism,—of that ceremonial religion which in its day indeed had been the instrument of Divine Providence towards higher blessings in store, and those for all men, but which, when those blessings were come, forthwith was disannulled in the Divine counsels "for the weakness and unprofitableness thereof."

202. And next the question may be asked whether there was after all any miracle in the case, as in the instance of most of the other extraordinary occurrences which have passed under review. The luminous

[u] Discourses on Prophecy, v. 2. § 2.

Crosses upon the garments and bodies of the persons present were apparently of a phosphoric nature; the Cross in the air resembled meteoric phenomena; the earthquake and balls of fire had a volcanic origin; and other marvellous circumstances are referable to electricity. This all may be very true, and yet it may be true also that the immediate cause, which set all these various agents in motion, and combined them for one work, was supernatural; just as the agency of mind on matter, in speaking, walking, writing, eating, and the like, is not subject to physical laws, though manifesting itself through them.[v] Again, even supposing that these phenomena were not in themselves miraculous, yet surely their concurrence with the

[v] "The mineral and metallic substances which, by their accidental fermentation, are wont to take fire and burst out in flame, were the native contents of the place from which they issued; but in all likelihood *they would have there slept*, and still continued in the quiet innoxious state in which they had so long remained, *had not* the breath of the Lord *awoke* and *kindled* them. But when the Divine Power had thus miraculously interposed to *stir up* the rage of these fiery elements, and yet to restrain their fury to the objects of His vengeance, He then again suffered them to do *their ordinary office;* because nature, thus directed, would, by the exertion of its own laws, answer all the ends of the moral designation." Warburt. Julian, p. 246. Again, "We see why *fire* was the scourge employed; as we may be sure *water* would have been, were the region of Judea naturally subject to inundations. For miracles, not being an ostentatious, but a necessary instrument of God's moral government, we cannot conceive it probable that He would *create* the elements for this purpose, but *use* those which already lay stored up against the day of visitation." Ibid. p. 250.

moral system of things, their happening at that time and place and in that subserviency to the declarations of ancient prophecy, is in itself of the nature of a miracle. It is observable too, that though the Cross in the air be attributable to meteoric causes, yet such an occurrence is after all very unusual ; now we read of three such occurrences in the course of the fifty years between Constantine's accession to power and Julian, during which period Christianity was effecting its visible triumph and establishment in the world ;— viz., the Cross at the conversion of Constantine, that which hung over Jerusalem in the reign of Constantius, and the Cross which forms part of the awful events now in question ; and while any accumulation of extraordinary phenomena creates a difficulty in finding a cause in nature adequate to their production, the recurrence of the same phenomena argues design, or the interference of agency beyond nature. It must be added, too, that the occurrence of a whirlwind, an earthquake, and a fire, especially reminds us of Elijah's vision in Horeb, and again of the manifestation of the Divine Presence in the first and fourth of the Acts, yet it does not appear as if the writers to whom we have referred had these events in their mind ; rather it is only by the union of their separate testimonies, each incomplete in itself, that the parallel is formed.[x]

[x] It should be observed that the *order* in which the miraculous phenomena have been arranged above is not found in the

203. Moreover the events in question did the work of a miracle; they defeated powerful enemies, who would not have been unwilling to detect imposture, and who would not have been deterred from their purpose by interruptions which are extraordinary only in a relation. If the purpose of the Scripture miracles be to enforce on the minds of men an impression of the present agency and of the will of God, His approval of one man or doctrine, and His disapproval of another, not even the clearest of those recorded in the Gospel could have secured this object more effectually than did the wonderful occurrence in question. And did we see at this day a great attempt made to reinstate the Jews as Jews in their own land, to build their Temple, and to recommence their sacrifices, did the enemies of the Catholic Church forward it, did heretical bodies and their officials on the spot take part in it, and did some catastrophe, as sudden and unexpected as the fiery eruption, befall the attempt, I conceive, whatever became of abstract definitions, we should feel it to be a Divine interference, bringing with it its own evidence, and needing no interpretation. It must be recollected, too, that certain of the miracles of Scripture, such as the destruction of Sodom, may be plausibly attributed to physical causes, yet without disparagement of their

original authorities; Warburton has been followed except in one instance.

Divine character. And lastly, as to the extravagance of some writers who have considered the miracle an artifice of the Christian body, the same scepticism which has wantonly ascribed it to combustibles of the nature of gunpowder, has at other times suggested a like explanation of the thunders and lightnings when the Law was given, and of the deaths of Korah, Dathan, and Abiram.

Section VIII.

RECOVERY OF THE BLIND MAN BY THE RELICS OF ST. GERVASIUS AND ST. PROTASIUS AT MILAN.

204. THE broad facts connected with this memorable interposition of Divine Power are these: St. Ambrose, with a large portion of the population of Milan, was resisting the Empress Justina in her attempt to seize on one of the churches of the city for Arian worship. In the course of the contest he had occasion to seek for the relics of Martyrs, to be used in the dedication of a new church, and he found two skeletons, with a quantity of fresh blood, the miraculous token of martyrdom. Miracles followed, both cures and exorcisms; and at length, **as** he was moving the relics to a neighbouring church, a blind man touched the cloth which covered them, and regained his sight. The Empress in consequence relinquished the contest; and the subject of the miracle dedicated himself to religious service in the Church of the Martyrs, where he seems to have remained till his death. These facts are attested by St. Ambrose himself, several times by St. Augustine, and by Pau-

linus, secretary to St. Ambrose, in his Life of the Saint addressed to St. Augustine.

205. This miracle, it is to be presumed, will satisfy the tests which Douglas provides for verifying events of that nature. That author lays down, as we have already seen, that miracles are to be suspected, when the accounts of them were first published long after the *time* or far from the *place* of their alleged occurrence; or, if not, yet at least were not then and there subjected to examination. Now in the instance before us we have the direct testimony of three contemporaries, St. Ambrose, St. Augustine, and Paulinus; two of whom at the least were present at the very time and place, while one of those two wrote his account immediately upon or during the events, as they proceeded. These three witnesses agree together in all substantial matters; and the third, who writes twenty-six years after the miracle, when St. Ambrose was dead, unlike many reporters of miracles, adds nothing to the narrative, as St. Ambrose and St. Augustine left it. Douglas observes in explanation of the third of his conditions, that we may suspect miracles of having "been admitted without examination, first, if they coincided with the favourite opinions and superstitious prejudices of those to whom they were reported, and who on that account might be eager to receive them without evidence; secondly, if they were set on foot, or at least were encouraged

and supported, by those who alone had the power of detecting the fraud, and who could prevent any examination which might tend to undeceive the world."[y] Now here all the power was on the side of those against whom the miracle was wrought ; and, though the popular feeling was with St. Ambrose, yet the whole city had had an Arian clergy for nearly twenty years, and could not but be in a measure under Arian influence. But however this might be, at least Ambrose had to cope with Arian princes armed with despotic power, an Arian court, an Arian communion lately dominant and still organised, with a bishop at its head. His enemies had already made attempts to assassinate him ; and again, to seize his person, and to carry him off from the city. They had hitherto been the assailants, and he had remained passive. Now, however, he had at last ventured on what in its effects was an aggressive act. As I have said, he has to dedicate a Church, and he searches for relics of Martyrs. He is said to find them ; miracles follow ; the sick and possessed are cured ; at length in the public street, in broad day, while the relics are passing, a blind man, well known in the place by name, by trade, by person, and by his calamity, professes to recover his sight by means of them.

206. Here surely is a plain challenge made to the enemies of the Church, almost as direct as Elijah's to

[y] Pages 28, 52.

the idolatrous court and false prophets of Israel. St. Ambrose supplies them with materials, nor do they want the good-will to detect a fraud, if fraud there be. Yet they are utterly unable to cope with him. They denied the miracle indeed, and they could not do otherwise, if they were to remain Arians; as Protestant writers deny it now, that they may not be forced to be Catholics. They denied the miracle, and St. Ambrose, in a sermon preached at the time, plainly tells us that they did; but they did not hazard any counter statement or distinct explanation of the facts of the case. They did not so much as the Jews, who, on the Resurrection, at least said that our Lord's Body was stolen away by night. They did nothing but deny,—except indeed we let their actions speak for them. One thing then they did; they gave over the contest. The Miracle was successful.

207. This miracle answers to Leslie's criteria also. It was sensible; it was public; and the subject of it became a monument of it, and that with a profession that he was so. He remained on the spot, and dedicated himself to God's service in the Church of the Martyrs who had been the means of his cure; thus by his mode of life proclaiming the mercy which had been displayed in his behalf, and by his presence challenging examination.

208. An attempt has lately been made to resolve this miracle into a mere trick of priestcraft; but

doubtless the Arians would have been beforehand with the present objector, could a case have been made out with any plausibility. This anticipation is confirmed by an inspection of the inferences or conjectures of which he makes the historical facts the subject. The blood, he says, was furnished by the blind Severus, who had been a butcher, and might still have relations in the trade. And since St. Ambrose translated the relics at once, instead of waiting for the next Sunday, this is supposed to argue that he was afraid, had the ceremony been postponed, of the fraud being detected by the natural consequence of the delay.

209. But all facts admit of two interpretations; there is not the transaction or occurrence, consisting of many parts, but some of them may be fixed upon as means of forcing upon it a meaning contrary to the true one, as is shewn by the ingenuity exercised in defence of clients in the courts of law. What has been attempted by the writer to whom I allude, as regards St. Ambrose, has been done better, though more wickedly, by the infidel author of the New Trial of the Witnesses as regards the History of the Resurrection. In such cases inquirers will decide according to their prepossessions;[z] if they are prepared to

[z] This has been dwelt on at length, supr. n. 71 to n. 80. Gibbon gives us a curious illustration of it in his remark on the miracle of the Confessors, which is presently to be related. He

believe that the Fathers and Doctors of the Church would introduce the blood of the shambles into a grave, and pretend that it was the blood of God's saints, and hire men first to feign themselves demoniacs and then to profess themselves dispossessed on approaching the counterfeit relics, they will be convinced in the particular case by very slight evidence, and will catch at any circumstances which may be taken as indications of what they think antecedently probable; but if they think such proceedings to be too blasphemous, too frightful, too provocative even of an immediate judgment, for any but the most callous hearts and the most reckless consciences to conceive and carry out, they would not believe even plausible evidence in their behalf. If it appears to them not unlikely that miracles continue in the Church, they will find that it is easier to admit than to reject what comes to them on such weighty testimony; but if they think miracles as improbable after a revelation is given, as they appeared to Hume before it, then they will judge with him that "a religionist may know his narration to be false, and yet persevere in it, with

says: "This supernatural gift of the African Confessors, who spoke without tongues, will command the assent of those, and of those only, who *already* believe that their language was pure and orthodox. But the *stubborn mind* of the infidel is *guarded by secret incurable suspicion;* and the Arian or Socinian, who has seriously rejected the doctrine of the Trinity, *will not be shaken by the most plausible evidence* of an Athanasian miracle." Ch. xxxvii.

the best intentions in the world, for the sake of promoting so holy a cause; or even where this delusion has no place, vanity, excited by so strong a temptation, operates on him more powerfully than on the rest of mankind in any other circumstances, and self-interest with equal force."[a]

210. There are circumstances, however, in this miracle, which may be felt as difficulties by those who neither deny the continuance of a Divine Presence in the Church, nor accuse her Pastors and Teachers of impious imposture. Yet it is difficult to treat of them, without entering upon doctrinal questions which are not in place in the present Essay. One or two of them, which extend to the case of other alleged miracles of the early Church, besides the one immediately before us, shall here be briefly considered, and that in the light which the analogy or the pattern of Scripture throws upon them, which is the main view I have taken of objections all along.

211. Now, first it may be urged that the discovery of the blood of the Martyrs is not after the precedent of anything we meet with in Scripture, which says very little of relics, and nothing of relics of such a character as this, involving as it does a miracle. What is the true doctrine about relics, how they are to be regarded, what is their use and their abuse, is no question before us. If it could be shown that the

[a] Essay on Miracles.

doctrine involved in the discovery of the Martyrs, is on Scriptural grounds such as plainly to prove either that it did not take place, or that it cannot be referred to Divine Agency, this of course would supersede all other considerations. Meanwhile I will but observe, as far as the *silence* of Scripture is concerned, that Scripture could not afford a pattern of the alleged miracle, from the nature of the case. The resurrection of the body is only a Christian dogma; and martyrdom, that is, dying for a creed, is a peculiarity of the Gospel, and was instanced among the Jews, only in proportion as the Gospel was anticipated. The blood was the relic of those whose bodies had been the temple of the Spirit, and who were believed to be in the presence of Christ. Miracles were not to be expected by such instruments, till Christ came; nor afterwards, till a sufficient time had elapsed for Saints to be matured and offered up, and for pious offices and assiduous attentions to be paid by others towards the tabernacles which they left behind them. Precedents then to our purpose, whether in Old or in New Testament, are as little to be expected, as precedents to guide us in determining the relations of the Church to the State, or the question of infant baptism, or the duty of having buildings for worship. Time alone could determine what the Divine purpose was concerning the earthly shrines in which a Divine Presence had dwelt: whether, as in the case of Moses and Elijah, they were to be withdrawn from the Church, or, as in the case of Elisha, to fulfil some purpose, even though the soul had departed; and if the latter, whether their bones were to be employed,—or whether their bodies would be preserved incorrupt, as St. Jerome reports of Hilarion,—or whether the Levitical sacrifices, which as types were once for all fulfilled when our Lord's blood was shed, were nevertheless to furnish part of the analogy existing between the Christian and the Mosaic Dispensations. Nor is there anything that ought to shock us in the idea that blood, which had become coagulate, should miraculously be made to flow. A very remarkable prototype of such an event seems to be granted to us in Scripture, in our Lord's own history. The last act of His humiliation was, after His death, to be pierced in His side, when blood and water issued from it. A stream of blood from a corpse can hardly be considered to be other than supernatural. And it so happens that St. Ambrose is the writer to remark upon this solemn occurrence in his comment on St. Luke, assigning at the same time its typical meaning. "Blood," he says, "undoubtedly congeals after death in our bodies; but in that Body, though incorrupt, yet dead, the life of all welled forth. There issued water and blood; water to wash, blood to redeem. Let us drink then what is our price, that by drinking we may be redeemed."[b]

[b] In. Luc. lib. x. § 135. Euthymius Zigab. says the same in

212. Another objection which has been made to the miracles ascribed by St. Ambrose to the relics which he discovered, is the encouragement which they are supposed to give to a kind of creature-worship, unknown to Scripture. This is strongly urged by the objector whom I just now had occasion to notice. He observes that miracles can be of no avail against the great principles of religious truth, such as the Being and Attributes of Almighty God; that no miracles can sanction and justify idolatry; if then the Nicene Miracles (so he calls them), "when regarded in the calmest and most comprehensive manner," "have constantly operated to debauch the religious sentiments of mankind, if they have confirmed idolatrous practices, if they have enhanced that infatuation which has hurried men into the degrading worship of subordinate divinities, we then boldly say that, whether natural or preternatural, such miracles are

loc. Joan. Theophylact. in loc. says that in order to place the miracle beyond doubt the water issued also. That the flowing of the blood was miraculous would appear from the description St. John gives of it, "*forthwith came there out;*" which implies a stream, and not a few drops. Calov. in Joan. xix. 35. Nor is there any reason to suppose that the water came forth by drops; yet the words just quoted are common to the blood and to the water. Again, the water was miraculous (for " medical men tell us that the fluid of the pericardium is yellow in colour, bitter in taste, and therefore different from what we mean by water," S. Basnag. Ann. 33. § 126; and the wound was most probably on the right side, as St. Augustine and the most ancient pictures and coins represent it, and the Arabic or Ethiopic version, vid. Grets. de Cruc. t. l. i. 35.

not from God, but from 'the enemy.'"c "Do you choose," he continues, "to affirm the supernatural reality of the Nicene Miracles? you then mark the Nicene Church as the slave and agent of the Father of Lies;" and then he proceeds to quote the charge of Moses to his people: "If there arise among you a prophet or a dreamer of dreams, and giveth thee a sign or a wonder, and the sign or the wonder come to pass, whereof he spoke unto thee, saying, 'Let us go after other gods which thou hast not known, and let us serve them,' thou shalt not hearken unto the words of that prophet or that dreamer of dreams; for the Lord your God proveth you, to know whether ye love the Lord your God with all your heart and with all your soul."

Lamp. in loc. Joan.), and therefore there is no reason for a strained interpretation only to escape believing that the blood was miraculous. Further, St. John's solemn asseverations, " He who saw it bare record," etc., which seems to intimate something miraculous, applies to the blood as well as the water. And moreover, in 1 John v. 6, the blood is insisted on even more than the water; "not by water only," etc. Another parallel to this miracle is to be found in the reported instances of blood flowing from a corpse at the approach of the murderer; vid. an instance introduced into a Scotch court as late as 1688, in the notes to the Waverley Novels, vol. xliii. p. 127. It is scarcely necessary to say that, whatever truth there may be in any such stories, or in certain others of which the blood of Martyrs is the subject, they are so encompassed by fictions and superstitions, that it seems hopeless at this day to trace the Divine Agency, as and when It really wrought, though we may believe in Its presence generally.

c Anc. Christ. Part vii. p. 361.

by the Relics of the Martyrs.

213. But the objection, which of course demands a careful consideration, admits of being met, perhaps of being overcome, by reference to an analogy contained in the Old Testament, to which the appeal is made. It is well known that the Divine revelations concerning Angels received a great development in the course of the Jewish Dispensation. When the people had lately come out of Egypt, with all the forms of idolatry familiar to their imaginations, and impressed upon their hearts, it did not seem safe, if we may dare to trace the Divine dealings in this matter, to do much more than to set before them the great doctrine of the Unity and Sovereignty of God. To have disclosed to them truths concerning angelic natures, except in the strictest subserviency to this fundamental Verity, might have been the occasion of their withdrawing their heart from Him who claimed it whole and undivided.[4] Hence, though St. Stephen tells us that they " received the Law by the disposition of Angels," and St. Paul that " it was ordained by Angels," in the Old Testament we do but read of "the voice of the trumpet exceeding loud," and its "waxing louder and louder," and " Moses speaking, and God answering him by a voice," and of " the Lord talking with them face to face in the mount." In like manner, when Angels appeared, it was for the most part in the shape of men;

[4] [Eusebius says this, contrasting Genesis with Daniel, Eccl. Theol. ii. p. 20, and vid. Suicer de Symb. Nic. pp. 89—91.]

or if their heavenly nature was disclosed, still they are called "wind" or "flame," or represented as a glory of the Lord, and so intimately and mysteriously connected with His Presence that it was impossible that God should be forgotten, and a creature worshipped. Thus it is said of the Angel who went before the Israelites, "Obey his voice, *for My Name is in him;*" and it was the belief of the early Church that the Second Person of the Holy Trinity did really condescend to manifest Himself in such angelic natures. Again, the title of "the Lord of hosts" does not occur till the times of Samuel, who uses it when he sends Saul against the Amalekites, whereas it is the ordinary designation of Almighty God in the Prophets who lived after the captivity.[d] And so again, in the Book of Daniel, Angels are made the ordinary instruments of Divine illumination to the Prophet, and are represented as the guardians of the kingdoms of the world, and that without any mention of the Divine Presence at all, which, on the contrary, had been awfully signified in the vision of Isaiah, when the Seraph touched his lips.

214. Still more striking is the difference of language in different parts of the inspired volume as to the doctrine of an Evil Spirit, whom even to name might have been to create a rival to the All-Holy Creator in carnal minds which had just left the house of

[d] Vid. e.g. Hagg. ii. 4—9 ; Zech. viii.

spiritual as well as temporal bondage. The contrast between the earlier and later books of the Old Testament in this point has often been observed. Satan is described in the Book of Job and in Micaiah's vision as appearing before God, and acting under His direction. Again, while in the Second Book of Samuel we are merely told that "the anger of the Lord was kindled against Israel, and He moved David against them to say, Go number Israel and Judah;" in the First Book of Chronicles we read that " Satan stood up against Israel, and provoked David to number Israel."

215. Yet, in spite of this merciful provision on the part of Almighty God, it would appear that the revelation of Angels, when made, did lead many of the Jews into an idolatrous dependence upon them. It is the very remark of Theodoret upon St. Paul's mention of Angel-worship in his Epistle to the Colossians, that " the advocates of the Law induced men to worship Angels, because the Law was given by them, and for humility-sake, and because the God of all is invisible and inaccessible and incomprehensible, so that it was fitting to procure the Divine favour through the Angels."[e] The Essenes, too, are said to

[e] In Col. ii. 18. Vid. also the passage from the Prædic. Petr. in Clem. Strom. vi. 5. and Origen. in Joann. tom. xiii. 17 ; also contr. Cels. v. 6, etc., Hieron. ad. Algas. Ep. 121. § 10 : vid. references to Rabbinical and other writings, Calmet. Dissert. 2. in Luc.

have paid to the Angels an excessive honour, and several of the early heresies, which did the same, sprang from the Jews. What place afterwards the invocation of Angels for magical purposes held in the practical Cabbala, as Brucker calls it, is well known.

216. Such is the history of the revelation of the doctrine of Angels among the Jews; and it is scarcely necessary to draw out at length its correspondence with the history of the introduction and abuse of several of the tenets and usages which characterize the Christian Church. In its origin, the Jewish as well as the Pagan institutions with which the Apostles were surrounded, suggested to them a cautious economy in the mode in which they set Divine truth before their disciples, lest a resemblance of external rites and offices, or of phraseology, between Christianity and the prevailing religions, should be the means of introducing into their minds views less holy and divine than those which they were inspired to reveal. It is on this supposition that some English divines even account for the omission in the New Testament of the words "priest," "sacrifice," and the like, in their plain Christian sense; as if the Jewish associations which attached to them would not cease till the Jewish worship had come to an end. The remark may obviously be extended to the miracle under review, so far as no parallel is found for it in

the New Testament. As the doctrine of priesthood might be almost necessarily Judaic in the minds of the Jewish converts, so that of piety towards Saints and Martyrs was in the minds of Pagans necessarily idolatrous; and it may be for this, as well as other reasons, that so little explicit mention is made in the New Testament of the honours due to Saints, as also of the Christian Priesthood, after the pattern of that silence, which has been above noticed, about the offices of good Angels and about the Author of Evil in the earlier books of the Old; and it may be as rash to say that a miracle was not from God because it was wrought by a Martyr's relics, or because such relics have in other instances been idolatrously regarded, as to say that the Prophet Daniel was not divinely inspired, because we hear nothing of Michael or Gabriel in the Books of Moses, or because the names of those Angels were afterwards superstitiously used in the charms of the Cabbalists. The holy Daniel's profound obeisance and prostrations before the Angel are a greater innovation, if it must so be called, on the simplicity of the Mosaic ritual, than the treasuring the blood of the Martyrs upon the ecclesiastical observances of the Apostles; and as no one would say that Daniel's conduct incurred the condemnation pronounced by Moses on those who introduced the worship of other gods, so much less was the reverence paid by St. Ambrose and other Saints to the relics of the Martyrs inconsistent with precepts which in their direct force belong to an earlier Dispensation.

217. There is a third difficulty, which may be raised upon the passage of history before us, not arising, however, out of the miracle, but out of the circumstances under which it took place. It may be represented as giving a sanction to a subject's playing the part of a demagogue, and heading a mob (as we may speak) against his lawful sovereign. The crowds which attended Ambrose, whether in the church which the Empress had seized, or on occasion of the translation of the relics, whold have been dispersed at this day among ourselves by the officers of the peace ; and with our present notions of law and of municipal and national order, not to say of the subserviency of the Church to the State, and our interpretations of the Scripture precepts concerning civil obedience, there is something strange and painful to us in the sight of a Christian Bishop placed in opposition to the powers that be. But it must be recollected, according to a former remark, that everything that happens has two aspects ; and the outside or political aspect is often the reverse of its inward or true meaning. We are used to put together the particulars which meet our eye, to parallel them with other transactions which bear a similar appearance, to suggest for them such motives of action as our own principles or disposition suggests, and thus to form what seems to us a philo-

sophical view of the whole case. And if our own habitual feelings and opinions, and the parallels to which we betake ourselves, are not of a very exalted nature, as may easily happen, while the subject contemplated, be it a person, or an act, or a work, is of such a nature, then we produce a theory as shallow, and as far from the truth, as a naturalist, who, judging of men by their anatomical peculiarities, should rank them among the brute creation. Every day brings evidence in great things or little, how incapable the run of men are of doing justice to minds of even ordinary refinement and sincerity, and how, rather than ascribe to them the honesty and purity of purpose which is the most natural and straightforward account of their actions, they will even go out of their way, and distort facts, thereby to be at liberty to impute petty motives; and much more will they catch at any circumstances which admit of being plausibly perverted into an evidence of such motives. Indeed, of such continual occurrence are instances of this sort, that in tales of fiction nothing is more commonly taken as a plot of the story than the troubles in which an innocent person is involved by an ingenious but perverse selection and collocation of his actions or of circumstances connected with him, to the detriment of his character.

218. As to the case immediately before us, it is enough to observe that an imputation of disloyalty, if

preferred against St. Ambrose, is only what the notorious Paine, I believe, throws out against the Jewish Prophets; and it is obvious what plausible materials are afforded by the history of Elijah and Elisha, in the hands of irreligious persons, for such a charge. Nor is it to be doubted that a secular historian, who heard the Prophet Jeremiah's public declaration on Nebuchadnezzar's invasion, "He that abideth in this city shall die, but he that goeth out, and falleth to the Chaldeans, shall live," would have decided that he was in the pay of the King of Babylon, and justified the Jews in their treatment of him. It must be recollected, too, that one charge against our Lord was that He "stirred up the people." We indeed have learned from the Gospel that He withdrew Himself from the multitude "when He perceived that they would come and take Him by force to make Him a king;" but a secular historian either would not know the fact, or might not believe the sincerity of His withdrawal, if He did. A more exact instance in point is afforded us in the history of St. John Baptist. No man surely has less of a political character upon him than this holy ascetic, as described in the Gospel; but it seems, according to Josephus, that Herod was of another mind, and the view he took of him as a popular leader is so curious that I will quote the words of a recent writer on the subject. "Herod," says Mr. Milman, "having formed an incestuous connection with the wife of his brother Herod Philip, his Arabian queen indignantly fled to her father, who took up arms to revenge her wrongs against her guilty husband. How far Herod could depend in this contest on the loyalty of his subjects was extremely doubtful It is possible he might entertain hopes that the repudiation of a foreign alliance, ever hateful to the Jews, and the union with a branch of the Asmonean line (for Herodias was the daughter of Herod the Great by Mariamne), might counterbalance in the popular estimation the injustice and criminality of his marriage with his brother's wife. The *influence* of John, according to Josephus, was almost *unlimited.* The subjects, and even the soldiery, of the tetrarch *crowded with devout submission* around the Prophet. *On his decision* might depend the *wavering loyalty* of the whole province. But John denounced with open indignation the royal incest, and declared the marriage with a brother's wife to be a flagrant violation of the law. Herod, before long, *ordered him to be seized and imprisoned* in the *strong fortress* of Machærus, on the *remote border* of his trans-Jordanic territory."[f]

219. Such was the light thrown upon the Holy Baptist by the secular events in which he was encompassed, in the opinion of one who nevertheless, as we know, "feared him, knowing he was a just man." And

[f] Hist. Christ. Vol. i. p. 176.

as St. John seemed to be a demagogue and a mere organ of the popular voice, yet spoke from heaven, so in like manner it need not take from the sanctity of St. Ambrose, or the truth of his cause, that the people sided with him, even tumultuously, and the Imperial Court accused him of insubordination.

Section IX.

THE POWER OF SPEECH CONTINUED TO THE AFRICAN CONFESSORS DEPRIVED OF THEIR TONGUES.

220. ARIANISM, though speedily exterminated from the Roman Empire, had taken refuge among the Barbarians of the North, who were then hanging over it, and soon to overwhelm it. Among these nations were the Vandals, who in the early part of the fifth century took possession of the Roman provinces on the African coast. Genseric forthwith commenced, and his successors continued, a terrible persecution of the Catholic Church, which they found there. Hunneric his son, to whose reign the miracle which is to be related belongs, began his series of cruelties by stationing officers violently to assault and drag off all Vandals whom they found attending the Churches, and by sending off the dependents of his court who were Catholics to work in the country as agricultural labourers. Others he deprived of their civil functions, stripped of their property, and banished

to Sicily and Sardinia. Next he summoned the nuns out of their convents, accused them of the vilest crimes, and submitted them to the most miserable indignities. Further, he caused them to be hung up without clothes, with weights to their feet, and to be tortured with red-hot irons in various parts of the body, in order to make them admit the charges he brought against them. His next measure was the wholesale cruelty of banishing a number of bishops, priests, deacons, and others, as many as four thousand nine hundred and sixty-one,[g] to the desert. He began by assembling them in the two towns of Sicca and Laribus; and in one or other of these places Victor, who has preserved the history of the transaction, saw them. His account is too horrible to be translated. They had been shut up, how long does not appear, in a small prison, and when Victor entered he sank up to his knees in the filth of the place. At length they set forth for the desert, with their faces and clothes in this defiled condition, chaunting the words, "Such glory have all His saints." They journeyed chiefly by night, on account of the heat of the days; when they flagged, their conductors goaded them and pelted them, or if this did not quicken them, they tied them by the feet, and dragged them after them along the rocky roads.

[g] The number is given differently; Gibbon says four thousand and ninety-six; Fleury four thousand nine hundred and sixty-six; that in the text is as it stands in the Bibl. Patr. Par. 1624.

Those who survived the journey found themselves in places abounding in venomous reptiles, and the food given them was the barley provided for the beasts of burden.

221. In the beginning of 484 Hunneric convened four hundred and sixty-six Catholic Bishops at Carthage, for the purpose of holding a disputation on the faith of Nicæa ; and, to intimidate them, he began by burning Lætus alive, who was one of their most learned members. This not succeeding, he dismissed them again to their homes, allowing them neither the beasts of burden on which they had come, nor their servants, nor their clothes, and forbidding all persons to lodge or feed them ; when they remonstrated, he set his cavalry to charge them. Jealous of their orthodoxy as a bond of union with the Catholic world, he next proposed to them to swear allegiance to his son and successor, and abstention from all ecclesiastical correspondence beyond sea. Forty-six refused it on the plea of our Lord's prohibition in the Sermon on the Mount ; three hundred and two, on the stipulation that their flocks and themselves should be restored to their churches, took it. The latter he distributed as serfs up and down the country, as having broken the Gospel precept against swearing ; the former he transported to Corsica to cut timber for his navy. Of the rest, twenty-eight had succeeded in escaping from Carthage, and eighty-eight conformed. A general

persecution followed, in which neither sex nor age was pitied, nor torture, mutilation, nor death was spared.

222. These particulars, which form but a portion of the atrocities which this savage was permitted to perpetrate, have here been mentioned, because they form a suitable antecedent, and (if the word may be used) a justification of the miracle which followed. It was no common occasion that called forth what was no common manifestation of the wonderful power of God. The facts, as stated by one who in such a case cannot be called a too favourable witness, were as follows: "Tipasa," says Gibbon, "a maritime colony of Mauritania, sixteen miles to the east of Cæsarea, had been distinguished in every age by the orthodox zeal of its inhabitants. They had braved the fury of the Donatists; they resisted, or eluded, the tyranny of the Arians. The town was deserted on the approach of an heretical Bishop; most of the inhabitants who could procure ships passed over to the coast of Spain; and the unhappy remnant, refusing all communion with the usurper, still presumed to hold their pious, but illegal, assemblies. Their disobedience exasperated the cruelty of Hunneric. A military Count was despatched from Carthage to Tipasa; he collected the Catholics in the Forum, and, in the presence of the whole province, deprived the guilty of their right hands and their tongues. But the holy Confessors continued

deprived of their Tongues.

to speak without tongues."[h] "The gift continued through their lives. Their number is not mentioned by any of the original witnesses; but is fixed by an old Menology at sixty."[i] Such was the miracle; the evidence on which it rests shall next be stated.

223. Victor, Bishop of Vite, who has been already mentioned, published in Africa his history of the persecution only two years after it took place. He says, "The King in wrath sent a certain Count with directions to hold a meeting in the forum of the whole province, and there to cut out their tongues by the roots, and their right hands. When this was done, by the gift of the Holy Ghost, they so spoke and speak, as they used to speak before. If however any one will be incredulous, let him now go to Constantinople, and there he will find one of them, a sub-deacon, by name Reparatus, speaking like an educated man without any impediment. On which account he is regarded with exceeding veneration in the court of the Emperor Zeno, and especially by the Empress."[k] It has been asked why Victor refers his readers to Constantinople, instead of pointing out instances of the miracle in the country in which it is said to have taken place.[1] But

[h] Hist. Ch. xxxvii.   [i] Ibid.
[k] Hist. Pers. Vand. iii. p. 613.

[1] This is suggested in the article on Miracles in the Encycl. Metrop. [*i.e.* Essay i. supr. p. 87, note f], in which I could wish some correction of opinion, but more of tone, in my treatment of the primitive miracles. The Essay aims, indeed, at bringing

persecution scattered the Catholics far and wide, as St. Gregory observes in a passage which is to follow; many fled the country; others concealed themselves. Under such circumstances, a writer would not know even where his nearest friends were to be found; and in this case Victor specified one of the Confessors who had been welcomed by an orthodox capital and court, and had the opportunity of exhibiting in security the miraculous gift wrought in him.

224. Æneas of Gaza was the contemporary of Victor. When a Gentile, he had been a philosopher and rhetorician, and did not altogether throw off his profession of Platonism when he became a Christian. He wrote a Dialogue on the Immortality of the Soul and the Resurrection of the Body; and in it, after giving various instances of miracles, he proceeds, in the character of Axitheus, to speak of the miracle of the African Confessors: " Other such things have been and will be; but what took place the other day, I suppose you have seen yourself. A bitter tyranny is oppressing the greater Africa; and humanity and orthodoxy have no influence over tyranny. Accordingly this tyrant takes offence at the piety of his subjects, and commands the priests to deny their glorious dogma. When they refuse, O the impiety! he cuts

out the characteristics of the evidence for the Scripture Miracles, in contrast with all others so considered; but Middleton and Douglas are unsafe guides, and it is no exaltation of Christ to lower His Saints.

out that religious tongue, as Tereus in the fable. But the damsel wove the deed upon the robe, and divulged it by her skill, when nature no longer gave her power to speak; they, on the other hand, needing neither robe nor skill, call upon nature's Maker, who vouchsafes to them a new nature on the third day, not giving them another tongue, but the faculty to discourse without a tongue more plainly than before. I had thought it was impossible for a piper to show his skill without his pipes, or harper to play his music without his harp; but now this novel sight forces me to change my mind, and to account nothing fixed that is seen, if it be God's will to alter it. I myself saw the men, and heard them speak; and wondering at the articulateness of the sound, I began to inquire what its organ was; and distrusting my ears, I committed the decision to my eyes. And opening their mouth, I perceived the tongue entirely gone from the roots. And astounded I fell to wonder, not how they could talk, but how they had not died." He saw them at Constantinople.

225. Procopius of Cæsarea was secretary to Belisarius, whom he accompanied into Africa, Sicily, and Italy, and to Constantinople, in the years between 527 and 542. By Belisarius he was employed in various political matters of great moment, and was at one time at the head of the commissariat and the fleet. He seems to have conformed to Christianity,

but Cave observes, from his tone of writing, that he was no real believer in it, nay, preferred the old Paganism, though he despised its rites and fables.[m] He wrote the History of the Persian, Vandalic, and Gothic War, of which Gibbon speaks in the following terms: "His facts are collected from the personal experience and free conversation of a soldier, a statesman, and a traveller; his style continually aspires, and often attains, to the merit of strength and elegance; his reflections, more especially in the speeches which he too frequently inserts, contain a rich fund of political knowledge; and the historian, excited by the generous ambition of pleasing and instructing posterity, appears to disdain the prejudices of the people and the flattery of courts."[n] Such is Procopius, and thus he speaks on the subject of this stupendous miracle: "Hunneric became the most savage and iniquitous of men towards the African Christians. For, forcing them to Arianize, whomever he found unwilling to comply, he burnt and otherwise put to death. And of many he cut out the tongue as low down as the throat,[o] who, even as late as my time, were alive in Byzantium, and talked without any impediment, feeling no effects whatever of the punishment. But two of them, having allowed themselves to hold converse with abandoned women, ceased to speak."[p]

[m] Cave, Hist. Liter. Procop.
[n] Hist. Ch. xl.
[o] Ἀπ' αὐτοῦ φάρυγγος.
[p] Bell. Vand. i. 10.

226. Our next witness, and of the same date, is the Emperor Justinian, who, in an edict addressed to Archelaus, Prætorian Præfect of Africa, on the subject of his office, after Belisarius had recovered the country to the Roman Empire, writes as follows: "The present mercy, which Almighty God has deigned to manifest through us for His praise and His Name's sake, exceeds all the wonderful works which have happened in the world; viz., that Africa should through us recover in so short a time its liberty, after being in captivity under the Vandals for ninety-five years, those enemies alike of soul and body. For such souls as could not sustain their various tortures and punishments, by rebaptizing they translated into their own misbelief; and the bodies of free men they subjected to the hardships of a barbaric yoke. Nay, the very churches sacred to God did they defile with their deeds of misbelief; some they turned into stables. We have seen the venerable men, who, when their tongues had been cut off at the roots, yet piteously recounted their pains. Others after diverse tortures were dispersed through diverse provinces, and ended their days in exile."[q]

227. Count Marcellinus, Chancellor to Justinian before he came to the throne, is the fourth layman to whose testimony we are able to appeal. He too, as two of the former, speaks as an eye-witness, and the

[q] Cod. Just. lib. i. tit. 30, ed. 1553.

additional circumstances, with which he commences seem to throw light upon Æneas's singular account that the Confessors spoke "more plainly than before." "Through the whole of Africa," he says in his Chronicon, under the date 484, "the cruel persecution of Hunneric, King of the Vandals, was inflicted upon our Catholics. For after the expulsion and dispersion of more than 334 Bishops of the orthodox, and the shutting of their churches, the flocks of the faithful, afflicted by various punishments, consummated their blessed conflict. Then it was that the same King Hunneric ordered the tongue to be cut out of a Catholic youth, who from his birth had lived without speech at all; soon after he spoke, and gave glory to God with the first sounds of his voice. In short, I myself have seen at Byzantium a few out of this company of the faithful, religious men, with their tongues cut off, and their hands amputated, speaking with perfect voice."

228. Victor, Bishop of Tonno in Africa Proconsularis, another contemporary, and a strenuous defender of the Tria Capitula, which were condemned in the Fifth Ecumenical Council, has left behind him a Chronicon also; which at the same date runs as follows: "Hunneric, King of the Vandals, urging a furious persecution through the whole of Africa, banishes to Tubunnæ, Macrinippi, and other parts of the desert, not only Catholic Clerks of every order,

but even Monks and laymen, to the number of about four thousand; and makes Confessors and Martyrs; and cuts off the tongues of the Confessors. As to which Confessors, the royal city, where their bodies lie, attests that after their tongues were cut out they spoke perfectly even to the end. Then Lætus, Bishop of the Church of Nepte, is crowned with Martyrdom, etc." It is observable from this statement that the miracle was recorded for the instruction of posterity at the place of their burial.

229. Lastly, Pope Gregory the First thus speaks in his Dialogues: "In the time of Justinian Augustus,[r] when the Arian persecution raised by the Vandals against the faith of Catholics was raging violently in Africa, some Bishops, courageously persisting in the defence of the truth, were brought under notice; whom the King of the Vandals, failing to persuade to his misbelief with words and offers, thought he could break with torture. For when, in the midst of their defence of the truth, he bade them be silent, but they would not bear the misbelief quietly, lest it might be interpreted as assent, breaking out into rage he had their tongues cut off from the roots. A wonderful thing, and known to many senior persons; for afterwards, even without tongue, they spoke for the defence of the truth, just as they had been accus-

[r] This date is a mistake of St. Gregory's; also he calls them Bishops.

tomed before to speak by means of it. . . . These then, being fugitives at that time, came to Constantinople. At the time, moreover, that I was myself sent to the Emperor to conduct the business of the Church, I fell in with a certain senior, a Bishop, who attested that he had seen their mouths speaking, though without tongues, so that with open mouths they cried out, 'Behold and see; for we have not tongues, and we speak.' And it appeared to those who inspected, as it was said, as if, their tongues being cut off from the roots, there was a sort of open depth in their throat, and yet in that empty mouth the words were formed full and perfect. Of whom one, having fallen into licentiousness, was soon after deprived of the gift of miracle."[s]

230. Little observation is necessary on evidence such as this. What is perhaps most striking in it is the variety of the witnesses, both in their persons and the details of their testimony, together with the consistency and unity of that testimony in all material points. Out of the seven writers adduced, six are contemporaries; three, if not four, are eye-witnesses of the miracle; one reports from an eye-witness, and one testifies to a permanent record at the burial-place of the subjects of it. All seven were living, or had been staying, at one or other of the two places which are mentioned as their abode. One is a Pope; a

[s] Dial. iii. 32.

second a Catholic Bishop; a third a Bishop of a schismatical party; a fourth an Emperor; a fifth a soldier, a politician, and a suspected infidel; a sixth a statesman and courtier; a seventh a rhetorician and philosopher. "He cut out the tongues by the roots," says Victor, Bishop of Vite; "I perceived the tongue entirely gone by the roots," says Æneas; "as low down as the throat," says Procopius; "at the roots," say Justinian and St. Gregory. "He spoke like an educated man, without impediment," says Victor of Vite; with "articulateness," says Æneas, "better than before;" "they talked without any impediment," says Procopius; "speaking with perfect voice," says Marcellinus; "they spoke perfectly even to the end," says the second Victor; "the words were formed full and perfect," says St. Gregory.

231. One of the striking points then in this miracle, as contained in the foregoing evidence, is obviously its *completeness*. We know that even deaf and dumb persons can be made in some sense to utter words; and there may be attempts far superior to theirs, yet wanting in that ease and precision which characterize the ordinary gift of speech. But the articulateness, nay, the educated accent of these Confessors is especially insisted on in the testimony. "A cure left thus imperfect," says Douglas, speaking of a Jansenist miracle, "has but little pretension to be looked upon as miraculous; because its being so imperfect naturally points

out a failure of power in the cause which brought it about."[t] Whatever be the truth of this position, it cannot be applied to the miracle under review.

232. The *number* on which it was wrought is another most important circumstance, distinguishing this history from others of a miraculous character. It both increases opportunities for testimony, and it prevents the interposition of what is commonly called chance, which could not operate upon many persons at once in one and the same way. This is the proper answer to Middleton's objection, that cases are on record of speech without a tongue, when no special intervention of Providence could be supposed. Not to say that a person *born* without a tongue, as in the instance to which he refers, may more easily be supposed to have found a compensation for her defect by a natural provision or guidance, than men who had ever spoken by the ordinary organ till they came suddenly to lose it. "If we should allow after all," says he, "that the tongues of these Confessors were cut away to the very roots, what will the learned Doctor [Berriman] say if this boasted miracle, which he so strenuously defends, should be found at last to be no miracle at all? The tongue, indeed, has generally been considered as absolutely necessary to the use of speech; so that to hear men talk without it might easily pass for a miracle in that credulous

[t] Page 111.

age."[u] And then he mentions the case of a girl born without a tongue, who yet talked as distinctly and easily as if she had enjoyed the full benefit of that organ, according to the report of a French physician who had carefully examined her mouth and throat, and who refers at the same time to another instance published about eighty years before, of a boy who at the age of eight or nine years lost his tongue by an ulcer after the small-pox, yet retained his speech,— whether as perfectly as before, does not appear.[5]

233. Now, taking these instances at their greatest force, does he mean to say that if a certain number of men lost their tongues at the command of a tyrant for the sake of their religion, and then spoke as plainly as before, nay, if only one person was so mutilated and so gifted, it would not be a miracle? if not, why does he not believe the history of these Confessors? At least he might believe that some of them had the gift of speech continued to them, though the numbers be an exaggeration. It is his canon, as Douglas assures us, that while the history of miracles is "to be suspected always of course, without the strongest evidence to confirm it," the history of common events is "to be *admitted of course*, without as strong reason to suspect it."[v] Now here all the reason or evidence is on the side of believing; yet he

[u] Page 184.   [5] [Vid. Note at the end.]
[v] Page 26. vid. supr. n. 73.

does not believe it; why? simply because, as common sense tells us, and as he feels, it *is* a miraculous story. It is far more difficult to believe that a number of men were forbidden to profess orthodoxy, did continue to profess it, were brought into the forum, had their tongues cut out from the roots, survived it, and spoke ever afterwards as they did before, *without* a miracle than *with* it. But Middleton would secure two weapons at once for his warfare against the claims of the Catholic Church :—it *is* a miracle, and therefore it is incredible as a fact; it is *not* a miracle, and therefore it is irrelevant as an argument.

234. Another remarkable peculiarity of this miracle is what may be called its *entireness*, by which I mean that it carried its whole case with it to every beholder. When a blind man has been restored to sight, there must be one witness to prove he *has been* blind, and another, that he *now sees;* when a cure has been effected, we need a third to assure us that no medicines were administered to the subject of it; but here the miracle is condensed in the fact that there is no tongue, and yet a voice. The function of witnessing is far narrower and more definite, yet more perfect, than in other cases.

235. A further characteristic of this miracle is its *permanence;* and in this respect it throws light upon a remark made in a former page to account for the deficiency of evidence which generally attaches to the

deprived of their Tongues.

Ecclesiastical Miracles. It was there observed that they commonly took place without notice beforehand, and left no trace after them ; and we could not have better or fuller testimony than that which happened to be found on the spot where they occurred.[x] The instance before us, however, being of a permanent character, and carrying its miraculousness in the very sight of it, admitted of being witnessed in a higher way, and so it is witnessed. Supposing the miracles of St. Gregory Thaumaturgus or St. Martin to have had advantage of similar publicity, at least they would have been disengaged from the misstatements and exaggerations which at present prejudice them ;—are we sure they would not have gained, instead, a body of testimony to their substantial truth ?

236. It may be thought a drawback on this miracle that it produced no impression on the brutal Prince who was the occasion of it. He continued the persecution. Yet it must be recollected that his death followed in no long time ; and that, under that horrible and loathsome infliction with which it has in other cases pleased Almighty God to visit those who have used their power, committed to them by Him in cruelties towards His Church.

237. And now, after considering this miracle, or that of the recovery of the blind Severus by the relics, as described in its place, or the death of Arius, how un-

[x] n. 103.

real does the remark appear with which Douglas concludes his review of the alleged miracles of the first ages! "I shall only add," he says, "that *if ever there were any accounts* of miracles, which passed current *without being examined into* at the first publication, and which consequently will not bear the test of the third rule which I laid down in this treatise, *this may be affirmed of the miracles* recorded by writers *of the fourth and fifth ages*, when Christianity, *now freed from the terrors of persecution*, and *aided by civil magistrates*, began to be corrupted by its credulous or ill-designing professors, and the foundation was laid of those inventions which have gathered like a snow-ball in every succeeding age of superstitious ignorance, till at last the sunshine of the Reformation began to melt the monstrous heap."[y] Surely, if there are miracles prominent above others in those times, in that number are the three which I have just specified; they are great in themselves and in their fame. What then is meant by saying that in Arius's death the Church was "aided by the civil magistrate?" or that she was "freed from the terrors of persecution" when Severus was restored to sight? or that the report of the power of speaking given to Reparatus and his brethren "passed current without being examined into?" But if these are true, why should not others be true also, whether at this day they have evidence

[y] Page 239.

sufficient for our conviction or not? That superstitions and imposture *accompanied* the civil establishment of Christianity, all will allow; but they could but obscure,—they could not reverse or undo,—and why should they prejudice?—that true work of God in His Church, of which they were but the mockery.

Conclusion.

238. MUCH stress has been laid throughout this Essay on the *differences* existing between the Miracles recorded in Scripture, and those which are found in Ecclesiastical History; but from what has come before us in the course of it, it would seem that those differences are for the most part merely such as *necessarily* attend the introduction of a religion to the world compared with its subsequent course, the miraculous agency itself being for the most part the same throughout. For instance, the miracles of Scripture are wrought by persons *conscious of their power and of their exercise of it;* for these persons are the very heralds of Almighty God, whom He has commissioned, whom He has instructed, and whom He has gifted for their work. The Scripture miracles are wrought *as evidence of revealed truth*, because they are wrought before that truth had as yet been received. They are *grave and simple* in their circumstances, because they are wrought by persons who know their gift, and who, as being under immediate Divine direction, use it without alloy of human infirmity or personal peculiarity. They

are *definite and certain*, drawn out in an orderly form, and finished in their parts, because they are found in that authoritative Document which was intended by God's Providence to be the pattern of His dealings and the rule of our thoughts and actions. They are *undeniably of a supernatural character*, not only because it is natural that the most cogent miracles should be wrought in the beginning of the Dispensation, but because the sacred writers have been guided to put into the foreground those works of power which are the clearest tokens of a Divine Presence, and to throw the rest into the distance. They have *no marks of exaggeration* about them, and are *none of them false or suspicious*, because Inspiration had dispersed the mists of popular error, and the colouring of individual feeling, and has enabled the writers to set down what took place, and nothing else. But when once Inspiration was withdrawn, whether as regards those who wrought or those who recorded, then a Power which henceforth was mysterious and inscrutable in operation, became doubly obscure in report; and fiction in the testimony was made to compensate for incompleteness in the manifestation.

239. In conclusion I will but observe what, indeed, is very obvious, but still may require a distinct acknowledgment; that the view here taken of the primitive miracles is applicable in defence of those of the medieval period also. If the occurrence of

miraculous interpositions depends upon the presence of the Catholic Church, and if that Church is to remain on earth until the end of the world, it follows, of course, that what will be vouchsafed to Christians at all times, was vouchsafed to them in the middle ages inclusively. Whether this or that alleged miracle be in fact what it professes to be, must be determined, as in the instances already taken, by the particular case; but it stands to reason, that, where the views and representations drawn out in the foregoing pages are admitted, no prejudice will attend the medieval miracles at first hearing, though no distinct opinion can be formed about them before examination.

240. On the other hand, I am quite prepared to find those views themselves condemned by many readers as subtle and sophistical. This is ever the language men use concerning the arguments of others, when they dissent from their *first principles*,—which take them by surprise, and which they have not mastered.

Note on Page 383.

March, 1870. Since the date of these Essays facts have been published, bearing upon the apparent miracle wrought in favour of the African confessors in the Vandal persecution, which have led me, in my "Apologia" (p. 306, ed. 2), to write as follows:

"Their tongues were cut out by the Arian tyrant, and yet they spoke as before. I insisted[z] on this fact as being strictly miraculous. Among other remarks (referring to the instances adduced by Middleton and others in disparagement of the miracle, viz., of 'A girl born without a tongue, who yet talked as distinctly and easily as if she had enjoyed the full benefit of that organ,' and of a boy who lost his tongue at the age of eight or nine, yet retained his speech, whether perfectly or not,) I said, 'Does Middleton mean to say that, if a certain number of men lost their tongues *at the command of a tyrant*, for the *sake of their religion*, and then spoke *as plainly* as before, nay, *if only one person was so mutilated* and so gifted, it would not be a miracle?'—p. 210. And I enlarged upon the minute details of the fact as reported to us by eye-witnesses and contemporaries.

"However, a few years ago an article appeared in *Notes and Queries* (No. for May 22, 1858), in which various evidence was adduced to show that the tongue is not necessary for articulate speech.

"1. Colonel Churchill, in his 'Lebanon,' speaking of the cruelties of Djezzar Pacha, in extracting to the root the

---

[z] That is, in my Second Essay, as supr. Ch. v. Sec. 9, especially at p. 383.

tongues of some Emirs, adds, 'It is a curious fact, however, that the tongues grow again sufficiently for the purposes of speech.'

"2. Sir John Malcolm, in his 'Sketches of Persia,' speaking of Zâb, Khan of Khisht, who was condemned to lose his tongue, 'This mandate,' he says, 'was imperfectly executed, and the loss of half this member deprived him of speech. Being afterwards persuaded that its being cut close to the root would enable him to speak so as to be understood, he submitted to the operation; and the effect has been that his voice, though indistinct and thick, is yet intelligible to persons accustomed to converse with him. . . . I am not an anatomist, and I cannot therefore give a reason why a man, who could not articulate with half a tongue, should speak when he had none at all; but the facts are as stated.'

"3. And Sir John McNeil says, 'In answer to your inquiries about the powers of speech retained by persons who have had their tongues cut out, I can state from personal observation that several persons whom I knew in Persia, who had been subjected to that punishment, spoke so intelligibly as to be able to transact important business. . . . The conviction in Persia is universal, that the power of speech is destroyed by merely cutting off the tip of the tongue; and is to a useful extent restored by cutting off another portion as far back as a perpendicular section can be made of the portion that is free from attachment at the lower surface. . . . I never had to meet with a person who had suffered this punishment, who could not speak so as to be quite intelligible to his familiar associates.' So far these writers.

"I should not, however, be honest, if I professed to be simply converted by their testimony, to the belief that there was nothing miraculous in the case of the African confessors. It is quite as fair to be sceptical on one side of the question as on the other; and if Gibbon is considered worthy of praise for his 'stubborn incredulity' in receiving the evidence for the miracle, I do not see why I am to be blamed, if I wish to be quite sure of the full appositeness of the recent evidence which is brought to its disadvantage. Questions of fact cannot be disproved by analogies or presumptions; the inquiry must be made into the particular case in all its parts, as it comes before us. Meanwhile, I fully allow that the points of evidence brought in disparagement of the miracle are *primâ facie* of such cogency, that, till they are proved to be irrelevant, Catholics are prevented from appealing to it for controversial purposes."

INDEX

Abbé Paris, cures at the tomb of, 33, 38, 44, 45, 59, 61, 64, 66, 90.
Æneas of Gaza, testifies to the miracle of the Confessors retaining the power of speech, 374.
African Confessors, miracle of the, 369 ; its *completeness*, 381 ; *number* on whom it was wrought, 382.
Alexander Pseudomantis, 81.
Alexander the coppersmith, 333.
Alypius, 335.
Ambrose, St., on the discovery of the two martyrs' bodies, 137 ; his character, 238; resists the Empress Justina in her attempt to enforce Arian worship, 348 ; discovers the relics of St. Gervasius and St. Protasius, *ib.*
Ammianus, his account of Julian's attempt to rebuild the Temple, 337.
Ananias and Sapphira, 166, 333.
Angel-worship, 361.
Antonine Column at Rome, 249.
Antony, St., 122 ; his combats with evil spirits, 158.
Apocryphal Accounts of Christ, 28.
Apollonius, miracles attributed to, 27, 36, 57, 62, 90, 159.
Arius, sudden death of, 134, 327.
Arnobius, his challenge to the heathen as to miracles, 66.
Athanasius, St., Life of St. Antony, 122.
Augustine, St., his *De Civitate Dei*, 129; passage against the Donatists, 142; keenness of his intellect, 238.
Aurea Legenda of Jacob de Voragine, 236.
Austin, 84.

Balaam's ass, 30.
Barrington, Lord, on the duration of the gift of miracles, 214.
Basil, St., miraculously informed of the death of the Emperor Julian, 57 ; on St. Gregory Thaumaturgus, 118.
Bede's Ecclesiastical History, 236.
Bentham, Jeremy, *Preuves Judiciaires*, 21, 45, 56, 58, 83.
Berkeley (Bishop) his *Alciphron*, 10.
Bernard, St., quoted, 208 ; his miracles, 219.
Bethesda, 34.
Blomfield, Bishop, Sermons, 135 ; quoted, 221.

Bryant, 25.
Butler, Alban, Lives of the Saints, 257.
Butler, Bishop, Analogy, 17, 71.

Calvin, on Saint Helena, 289.
Campbell on Miracles, 5, 50.
Chinese painters, their method of drawing, 82.
Chrysostom, St., on Miracles, 136.
Clarke, Dr., on the site of the Holy Sepulchre, 302.
Claudius Apollinaris, his Apology for Christianity lost, 241.
Clement, St., of Alexandria, quoted, 139.
Cock-lane ghost, 61.
Constantine's Luminous Cross, 134, 271 ; his letter to Macarius, 291.
Cyprian, divine admonition to, 37; his description of the demoniacs, 132; account of a lapsed communicant, 134.
Cyril, St., of Jerusalem, on the discovery of the Cross, 293.

Davison's Discourses on Prophecy, quoted, 343.
Demetrian, 132.
Dio Cassius, on the miracle of the Thundering Legion, 248.
Doddridge on Acts, quoted, 64.
Domitian, assassination of, 57.
Donatus, 143.
Douglas, Bishop, his Criterion, 34, 42, 60, 61, 64, 106, 177.

Ecclesiastical Miracles, 97.
Eleazar, charm wrought by, 27.
Elijah's sacrifice, 31, 32; miracles, 88, 91, 332.
Elisha's miracles, 81, 91, 161, 163, 167, 232.
Elymas, 333.
Empedocles, 27.
Essenes, the, 361.
Eusebius, 123, 134, 241; his account of Narcissus, 256; of Constantine's Luminous Cross, 281 ; of the discovery of the Holy Cross, 290; and Sepulchre, 305.
Eve's temptation by the serpent, 30.

Fabricius, quoted, 279.
Farmer on Miracles, 12, 26, 33, 50, 55.
Fleetwood on Miracles, 53.
Fleury's Ecclesiastical History, 99.
Francis, St., tears of, 256.

Gelasius, Pope, his warning to the faithful against apocryphal works, 235.
Genseric, 369.
Gervasius, St., discovery of the relics of, 134; miracles wrought by them, 348.
Gibbon, his mock defence of the miracle wrought in the case of the Confessors, 87 ; on the first converts, 89 ; on the miracles of Moses and Joshua, 165 ; on the silence of the Saints as to their gift of miracles, 219; on the appearance of the Cross to Constantine, 282, 285 ; on the death of Arius, 331 ; on the miracle of the African Confessors, 352 ; on the persecution of Hunneric, 372 ; on Procopius, 376.

Index. 397

Graves, Dr., Lectures on the Pentateuch, 37 ; quoted, 40.
Gregory, St., of Neocæsarea (Thaumaturgus), 117, 236 ; miracle on the course of the Lycus, 261.
Gregory, St., of Nyssa, 118; his account of St. Gregory Thaumaturgus, 261.
Gretzer, *de Cruce*, quoted, 273.
Grotius, Hugo, 114.

Heber, Bishop, his article in the *Quarterly Review* on the site of the Holy Sepulchre, 302.
Helena, Saint, her discovery of the Holy Cross, 287.
Herod, 366.
Herodotus, fables related by, 56.
Hezekiah, recovery of, 66 ; site of the pool of. 311, 317-323.
Hilarion, his cures of wounds, 66 ; various miracles wrought by him, 126.
Hohenlohe, Prince, his cures stopped by authority, 45.
Hume on Miracles, 10 ; quoted, 14, 16, 20, 26 ; his argument from general experience, 54 ; argument against miracles generally, 155 ; their *impossibility*, 175 ; quoted, 354.
Hunneric's persecution, 33, 87, 369-372.

Jansenists, ruin of, 44 ; their cures unsatisfactory, 60, 81.
Januarius, St., liquefaction of the blood of, 60, 63.
Jeremiah, his public declaration on Nebuchadnezzar's invasion, 366.
Jerome, St., his Life of Hilarion, 126, 162.
Jerusalem, site of, considered, 309.
Jesus, the Son of Sirach, 147.
Jewish Miracles, express purpose and one grand object of, 23 ; evidence for, 91.
Jonah and the whale, 30.
Jones on the Figurative Language of Scripture, 26; on the Canon, 28, 39, 235.
Jortin on the Ecclesiastical Miracles, 181, 190, 257.
Josephus, 27, 366.
Joshua, commands the Sun to stand still, 81.
Irenæus, St., 131, 140, 214, 224.
Isidore of Pelusium, 138.
Julian, Emperor, 57, 67; upbraids the Christians with their worship of the wood of the Cross, 275 ; Fiery Eruption on his attempt to rebuild the Jewish Temple, 334.
Justina, Empress, 348.
Justinian, Emperor, edict to Archelaus, 377.
Justin, St., on the Incarnation, 224.

Korah, Dathan, and Abiram, 347.
Koran, boasted elegance of the, 62.

Lardner, Dr., on St. Gregory Thaumaturgus, 262 ; on the Emperor Julian's attempt to rebuild the Temple, 339-341.
Lavington's *Enthusiasm of Methodists and Papists*, 28.
Lazarus, restoration of, 60.
Lee, Professor, Persian Tracts, 76.
Leland's *View of Deistical Writers*, 14.

Livy, prodigies of, no part in the action of his history, 36.
Loyola, 76.
Lycus, changed in its course by St. Gregory, 261.
Lyttelton, Lord, on St. Paul's conversion, 231.

Macrina, St., 261, 268.
Mahomet's night-journey to heaven, 65; miracles of, 76.
Marcellinus, Count, testifies to the miracle of the Confessors retaining their power of speech, 378.
Marcus Antoninus, 134, 242.
Martin, St., miracles of, 127, 163, 209.
Maxentius, Constantine's engagement with, 271, 278, 281.
Melchior Canus, 236.
Middleton's Free Enquiry, 29, 42, 57, 60, 79, 131, 154, 164, 206, 384.
Milman, Dean, on the history of Samson, 168; on the apparition of the Cross to Constantine, 251; on Herod and John the Baptist, 367.
Milner's Church History, 87.
Miracle, idea and scope of a, 4; antecedent credibility of considered as a Divine interposition, 13; criterion of, 49; *et sæpius.*
Miracles of Scripture, characterized, 388.
Montanus, trances of, 64.
Moses, divides the Red Sea, 66; miracles of, 88, 163.
Mosheim's Ecclesiastical History; 41, 86, 90, 245.
Moyle, on the miracle of the Thundering Legion, 245-247, 250.

Narcissus, Bishop of Jerusalem, changes water into oil, 134, 255.
Natalis, 123.
Nazarius, his panegyrical oration upon the Emperor Constantine, 277.
Neander's Church History, 245.
Newman, Dr., "Apologia," passage quoted from, 391-393.

Optatus of Milevis, 145.
Origen, 137, 140; quoted, 189, 220.
Osburn's *Errors of the Apostolic Fathers*, 139.

Paine, the notorious, 366.
Paley's Evidences, 44, 59, 79, 89, 91; quoted, 329-330.
Palladius, 237, 238.
Papias, 131.
Paulinus, St., on the discovery of the Cross, 299.
Paul the Hermit, buried by lions, 29.
Penrose on Miracles, quoted, 43.
Phidias, figure of on Minerva's shield, 37.
Philostratus, his account of Apollonius, 75, 159.
Pliny, on fountains of oil, 258.
Polycarp, St., martyrdom of, 29; fragrance issues from, 133.
Procopius of Cæsarea, testifies to the miracle of the Confessors retaining their power of speech, 375.
Protasius, St., discovery of the relics of, 135; miracles wrought by, 340.
Protestant habits of thought, 176.
Pythagoras, 27.

Index. 399

Quarterly Review, on the discovery and site of the Holy Sepulchre, 302, 303.

Recovery of the Blind Man, Severus, by the Relics of St. Gervasius and St. Protasius, 348.
Religion, its prepossessions always the strongest, 86.
Robinson, Professor, quoted, 289, 295-297, 321-325.

Sabbath-day's journey, space of, 308-309.
Samson, history of, 168.
Samuel, invokes a storm to defeat the Philistines, 253.
Saragossa, Cathedral of, 87.
Scripture, compared to a garden of Eden, 151.
Serapis, worshippers of, 87.
Sergius Paulus, 39.
Simon Magus, miracles of, 28.
Socrates, Ecclesiastical History, quoted, 341.
Sodom, destruction of, 172.
Speculum Exemplorum, 236.
Stephen, St., miracles at his shrine at Hippo, 130.
St. George, the patron Saint of England, 235.
Stillingfleet, 32, 59.
Sulpicius, his account of St. Martin, 127, 209, 234.
Sumner, Archbishop, *Records of Creation*, 9.

Tacitus, 34.
Taylor, Isaac, his *Ancient Christianity*, 135 ; on St. Ambrose, 238; quoted, 292, 297 ; on the Nicene miracles, 358.
Tentative Miracles, 220.
Tereus, 375.
Tertullian, his account of the vision of an Angel, 37 ; his *De Pudicitiâ*, 139, quoted, 225, 242.
Theodoret's Religious History, 237.
Theodotus, heresy of, 123 ; writings of, 139.
Theophilus, St., 203.
Thundering Legion, the, 241.
Tillemont, 237, 300.
Tillotson, Archbishop, his *decisive* argument against the Real Presence, 109.
Tongue, the, recent instances of its growing again after extraction, sufficiently for purposes of speech, 392.

Van Mildert's Boyle Lectures, 53.
Vespasian, cures ascribed to, 34, 38, 77, 87.
Victor, Bishop of Vite, testifies to the miracle of the Confessors retaining their power of speech, 373.
Victor, Bishop of Tonno, testifies to the miracle of the Confessors, 378.
Vince on Miracles, 18, 20 ; a valuable treatise, 70.
Voltaire, his objection to miracles as arguing mutability in the Deity, 21.

Warburton, Bishop, *Divine Legation*, 18, 30 ; Sermon on Resurrection, 34 ; quoted, 44 ; his test of true miracles, 106 ; writes in defence of the miraculous character of the fiery eruption which defeated Julian's attempt to rebuild the Temple, 334.

Water changed into oil at the prayer of St. Narcissus, 255.
Whately, Archbishop, his Treatise on Rhetoric, 14.
Whiston, quoted, 45.
White, Blanco, *Against Catholicism*, 38.

Xavier, 79.

Zeno, 87, 373.
Zoroaster, extraordinary works attributed to, 27, 31.

FINIS.

EDITOR'S NOTES

Dedication
Frederic Rogers (1811–1889), raised to the peerage as Lord Blachford in 1871, was one of Newman's favourite pupils at Oriel, whom Newman thought one of the most able and intelligent of all his friends. A barrister of Lincoln's Inn, he was Permanent Under-Secretary of State for the Colonies from 1860 to 1871. When Newman, travelling in Sicily in 1833, saw in an old newspaper that Rogers had been elected as a Fellow of Oriel he 'kissed the paper rapturously'. When Hurrell Froude died it was at Rogers' suggestion that Newman chose the Breviary from Hurrell Froude's books. It was Rogers whom Newman invited to write a critical article on the works of Jeremy Bentham for *The British Critic*, which appeared in 1840 as 'Utilitarian Moral Philosophy' (BC, 28 July 1840, pp. 93–125). A supporter of the Tractarian movement Rogers was distressed at Newman's move to Rome, and did not see him for some twenty years. They had an emotional meeting and Newman noted that 'It was a sad pleasure to find how closely we agreed on a number of matters ... It was almost like two clocks keeping time' (*L&D*, XX, p. 513).

p. vii. *Encyclopaedia Metropolitana*: The *Encylopaedia Metropolitana* was edited from 1822 to 1836 by the Revd Edward Smedley. In the spring of 1824 Newman had been asked by Whately (a regular contributor) to write an article on Cicero for the *Encyclopaedia* at short notice, as Smedley had been let down by Julius Hare whose submitted article had been found wanting. Newman noted how after working with his private pupils till evening he had then worked on the article on Cicero until four in the morning, and then walked from Oxford to Over Worton, a distance of eighteen miles, to breakfast with his former school master at Ealing, the Revd Walter Mayers (*L&D*, I, p. 175n.). Newman noted that he wrote the Cicero article in six weeks without previous engagement (H. Tristram (ed.), *John Henry Newman Autobiographical Writings*, London, 1955, p. 10). It was later republished in his *Historical Studies,* I, pp. 239–300.

p. vii. *Apollonius of Tyana*: (d. *c*.98). Neopythagorean philosopher, whose 'virtuous life and reforming religious tendencies were constantly exaggerated after his death so that it became possible for anti-Christian writers to compose biographies of him consciously parallel with the Gospel life of Christ'. Particularly notable was the *Life* written by Flavius Philostratus (*c*.220), which was drawn on by Hierocles, Governor of Bithynia *c*.303, whose life of Apollonius occasioned a refutation by Eusebius of Caesarea (cf. *ODCC*, loc. cit.). Newman was invited to write on Apollonius for the *Encyclopaedia Metropolitana* of which Tom Mozley noted: 'Newman wrote about this time an elaborate article on Apollonius Tyanaeus for an Encyclopaedia, drawing the line strongly between true and fictitious miracles. He had early faced fairly the question of evidences, by the study of infidel writers. He was one of the few people who could be called thoroughly acquainted with Gibbon's great work ... He knew well Hume's Essays' (T. Mozley, *Reminiscenes chiefly of Oriel College and the Oxford Movement,* London, 1882, I, p. 40).

p. vii. *Fleury's Ecclesiastical History*: Claude Fleury (1640–1723) author of *Histoire ecclésiastique* in 20 volumes (1691–1720), the first large-scale history of the Church, in which he was assisted by the Maurist historians, Jean Mabillon and Bernard de Montfaucon. By the time of his death the history had been brought to 1414. It was continued to 1778 by J. C. Fabré and others. Hugh James Rose, who wished to produce a vast collaborative ecclesiastical history, thought that if that project was unable to be pursued then a translation of Fleury would do almost as well. Newman wrote to Hurrell Froude on 9 August 1835: 'Rose is set upon having a standard history to supplement Mosheim. He has pitched upon Fleury which about a dozen men are to abridge or retrench, translate, prove references of, put notes to, etc. It is a good plan.' Newman played his part in this with an annotated translation of Fleury's history into English, beginning with the Council of Constantinople in 381 where his own *The Arians of the Fourth Century* (which he had hoped to revise) had left off. His translation of Fleury was published in three volumes between 1842 and 1844. The second *Essay on Miracles* was to serve as a preface to the translation of Fleury but was published separately. Newman commented that the translation of Fleury had 'a good deal to do with unsettling me in my Anglicanism'.

ESSAY I: THE MIRACLES OF SCRIPTURE COMPARED WITH THOSE REPORTED ELSEWHERE, AS REGARDS THEIR NATURE, CREDIBILITY, AND EVIDENCE

p. 3. *antecedent Credibility*: Newman was introduced to the argument from antecedent probability by Richard Whately, who first put it into systematic shape in his *Elements of Rhetoric*, (cf. note on p. 14) which had appeared in the *Encyclopaedia Metropolitana* and was printed in book form in 1828. Newman, who noted his debt to Whately in the *Apologia*, wrote of how Whately had shown him some manuscript dialogues on Logic, which Newman copied out, and which Newman worked on at Whately's suggestion for the *Encyclopaedia Metropolitana* (*L&D*, XV, p.176). In *The Elements of Rhetoric* Whately wrote: 'The Antecedent Probability that a Revelation should be given to man, and that it should be established by miracles, all would allow to be, considered by itself, in the absence of strong direct testimony, utterly insufficient to establish the Conclusion. On the other hand, miracles considered abstractedly, as represented to have occurred without any occasion or reason for them being assigned, carry with them such a strong improbability as could not be wholly surmounted even by such evidence as would fully establish any other matter of fact. But the evidence of the former class, however insufficient alone towards the establishment of the Conclusion, have very great weight in preparing the mind for receiving the other Arguments: which again, though they would be listened to with prejudice if not so supported, will then be allowed their just weight (Richard Whately, *Elements of Rhetoric*, Oxford, 1828, p. 84).

Behind Whately's argument lies that of Bishop Butler who in *The Analogy of Religion* had argued from the presumption established by the analogy of nature to the probability of revelation. Antecedent Probability became one of Newman's strongest apologetic planks. As he puts it in a letter of 1853, 'If I have brought out one truth in anything I have written, I consider it to be the *importance of antecdent probability* in conviction. It is how you convert factory girls as well as philosophers' (*L&D*, XV, p. 381). For further discussion see 'The Argument from Antecedent Probability', Robin C. Selby, *The Principle of Reserve in the Writings of John Henry Cardinal Newman*, Oxford, Oxford University Press, 1975, pp. 75–88.

p. 5. *Campbell, On Miracles*: George Campbell (1719–1796) Scottish theologian, published *A Dissertation on Miracles* in 1762. Published in a new edition in 1823, Newman read it in 1825 when he was engaged in epistolary argument with his atheist brother, Charles, as well as writing the essay on miracles. Edward Hawkins had noted the books on miracles in the window seat in Newman's rooms and commented on 28 August, 'I hope by this time your Essay on Miracles, a priori and a posteriori parts, and all the contents of all the books in the window-seat, are in a beautiful state of effervescence.' (*L&D*, I, pp. 244, 252, 255). Leslie Stephen classes Campbell, together with William Adams and John Douglas, as a trio of apologists equally opposed to any continuing manifestation of supernatural agency and any denial of its earlier manifestation (see *US*, p. 381n).

p. 8. *evidences*: Archdeacon William Paley (1743–1805) published *A View of the Evidences of Christianity* in 1794. 'Though this work amounted to little more than a compilation of standard 18th century arguments, its effective presentation of the facts and pellucid style made it extremely popular'(*ODCC*, loc. cit.). Paley's evidence theology, because it presented what was in effect a utilitarianism with supernatural sanctions, was both attractive and limited. Newman characteristically notes that 'The evidences of Revelation are cumulative ... they gain strength from each other.' Newman's own copy of Paley's *Evidences* is dated 1819 and is partly interleaved and contains many notes. One of these, dated 13 January 1836, comments that 'Paley assumes a miracle as the only way of ascertaining a revelation – true, *ascertaining* – but why need we ascertain? Faith lies in *acting upon* what is before one, before *ascertaining*.' It leads to the position, as St Thomas wanting proof of the Resurrection, 'I will not believe unless it is proved to me.' For a detailed discussion of Newman and evidence theology see the introduction of J. D. Earnest and Gerard Tracey to their critical edition of Newman's *University Sermons*, Oxford University Press, 2006, pp. lxxviff. In Newman's 1839 sermon 'Faith and Reason contrasted as habits of mind' he reveals his scepticism about evidence theology: 'We see what divines mean, who have been lead to depreciate what are called the Evidences of Religion. The last century, a time when love was cold, is noted as being especially the Age of Evidences; and now, when more devout and zealous feelings have been excited, there is ... a disposition to think lightly, as of the eighteenth century, so of its boasted demonstrations.' 'When persons disparage the Evidences, – viz. they consider that, as a general rule, religious minds embrace the Gospel mainly on the great antecedent probability of a Revelation, and the suitableness of the Gospel to their needs; on the other hand that on men of irreligious minds, Evidences are thrown away.' (J. D. Earnest and Gerard Tracey (eds), John Henry Newman, *Fifteen Sermons preached before the University of Oxford*, Oxford, 2006, p.140).

p. 9. *Sumner's "Records of Creation"*: John Bird Sumner (1780–1862), a convinced Evangelical, Bishop of Chester 1828 to 1848 when he succeeded William Howley as Archbishop of Canterbury. His *Apostolical Preaching considered in an examination of St Paul's Epistles* (1815) was given to Newman in August 1824 by Edward Hawkins, later Provost of Oriel, whom Newman served as curate at St Mary's. Newman commented in the *Apologia* that this was the book 'from which I was led to give up my remaining Calvinism, and to receive the doctrine of Baptismal Regeneration'. Sumner's *Treatise on the Records of the Creation* (1816) was amongst the books studied in the 'private lectures in divinity' by Charles Lloyd which Newman attended in 1823 and 1824. Newman noted that it was necessary to get up the books thoroughly as 'Dr Lloyd made the lecture catechetical, taking very little part in it himself, beyond asking questions, and requiring direct, full and minutely accurate answers' (*AW*, pp. 70–1). Newman noted Sumner's appointment to Chester 'with great pleasure' (*L&D*, II, p. 85).

p. 10. *Hume, On Miracles*: David Hume (1711–1776) Scottish philosopher and sceptic. Newman read his *Essay on Miracles* on 15 July 1825, and Hume's *Essay on Liberty* on 28 July the same year (*L&D*, I, pp. 242, 248).

p. 10. *Berkeley's "Minute Philosopher"*: George Berkeley (1685–1753), Bishop of Cloyne 1734–53, author of a number of philosophical treatises in which he upheld a metaphysic of subjective idealism, holding that *esse est percipi*, i.e. that the affirmation that material things are real means no more than that they are perceived, though material things continue to exist when we do not perceive them as they are objects of the thought of God. His book *Alciphron, or the Minute Philosopher* (1733) was a finely written critique of freethinking. In *The Grammar of Assent* Newman noted that 'the ratiocinative faculty ... as found in individuals, is not a general instrument of knowledge' but operates in particular ways according to the subject matter with which it is concerned. Skill in one area does not mean skill in another, mathematical ability does not mean historical. Berkeley is cited as an example: *The Minute Philosopher* with approval, the *Analyst* (1734), in which Berkeley attacked higher mathematics as leading to freethinking, with disapproval (Newman, *An Essay in Aid of a Grammar of Assent,* ed. I. T. Ker, Oxford, 1985, p. 219). In a letter of 18 May 1834 Newman writes to his sister, Jemima: 'As to Berkeley, I do not know enough to talk – but it seems to me, while a man holds the moral governance *of God as existing in and thro' his conscience*, it matters not whether he believes his senses or not. For at least he will hold the external world to be a *divine* intimation, a scene of trial (whether a reality or not) just as a child's game may be a trial. I have tried to say this in the Arians, ch. I § 3. I conceive Hume *denied* conscience, Berkeley confessed it – To what extent B. denied the existence of the external world, I am not aware – nor do I mean to go so far myself (far from it) as to deny the existence of matter – tho' I should deny that *what we saw* was more than accidents of it – and say that space perhaps is but a condition of the objects of the senses – not a reality' (*L&D*, IV, p. 253).

p. 12. *Farmer, On Miracles*: Hugh Farmer (1714–1787). A pupil of Philip Doddridge, Farmer was an Independent minister and theological writer, who published, as a response to Hume, *A Dissertation on Miracles, Designed to Shew, That They Are Arguments of a Divine Interpretation, and Absolute*

Proofs of the Mission and Doctrine of a Prophet, 1771, which Newman began to read on 3 August 1825 and finished on 10 August, a day on which he noted that he 'looked over articles on Miracles' in the *Encyclopaedia Britannica* and on Methodism' (*L&D*, I, pp. 249–50). Earnest and Tracey note Leslie Stephen's comment that Farmer 'illustrates the process by which Protestant Rationalism developed into a wider scepticism ... Farmer, like the whole evidence school, imagines that, by isolating and removing to a distance the manifestations of divine power he is really strengthening the evidence'. *University Sermons,* p. 381, citing L. Stephen, *History of English Thought in the Eighteenth Century,* 1876, I, pp. 393–5.

p. 14. *Whately, Treatise on Rhetoric*: Richard Whately (1787–1863) entered Oriel College in 1805 and was a Fellow of the College from 1811 to 1821. His *Elements of Rhetoric,* published in book form in 1828, was, like his earlier *Treatise on Logic,* with which Newman assisted him, first written for the *Encyclopaedia Metropolitana*. The *Elements of Rhetoric* were the first place in which Whately set out systematically his thoughts on antecedent probability, noting in the preface that 'a brief outline of the principal part of the ... Work was sketched out several years ago for the private use of some young friends'. Selby suggests that it is probable that Newman first came upon the argument in this manuscript or in conversation with Whately. R. C. Selby, *The Principle of Reserve in the Writings of John Henry Cardinal Newman,* Oxford, 1975, p. 77.

p. 14. *Leland, "Supplement to View of Deistical Writers"*: John Leland (1691–1776), a minister and divine in Aberdeen who attacked the Deists in *A View of the principal Deistical Writers that have appeared in England during the last and present Century* (1754–6) Newman noted reading Leland 'on Miracles à priori' on 27 July 1825 and returned to his work as he wrote the *Essay on Miracles,* noting on 15 February 1826, 'looked over Douglas, B. White, Jenkin, Leland etc, for miracles' (*L&D*, I, pp. 248, 276).

p. 17. *Butler's "Analogy"*: Joseph Butler (1692–1752), born at Wantage, son of a well-to-do Presbyterian draper, educated first at a dissenting academy, and then, after he had joined the Church of England, at Oriel College, Oxford, to which he went up in 1714. After graduating from Oxford he was appointed Preacher at the Rolls Chapel, where he preached the series of sermons on moral virtue for which he is now best known. He moved to the Diocese of Durham in 1722, first to the parish of Haughton near Darlington, and then to the wealthier living of Stanhope in 1726. During his time there he wrote *The Analogy of Religion,* which was published in 1736. In 1738 he became Bishop of Bristol, and two years later was made also Dean of St Paul's. In 1750 he became Bishop of Durham. The full title

Editor's Notes

of Butler's *Analogy* is *The Analogy of Religion, Natural and Revealed, to the Constitution and Course of Nature*. Terence Penelhum notes that 'the analogy of the title is not between natural religion and revealed religion, but between both natural *and* revealed religion, on the one hand, and the constitution and course of nature on the other' (T. Penelhum, *Butler*, Routledge, London, Boston & Henley, 1985, p. 96). Penelhum comments that 'Butler sees our ignorance of the details of God's providence as similar to our ignorance of undiscovered details of the system of nature, about which some real though limited knowledge is possible. (A striking illustration of this is his suggestion that although miracles may be unpredictable by natural law, they may be fully intelligible as manifestations of some higher laws of which we may be ignorant). '*Analogy*, II, iv, 4/4' (Ibid., p. 95).

p. 18. *Divine Legation* (Warburton): William Warburton (1698–1779), Bishop of Gloucester 1757–79. His *Alliance between Church and State* (1736) defended the Establishment of the Church of England on largely utilitarian grounds. *The Divine Legation of Moses* (1737–41) upheld the Divine origin of the Mosaic Law against the Deists on the grounds that the Mosaic Law contained no doctrine of eternal life. As future rewards and punishments were, Warburton believed, essential to human wellbeing its absence from the Mosaic Law could only be explained by a special Divine inspiration. He was strongly opposed to the 'enthusiasm' of Methodists publishing *The Doctrine of Grace* (1762) against John Wesley. Newman read Book IX of the *Divine Legation* about miracles on 28 July 1825 (*L&D*, I, p. 248).

p. 18. *Vince, On Miracles*: Samuel Vince (1749–1821), mathematician and divine, and professor of astronomy at Cambridge; author of *The Credibility of Christianity Vindicated, in answer to Mr Hume's Objections* (1798). Newman read Vince's *Elements of Astronomy* and *Hydrostatics* when studying for his final examinations in November 1820 (*L&D*, I, pp. 94). Newman noted (5 August 1825) that he 'read Vince on miracles à priori part' (*L&D*, I, p. 249). In *The Grammar of Assent*, pp. 206–7, Newman discusses Vince's resort to argument from 'independent probabilities in connection' (see *US*, p. 415n).

p. 21. *Voltaire*: Newman identifies 'another writer, notorious for his irreligion' as Voltaire, the pseudonym of François-Marie Arouet (1694–1778), the leader of the French 'Philosophes'. In the *Apologia* Newman records that, when he was fourteen, he had read the sceptical works of Tom Paine attacking the Old Testament and had also recollected 'copying out some French verses, perhaps Voltaire's, against the immortality of the soul, and saying to myself, "How dreadful, but how plausible!" (*Apo*, 1864, p. 58).

p. 21. *Bentham*: Jeremy Bentham (1748–1832), utilitarian philosopher. In Newman's *University Sermons* the most polemical passages are aimed at Bentham and the Utilitarians, viz. 'The founder of the recent Utilitarian School insists, that all evidence for miracles, before it can be received, should be brought into a court of law, and subjected to its searching forms:- this too is to imply that Reason demands exact proofs, but that Faith accepts inaccurate ones' (Sermon X, 'Faith and Reason contrasted as Habits of Mind', *US*, p. 132). Later in the same sermon Newman combines his critique of the evidence theology of Paley with a similar critique of Bentham's utilitarianism with respect to miracles, viz. '[Paley] here asks leave to do only what the Utilitarian writer ... demands should be done, namely, to bring his case (as it were) into court; as if trusting to the strength of his evidence, dispensing with moral and religious considerations on one side or the other, and arguing from the mere phenomena of the human mind, that is the inducements, motives, and habits according to which man acts. I will not say more of such a procedure than that it seems to me to be dangerous. As miracles, according to the common saying, are not wrought to convince Atheists, and, when they claim to be evidence of a Revelation, presuppose the being of an Intelligent Agent to whom they may be referred, so Evidences in general are grounded on the admission that the doctrine they are brought to prove is, not merely not inconsistent, but actually accordant with the laws of His moral governance. Miracles, though they contravene the physical laws of the universe, tend to the due fulfilment of its moral laws' (*US*, p. 139). In 1841 in the *Tamworth Reading Room Letters* Newman attacks with coruscating irony the utilitarian, Benthamite principle that knowledge was able of itself to effect moral transformation. 'Let Benthamism reign, if men have no aspirations; but do not tell them to be romantic, and then solace them with glory; do not attempt by philosophy what once was done by religion.' (*DA*, London, 1888, p. 292.)

p. 22. *a system which is but partially revealed*: Although a firm believer in Revelation, Newman recognised that the pattern of Revelation was one of gradual unfolding, anticipations followed by fulfilment. This was true of the relation of the Old Testament to the New, and to subsequent development of Christian doctrine (the *Essay on Development* notes as one of the tests of development, 'early anticipation'). Newman also links the sense of a partial and gradual revelation with the theme of economy, and of the pastoral character of God's self-disclosure. In St John's Gospel (16:12), Jesus tells his disciples that he has many things to say to them, but they cannot bear them yet. In Tract LXXIII, 'On the Introduction of

Editor's Notes

Rationalistic Principles into Religion' (1836, reprinted in *Ess.* I, 1872, pp. 30–99), Newman is clear that Revelation and Mystery belong together: 'No revelation can be complete and systematic, from the weakness of the human intellect; *so far as* it is not such, it is mysterious ... A Revelation is religious doctrine viewed on its illuminated side; a Mystery is the self-same doctrine viewed on the side unilluminated. This Religious Truth is neither light nor darkness, but both together; it is like the dim view of a country seen in the twilight, with forms half extricated from the darkness, with broken lines, and isolated masses. Revelation, in this way of considering it, is not a revealed *system*, but consists of a number of detached and incomplete truths belonging to a vast system unrevealed, of doctrine and injunctions mysteriously connected together; that is, connected by unknown media, and bearing upon unknown portions of the system. And in this sense we see the propriety of calling St John's prophecies, though highly mysterious, yet a revelation'(*Ess.* I, pp. 41–2).

p. 26. *Jones, On the Figurative Language of Scripture*: William Jones 'of Nayland' (1726–1800), educated at Charterhouse and University College, Oxford, was a close friend and contemporary of George Horne, later Dean of Canterbury and Bishop of Norwich. Like Horne, whose biography he wrote, he was influenced by the writings of John Hutchinson, and taught a sacramental and mystical interpretation of orthodox Christianity. Ordained in 1751, he became rector of Pluckley in Kent in 1765 and then, in 1777, Perpetual Curate of Nayland in Suffolk. In 1786 Jones published *A Course of Lectures on the Figurative Language of Holy Scripture, and the Interpretation of it from Scripture Itself*, which he had delivered in Nayland parish church the same year. In these lectures Jones argued that Scripture consisted not merely of words, 'but of signs or figures taken from visible things'; 'The world which we now see becomes a sort of commentary on the mind of God, and explains the world in which we believe.' As Peter Nockles comments, in Jones' *Lectures* 'The argument of Pusey's *Lectures on Types* of half a century later was strikingly prefigured' (*The Oxford Movement in Context: Anglican High Churchmanship 1760–1857*, Cambridge University Press, 1994, pp. 207–8). Nockles also notes that 'It was only with Jones of Nayland's foundation of the *Society for the Reformation of Principles* in 1792 that High Churchmen had their own organisation and ideology' (p. 271). Newman refers in the *Apologia* to 'the admirable works of Jones of Nayland' in which he learnt that the truths in Scripture are expressed mysteriously rather than directly. It was from the writings of Jones and Thomas Scott that Newman compiled 'a collection of Scripture texts in proof of the doctrine [of the Trinity], with remarks (I think) of my own upon them before I was sixteen' (p. 60).

p. 27. *Zoroaster*. The putative founder of Zoroastrianism, and the author of the *Gathas*, the hymns which comprise the oldest part of the *Avesta*. Zoroaster's dates are uncertain, ranging from the early sixth century BC to sometime in the middle or the end of the second millennium before Christ. Zoroastrianism, with its veneration of fire and dualist theology, became the dominant religion of Iran, where the Zoroastrian priests were known as *magi*.

p. 27. *Empedocles*: Philosopher of Agrigentum in Sicily who flourished *c.*460 BC. His works in verse are known only in fragments.

p. 27. *Apollonius*: see note to p. viii.

p. 27. *Josephus, Eleazar*: In *Antiquities* VIII, §46–9 Josephus gives the following account: 'I have seen a certain Eleazar, a countryman of mine, in the presence of Vespasian, his sons, tribunes, and a number of other soldiers, free men possessed by demons, and this was the manner of the cure: he put to the nose of the possessed man a ring, which had under its seal one of the roots prescribed by Solomon, and then, as the man smelled it, drew out the demon through his nostrils, and, when the man at once fell down, adjured the demons never to come back into him, speaking Solomon's name and reciting the incantations which he had composed. Then, wishing to convince the bystanders and prove to them that he had power, Eleazar place a cup or footbasin full of water a little way off and commanded the demon, as it went out of the man to overturn it, and make known to the spectators that he had left the man. And when this was done, the understanding and wisdom of Solomon were clearly revealed.'

p. 28. *Lavington, Enthusiasm of Meth. and Papists comp.*: George Lavington (1684–1762) Bishop of Exeter 1747–62. He published *The Enthusiasm of Methodists and Papists compared* in three parts between 1749 and 1751, mocking 'the seraphic rhapsody of the divine love' which he said the Methodists had borrowed from the papists. He attacked Methodists as being 'field preachers, fanatical opponents of diversion, superstitious proponents of casting of lots, prophesying, cures and miracles, practitioners of private confession, pretenders to visions, trances, and ecstasies, who believed themselves to be continually contending with the Devil ... [They were led] to a "wild and pernicious *Enthusiasm*" which undermined the bases of "*true Religion*" (B. Semmel, *The Methodist Revolution*, 1974, p.16). Extensively read, Lavington's work was strongly attacked by John Wesley who accused Lavington not only of ignorance but of downright deception in his manipulation of passages extracted from Wesley's *Journal*. Lavington ranked Wesley with Dominic and Ignatius Loyola,

Editor's Notes

viewed pejoratively by Protestants, and with Antoinette Bourignon, one of the most despised of the 'mystics', whose teachings Church of Scotland ministers were for a considerable period required to repudiate. On Christmas Eve 1825 Newman noted that he had 'looked over Apocryphal Gospels, Lavington's Papists and Methodists for miracles' (*L&D*, I, p. 271).

p. 28. *apocryphal accounts of Christ*: The Apocryphal Gospels comprise those early Christian books outside the Canon of the New Testament similar in form or content to the canonical Gospels. Some, such as the Gospel of Thomas, may embody trustworthy traditions, others are clearly composed to support Gnostic and other heretical positions.

p. 28. *Jones, On the Canon*: For Jones of Nayland see *supra* on p. 21.

p. 29. *Polycarp*: (*c*.69–*c*.155), Bishop of Smyrna. A letter addressed to him by St Ignatius of Antioch survives, as well as his own epistle to the Philippians. Martyred in 155 or 156 his trial and martyrdom are described in the *Martyrium Polycarpi*. According to Irenaeus Polycarp 'had intercourse with John and with the rest of those who had seen the Lord'.

p. 29. *The Miracles of the Romish Breviary*: Newman did not possess a Breviary until 1836, when he selected Froude's copy of it on being asked to choose books from Hurrell Froude's library after his death. He would, however, have known of the Breviary from the lectures of Charles Lloyd, Regius Professor of Divinity, and afterwards Bishop of Oxford. In Tract 75, 'On the Roman Breviary as embodying the substance of the devotional services of the Church Catholic', which Newman wrote in 1839, he notes that the inclusion in the Breviary of popular legends of saints posed difficulties for Anglicans, but observed that the edition of the Breviary by Cardinal Quiñones that had influenced Cranmer had omitted these legends (Tract 75, p.13). When S. F. Wood and Robert Williams were corresponding with Newman about a translation of the Breviary, Williams posed Newman the question whether such material should or should not be included. The choices were either to take 'the credulousness of the compilers' own mind as the proper standard', or to boldly reject 'all supernatural events since the apostles' days as untrue'. (Donald A. Withey, *John Henry Newman: The Liturgy and the Breviary: Their influence on his life as an Anglican,* Sheed & Ward, London, 1992, p. 45 and passim.)

p. 29. *Paul the Hermit*: St Paul of Thebes (d. *c*.340), traditionally the first Christian hermit. During the Decian persecution (249–251) he fled to the desert where he is said to have lived for some hundred years of prayer and penitence in a cave. A Coptic monastery dedicated to him is found in the Eastern desert.

p. 29. *the Miracles ascribed by some to Mahomet*: The miracles of Mahomet which Newman cites are not referred to in the Muslim scripture, the Qu'ran, but are rather part of the later Islamic tradition, the Hadith, which was collected in the ninth century CE and whose status and authority are to some extent contested. The mainstream Muslim opinion is that it was the Qu'ran itself, with its inimitable language, which was the miracle given by God to Muhammad, and while the stories referred to by Newman are passionately believed in by many elements of the Muslim community, they should perhaps be seen as part of a process of developing devotion to the person of Muhammad, rather than to his message. Cf. Gril, D., 'Miracles' in J. D. McAuliffe (ed.), *The Encyclopaedia of the Qu'ran*, vol. 3, Leiden, Brill, 2003.

p. 29. *Middleton, Free Enquiry*: Conyers Middleton (1683–1750), Cambridge divine, whose *A Free Inquiry into the Miraculous Powers, Which are supposed to have subsisted in the Christian Church, From the Earliest Ages through several successive Centuries* (1749), which argued against the persistence of miraculous powers in the Church's second century, provoked much criticism for its latitudinarian views. Newman read it on 3–4 January 1826 (*L&D*, I, p. 271). Middleton noted that miracles cited by Fathers of the Church in the fourth century 'said to be wrought in confirmation of some favourite institutions of those days, which, in the judgement of all the learned and candid Protestants, are manifestly fictitious and plainly incredible'. (*Free Inquiry*, p. lxxvi cited F. McGrath (ed.), J. H. Newman, *The Church of the Fathers*, Leominster and Notre Dame, 2002, p. lv). In the *Apologia*, in commenting on his drifting towards liberalism, Newman writes that 'In writing on the Scripture Miracles in 1825–6, I had read Middleton on the Miracles of the early Church, and had imbibed a portion of his spirit' (p. 74).

p. 30. *the Book of Tobit*: One of the apocryphal books of the Old Testament originally written in either Hebrew or Aramaic, it is dated to *c*.200 BC. Tobit became poor and blind in his old age, and prayed to God to deliver him. Remembering a debt due to him from a friend in Media he sent his son Tobias there with a companion, who was later revealed as the angel Raphael. With the angel's assistance Tobias rescued his kinswoman, Sarah, from the power of a demon. He does so by burning on incense the liver and heart of a fish he had miraculously caught, which the angel instructs him is for driving out demons by fumigation (Tobit 6:7,16–17). Raphael recovered the debt and then enabled Tobias to heal the aged Tobit of his blindness. The attractive story made Tobit one of the most popular books of the Bible, and it was frequently quoted by the Fathers from the time of Polycarp.

p. 30. *Philostr.*: Flavius Philostratus, a native of Lemnos, who flourished *c.*200 AD, teaching rhetoric at Athens and then at Rome. Author of the *Life of Apollonius.*

p. 30. *Justin Martyr*: Justin (*c.*100–*c.*165) was an early Christian apologist, who was born of pagan parents at Flavia Neapolis (ancient Shechem). Converted to Christianity *c.*130 he is the most significant of the early Christian apologists. Arguing that Christianity fulfilled not only Jewish prophecy, but also Greek philosophy, Justin developed his doctrine (most likely derived from Stoic sources) of the Λογος σπερματικος, the 'generative' or 'germinating' Word, by which the seed of truth was sown in every human being, but which had become incarnate in Jesus Christ. It was Christ who taught the whole truth and delivered mankind from the power of the demons. Justin's *First Apology* gives one of the earliest accounts of the celebration of the Eucharist. Justin's *Dialogue with Trypho* argues that the fulfilment of the Old Testament prophecies in Christ proves the transitoriness of the Old Covenant, and the vocation of the Gentiles to take the place of Israel. Justin uses Middle Platonic ideas to interpret the Old Testament theophanies as manifestations of the Logos.

Justin was important to Newman in the development of his understanding of the 'dispensation of paganism'. Reading the Fathers chronologically on Lloyd's suggestion Newman criticised Justin for being 'almost silent' on the Atonement, and could not find any 'definite allusion to the doctrine of the Holy Spirit's renovating *influences*'. (See Francis McGrath, FMS, *John Henry Newman: Universal Revelation,* Burns & Oates, Tunbridge Wells, 1997 and in Australia by John Garratt Publishing, Mulgrave, Victoria, 1997.)

p. 31. *Brucker*: Jacob Brucker (1696–1770), author of *Historia Critica Philosophiae.* Newman read his work in September 1825, with particular reference to Apollonius and Philostratus (*L&D*, I, p. 271).

p. 32. *Stillingfleet, Orig. Sacr.*: Edward Stillingfleet (1635–1699), a man of latitudinarian views he was appointed Bishop of Worcester after the Revolution of 1689. His *Origines Sacrae,* published in 1662, was an apologetic work concerned with the Divine authority of Scripture. Stillingfleet argued that in his capacity as a lawgiver Moses was a faithful witness because his knowledge of God's will is attested by miracle. 'Now what conviction there can be to any sober mind concerning Divine Authority in any person without such a Power of Miracles going along with him, when he is to deliver new Doctrine to the World to be believ'd, I confess I cannot understand.' He argued that the miracles of Moses were calculated to terrify Israel and so win them from idolatry. By contrast the miracles of Christ showed God's goodness. 'Those terrible Signs of Mount Sinai being very suitable to the severity and rigour of the Law: and the gracious Miracles of our Saviour to the sweetness and grace of the Gospel.' The many miracles of Christ demonstrate that the goodness of God is strong to penetrate within the citadel of sin, and to conquer the hostile powers that hold man in chains. (cf. W. C. de Pauley, *The Candle of the Lord: studies in the Cambridge Platonists,* SPCK (Church Historical Society), 1937, pp.193, 202–3.)

p. 33. *long after the real age of Miracles was past*: In this first *Essay* on Miracles Newman still holds with the contemporary Protestant view that miracles belonged to the apostolic age and were evidence of divine revelation.

p. 33. *relics*: Springing from the natural reverence for what remains of someone loved, the material remains of a saint after death, especially of the martyrs, became an object of veneration. In the Old Testament miracles were worked through the bones of Elisha (2 Kings 13:21). St Jerome defended the cult of relics saying that the relics of the martyrs were to be honoured for the sake of the One whose martyrs they were. When St Thomas Aquinas laid the theological foundation of the cult of relics he followed Jerome and Augustine in stressing the special dignity of the bodies of the saints as temples of the Holy Spirit and also the miracles associated with them as indicating God's sanction and approval. At the Reformation abuses connected with relics led to the destruction of many shrines.

p. 33. *Abbé Paris*: François de Pâris (1690–1727), son of a magistrate of the *parlement* and a Jansenist, entered the Oratorian seminary of Saint-Magloire in 1713. Disfigured by smallpox the previous year he had thanked God for the affliction. Ordained deacon in 1716 he followed a life of abject poverty. He died in 1727 and was buried in the cemetery of the church of Saint-Médard. Miracles of healing began to take place at his tomb and, following an investigation by Cardinal Noailles, he was accorded the title of *bienheureux*. Noailles' successor, Vintimille, banned the cult, which led to a sharp reaction of pilgrimages to the tomb, convulsions, and healings (seventy were attested in 1731). In 1732 a royal edict closed the cemetery of Saint-Médard. For an account of the cult of the Abbé de Pâris, the associated miracles and the Jansenist context see John McManners, *Church and Society in Eighteenth-Century France,* II, *The*

Religion of the People and the Politics of Religion, Clarendon Press, Oxford, 1998, pp. 422–55.

p. 34. *Griesbach*: Johann Jakob Griesbach (1745–1812), professor of New Testament at Jena from 1775 until his death. 'He was the first critic to make a systematic application of literary analysis to the Gospels' arguing that Mark was the third of the Gospels and was dependent on Matthew and Luke.

p. 34. *Douglas, Criterion*: John Douglas (1721–1807) Bishop of Carlisle 1787–91, Bishop of Salisbury 1791–1807. In 1752 he published the *Criterion* attacking Hume's argument against miracles. In a later work, *An Apology for the Clergy* (1755) he attacked the Hutchinsonians. Newman notes that on 2 August 1825 he 'read Douglas, Monboddo, Tucker, Rutherforth, Bryant's Authenticity, Watson against Gibbon, all as far as à priori on miracles is concerned' (*L&D*, I, p. 249). Later that same month he noted reading Douglas's *Criterion* (*L&D*, I, p. 255).

p. 34. *Warburton, Sermon on Resurrection*: William Warburton (1698–1779), Bishop of Gloucester (1779–79). In *The Alliance between Church and State* (1736) he defended the Establishment of the Church of England. In *The Divine Legation of Moses* (1737–41) he upheld the Divine origin of the Mosaic law against the Deists on the curious grounds that it contained no doctrine of eternal life. The absence of a doctrine of future rewards and punishments being in his view essential to the well-being of humanity, its absence from the Old Testament could only be explained by a special Divine inspiration. He was a noted opponent of the 'enthusiasm' of Methodists. In 1727 he published anonymously *A Critical and Philosophical Enquiry into the causes of Prodigies and Miracles*.

p. 34. *Fleetwood*: William Fleetwood (1656–1723), Bishop of St Asaph (1708–14), Bishop of Ely (1714–23). Educated at Eton and King's College, Cambridge, he was regarded as one of the best preachers of his time. His *Chronicum preciosum* (1707), an account of English coinage, and one of the first works to tabulate comparative prices in different ages, provided data for Adam Smith in his *Wealth of Nations* (1776). His sermons often dealt with economic issues. He published *An Essay on Miracles* in 1701.

p. 36. *Phidias on Minerva's shield*:
Phidias, the famous sculptor of the fifth century BC and friend of Pericles who carved the ivory and gold statue of Minerva that stood inside the Parthenon, was charged with having insulted the goddess by carving on her shield a likeness of himself and of Pericles.

p. 37. *Graves, On the Pentateuch*: Richard Graves (1763–1829) was Dean of Ardagh and Regius Professor of Divinity at Trinity College, Dublin, from 1819 until his death. His *Lectures on the Four Last Books of the Pentateuch; designed to show the divine origin of the Jewish religion, chiefly from internal evidences* was a standard work which Newman noted that he had studied in 1824 in the class organised by Charles Lloyd which he attended with three other fellows of Oriel: Jelf, Ottley and Pusey, together with four students of Christ Church (*AW*, pp. 71, 197). He commended it to his pupil John Marriott as a key work on the Mosaic Law, together with John Bird Sumner's *Records of Creation and the Moral Attributes of the Creator* (London, 1816) and Moses Lowman, *A Rationale of the Ritual of the Hebrew Worship, in which the design and usefulness of that Ritual is explained and vindicated* (London, 1748) as necessary reading for understanding St Paul's epistles. 'It is not possible to enter rightly into them without some first acquaintance with the Mosaid Law – i.e. the last 4 books of the Pentateuch. After this go to St Paul's epistles. And then try to draw up some system of the Christian doctrines.' (JHN to John Marriott, 15.viii.1830, *L&D*, XXXII (Supplementary Letters), ed. F. J. McGrath, Oxford, 2008, pp. 4, 5).

p. 37. *Tertullian's account of the vision of an Angel*: Tertullian (Quintus Septimius Florens Tertullianus *c*.160–*c*.225), a North African theologian, the author of many theological, polemical and ascetic works, whose rigorist strain took him into Montanism. In his treatise, *On the Veiling of Virgins,* he records that 'the Lord has, even by revelations, measured the space for the veil to extend over. For a certain sister of ours was thus addressed by an angel, beating her neck, as if in applause: "Elegant neck, and deservedly bare! It is well for thee to unveil thyself from the head right down to the loins, lest withal this freedom of thy neck profit thee not!"' (*On the Veiling of Virgins,* xvii).

p. 37. *Cyprian*: St Cyprian (d. 258), Bishop of Carthage. In Epistle lxii to Caecilius, Cyprian argues strongly for the tradition of the mixed chalice of mingled wine and water as the appropriate Eucharistic element.

p. 38. *the cures ascribed to Vespasian*: Newman probably has in mind Hume's comment in his *Essay on Miracles* in which he writes, 'One of the best attested miracles in all profane history is that which Tacitus reports of Vespasian, who cured a blind man in Alexandria by means of his spittle, and a lame man by the mere touch of his foot.' Hume notes that Suetonius gives a similar account in his life of Vespasian. (D. Hume, *Essay concerning Human Understanding,* X.ii.96.)

p. 38. *Eclectic prodigies*: The Eclectic philosophers is the name given to Ammonius Saccas and his disciples, later more usually known as the Neoplatonists. In his comprehensive *Biblical and Theological Dictionary* compiled largely from conservative sources, Richard Watson (1737–1816), a Methodist theologian, noted that the Eclectics were 'a sect of ancient philosophers who professed to select whatever was good and true from all the other philosophical sects ... The Eclectic system was brought to perfection by Ammonius Saccas, who blended Christianity with his philosophy, and founded the sect of the Ammonians, or Neo Platonists, in the second century' (*A Biblical and Theological Dictionary explanatory of the History, Manners and Customs of the Jews, and neighbouring nations . . .an exposition of the Principal Doctrines of Christianity, and notes of Jewish and Christian Sects and Heresies*, 1832, 2nd edn). Some writers claimed that miraculous healings were effected by members of this group by the use of charms and thaumaturgical arts.

p. 38. *Blanco White, Against Catholicism*: Joseph Blanco White (1775–1810); born in Seville of an Irish Roman Catholic family and ordained to the priesthood in 1800 he came to England in 1810, having been troubled by religious doubts. He was for a time attached to Oriel College where he was a member of the Common Room. He later became a Unitarian. The work to which Newman refers is White's *Practical and Internal Evidence against Catholicism, with occasional strictures on Mr Butler's Book of the Roman Catholic Church: in six letters addressed to the impartial among the Roman Catholics of Great Britain and Ireland*, (London, 1825). Written against Charles Butler whose *Book of the Roman Catholic Church* (1824) had itself been a riposte to the poet Robert Southey's *Book of the Church* (1824), a defence of the Church of England. White dealt not with abstract theories, but drew rather on his own experience in Spain to condemn what he perceived as the practical effects of the Catholic system. In violent language he dismissed scholastism as 'intellectual garbage', 'monkish' devotional practices as 'drivelling imbecility', and there are savage attacks on credulity and superstition. Martin Murphy comments: 'It is ... the work of a rationalist of the enlightenment outraged by the fact that the whole apparatus of monks and mediaevalism which he disdained as part of a dark, barbaric age was now, in England, moving into romantic fashion.' (Martin Murphy, *Blanco White: self-banished Spaniard*, Yale University Press, New Haven & London, 1989, pp.132–3.)

p. 41. *Socinian*: Latinised as Socinus, Fausto Sozzini (1539–1604) was an early advocate of Unitarianism and consequently denied the divinity of Christ. As Newman notes, the consequences of a Unitarian doctrine is to reduce Christ to a religious teacher – 'It prunes away the Christian system till little is left for miracles to attest.'

p. 41. *Hunneric's persecution*: Eldest son and successor (in 477) of Genseric, King of the Vandals, a strong supporter of the Arians and a fierce persecutor of orthodox Christians. He died in 484. In his work *de Persecutione Vandalica*, Victor Vitensis reports the miracle to which Newman alludes, which occurred at Typasa, a seaport town in Mauretania, where the Catholics who were not able to flee from the newly appointed Arian bishop met together to celebrate the Eucharist, having refused to subscribe to Arian doctrine. Hunneric ordered their tongues to be cut out but they continued to speak as plainly as before. In his *Dictionary of Christian Biography and Literature to the end of the sixth century*, (London, John Murray, 1911), Henry Wace states that it has generally been considered not only a miracle, but 'the most remarkable one on record after apostolic times', noting the number and variety of witnesses – notably, as well as Victor himself, Aeneas of Gaza, Justinian, Marcellinus, Procopius, Victor Tununensis, and Pope Gregory the Great, all of whom are referred to by Newman.

p. 41. *Mosheim, Eccl. Hist.*: Johann Lorenz von Mosheim (1694–1755) historian and divine, professor first at Helmstedt and then at Göttingen. 'His historical work was marked by a hitherto unprecedented objectivity and penetration, and he may be considered the first of modern ecclesiastical historians. His *Institutiones historiae ecclesiasticae* (1726; Eng. tr. 1841) went through many editions and revisions' (ODCC, loc. cit.). His *Commentationes et Orationes* (1751) treats of Apollonius of Tyana at some length.

p. 43. *Penrose*: John Penrose (1778–1859), divine, author of *The Use of Miracles in proving the Truth of a Revelation* (1824), a work Newman notes reading on 18 August 1825 (*L&D*, I, p. 252).

p. 44. *Jansenist*: The theological school following the teaching of Cornelius Jansen (1585–1638) whose teaching, set out in his *Augustinus* (1640), was marked by a theological pessimism that led to a movement of general harshness and moral rigorism. The miracles to which Newman refers centred on the tomb of the Abbé de Paris in the cemetery of Saint-Médard, on whom see the note on p. 33 above.

p. 44. *Council of Laodicea*: Nothing definite is known of the Council of Laodicea which is dated *c*.365. A collection of fifty-nine canons is known as the Canons of Laodicea and deal with the treatment of heretics, liturgy, penance, Church Order, and the observance of Lent. In some texts a list of canonical scriptures is appended which excludes the Old Testament Apocrypha and the Book of Revelation.

p. 45. *Whiston*: William Whiston (1667–1752), mathematician and theologian who succeeded Isaac Newton as Lucasian professor of mathematics at Cambridge. His Arianising views led to his expulsion from the university in 1710. In 1747 he left the Church of England to join the General Baptists. The author of a large number of treatises he is now particularly remembered for his translation of Josephus.

p. 47. *analogy of nature*: An allusion to the theory set out in Bishop Butler's *The Analogy of Religion, Natural and Revealed, to the Constitution and Course of Nature* (1736), in which Butler argued against the Deists that both Natural and Revealed Religion are positively reasonable, noting that objections to particular religious beliefs lost their force when it was recognised that exactly the same objections could be raised in relation to non-religious beliefs concerning nature.

p. 51. *Sherlock*: William Sherlock (1641–1707), Dean of St Paul's. Best known for his *Practical Discourse concerning Death* (1689), he upheld the Divine Right of Kings and taught the duty of passive obedience. In 1688 he initially sided with the Nonjurors, but two years later took the oath of allegiance to William and Mary and was made Dean of St Paul's the following year. Following the publication of his *Vindication of the Doctrines of the Trinity and of the Incarnation* (1690) he was accused of teaching Tritheism.

p. 51. *Clarke*: Samuel Clarke (1674–1729), fellow of Caius, Cambridge and a disciple of Isaac Newton. In 1704–5 he delivered two sets of Boyle Lectures in defence of rational theology against the empiricism of John Locke, published later with the title, *A Discourse concerning the Being and Attributes of God, the Obligations of Natural Religion, and the Truth and Certainty of the Christian Revelation*. Although critical of the Deists he sympathised with some aspects of their teaching. (*ODCC*, loc. cit.).

p. 51. *Locke*: John Locke (1632–1704), philosopher and defender of free inquiry and toleration who, influenced by Descartes, developed a system which combined Christian rationalism and empiricism. 'His ideal was a national Church with an all-embracing creed that made ample allowance for individual opinion, on the grounds that human understanding was too limited for one man to impose his beliefs on another ... The substance of his philosophical thought is contained in the famous *Essay concerning Human Understanding* (1690). In it he attacks the Platonist conception of 'innate ideas'. The human mind is a *tabula rasa* and all our ideas come from experience, i.e. from sensation or reflection, knowledge through reason being, according to him, a 'natural revelation'. Pure reality cannot be grasped by the human mind; consequently there is no sure basis for metaphysics, and substance is 'an uncertain supposition of we know what'. The spirituality of the soul, though not certain, is at least probable, the existence of God, on the other hand, can be discovered with certainty by reason, and His law gives men their rule of conduct. (*ODCC*, loc. cit.). In defending the reasonableness of Christianity (*The Reasonableness of Christianity as Delivered in the Scriptures*, 1695), Locke accepted the miracles recorded in Scripture as proofs of Christianity's divine origin. Locke treated further of miracles in the posthumously published *A Discourse on Miracles* (1706). Newman read Locke in the summer of 1818 along with Gibbon. Locke taught Newman his epistemology though he later, in *The Grammar of Assent*, took issue with some aspects of this; what endured was the subjective element in Newman's thought, which derived ideas from the impressions made on the mind by the senses with the implication that what is real for us is private and personal to ourselves. Newman paid tribute to Locke in the *Grammar*, writing that he had 'so high a respect both for the character and the ability of Locke, for his manly simplicity of mind and his outspoken candour, and there is so much in his remarks upon reasoning and proof in which I fully concur, that I feel no pleasure in considering him in the light of an opponent to views, which I myself have ever cherished as true with an obstinate devotion'. (I. T. Ker (ed.), John Henry Newman, *An Essay in Aid of a Grammar of Assent*, Clarendon Press, Oxford, 1985, p. 107). Despite Newman's epistemological indebtedness to Locke, Newman, in the end, concluded that Locke's simple and straightforward epistemology would not do. As Basil Mitchell notes Newman came to have three substantial objections to it: (1) it was excessively cerebral, making faith the outcome of an intellectual argument; (2) it effectively restricted faith to those intellectually capable of following the argument; (3) the person to whom the argument was addressed was an isolated individual, belonging to no community, and standing in no tradition. (Basil Mitchell, 'Newman as a Philosopher' in Ian Ker and Alan G. Hill, *Newman after a hundred years,* Clarendon Press, Oxford, 1990, pp. 224–5). As Vargish notes it may have been Joseph Milner, whose church history significantly influenced Newman, who led him to see where Locke's philosophy led. Locke '"led the fashion in introducing a pompous parade of *reasoning* into religion". Reason was once the submissive handmaid of Christianity; now she usurps its function. The train of influence moves from Locke to Hume, "a gradual melancholy declension from evangelical simplicity"'. (Thomas Vargish, *Newman: the Contemplation of Mind,* Clarendon Press, Oxford, 1970, p. 8, citing Joseph Milner, *Gibbon's*

Account of Christianity Considered with some Strictures on Hume's Dialogues Concerning Natural Religion, Lincoln, 1808). On 28 July 1825, Newman notes that he read Locke, Clarke and Tucker on Miracles' (*L&D*, I, p. 248).

p. 51. *Prideaux*: Humphrey Prideaux (1648–1724), Dean of Norwich from 1702. He welcomed the revolution of 1688 and supported changes in the Prayer Book in the hope that it would be inclusive to Dissenters. In 1697 he published a *Life of Mahomet*, which was really a work aimed at the Deists, and, in 1716–18, *The Old and New Testaments connected in the History of the Jews*, an account of the Jewish people in the last centuries before the Christian era. Newman studied his *Connexion* in 1824 in the class organised by Charles Lloyd (*AW*, pp. 71, 197).

p. 51. *Chandler*: Edward Chandler (1668?–1750) Bishop of Lichfield 1717–30, when he was translated to Durham. At Lichfield he published polemical works in opposition to the deist, Anthony Collins: *A Defence of Christianity from the Prophecies* (1725) and *A Vindication of the Defence of Christianity* (1728), which defended the typological interpretation of Old Testament prophecies, and also defended miracles. Newman's criticism points to what he sees as the essentially circular nature of the argument employed by Chandler and others appealing to miracles to support doctrine, and then doctrine to support the miracle.

p. 53. *Van Mildert's Boyle Lectures*: William van Mildert (1765–1836), Bishop of Durham 1826–36 having previously been Regius Professor of Divinity at Oxford, Bishop of Llandaff and Dean of St Paul's. An old High Churchman and the last of the Prince-Bishops of Durham, his Boyle lectures of 1802–5 were published in 1806 under the title *An historical review of the rise and progress of Infidelity, with a refutation of its principles and reasonings.* In an earlier Ascension Day sermon in 1792, as Elizabeth Varley notes, there was 'an early airing [of] a key theme of his Boyle Lectures ... restating Leslie's anti-Deist argument that the miracles performed by Jesus and his disciples, and the miraculous events surrounding the Saviour's life, constituted an incontestable divine endorsement of the whole Christian revelation, compelling belief in Jesus' divinity and acceptance of all his teachings'. (E. A. Varley, *The Last of the Prince Bishops: William Van Mildert and the High Church Movement of the early nineteenth century,* Cambridge, 1992, p. 23). Newman noted on 25 July 1825 that he had begun 'to run through Van Mildert's Boyle Lectures,' which he finished doing the next day. (*L&D*, I, p. 245).

p. 54. *opposite probabilities*: Newman notes that Hume's argument from general experience indicates that the ordinary powers of nature cannot be responsible for miraculous works. It is a matter of balancing unknown causes on the one hand, and the known power of God on the other. If with Bishop Butler probability is the guide of life, then with miracles we are faced with considering the balancing of opposite probabilities.

p. 56. *Herodotus, Cyclops, Centaurs, Scythians, Scylla and Charybdis*: Herodotus of Halicarnassus (*c*.484BC–*c*.425BC), author of *The Histories* ('ιστορια —enquiries) focuses on the origins of the Greco-Persian wars of 490BC and 480–479BC. Herodotus describes many wonders and strange occurrences of which Newman notes the Cyclops – a primordial race of giants each with a single eye in the middle of the forehead; Centaurs – half horse, half human; the Scythians whose customs and culture are described at the beginning of Book IV of *The Histories*; and Scylla and Charybdis, the dangerous rock and whirlpool in the Straits of Messina.

p. 57. *St. Basil . . . Emperor Julian*: St Basil the Great (*c*.330–79) one of the three Cappadocian Fathers who had known the emperor Julian (Flavius Claudius Julianus, 'Julian the Apostate', 332–363), when studying in Athens together with Gregory of Nazianzus. When Julian died in 363 during a campaign against the Persians, visions announced his death. The church historian, Sozomen, recounts how Didymus, a Christian philosopher of Alexandria, who had been fasting and praying that God would remove the apostate, had a vision of white horses and riders traversing the air and a voice said, 'Go and tell Didymus that Julian has been slain and just this hour; let me communicate this intelligence to Athanasius, the bishop, and let him arise and eat' (Sozomen, *Ecclesiastical History*, VI.2). It is possible that Newman is alluding to this story rather than to St Basil.

p. 58. *Croesus*: Last king of Lydia, reigned 560–546 BC, famed for his wealth. Defeated by Cyrus, King of Persia, Croesus was condemned to be burnt to death, but, remembering the words spoken to him by the Athenian, Solon, that no man should be called happy until he had finished his life happily, he called out Solon's name as he was about to be burnt, and Cyrus, being told of the story, spared the life of Croesus.

p. 59. *Miracles of Electricity*: The discovery of electricity and galvinism not surprisingly aroused considerable interest. Thomas Jefferson Hogg, the friend and contemporary of the poet, Shelley, describes how Shelley not only 'read treatises on magic and witchcraft' but also 'those more mundane ones detailing the miracles of electricity and galvinism'. Hogg also describes how Shelley experimented with electrical charges when at Oxford in 1810.

p. 59. *cures of scrofula by the King's touch*: There was a long tradition that scrofula, a disease producing glandular swellings known as 'the King's evil', could be cured by royal touch. There is evidence of the practice of curative touching in France. In England it was practised under Henry I and Henry II. James I and Charles I practised it, the last English sovereign to do so being Queen Anne. A form of service for the touching was often included in the Book of Common Prayer between the reign of Charles I and 1719.

p. 60. *liquefaction of St. Januarius's blood*: St Januarius, Bishop of Benevento, patron saint of Naples, of whom little is known. He is renowned for the 'liquefaction' of his blood, kept in a small glass phial, which is believed to occur on several occasions in the year.

p. 61. *Hey's Lectures*: John Hey (1734–1815) Norrisian professor of Divinity at Cambridge and Fellow of Sidney Sussex College. His *Lectures in Divinity* (1796) were edited by Thomas Turton, Regius Professor of Divinity at Cambridge (1827) and Bishop of Ely 1845–64. Hey's stress on the need to assent to what God has revealed to us, even though we do not as yet understand it, led him to endorse those expressions of Scripture in doctrine and devotion, including creeds, which few if any could comprehend. 'In assenting to that which is unintelligble – including the doctrine of the Trinity – they acknowledge the *mysterious* in religion: "a design of God not yet executed or made manifest". Hey's lectures were recommended to their pupils by the Tractarians. Both his scrupulous reasoning and his frank acknowledgement of mystery left their mark upon the Oxford Movement.' (John Hey, *Oxford Dictionary of National Biography*, loc. cit. [A. M. C. Waterman]). Newman notes reading Hey 'on Miracles à priori' on 27 July1825 in preparation for writing on miracles (*L&D*, I, p. 248).

p. 61. *The Cock-lane ghost*: In January 1762 William Kent, a young man from Norfolk, married (first) Elizabeth Lynes, who died in childbirth. Kent then eloped to London with Fanny Lynes, his dead wife's sister, where they lodged in Cock Lane near Smithfield market. Fanny heard mysterious scratchings in the bedroom and believed it was the ghost of her sister warning her of her own impending death. After her death the scratchings increased, and the landlord, William Parsons, began communicating with the ghost, who claimed that she (Fanny Kent) had died of arsenic poisoning in a premediatated murder by her husband, William. The house in Cock Lane became a popular attraction, William Parsons charging those who wanted to 'talk' with the ghost. Samuel Johnson was amongst those who investigated, when they discovered that Parsons' daughter was hiding a wooden clapper under her clothes and using it to produce the ghostly sound.

p. 62. *elegance of style of the Koran*: Newman rightly cites the Muslim claim that the Qur'an's elegance of style was a sign of it being a divine revelation. This is based on a number of verses in the Qur'an where Muhammad's detractors are challenged to bring a message like it, e.g in 2:23 'If you doubt what we (i.e. God) have sent down to our servant (i.e. Muhammad), then bring a sura like it.' The failure of Muhammad's detractors even to try to do this is interpreted as evidence, or proof, of the *i'jaz* or immutablity of the Qur'an. See R. C. Martin, 'Immutability' in J. D. McAuliffe (ed.), *The Encyclopaedia of the Qur'an,* vol. 2, Leiden, Brill, 2002.

p. 64. *Montanus*: The founder of a charismatic movement in Phrygia in the second century. Montanus and his associates believed themselves to be vehicles of a new effusion of the Holy Spirit, and in the oracles of their prophets believed that there was a revelation that supplemented 'the ancient scriptures'. The Montanists believed that the holy city, the new Jerusalem, would descend from heaven at Pepuza, and Epiphanius records how this was revealed in a dream to Prisca, one of the Montanist prophetesses, to whom Christ appeared in a dream when she was asleep, in the form of a shining female figure, and 'caused wisdom to sink into her heart and revealed to her that this was a holy place, and here would Jerusalem descend out of heaven'. Epiphanius also records that men and women used to sleep in the temple at Pepuza in the hope that Christ would appear to them as he had done to Prisca. (Epiphanius, *Panarion*, §48).

p. 65. *Mahomet's pretended night-journey*: Sura 17 vv.1 and 60 of the *Qu'ran* tells how Muhammad resting in the Ka'aba at Mecca, *c.*620, is visited by the archangel Gabriel, who brings him the winged steed Buraq who carries Muhammad to the farthest mosque the al-Aqsa mosque in Jerusalem – the name al-Aqsa means literally 'the further mosque'. ('Praise be to God, who took his servant by night from the holy mosque [i.e. Mecca] to the further mosque') (i.e. Jerusalem) (Sura 17 :1 of the Qur'an). This journey is known as the *Isra*, which is followed by the *Mi'raj* in which Buraq takes Muhammad to the heavens to meet with the earlier prophets and with Allah. Islamic opinion differs as to whether it was a physical journey or a dream. See M. Sells, 'Ascension' in J. D. McAuliffe (ed.), *The Encyclopaedia of the Qur'am,* vol.1, Leiden, Brill, 2001.

p. 66. *Hilarion's cures of wounds as mentioned by Jerome*: St Hilarion (*c.*281–371), the founder of the anchorite life in Palestine. Converted to Christianity at Alexandria he retired to the Egyptian desert under the influence of St Antony. From 306 he led a life of extreme asceticism at Maiuma near Gaza, where his fame and miraculous gifts became widely known. To escape the crowds who came to see him he returned to Egypt, and latterly to Libya, Sicily and Cyprus where he died. He was well known to St Epiphanius, from whom St Jerome gleaned much of the details of his life. Among the miracles recounted in Jerome's *Life of Hilarion* are some in which Hilarion effects cures by anointing with oil.

p. 70. *Vince*: See *supra*, p.18.

p. 75. *the Empress Julia:* Julia Domna (d. 217) second wife of the Roman emperor Septimius Severus (reigned 193–211). Born in Syria, she gathered around her in Rome a group of philosophers and intellectuals of which we know from the writings of Philostratus. 'She was wont to pass whole days surrounded by troops of grammarians, rhetoricians and sophists.' At her command Philostratus wrote the life of Apollonius of Tyana.

p. 76. *Loyola*: St Ignatius Loyola (1491–1556); founder of the Society of Jesus.

p. 77. *notorious insincerity and frauds of the Church of Rome*: Anti-Catholic polemic characteristically portrayed the Roman Catholic Church, and particularly the papacy and the Jesuits as scheming, deceitful and insincere. It was an accusation later brought against Newman by Charles Kingsley with his assertion that 'truth had never been a virtue with the Roman priesthood', accusing Newman of having been a crypto-Catholic before his conversion – an accusation which gave Newman the opportunity to write the *Apologia pro vita sua* to rebut Kingsley.

p. 77. *Prince Hohenlohe*: Alexander Leopold Hohenlohe (1794–1849); ordained priest in 1815, he did pastoral work in Stuttgart and Munich, becoming a canon of Bamberg in 1821. Having been cured of a severe pain in the throat, by the prayers of a devout peasant, he felt called to exercise a healing ministry himself, and there were a series of miraculous cures which were believed to result from his prayer. He became titular bishop of Sardica in 1844.

p. 79. *Gregory Thaumaturgus*: St Gregory Thaumaturgus (*c*.213–270), Gregory the Wonder-worker; coming from a prosperous pagan family at Neocaesarea in Pontus, he became a disciple of Origen at Caesarea in Palestine. He returned to Neocaesarea as bishop and converted its pagan population. The many miracles attributed to him led to his title of Thaumaturgus.

p. 79. *Xavier*: St Francis Xavier (1506–1552). One of the original members of the Jesuits, from 1542 he preached in Goa, Malacca, and Sri Lanka and in 1549 landed in Japan, where he founded the Church.

p. 81. *Alexander Pseudomantis*: Newman takes this from Hume's *Essay on Miracles* in which he writes, 'It was a wise policy in that the false prophet, Alexander, though now forgotten, was once so famous, to lay the first scene of his impostures in Paphlagonia, where, as Lucian tells us, the people were extremely ignorant and stupid, and ready to swallow even the grossest delusion.' Alexander, Hume adds, 'was enabled to proceed, from his ignorant Paphlagonians, to the enlisting of votaries, even among the Grecian philosophers, and men of the most eminent rank and distinction in Rome' (*Essay on Human Understanding,* X.ii.94).

p. 81. *the Paphlagonians*: Region of southern Asia Minor. See note on Alexander Pseudomantis above.

p. 83. *the facility with which the Japanese ascribed the ascent of a balloon, which they witnessed at St. Petersburgh, to the powers of magic*: Etienne Gaspard Robertson (1763–1837), a Belgian balloonist, who was the first to note the precise calculation of gas expansion with altitude, made a balloon ascent from St Petersburg in January, 1804. It is unclear to what Newman's comment about the Japanese believing this to be by the power of magic refers.

p. 84. *Less, Opuscul*: Gottfried Less (1736–1797) Professor of Theology at Göttingen, Newman asked Pusey, who was in Göttingen, to read and comment on Less's work on miracles for him.

p. 85. *Jenkin, On the Christian Religion*: Robert Jenkin (1656–1727), Master of St John's College, Cambridge and Lady Margaret Professor of Divinity, 1711–27. A Nonjuror under William and Mary, he took the oaths under Queen Anne. He published an *Historical Examination of General Councils* (1688) which was reprinted by Edward Gibbon. Newman noted that he read Jenkin on 28 July 1825 for his essay on Miracles for the *Encyclopaedia Metropolitana* (*L&D*, I, p. 248) and on 15 February 1826 he noted that he had 'looked over Douglas, B.White, Jenkin, Leland, etc. for miracles (*L&D*, I, p. 276).

p. 87. *The professed cures of Vespasian were performed in honour of Serapis*: Serapis was a Greco-Roman deity of the sun, whose cult at Memphis was associated with that of the sacred Egyptian bull, Apis. He was a favourite deity of the Emperor Caracalla. Tacitus records how when Vespasian was at

Editor's Notes 427

Alexandria a blind man threw himself at Vespasian's feet imploring him to heal his blindness and saying he had been commanded to do this by Serapis. A man with a withered hand also asked to be cured, similarily instructed by Serapis. After some hesitation Vespasian did what was asked and both men recovered (Tacitus, *Histories,* 4.81).

p. 87. *Victor Vitensis*: Bishop of Vita in North Africa in the late fifth century, and author of the *Historia Persecutionis Africanae Provinciae,* a history of the persecution of the Catholic Church in Africa by the Arian Vandals under Gaiseric and Hunneric.

p. 87. *Zeno*: (*c*.450?–491), Emperor of the East from 474, and author of the *Henoticon* (482) which atttempted (unsuccessfully) to reconcile the Monophysites, leading to another schism between Rome and Constantinople.

p. 87. *Milner's Church History*: Joseph Milner (1744–1797), Evangelical divine, and author of a *History of the Church of Christ*. This was largely put into shape and extended by his brother, Isaac Milner, Dean of Carlisle, and published in stages between 1794 and 1809. It stood in the pietist/Evangelical tradition of church history which saw the providential shaping of the Church by converted leaders. It was also one of the few Evangelical works to quote extensively from the Fathers. Newman read Milner as a schoolboy in 1816 writing in the *Apologia* that 'I read Joseph Milner's Church History, and was nothing short of enamoured of the long extracts from St Augustine, St Ambrose, and the other Fathers which I found there. I read them as being the religion of the primitive Christians.' He believed that Milner's introducing him to the Fathers saved him from 'the cold Arminian doctrine' which was 'the first stage of Liberalism'. 'An imaginative devotion to them and to their times had been the permanent effect upon him of reading at School an account of them and extracts from their work in Joseph Milner's Church History ... the first centuries were his *beau idéal* of Christianity' (*AW*, p. 83). As Newman told Henry Wilberforce in 1846: 'St Ambrose in Milner's history was one of the first objects of my veneration' (*L&D*, XI, p. 252). See J. D. Walsh, 'Joseph Milner's Evangelical Church History', *Journal of Ecclesiastical History,* 9 (1959), pp.174–87). He noted in the *Apologia* that it was from Milner's description of the Day of Pentecost 'as marking "the first of those *Effusions* of the Spirit of God, which from age to age have visited the earth since the coming of Christ"' that was an important plank in his coming to admit the possibility of ecclesiastical miracles (*Apologia,* p. 83).

ESSAY II: THE MIRACLES OF EARLY ECCLESIASTICAL HISTORY, COMPARED WITH THOSE OF SCRIPTURE, AS REGARDS THEIR NATURE, CREDIBILITY AND EVIDENCE

In his first *Essay* Newman had confined himself to the miracles of Scripture, rebutting the attacks of sceptics, but bound by the common Protestant position that the miracles of Scripture were the evidence of Divine revelation, but that miracles ceased with the end of the apostolic period. In this second *Essay* Newman is no longer bound by this limitation, and seeks to evaluate the miracles reported from the early centuries of the Church. As the title indicates Newman is interested in comparing significant miracles reported in the early centuries of the Church with the miracles of Scripture. He is not concerned with a general defence of miracles from any period of church history, nor does he either in the title or the *Essay* itself in any way endorse all miraculous claims. He is concerned with the 'nature, credibility and evidence' of a particular set of reported miracles.

pp. 97–8. *The momentary yet recurring tokens of that conflict between good and evil, which is waging in the world of spirits from age to age*: Newman had a strong sense both of the supernatural and of a cosmic conflict between good and evil. This was evidenced particularly in his early polemic against Rome as the Antichrist, and as this was transferred later to liberalism. (See Sheridan Gilley, 'Newman and Prophecy, Evangelical and Catholic', *The Journal of the United Reformed Church History Society*, III (March 1985), pp.160–88).

p. 100. *that there was no Age of Miracles, after which miracles ceased*: Newman clearly takes up a new position from that defended in his first *Essay*, being clear that reported miracles have to be judged on evidential criteria rather than the drawing of a line between the scriptural miracles of the Old Testament, of the Gospels and the apostolic age, and any alleged miracles described subsequently.

p. 101. *antecedent probability*: See note on 'antecedent credibility' *supra*, p. 3.

p. 106. *Dr. Middleton and his opponents, in a late controversy concerning miracles*: For Newman's reading of Conyers Middleton's *Free Inquiry into the Miraculous Powers in the Christian Church*, see note *supra*, p. 29.

p. 106. *Bishop Douglas*: See note *supra*, p. 34.

p. 109. *Archbishop Tillotson's [argument] against the Real Presence*: John Tillotson (1630–1694), Archbishop of Canterbury 1691–94 in succession to the Nonjuror, William Sancroft. A notable preacher, strongly opposed to Roman Catholics, he urged a policy of comprehension which would allow nonconformists a place in the Established Church. He held Zwinglian ideas about the Eucharist. Newman will have noted Hume's reference to Tillotson's Eucharistic doctrine in the first paragraph of his *Essay on Miracles.* Hume takes up Tillotson's argument against the doctrine of the Real Presence in which he states that, unlike the testimony of the Apostles, 'who were eye-witnesses to those miracles of our Saviour, by which he proved his divine mission', the doctrine of the Real Presence is contrary to the evidence of our senses which, in Tillotson's reference to the eyewitness testimony of the Apostles to miracles, is that on which the truth of Christianity is based. Hume comments that 'Our evidence, then, for the truth of the *Christian* religion is less than the evidence for the truth of our senses; because even in the first authors of our religion, it was no greater; and it is evident it must diminish in passing from them to their disciples; nor can anyone rest such confidence in their testimony, as in the immediate object of his senses'(X.i.86). In his thirteenth University Sermon, 'Implicit and Explicit Reason' (1830) Newman condemns Tillotson for inaccurately worded assertions which may lead to great error, citing Tillotson's comments that 'Nothing ought to be received as a divine doctrine and revelation, *without good evidence* that it is so, without some *argument* sufficient to *satisfy* a prudent and considerate man' (*Sermons*, ii, p. 260). And further, 'Faith ... is an assent of the mind to something revealed by God: now all assent must be *grounded upon evidence*; that is, no man can believe anything, unless he have, or think he hath, some *reason* to do so. For to be confident of a thing without reason is not faith, but a 'presumptuous persuasion and obstinacy of mind' (*Sermons*, iv. p. 42). Newman comments 'such assertions either have an untrue meaning or are unequal to the influences which the writers proceed to draw from them' (*US*, pp.178–9).

p. 114. *Grotius*: Hugo Grotius (1583–1645), Huig de Groot, a Dutch jurist and theologian, sometimes known as 'the Father of international law'. He visited England in 1613, where he met with John Overall, the Dean of St Paul's and Lancelot Andrewes, who appreciated his Arminianism and interest in church history. Much concerned with church unity he was attracted by the Anglican Liturgy, episcopacy and the Anglican respect for tradition.

p. 114. *Barrow*: Isaac Barrow (1630–1677), Anglican divine, classical scholar and mathematician. He was Lucasian Professor of Mathematics at Cambridge, in which position he was succeeded by Sir Isaac Newton and subsequently Master of Trinity College, Cambridge, 1672–77. He was described as 'low in stature, lean, of a pale complexion' slovenly in his dress and an inveterate smoker. In 1832 Newman gave Barrow's *Works* to his Oriel friend Robert Francis Wilson commenting that 'I felt Barrow was so good a writer that I could do no wrong in selecting it.' When Newman visited Wilson many years later in 1876 Wilson showed him the copy of Barrow's works that he had given him (*L&D*, III, p. 31, 13. iii.1832).

p. 114. *Dodwell*: Almost certainly in this context William Dodwell (1709–1785) rather than his father Henry Dodwell (1641–1711), a leading Nonjuror, or William's brother, also Henry Dodwell (1706–1784), the author of a satirical attack on William Law and orthodox apologists for Christianity in his book *Christianity not founded on Argument* (1741), William Dodwell, rector of Shottesbrooke in Berkshire and later Archdeacon of Berkshire, was one of the staunchest defenders of orthodoxy in the eighteenth century, maintaining that Trinitarianism was 'the very essence of the Christian Religion, the foundation of the whole Revelation, and connected with every part of it'. In *A free answer to Dr Middleton's free inquiry into the miraculous powers of the primitive church* (1749) he 'defended the church Fathers and contested each of Middleton's four main criticisms of the primitive church and its use of miracles; there were occasions, he insisted, when they could be convincingly vindicated "to the satisfaction of men of sense"' (*Oxford Dictionary of National Biography*, William Dodwell, loc.cit. [Nigel Aston]).

p. 117. *St. Gregory of Neocaesarea*: St Gregory Thaumaturgus ('the wonderworker') (*c*.213–*c*.270), see *supra* p. 79.

p. 122. *St. Athanasius's biographical notice of St. Anthony*: St Antony of Egypt (*c*.251–356) regarded as the founder of Christian monasticism in its eremitic expression. A supporter of the Nicene party in the Arian controversy, he was closely associated with Athanasius, Bishop of Alexandria and the champion of the Nicene cause, he was a friend of the monks Pachomius and Serapion, as well as Athanasius who quite possibly wrote the life of Anthony traditionally attributed to him.

p. 123. *Natalis*: Nothing is known of Natalis (or Natalius) except what Eusebius records in his *Church History* (v. 28) where he is described as a disciple of Theodotus the cobbler, who was excommunicated by Pope Victor for maintaining that Christ was 'a mere man'. Having been persuaded to be chosen as bishop for this heretical group, Natalis was warned through a series of visions not to link himself with this group. 'But as he paid little regard to the visions, because he was ensnared by the first position among them and by that shameful covetousness which destroys a

Editor's Notes 431

great many, he was scourged by holy angels, and punished severely through the entire night.'

p. 126. *Hilarion*: St Hilarion (*c*.291–371), cf. *supra* p. 66.

p. 127. *Sulpicius*: Sulpicius Severus (360?–430?), historian and hagiographer and author of the *Life of Martin* (396), which portrays Martin as a man of God attested by miracles. In a later work, the *Dialogues* (*c*.405) Martin's thaumaturgical powers are compared favourably with those of the Egyptian ascetics.

p. 127. *St. Martin*: St Martin (d. 397), Bishop of Tours and Patron saint of France.

p. 127. *St. Hilary*: (*c*.315–367/8), Bishop of Poitiers from *c*.350, and the leading Latin theologian of his day. *De Trinitate,* written against the Arians, is a major exposition of Trinitarian theology. St Martin was as a young man his spiritual student.

p. 129. *St Augustine, De Civitate Dei*: The twenty-two books which make up *The City of God* (*De Civitate Dei*) were written between 416 and 422. In Book XXII, which is concerned with the end of the City of God, the eternal happiness of the saints, and the resurrection of the body, Augustine writes in chapters 8–10 of the 'miracles which were wrought that the world might believe in Christ, and which have not ceased since the world believed', and particularly of miracles associated with the martyrs.

p. 131. *Papias*: Papias (*c*.60–130), Bishop of Hierapolis, cited by Eusebius for the valuable oral traditions in his writings concerning the origins of the Gospels of Matthew and Mark. Eusebius records that Philip the Apostle resided at Hierapolis and Papias heard 'from the lips of Philip's daughters, the resurrection of a dead person in his own lifetime, and a further miracle that happened to Justus, surnamed Barsabas, who swallowed a dangerous poison and by the grace of the Lord was none the worse'. (*Church History*, 3.39.11).

p. 131. *Irenaeus*: Irenaeus (*c*.130?–*c*.200), Bishop of Lyons and author of *Adversus Haereses,* a detailed attack on Gnosticism, and the *Demonstration of the Apostolic Preaching*. In *Adversus Haereses* II, xxxi, Irenaeus argues against the Gnostics Simon and Carpocrates, that 'they can neither confer sight on the blind, nor hearing on the deaf, nor chase away all sorts of demons'. They cannot raise the dead, 'as the Lord raised them, and the apostles did, by means of prayer, and has been frequently done in the brotherhood on account of some necessity – the entire Church in that particular locality entreating [the boon] with much fasting and prayer, the spirit of the dead man has returned, and he has been bestowed in answer to the prayers of the saints'. (ANCL (Ante-Nicene Christian Fathers), I, p. 507; A.Cleveland Coxe, the translator and the editor adds in a footnote that 'On the sub-apostolic age and this subject of miracles, Newman, in spite of his sophistical argumentation, may well be consulted for his references.')

p. 132. *Whitby*: Daniel Whitby (1637/8–1726), Anglican divine. Well read in the Fathers, after the revolution of 1688 he was close to Gilbert Burnet, his bishop at Salisbury. His *Paraphrase and Commentary on the New Testament* (1703) became an eighteenth-century classic. Whitby was an exponent of Whig theories of contract and resistance and maintained a strong Arminian position, denying any imputation of Adam's sin to his posterity. He was strongly hostile to 'Popery' and looked for reconciliation with the Nonconformists. His last (posthumous) work shows that he had come to hold an Arian theology. (*ODNB*, loc. cit. [Jean-Louis Quantin].)

p. 133. *Narcissus*: Bishop of Jerusalem in the third century. Eusebius (*Church History,* VI.9) records the miracles of Narcissus including that to which Newman refers. 'They relate the following wonder as performed by him. They say that the oil once failed while the deacons were watching through the night at the great paschal vigil. Thereupon the whole multitude being dismayed, Narcissus directed those who attended to the lights, to draw water and bring it to him. This being immediately done he prayed over the water, and with firm faith in the Lord, commanded them to pour it into the lamps. And when they had done so, contrary to all expectation by a wonderful and divine power, the nature of the water was changed into that of oil. A small portion of it has been preserved even to our day by many of the brethren there as a memento of the wonder.' See Section II of Chapter V of the *Second Essay on Miracles.*

p. 134. *the thundering Legion*: Eusebius records (*Church History,* v. 5) that the soldiers of the Melitene Legion, in the time of Antoninus Pius, knelt on the ground and prayed to God, and immediately afterwards lightning drove the enemy to flight, and a shower refreshed the soldiers who had prayed. As a consequence the legion became known as 'the Thundering Legion'. See Section I of Chapter V of the *Second Essay on Miracles*.

p. 134. *death of Arius*: Sozomen records (*Ecclesiastical History,* II.xxx.) that fearing that Arius would be re-admitted to the Church, Alexander, Bishop of Constantinople, prayed that this should not happen. Arius was

Editor's Notes

'compelled by a want of nature to enter a place appointed for such emergencies, and here he lost at once both his restoration to communion and his life'. See Section VI of Chapter V of the *Second Essay on Miracles*.

p. 134. *St. Gervasius and St. Protasius*: The proto-martyrs of Milan, about whom little is known. Many miraculous healings took place at their shrine to the discomforture of the Arians.

p. 135. *speech granted to African confessors*: See Section IX of Chapter V of the *Second Essay on Miracles*.

p. 135. *Brook's Defens. Miracl. Eccl.*: Zachary Brooke (*sic* not 'Brook' as Newman has it) (1715/16–1788). Educated at Stamford School, he became a fellow of St John's College, Cambridge. He was elected to the 'valuable sinecure' of the Lady Margaret Professorship of Divinity in 1765 as a *quid pro quo* for ceding the Mastership of St John's to a rival in the fellowship, W. S. Powell. In his *Defensio miraculorum: quae in Ecclesia Christiania facta esse perhibentur post tempora Apostolorum* (Cambridge, 1748), the work cited by Newman, and described as 'a brief work of considerable erudition', he attacked the scepticism of Conyers Middleton's *Free Enquiry* (*ODNB*, loc. cit).

p. 135. *Isaac Taylor*: Isaac Taylor of Stanford Rivers (1787–1865), best known for his *Natural History of Enthusiasm* (1829), and a lifelong student of the early Church (he is said to have coined the word 'patristic'). His *Ancient Christianity* (1839–40) was a lengthy attack on the use made of the Fathers in the *Tracts for the Times*.

p. 135. *Blomfield*: Charles James Blomfield (1786–1857), Bishop of London 1828–57. Blomfield established an early reputation as a classical scholar and might be best characterised as a pragmatic High Churchman, who could have hesitations about Catholic Emancipation and yet support the Jerusalem Bishopric.

p. 136. *St. Chrysostom*: St John Chrysostom (*c*.347–407), Bishop of Constantinople. One of the greatest Christian expositors of Scripture, his sermons 'combine a great facility for seeing the spiritual meaning of the author with an equal ability for immediate practical application'. (*ODCC*, loc. cit.)

p. 137. *St. Ambrose*: Ambrose (*c*.339–397), Bishop of Milan, a staunch upholder of orthodoxy against Arianism, who had a strong influence on St Augustine. He did much to encourage asceticism and the cult of the martyrs.

p. 138. *Isidore of Pelusium*: Isidore, ascetic and exegete (d. *c*.440), lived in a monastery not far from Pelusium on the eastern estuary of the Nile. During the Third Council of Ephesus he corresponded with Cyril of Alexandria and admired the Cappadocians and St John Chrysostom. A large amount of his correspondence survives.

p. 138. *Pope Gregory*: Gregory the Great (*c*.540–604), Pope from 590. His 'Dialogues' (*c*.593) relate the lives and miracles of Italian saints, including St Benedict; they provided models of holiness for Gregory's contemporaries taken from saints close to them (*ODCC*, loc.cit.).

p. 139. *St. Clement of Alexandria*: Clement (*c*.150–*c*.215), theologian and teacher, who had a significant influence on Newman, who wrote in the *Apologia* 'The broad philosophy of Clement and Origen carried me away; the philosophy, not the theological doctrine ... some portions of their teaching, magnificent in themselves, came like music to my inward ear, as if the response to ideas, which, with little external to encourage them, I had cherished so long. These were based on the mystical or sacramental principle, and spoke of the various Economies or Dispensations of the Eternal.' (For the influence of Clement on Newman see Robin C. Selby, *The Principle of Reserve in the Writings of John Henry Cardinal Newman*, Oxford University Press, 1975, pp. 4–7, 11, 21.)

p. 139. *Mr. Osburn*: A Protestant controversialist, W. Osburn published *Doctrinal Errors of the apostolical and early Fathers* in 1835. Newman wrote to J. W. Bowden on 28 August 1836 saying that Manning feared that 'Mr Osborn and the Record are doing harm. Yet I can hardly think so – so that they rouse people to think, it is every thing' (*L&D*, V, p. 345). Newman followed this with a letter to Manning (4 September 1836): 'As to Mr Osburn, he is so insufferably profane, that I cannot help thinking that if that, and one remark, which you are familiar with, be put before well disposed people, they would eschew him and his opinions. My first remark then would be, that "Mr Osburn accuses St Barnabas, Apostle and Martyr, of silliness, weakness, obscenity etc" – Is not this quite enough to over throw his whole book with any Clergyman, if not layman? – Well, all that will remain then, is the impression that "these Fathers are strange men after all, Platonists, etc.etc."' Newman told Manning that he would like to have reviewed Osburn's book in the *British Critic*, but it had already been reviewed. 'Mr O. is too vile and abominable (reviewed as an author) to touch with a pair of tongues in propriâ personâ' (*L&D*, V, pp. 348–9). In his essay on 'The Theology of the Seven Epistles of Ignatius', originally published in the *British Critic* and reprinted in *Ess*. I (London, Basil Montagu Pickering, 1872, pp.186–260), Newman criticises Osburn for his judgement on Ignatius, that 'no consideration, either of reason or Scripture, seems to have power for a moment to check the mad career of his turgid and bloated, but often eloquent, declamation; or to deter him from working up his exhortations to the highest pitch of hyperbole' (I, p. 210).

p. 139. *Bishop of Lincoln*: John Kaye (1783–1853), Bishop of Lincoln (1827–53). As Regius Professor of Divinity at Cambridge he recommenced lecturing, concentrating on the Fathers, thus contributing to the revival in patristic studies. His lectures on Clement of Alexandria were published in 1835. Newman told Hugh James Rose in December 1835 that he had noted that Kaye had maintained that Clement had held the doctrine of the *Disciplina Arcani*, as did Newman himself (*L&D*, V, p. 178).

p. 142. *Donatists*: A schismatic body in the Church in North Africa, who refused to accept the consecration of Caecilian as Bishop of Carthage on the grounds that his consecrator, Felix of Aptungi, had been a *traditor*, who had handed over the Scriptures during the persecution under Diocletian. Augustine led the theological attack against Donatist rigorism. Newman, who allowed that the miracles of Scripture were part of the evidence for revealed truth, held that this was not the case with Ecclesiastical Miracles. 'The object of Ecclesiastical Miracles is not, strictly speaking, that of evidencing Christianity' (*Miracles,* p.146).

p. 145. *Circumcelliones*: A fourth-century fanatical North African group, concentrated especially in Numidia, who were known as Circumcelliones because they lived around (*circum*) the martyrs' shrines (*cellae*), who became linked with the Donatists.

p. 145. *Optatus of Milevis*: (*fl.*370) Bishop of Milevis in North Africa. Largely known for his writings against the Donatists, which formed the basis of St Augustine's anti-Donatist writings.

p. 154. *Divine Economy*: Economy ('οικονομια)is literally 'household management'. It comes to mean 'dispensation' or how things are ordered. Newman believed that the inability of the finite human mind to comprehend infinite divine realities necessitated a reserve in both God's self-communication, and in the human communication of revealed truth. Revelation was at the same time a mystery. Nonetheless Divine realities may be partially represented, and that representation was 'economy'. Selby notes that it is a word in its theological usage in English that is first attributed to Newman himself, where, in *The Arians of the Fourth Century*, he maintained that 'The word economy might be used for the general system of Providence, or for the work of creation, as opposed to the absolute perfection of God' (R. C. Selby, *The Principle of Reserve in the Writings of John Henry Cardinal Newman*, Oxford University Press, 1975, p. 59 et seq.).

p. 175. *Leslie*: Charles Leslie (1650–1722), Nonjuring divine and controversialist. Deprived of his living as Chancellor of Connor for refusing to take the oath of allegiance to William III. He wrote against the Quakers (*A Snake in the Grass* (1696)) and was the author of a major attack on Deist philosophy, *A Short and Easy Method with the Deists* (1698). A strong defender of the divine authority of the Church and of patriarchal theories of government, he followed the Pretender to Rome, though protesting his loyalty to the Church of England. He returned to Ireland a year before his death.

p. 181. *Jortin*: John Jortin (1698–1770), ecclesiastical historian. The son of Renatus Jortin, a Huguenot refugee, he held various appointments in London, becoming Archdeacon of London in 1764. He published *Remarks on Ecclesiastical History* in several volumes from 1751 and a *Life of Erasmus* in 1758.

p. 189. *cumulative force*: Newman's citing of ecclesiastical miracles having a cumulative force is of a piece with his more general apologetic which appealed to cumulative arguments for the truth of Christianity.

p. 189. *Orig. contr. Cels.*: Origen (*c*.185–*c*.254), one of the Alexandrian theologians whose philosophy influenced Newman. His *Contra Celsum*, written in defence of Christianity against the pagan philosopher, Celsus, dates from the middle of the third century. Celsus criticised much of the biblical history for its miracles.

p. 190. *Tillemont*: Louis Sébastien Le Nain de Tillemont (1637–1698), French church historian, whose *Mémoires pour servir à l'histoire ecclésiastique des six premiers siècles* (1693–1712) gathered together a huge range of patristic material. It was much used by Gibbon for his *Decline and Fall of the Roman Empire*. Newman was presented with the sixteen volumes of Tillemont's *Mémoires* by Frederick Rogers in 1833 after his return from his Sicilian journey. He told Rogers: 'You have no notion how useful your Tillemont already is. The "Church of the Fathers" is in great measure drawn up from it.' (*L&D*, IV, p. 36, Newman to Rogers, 31 August 1833). In 1868 Newman told Mrs William Hill Buckle, who had asked his advice about a book on the history of the Church that she was writing, that Tillemont was the best source he could recommend 'for history, chron-ology and geography ... he religiously gives his authorities for every half sentence of his elaborate work' (27.x.1868). Gibbon had also relied heavily on Tillemont when writing his *History of the Decline and Fall of the Roman Empire,* describing Tillemont as one 'whose inimitable accuracy almost assumes the character of genius', who helped him safely through the treacherous terrain of Roman politics with the patience and sure-footedness of an Alpine mule which could be trusted even on the 'most slippery paths' (*L&D*, XXXII, 2008, p. 290).

p. 208. *St. Bernard*: St Bernard (1090–1153), Abbot of Clairvaux, one of the chief centres of the Cistercian Order. Newman quotes from Bernard's *Sermones per annum*, Bernard's sermons for the feast days of the liturgical year.

p. 208. *Kuinoel*: Christian Gottlieb (Theophilus) Kuinoel (1768–1841), professor at Liepzig and Giessen. His works include his *Commentarius in libri Novi Testamenti historicos* and his *Philological Commentary on the New Testament* (1828).

p. 214. *Lord Barrington*: John Shute Barrington, First Viscount Barrington (1678–1734), politician and Christian apologist, and father of Shute Barrington, Bishop of Durham. He argued for the relief of Dissenters, and towards the end of his life published *An Essay on the Several Dispensations of God to Mankind* (1725) and *Miscellanea sacra, or, A new method of considering so much of the history of the apostles as is contained in scripture.* It is these to which Newman is probably referring, and which he would most likely have known in George Townsend (ed.), *The Theological Works of the First Viscount Barrington* (1828).

p. 230. *Lord Lyttelton*: William Henry Lyttelton (1782–1837), third Baron Lyttelton, student of Christ Church, Oxford, 1800–12. A considerable Greek scholar he was a favourite of Cyril Jackson, the Dean. From 1807 to 1820 he was Member of Parliament for Worcestershire. He was 'a staunch Whig, a bad speaker, and a good conversationalist' (*Oxford Dictionary of National Biography*, loc. cit.).

p. 235. *Pope Gelasius*: (d. 496); he succeeded Felix III as Pope in 492. He staunchly upheld the Roman primacy, wrote a treatise on the two natures of Christ, and many letters on practical matters, but did not compile the Gelasian Sacramentary, long attributed to him.

p. 235. *St. John Damascene*: St John of Damascus (*c*.655–780), Greek theologian and Doctor of the Church, a strong defender of images in the Iconoclastic Controversy.

p. 235. *St. Bridget*: St Bridget (Birgitta) of Sweden (*c*.1303–1373). After marriage and a pilgrimage to Compostela, shortly after which her husband died, she received a series of revelations, which included directions about the founding of a new religious Order. In 1349 she went to Rome, where she lived until her death, campaigning for the reform of the Church and the foundation of her Order. Her revelations are an outstanding example of the affective spirituality of her time (*ODCC*, loc. cit.).

p. 235. *St. Mathildis*: St Mechtild of Magdeburg (*c*.1207–1282), author of a book of mystical Revelations, she became a Beguine at Magdeburg, and later, *c*.1270, a nun at the Cistercian-inspired convent of Helfta (*ODCC*, loc. cit.)

p. 235. *Baron*: Cesare Baronius (1538–1607), a member of the Oratory and an ecclesiastical historian whose *Annales Ecclesiastici* – a history of the Church in twelve volumes divided into chapters, each covering a year, was designed as a Catholic response to the Protestant church history of the Centuriators of Magdeburg, By the time of his death the work had only reached the year 1198, and subsequent attempts to complete it proved fruitless. In 1586 and 1589 he published new and corrected editions of the Roman martyrology.

p. 236. *Emperor Trajan was delivered from the place of punishment at the prayers of St. Gregory the First*: The earliest life of St Gregory the Great (540–604), written at Whitby in 710, records how Gregory prayed for the release of Trajan from hell and God granted his prayer. The *Golden Legend* repeats the story, and it was used by Dante in *Purgatorio* 10.

p. 236. *Melchior Canus*: Melchior Cano (?1509–1560), Spanish Dominican theologian, who took an active part in the debates on the Eucharist and Penance at the Council of Trent. He defended Philip II's anti-papal policy.

p. 236. *St. Gregory's Dialogues*: The *Dialogues* (*c*.593) relate the lives and miracles of Italian saints. See *supra* p. 138.

p. 236. *Ecclesiastical History of Bede*: The Venerable Bede (*c*.673–735), the leading scholar of Anglo-Saxon England. His *Historia Ecclesiastica Gentis Anglorum* (completed in 731) is one of the great works of mediaeval

Editor's Notes

historiography and the single most important source for our understanding of early England' (*ODCC*, loc. cit.).

p. 236. *Speculum Exemplorum and the Aurea Legenda of Jacobus de Voragine*: James of Voragine or Varazze (*c*.1230–1298). A member of the Dominican Order, he compiled a series of saints' lives and short treatises on the Christian festivals to be a source book for preachers. It became immensely popular and was translated into many languages. In the sixteenth century it was attacked by Protestants and by some Catholics, such as J. L. Vives and Melchior Cano because it was feared that the large number of improbable tales it contained would endanger true religion. The Broad Church divine, Bishop Connop Thirlwall of St David's, attacked Newman for his 'extravagant credulity' expressed in his series of Saints' Lives. Thirlwall wrote pungently of what he saw as Newman's 'utter want of historical tact and judgment, which alone enables us to believe the sincerity of his professed all-absorbing credulity. He was in this respect a born Papist, and finds his natural element in the Golden Legend. The conception that all the work of the universe, all mechanical, physical, chemical, and physiological movements, from planetary and sidereal rotations to the dislocations of the molecules of an atom, are carried on by the agency of an order of personal beings, is one which my mind utterly rejects, and I believe that no mind could attempt to realize it without feeling itself in danger of losing its senses. Surely it is one thing to believe that all is regulated by a Supreme Will, and quite another thing to believe that this Will employs a machinery like that of the "Rape of the Lock"'. (See John Connop Thirlwall, Jr., *Connop Thirlwall, historian and theologian,* London, 1936, p. 208, citing Connop Thirlwall, *Letters, Literary and Theological* (ed. Perowne and Stokes), London, 1881.)

p. 237. *schools of St. Dominic and the Oratory*: The Dominican Order of friars, founded by St Dominic in 1220. Jacob of Voragine, the author of the *Golden Legend*, was a Dominican. The Oratorians were founded by St Philip Neri in Rome in 1575, and Newman founded the Oratory in England following his reception into the Roman Catholic Church. Cesare Baronius (see note on p. 235 above), one of the most significant Catholic church historians, was an Oratorian.

p. 237. *Palladius in his Lausiac*: Palladius (*c*.364–between 420 and 430), historian of early monasticism. A pupil of Evagrius Pontus, he became Bishop of Helenopolis in Bithynia and later Bishop of Aspouma in Galatia. His 'Lausiac' (so-called from its dedication to Lausus, the chamberlain of Theodosius II) history of the 'Friends of God' is the most valuable single writing that survives in the history of early monasticism. It includes a number of miraculous stories.

p. 237. *Theodoret*: (*c.* 393–*c.*460), Bishop of Cyrrhus. Educated in Antioch and a friend and admirer of Nestorius, he was a strong defender of an Antiochene Christology. Amongst his many writings are his *Religious History* consisting of a number of biographies of monks, and a *Church History* which continues the work of Eusebius down to 428, valuable for its use of many authentic documents.

p. 237. *miracles of St. Stephen*: St Stephen, the first martyr, whose stoning is recorded in the Acts of the Apostles, had many miracles attributed to him, including the later finding of his relics. Some are recounted by James of Voragine in the *Golden Legend*.

p. 237. *The Bollandists*: The Jesuit editors of the *Acta Sanctorum* named after John van Bolland (1596–1665) the founder and first editor of the work, conceived as a critical edition of the lives of the saints.

p. 237. *Alban Butler's Saints*: Alban Butler, a Catholic priest who published the lives of over 1600 saints in *the Lives of the Fathers, Martyrs and other principal Saints, compiled from original Monuments and other authentic records, illustrated with the renarks of judicious modern critics and historians* (1756–59). Although based on wide research the primary aim is edification.

p. 237. *Geddes' Tracts*: Michael Geddes (*c.*1647–1713), for a time chaplain to the English factory at Lisbon, was made chancellor of Salisbury by Bishop Gilbert Burnet. The author of histories of the Churches of Malabar and Ethiopia, proving that there were ancient churches not under the authority of the papacy, his *Miscellaneous Tracts* (1714) went through several editions, and expressed Geddes' scepticism about miracles and marvels recounted in Catholic histories. The incomplete *The most Celebrated Popish Ecclesiastical Romance, being the Life of Veronica, of Milan* (1716) is in the same vein.

p. 241. *Claudius Apollinaris, Bishop of Hierapolis*: Christian apologist and writer of the second century of whom some fragmentary works remain, cited by Eusebius in his *History,* V.5, for the story of the Thundering Legion.

p. 242. *Melitene legion*: Melitene (present day Malatya) in Asia Minor. The legion was named the Thundering Legion either because of the story told by Eusebius quoting Claudius Apollinaris, or because a thunderbolt was the emblem on their shields.

p. 244. *Moyle's Posthumous Works*: Walter Moyle (1672–1727), Cornish politician and writer on classical themes. His *Essay on the Constitution of the*

Roman Government was at the time the most detailed study of the causes of the rise and fall of republican Rome, and won the praise of Edward Gibbon. (See *ODNB*, q.v.). Much of his writing was only published posthumously.

p. 244. *Jablonski*: Paul Ernst Jablonski (1693–1757), professor of theology and philosophy at the university of Frankfort on the Oder. Newman refers to his *Opuscula, quibus lingua et antiquitas aegyptiorum, difficilia librorum sacrorum loca et historiae ecclesiasticae capita illustrantur*. This work was recently republished by the Adamant Media Corporation (2001).

p. 245. *Scaliger*: Joseph Scaliger (1540–1609), religious scholar and classical historian.

p. 245. *Valesius*: Henricus Valesius, the Latin form of Henri Valois (1603–1676), French philologist and student of classical and ecclesiastical historians, who edited the church histories of Eusebius, Socrates and Sozomen. The edition of Sozomen in the *Nicene and Post-Nicene Christian Fathers,* Second Series, II, translates Valesius' remarks on Sozomen's life and writings (pp. 233–4, 1997 reprint).

p. 245. *Witsius*: Hermann Witsius (Herman Wits) (1636–1708), Dutch Protestant theologian. His most famous work was *The Economy of the Covenants between God and Man* (1677). Newman cites his *Diatribe de septem epistolarum apocalypticum sensu historico et prophetico* (Franeker, 1678).

p. 245. *Milman*: Henry Hart Milman (1791–1868), Dean of St Paul's, known particularly for his *History of Latin Christianity* (1855), which did much to encourage the study of mediaeval life, history and institutions.

p. 245. *King*: William King (1650–1729), Archbishop of Dublin. He engaged in controversies with both Roman Catholics and Presbyterians, his most important work being *De Origine Mali* (On the Origin of Evil) in which he endeavoured to reconcile the existence of evil (especially moral evil) with an omnipotent and beneficent Deity.

p. 245. *Neander*: Johann August Wilhelm Neander (1789–1850), ecclesiastical historian. Born a Jew, David Mendel, he became a Christian under the influence of Schleiermacher, and took the name of Neander on his baptism in 1806. His *General Church History* (1826–1852) which traced the history of the Church from the beginning to *c.*1450, utilised many original sources, but, unlike Mosheim's church history, which was primarily centred on institutions, Neander was concerned with persons, seeking to show the interpenetration of human life by the Divine. He was a convinced Protestant who regarded the priesthood and other outward ordinances as dangerous to Christian simplicity. (*ODCC*, loc. cit.)

p. 246. *G. Vossius*: Latinised form of Gerhard Jan Voss (1577–1649), a Dutch humanist theologian, and a friend of Hugo Grotius with whom he shared the belief that only a profound study of Christian antiquity could solve the religious disputes of the day. He was one of the first scholars to apply historical method to Christian dogmatics.

p. 246. *Pagi*: Antoine Pagi (1624–1699), Conventual Franciscan and French ecclesiastical historian who devoted himself to correcting the errors in the *Annales ecclesiastici* of Baronius, the whole work being edited in four volumes by his nephew, François Pagi.

p. 248. *Dio Cassius*: Cassius Dio (164–c.235) in his *Roman History*, LXII, 9–10, recounts the story of the Thundering Legion.

p. 248. *Julius Capitolinus*: One of a number of authors of the *Historia Augusta* (written in the late third or early fourth century), a series of biographies of Roman emperors. Julius Capitolinus is cited as the author of the biography of Marcus Aurelius, though nothing further is known about him, or a number of the other authors cited.

p. 249. *Antonine column at Rome*: Column erected in Rome by Marcus Aurelius between 180 and 196, with reliefs showing Roman victories in Armenia, Persia and Germany.

p. 251. *Tertullian*: Quintus Septimius Florens Tertullianus (*c*.160–*c*.225), North African theologian and Christian apologist. His *De Corona Militari* discusses the legitimacy of Christians serving in the army.

p. 252. *W. Lowth*: See note to p. 300.

p. 256. *St. Francis*: The *Little Flowers of St Francis*, iii, recount how St Francis had become nearly blind through weeping and penance.

p. 258. *Pliny*: Gaius Plinius Caecilius Secundus (*c*.61–*c*.112), Roman senator and man of letters. Amongst his letters are correspondence he had when he was governor of Bithynia with the Emperor Trajan, in which he reports that Christianity had spread so widely that the pagan cults were falling into neglect. His own investigation of Christianity had resulted in no evidence of criminal acts (*flagitia*). The correspondence throws interesting light on contemporary Christian practices, perhaps including the agape. Christians were not to be sought out, though they could still be accused of being Christians, even if anonymous information should rightly be disregarded (*ODCC*, loc. cit.).

p. 258. *Hardouin*: Jean Hardouin (1646–1729), Jesuit historian, who edited Pliny's *Natural History* (1685 and 1723). Sceptical about many classical writers, as about the authenticity of many early Christian writings, he believed Pliny's *Natural History* to be authentic.

p. 259. *Essay towards a Grammar of Assent, Ch. iv.§ 2*: Newman added this reference to the *Grammar of Assent* (published in 1870) on the republication of his two *Essays on Miracles* in 1875. The section of the *Grammar* to which he refers deals with Real Assents as contrasted with Notional Assents, which he has previously discussed. So Newman writes: 'In its notional assents as well as in its inferences, the mind contemplates its own creations instead of things; in real, it is directed towards things, represented by the impressions which they have left on the imagination. These images, when assented to, have an influence both on the individual and on society which mere notions cannot exert.' A little later in the same paragraph he speaks of how the religious sense, carefully cultivated, enables us rightly to apprehend the Holy Scriptures. 'To the devout and spiritual, the Divine Word speaks of things not merely of notions ... Hence the practice of meditation on the Sacred Text; so highly thought of by Catholics. Reading, as we do, the Gospels from our youth up, we are in danger of becoming so familiar with them as to be dead to their force, and to view them as a mere history. The purpose, then, of meditation is to realize them; to make the facts which they relate stand out before our minds as objects, such as may be appropriated by a faith as living in the imagination which apprehends them' (I. T. Ker (ed.), John Henry Newman, *An Essay in Aid of a Grammar of Assent*, Clarendon Press, Oxford, 1985, pp. 55–7). This parallels exactly what Newman wrote earlier in the second *Essay on Miracles*, 'Here we see the use of reading and studying the Gospels in order to true belief in our Lord; and, again, of acting upon His words, in order to true belief in them.'

p. 261. *St. Macrina*: St Macrina (*c*.327–380), the elder sister of St Basil the Great and St Gregory of Nyssa. She established a flourishing community on the family estate in Pontus (*ODCC*, loc. cit.).

p. 262. *Lardner*: Nathaniel Lardner (1684–1768), Nonconformist Independent minister known particularly for his book, *The Credibility of*

Gospel History (14 vols, 1727–57) in which he endeavoured to reconcile the discrepancies in the biblical narratives. His interpretation was based on patristic texts as well as on the commentaries of Grotius.

p. 262. *Firmilian*: St Firmilian (d. 268), Bishop of Caesarea in Cappadocia from *c*.230. He was a great admirer of Origen and supported Cyprian against Pope Stephen I in his doctrine that baptism could be validly performed only within the confines of the Church, and that heretics on joining the Church must therefore be 'rebaptized' (*ODCC*, loc. cit.).

p. 262. *Helenus*: Bishop of Tarsus in Cilicia, who apparently gathered a Synod at Antioch to enlist support for Novatian. He attended the synods of Antioch that condemned Paul of Samosata, at the latter of which he presided instead of the recently deceased Firmilian. (Eusebius, *Ecclesiastical History,* V I.46; V II, 5, 28, 30.)

p. 262. *Jerome's letter to Magnus*: Letter LXX of Jerome is addressed to Magnus, an orator of Rome, and is largely concerned with Jerome's response to the criticism made by Magnus that Jerome was too fond of quoting from pagan writers. Jerome lists a catena of notable Christian writers who 'so frequently interweave in their books the doctrines and maxims of the philosophers that you might be at a loss which to admire most, their secular erudition or their knowledge of the Scriptures'. Amongst those cited by Jerome is Gregory Thaumaturgus ('the wonderworker'); 'A man endowed with apostolic miracles as well as apostolic virtues' (*N&PNF,* VI, pp. 149–51).

p. 271. *Maxentius*: Roman emperor from 306 to 312, defeated by Constantine at the Battle of the Milvian Bridge.

p. 271. Philostorgius: (*c*.368–*c*.439), an Arian ecclesiastical historian. His principal work is a history of the Church for the period of *c*.300 to 430 written from an Arian standpoint, which includes valuable descriptions of several of the chief Arian personalities.

p. 271. *Nicephorus*: Nicephorus Callistus (*c*.1256–*c*.1335), Byzantine historian and author of a church history in eighteen books covering the period from the birth of Christ to the death of the Emperor Phocase in 610. It is an important source for certain of the early controversies and legends. Translated into Latin in 1555 it played an important part in the controversial literature of the time, furnishing material for the defence of images and relics (*ODCC*, q.v.).

p. 271. *Zonaras*: Johannes Zonaras, twelfth-century Byzantine canonist and historian, and author of a universal history in eighteen books (*ODCC*, q.v.).

p. 271. *Emperor Leo*: Leo III (*c*.675–741), Byzantine emperor often known as 'the Isaurian', an initiator of the Iconoclastic Controversy.

p. 271. *Brentius*: Johan Brentz (1499–1570), a rerformer of Württemberg and compiler of the Württemberg Confession; a prolific writer, he was the author of two catechisms, several biblical commentaries, sermons, and polemical treatises (*ODCC*, q.v.). Cranmer appealed to him to confute the views of the Swiss Reformers.

p. 271. *Rivetus*: André Rivet (1572-1651), French Huguenot theologian, professor of theology at Leiden, Rivet was a rigid Calvinist and the author of numerous theological works.

p. 273. *Gretzer de Cruce*: Jacob Gretzer (1562–1625), Jesuit theologian, who wrote extensively on the Cross of Christ.

p. 274. *Cornel. a Lapid.*: Cornelius a Lapide (1567–1637), Cornelis Cornelissen van den Steen, a Flemish Jesuit biblical exegete, the author of commentaries on all books of the Bible except the Psalms and Job. 'His works have owed their enduring popularity ... to their clarity, deep spirituality, and allegorical and mystical exegesis, buttressed by a wide erudition which enabled the author to draw extensively on the Fathers and mediaeval theologians'(*ODCC*).

p. 274. *Maldonat.*: Maldonatus, the Latinised name of Juan Maldonado (1533–1583), Spanish Jesuit theologian and exegete, who taught at the Jesuit college in Paris. His commentaries on the Gospels were held in high repute.

p. 276. *Burton*: Edward Burton (1794–1836), Regius Professor of Divinity at Oxford and patristic scholar, succeeding Charles Lloyd when the latter became Bishop of Oxford. He published *Thoughts on Church Reform* in 1831 admitting the need for church reform. Newman appreciated Burton's initial defence of Church and University in the context of the proposal to admit dissenters to the University in 1834 (*L&D*, IV, p. 268) but was caustic about his changing sides – 'Burton has ratted' (*L&D*, IV, p. 360). Newman noted his disapproval of the Theological Society he had founded (*L&D*, V, p. 191). Burton's unexpected death in 1836 caused concern to Newman, who, whilst not wholeheartedly supporting Burton, was fearful of a liberal appointment to the Regius Chair by a Whig government. The appointment of R. D. Hampden proved that Newman's concerns were justified.

p. 278. *Nazarius*: Latin rhetorician and panegyrust, said by Ausonius to have been professor of rhetoric at Burdigaia (Bordeaux). He was undoubtedly the author of a speech delivered in 321 in celebration of the fifteenth anniversary of the accession of Constantine, but the speech to which Newman refers, delivered in 313 at Augusta Trevirorum (Trier), although often attributed to him is now doubted because of differences of style, vocabulary and the distinctively Christian colouring.

p. 278. *Socrates*: (*c*.380–450), Church historian, author of a history of the Church designed as a continuation of the work of Eusebius.

p. 279. *Père de Grainville*: A Jesuit author of a dissertation on the conversion of Constantine noted by Gibbon in vol. II, Chapter XX of his *Decline and Fall of the Roman Empire*.

p. 282. *Optatianus Porphyrius*: Pubilius Optatianus Porphyrius, Prefect of Rome 329–33, Latin poet attributed with inventing acrostics and an admirer of Constantine.

p. 287. *St. Helena*: (*c*.255–*c*.330), mother of the Emperor Constantine, and a zealous supporter of Christianity. 'In 326, at a great age she made a visit to the Holy Land, where she founded the basilicas on the Mount of Olives and at Bethlehem, and, according to later traditions, discovered the cross on which Christ was crucified' (*ODCC*, q.v.).

p. 287. *Velser*: Marcus Velser of Augsburg (1558–1614).

p. 287. *S. Basnage*: Newman has the wrong initial. Jacques Basnage (1653–1723) was a Calvinist theologian and Church historian. Leaving his native town of Rouen after the revocation of the Edict of Nantes he resided in the Netherlands where in 1690 he published a history of the Reformed churches and a two-volume history of the Church.

p. 288. *Hadrian*: Roman emperor from 117 to 138, who built the city of Aelia Capitolina on the ruins of Jerusalem, turning it into a pagan city.

p. 288. *Hosius*: Hosius or Ossius (*c*.356–357/8), Bishop of Cordoba. It was as a result of his report that the Emperor Constantine summoned the Council of Nicaea, in which Hosius played an important role. He presided at the anti-Arian Council of Sardica in 343. Banished to Sirmium in 355 for his support of Athanasius, he was restored to his diocese after communicating with the Arians at the so-called 'Blasphemy' of Sirmium. According to Athanasius he repudiated his action before his death.

p. 288. *Nicomedia*: City now known as Izmit at the head of the Gulf of Izmit on the sea of Marmara. It served for a time as the imperial capital, which enabled Eusebius, formerly Bishop of Berytus (Beirut) and then Bishop of Nicomedia, who had been a fellow student with Arius of Lucian of Antioch, to exercise an Arianizing influence. Although he signed the Creed of Nicaea at the Council in 325 he was exiled shortly afterwards for his support of Arius. On his return in 328/9 he lead the struggle against Athanasius and secured his deposition at the Synod of Tyre (335). In 337 he baptised the dying Constantine. Translated to Constantinople in 339, he continued to influence the Church in an Arian direction (*ODCC*, 'Eusebius of Nicomedia', loc. cit.).

p. 289. *Professor Robinson*: Edward Robinson (1794–1863), an American biblical scholar, who studied Hebrew and theology at Göttingen, Halle and Berlin. 'Robinson's most original contribution to biblical studies ...was his research into the geography of the Middle East. In 1837 he travelled to Palestine, Syria and the Sinai, after having accepted a professorship in Biblical Literature at Union Theological Seminary, New York, on the understanding that he would not take up his post until his explorations in the Middle East were completed and written up. In collaboration with Eli Smith, an Arabic-speaking American missionary, he undertook a detailed survey of the region, "recording the Arabic toponyms [place names] and proposing and discussing numerous identifications with localities known from the Bible and other ancient sources. He also carefully evaluated the evidence for the reliability of traditional locations of the birthplace, trial, crucifixion and burial of Jesus, as well as other celebrated pilgrimage sites. His work was characterized by scrupulous personal observation of the terrain and profound knowledge of the written evidence"' (*L&D*, IX, p. 821). In a letter of 22 July 1842, Newman asked R.W. Church to check Robinson's *Biblical Researches in Palestine, Mount Sinai and Arabia Petraea* (1841) 'on which a good deal depends. Does he give the *distance* of Scopus or Tophim. The hill on the north of Jerusalem, from the city? i.e. *his own* distance of it? Next the *monument* <(not palace)> of Helena Queen of the Adiabeni on the norther was near Psephinus – I believe there are no remains of it. Has he found any? And *what distance* does he put the monument from the city?' Newman suggests that rather than Church answering his queries he could simply send Robinson's volumes to him, which it is likely Church did (*L&D*, IX,

p. 46). In the second *Essay* Newman took issue with some of Robinson's conclusions, and asked J. H. Parker, the publisher, to ensure that Robinson and Ogilby, the Professor of Ecclesiastical History at the General Seminary, were sent copies of the *Essay* (*L&D*, IX, p. 56).

p. 291. *Constantine's Letter to Macarius*: In his *Life of Constantine*, Eusebius quotes the text of the letter written by Constantine to Bishop Macarius of Jerusalem concerning the building of the Church of the Resurrection. Having earlier described the discovery of the Holy Sepulchre (III, xxviii), Constantine writes to Macarius that the discovery was miraculous, 'Indeed, the nature of this miracle as far transcends the capacity of human reason as heavenly things are superior to human affairs' (III, xxx).

p. 291. *the proposed Martyry or Church of the Resurrection*: In the latter part of his letter to Bishop Macarius, Constantine describes what he proposes for the building of the church to mark the site of the newly discovered Holy Sepulchre (III, xxxi–xxxii).

p. 292. *the Centuriators*: The Magdeburg authors of a church history, *Historia Ecclesiae Christi,* divided by centuries from the beginning to 1400, which set out a Lutheran and anti-Roman account of Church history in which pure New Testament Christianity came progressively under the power of the Papal Antichrist until delivered by Martin Luther. Matthias Flacius Illyricus (1520–1575) was the leading force behind the compiling of this history, which was innovative in scope but vulnerable to the criticisms of Cesare Baronius (1538–1607), whose *Annales Ecclesiastici* provided a Catholic response.

p. 292. *Dallaeus*: The Latinised name of Jean Daillé (1594–1670), a French Reformed theologian. He was the author of *Traité de l'employ des saints Pères* (1632) which rejected the authority of the Fathers as irrelevant, arguing that all Christian doctrines are implicitly stated in Scripture or can be deduced from it.

p. 292. *Montfaucon*: Bernard de Montfaucon (1655–1741), monk of the Maurist Benedictine congregation, and a leading patristic scholar, editing St Athanaius, Origen's Hexapla and Chrysostom. He virtually created the science of Greek palaeography and in his *Bibliotheca Bibliothecarum* (1739) he collated a mass of material on French historical antiquities.

p. 293. *St. Cyril of Jerusalem*: St Cyril (*c.*315–187), Bishop of Jerusalem from about 349. His most important work is a set of catechetical instructions delivered to the candidates for Baptism on Easter Eve as their

Editor's Notes 449

instruction during Lent. They provide a very full picture of the preparation for baptism and material for reconstructing the baptismal liturgy in use in Palestine in the fourth century. Cyril 'affirms the value and efficacy of Baptism with its anointing, renunciations, washing-away of sins, and laying on of hands' (*ODCC*, loc. cit.).

p. 297. *Methodius of Tyre*: (d. *c*.311). An opponent of Origen who, according to Jerome, was Bishop of Olympus in Lycia and afterwards Bishop of Tyre. A number of his works survive, and, although there is a query about whether he was Bishop of Tyre as Jerome asserts, Newman's point is that Eusebius' failure to mention him is not conclusive in relation to his existence.

p. 297. *Martyrdoms of Perpetua and Felicitas*: The *Passion of St Perpetua and St Felicitas* is a contemporary record of the martyrdom in 203 of Perpetua and her slave Felicitas in Carthage. It was possibly edited by Tertullian.

p. 299. – *St. Paulinus*: St Paulinus (353/5–431), Bishop of Nola. From a wealthy Aquitaine family, after his conversion he went to live with his wife in northern Spain. After the death of his eldest son he and his wife took a vow of continence, Paulinus being ordained to the priesthood. In 395 he and his wife left Spain to live a monastic life near the shrine of St Felix at Nola in the Campania, where he was later made bishop. He conducted a wide-ranging correspondence with many of the most notable Christians of his day. A skilled poet, he wrote many poems for the annual celebrations in honour of St Felix, which throw considerable light on the cult of the saints in his day.

p. 299. *Rufinus:* Rufinus Tyrannius or Turrianus (*c*.345–411), monk, historian and translator of Greek theological works into Latin, amongst them the ecclesiastical history of Eusebius which he brought up to the death of the Emperor Theodosius with the addition of two additional chapters. He wrote a monastic history (*Historia Monachorum*) and, at the invitation of Paulinus of Nola, wrote a commentary of the Benedictions of the Twelve Patriarchs in Genesis 49.

p. 300. *W. Lowth*: William Lowth (1660–1732), prebendary of Winchester and author of a *Commentary on the Prophets* (1714–25). His son, Robert Lowth, was successively Bishop of St David's, Oxford and London and is chiefly remembered for his study of the forms of Hebrew poetry.

p. 302. *Bishop Heber*: Reginald Heber (1783–1826), Bishop of Calcutta, to which he was appointed in 1823, and a notable hymn writer. A Fellow of All Souls he served after his ordination in 1807 as vicar of Hodnet in

Shropshire. In 1815 he delivered the Bampton Lectures on *The Personality and Office of the Christian Comforter*. A regular contributor to the *Quarterly Review*, he had corresponded in 1813 with George Wilkins, the author of *The History of the Siege of Jerusalem*, indicating a close knowledge of Josephus, and told Wilkins that he had kept one of his engraved pedigrees of the Herod family, 'and one of your elegant plans of Jerusalem. I have paid considerable attention to the very perplexed account which Josephus gives us as to the fortifications of his native city, and have compared it with the different ideas of Villalpandus, Calmet, Clarke, &c., and it is no flattery to say that your system reconciles the difficulties better than any other which I have met with' ([A. Heber], *The Life of Reginald Heber, D.D., Lord Bishop of Calcutta*, New York, 1830, I, p. 408). Newman corresponded with him in November 1824, when Heber offered to propose Newman for membership of the Athenaeum (of which Heber was a founder member) 'as a candidate for election *without ballot*'. Newman declined. Heber subsequently contributed £100 for Newman's collection for St Clement's Church (*L&D*, I, pp. 198–9, 206).

p. 308. *Lightfoot*: John Lightfoot (1602–1675) a biblical and rabbinic scholar and Master of St Catherine's College, Cambridge, who opposed the extreme Presbyterians in the Westminster Assembly (1643). In his *Horae Hebraicae et Talmudicae* (1658–78) he endeavoured to show the bearing of Jewish studies on the interpretation of the New Testament. Gibbon thought that Lightfoot had worked so long among Jewish texts that he had become 'the Christian Rabbi'. He provided 'Chorographical Observations' to Brian Walton's polyglot Bible of 1657, and it is to these that Newman refers.

p. 308. *Beza*: Theodore Beza (1519–1605), Calvinist theologian, originally (like John Calvin) a student of law, he went to Geneva in 1548, where he formally renounced the Catholic faith. In 1554 he defended the burning of Servetus. From 1558 to 1595 he served as a professor in the Geneva academy and succeeded Calvin as head of the Genevan Church on Calvin's death in 1563. He defended the orthodox doctrine of the Trinity against Socinus, and the view that in the Eucharist the Holy Spirit makes Christ's divine (though not his human) nature present to the faithful. He gave his name to the Codex Bezae of the Gospels and Acts, and his own work on the New Testament was widely influential all over Europe in the seventeenth century. 'He is usually considered to have hardened Calvin's doctrine of predestination by arguing that ... even the Fall was part of God's eternal plan; it followed the election of some to salvation and others to damnation, the atoning death of Christ being offered only for the former' (*ODCC*, loc. cit).

p. 308. *Poole's Synopsis*: Matthew Poole (1624?–1679), biblical commentator and a supporter of Presbyterian ordination, who resigned his living following the passing of the Uniformity Act in 1662. He nonetheless maintained good relations with Church of England leaders, one of whom, William Lloyd, later Bishop of Worcester, together with Archbishop Tillotson, encouraged him in his *magnum opus,* the *Synopsis criticorum aliorumque sacrae scripturae interpretum* which first appeared in 1669. 'The work constituted an important compendium of biblical commentary and exegesis, condensing into brief notes a great deal of study ... He used rabbinical sources and Roman Catholic texts extensively, but ... little was taken from Calvin and nothing from Luther' (*ODNB*, loc. cit.).

p. 308. *Spanheim*: Friedrich Spanheim the Younger (1632–1707), a Reformed theologian and professor at the University of Leiden, where his father, also Friedrich Spanheim, had likewise been professor, published his *Introductio ad geographiam sacram patriarchalem* in 1679.

p. 309. *De Dieu*: Louis de Dieu (1590–1642), a minister of the Dutch Reformed Church and a learned Orientalist, renowned for his interpretation of biblical texts based on a wide and profound linguistic learning.

p. 310. *Mounts Sion and Moriah*: Mount Moriah is an elongated ridge, which includes the Temple mount, with Mount Sion a separate hill.

p. 310. *Bezetha*: A part of Jerusalem north of the Temple area in which is situated the Pool of Bethesda and part of the Via Dolorosa.

p. 310. *Agrippa*: Herod Agrippa II (*c.*27–100), the seventh and last ruler of the family of Herod the Great, who enlarged the Hasmonaean palace in Jerusalem. Acts 26 records Paul's appearance before Agrippa and his wife Bernice.

p. 311. *Acra*: A fortress or citadel built by Antiochus Epiphanes after his capture of Jerusalem in 168 BC, which stood on a hill higher than the temple.

p. 311. *Gennath*: The Garden gate. Josephus speaks of the second wall taking its beginning from the gate called Gennath, and encompassing the northern quarter of the city until it reached the Antonia fortress (*Jewish Wars,* V, iv).

p. 311. *Antonia*: Part of the fortress-castle which stood on a high rock at the north-west corner of the Temple area in Jerusalem. It was strengthened by Herod the Great who changed its name to the Tower of Antonia in honour of his friend, Mark Anthony.

p. 311. *pool of Hezekiah*: Hezekiah was the twelfth king of Judah (*c.*715–687 BC). He constructed a tunnel (still surviving) which brought the waters of the spring of Gihon inside the walls of Jerusalem. The pool of Hezekiah, as Newman notes, is situated to the south-west of the Holy Sepulchre.

p. 313. *Sion*: Newman's long footnote draws extensively on Josephus, *Antiquities* and the *Jewish War*, but also cites geographical evidence from William of Tyre, the thirteenth-century Archdeacon and later Archbishop of Tyre in the Latin Kingdom of Jerusalem, author of *Historia Hierosolymitana*, a general history of the Crusades and the Kingdom of Jerusalem down to 1184, a work noted for its accuracy. John Lightfoot (1602–1675), whom Newman also cites, is regarded as the founder of modern Hebraic scholarship, Gibbon describing him as 'the Christian Rabbi'. 'His work displays an archaeological, historical, philosophical and even anthropological study of the biblical past' (*ODNB*, loc. cit.). For Lightfoot see *supra* p. 308.

p. 313. *Manasseh*: Son of Hezekiah, King of Judah (*c.*687–642), his reign is recounted in 2 Kings 21:1–8 and 2 Chronicles 33:1–20.

p. 314. *Iturea and Idumaea*: Iturea is the region south-east of Mount Hermon and north-east of the Sea of Galilee, corresponding to what is today known as the Golan Heights. It was part of the tetrachy of Philip (see Luke 3:1) and was given by Caligula in AD 40 to Herod Agrippa I along with Trachonitis and the title of king. When Herod Agrippa died, Iturea was incorporated into the Province of Syria. Idumea – the biblical Edom, south of the Dead Sea – was conquered by Herod the Great and incorporated into his kingdom, after his being made King of the Jews by the Emperor Augustus in 40 BC.

p. 326. *the relics of St. Cuthbert*: St Cuthbert (*c.*636–687), Bishop of Lindisfarne and a solitary on the Farne Islands. His body was taken by the Lindisfarne community to Durham because of the threat from Scandinavian invasions. The cult around his tomb in Durham Cathedral became one of the most important of the Middle Ages. His pectoral cross, portable altar, coffin reliquary and other objects survived the destruction of his shrine at the Reformation and were recovered when his tomb was opened in 1827.

Editor's Notes

p. 326. *the coffin of Bishop Coverdale*: Miles Coverdale (1487/8–1569), translator of the Bible and briefly Bishop of Exeter. He was one of the consecrators of Matthew Parker, and a leader of the Puritan party. He was buried in St Bartholomew by the Exchange in the City of London. When that church was pulled down to make room for the Royal Exchange, Coverdale's remains were exhumed and he was reburied in the Church of St Magnus the Martyr, London Bridge. In *Notes and Queries* (25 December 1852) there is the following response to a query about the exhumation. 'When the church of St Bartholomew the Less was about to be demolished, particular search was made for the remains of the Reformer; and on the 21st September, 1840, a skeleton was found under the floor of the church, in the precise spot where, from tradition, it was expected that his body would be discovered. These remains were removed with the greatest care, and were re-interred on the 4th October in a vault prepared for them in the south aisle of the Church of St Magnus, London Bridge.' The entry refers to a pamphlet published in 1840 containing account of the search (N. Whittock, *A correct account of the Exhumation of the remains of Myles Coverdale, sometime Bishop of Exeter and Rector of St Magnus the Martyr, London Bridge, who was interred in the church of St Bartholomew near the Exchange*). Newman may well have known either this pamphlet or the contemporary news reports.

p. 337. *Alypius of Antioch*: A geographer and vicarius of Roman Britain, who came from Antioch and served under Constantius II. Julian commissioned him to rebuild the Temple at Jerusalem, but was prevented, as Newman notes, citing Warburton, *Julian, Or a Discourse concerning the earthquake and fiery eruption which defeated that Emperor's attempt to rebuild the Temple at Jerusalem,* 1750, a work in which Warburton also criticised Hume's essays on miracles.

p. 338. *De la Bleterie*: John Philip René de la Bletherie (1696–1772). Born at Rennes in Brittany he joined the congregation of the Oratory. He wrote the *Life of the Emperor Julian* (1735), which was translated into English in 1746.

p. 340. *Prudentius*: Aurelius Prudentius Clemens (348–c.410), Latin poet and hymn writer. The *Peristephanon* consists of hymns in praise of a number of Spanish and Italian martyrs. The translation of his hymn *Corde natus ex parentis* ('Of the Father's heart begotten') is well known as a Christmas hymn.

p. 342. *Mr. Davison*: John Davison (1777–1834). Fellow of Oriel from 1798 to 1818, when he became first rector of Washington, Co. Durham, and then in 1826 rector of Upton-upon-Severn, and in the same year a prebendary of both St Paul's and Worcester cathedrals. A silent Northcountryman, sharing the same conservative and High Church principles as John Keble's with whom he was a contemporary as a Fellow of Oriel, he persuaded Keble to publish his celebrated collection of devotional poetry, *The Christian Year*. Keble edited Davison's *Remains* after Davison's death, which was for Keble a great loss, as he wrote to Newman 'To those who knew his kindness as I did the loss is humanly speaking irreperable' (*L&D*, IV, p. 248n). In 1825 Newman read Davison's two significant works, *Discourses on Prophecy* (1824) and *An Inquiry into the Origins and intent of Primitive Sacrifice* (1825). Newman's last contribution to *The British Critic* in 1842 was an essay on Davison, which was reprinted in *Ess.* II (1872), pp. 375–420. Newman described Davison in this essay as 'One of the most original thinkers of his day, deep, serious, reverential, various ... a man of the cast of Hooker and Butler, fitted to be a doctor of the Church, yet confined pretty much to the contemplation of the first principles of Christian doctrine, and allowed but once or twice to give utterance to the truths on which he lived, and to manifest the flame which burned unceasingly within him' (*Essays* ii, pp. 375–6). In his *Discourses on Prophecy* Davidson connects miracles and prophecy noting that 'the force which has been ascribed to single miracles, may be ascribed to single prophecies'. Davison argues that 'It has been urged by the defenders of Revelation ... that any one unquestionable miracle would in the eye-witness of that miracle be sufficient to prove a revelation attested by it, a suitable moral end of both being supposed. The miracle granted, the inference from it could not be resisted. The acknowledgement of the supernatural agency must be followed by an admission of the doctrine. It is but the connexion which subsists between the lightning and the thunder; when we see the flash, we know the thunder, which follows, comes from the same cloud'(John Davison, *Discourses on Prophecy, in which are considered its structure, use, and inspiration,* London, John Murray, 1834, pp. 537–8).

p. 347. *Korah, Dathan and Abiram*: In Numbers 16 Korah, Dathan and Abiram rebelled against Moses and as a result the earth opened and swallowed them up. Psalm 106:17 records how 'the earth opened and swallowed up Dathan, and covered the congregation of Abiram'.

p. 348. *St. Gervasius and St. Protasius*: The proto-martyrs of Milan. Nothing certain is known about them, though a later tradition said that they were martyred in the latter half of the second century. In his life of Ambrose (*Vita Ambrosii* 14) St Paulinus tells how their relics were discovered by St Ambrose in the church of Sts Felix and Nabor, Ambrose transferred them to his new basilica. A blind man called Severus, who had formerly been a butcher, recovered his sight by touching the fringe of the pall which covered the relics. In Ep.77 Ambrose describes other marvels which attended the translation of the relics (*Corpus Scriptorum Ecclesiasticorum Latinorum,* vol. 82, part 3).

p. 348. *Empress Justina*: (d. *c.*388), the second wife of Emperor Valentinian I (reigned 364–75) and mother of Valentinian II (reigned 375–93). A supporter of Arianism, she engaged in sharp conflict with St Ambrose, and was eventually defeated.

p. 363. *the Cabbalists*: The Kabbala was an esoteric and symbolic system of interpretation of the Old Testament, sometimes described as a Jewish theosophy, which revealed a hidden wisdom such as the creation of the world by emanations from the Godhead. It was most influential in the later Middle Ages and the Renaissance when there was also a Christian form of Kabbala practised by Reuchlin and Paracelsus.

p. 369. *the Vandals*: A Germanic tribe who, under their king Gaiseric, crossed from Spain to Africa in 435. A few years later they had taken Carthage, setting up an independent kingdom in North Africa, the granary of Rome. Their rule was later extended to Sicily, Sardinia, Corsica and the Balearics and in 455 they captured and sacked Rome, including among the booty taken to Carthage the Menorah, the seven-branched candlestick from the Jerusalem Temple seized by Titus when Jerusalem fell in AD 70.

p. 369. *Genseric*: (428–477), King of the Vandals, a variant of Gaiseric.

p. 370. *Sicca and Laribis*: Sicca Veneria (modern El Kef) an important town in Numidia in Roman proconsular Africa, on the road from Carthage to Hippo Regius. Lares (Laribis) is another important town nearby.

p. 373. *the article on 'Miracles' in the Enycl. Metrop.*: Newman had commented on the story of speech being restored to the African confessors, who spoke despite their tongues being cut out, in his first *Essay* (p. 87) and had referred both to Milner's *Church History* and to Gibbon. In his note he comments, in a way reminiscent of Augustine's *Retrectationes*, that he has moved to a position 'in which I could wish some correction not of opinion, but of tone, in my treatment of the primitive miracles'. Admitting that the first *Essay* was concerned with establishing the uniqueness and evidential character of the miracles of Scripture, Newman now characterises not only Conyers Middleton but also, perhaps more surprisingly, Bishop John Douglas, whom he had earlier read with profit, as 'unsafe guides'. The lapidary phrase, that 'it is no exaltation of Christ to lower His Saints', sums up the changed position which Newman has reached.

p. 373. *Emperor Zeno*: Zeno (*c*.450?–491), Emperor of the East from 474. He took an active part in attempting to reconcile the non-Chalcedonian churches, publishing his *Henoticon* in 482, which failed to achieve its purpose and occasioned a new schism between Constantinople and Rome. In 468 a naval expedition he sent from Constantinople against the Vandal kingdom was utterly destroyed in a naval battle.

p. 374. *Aeneas of Gaza*: (d. 381). A Christian philosopher who studied under Hierocles the Neoplatonist at Alexandria. A strong supporter of Platonist and Neoplatonist doctrines. The dialogue referred to by Newman is entitled *Theophrastus*. Despite Newman's saying that he did not altogether throw off his profession of Platonism when he became a Christian, he rejected Platonist ideas concerning the pre-existence of the soul and the eternity of the world.

p. 375. *Procopius of Caesarea*: A mid sixth-century Byzantine historian, born at Caesarea, later moving (*c*.542) to Constantinople where he practised as an advocate and rhetorician. He became secretary to Justinian's general, Belisarius, whom he accompanied in his campaigns against the Persians, the Vandals, and the Ostrogoths. His historical writing, notably his *History of the Wars*, is of considerable value as that of an impartial eye witness. His *Secret History* is a valuable source for Justinian's reign. Gibbon considered him a reliable witness, noting that of his strange anecdotes 'A part may be true because probable, a part true because improbable. Procopius must have *known* the former, and the latter he could scarcely *invent*' (cited Procopius, *The Secret History* (ed and tr. G.A. Williamson) Penguin, Harmondsworth, 1966, p. 30).

p. 375. *Belisarius*: Justinian's general who led the campaign of reconquest for the Byzantine empire against the Vandals in Africa. The Vandal king Gelimer was forced to surrender and in 534 Belisarius made a triumphant entry into Constantinople, bringing with him the great seven-branched candlestick (the *menorah*) which Titus had taken to Rome from Jerusalem, and which a Vandal king had subsequently taken to Carthage. Belisarius then took Sicily and invaded Italy, where he took Naples and, after a long siege, Rome, and then captured Ravenna and took Vitiges, the Ostrogoth king, prisoner to Constantinople in 540. His campaigns are described by his secretary Procopius.

Editor's Notes

p. 377. *Emperor Justinian*: Justinian I (*c*.483–565), Roman Emperor from 527. The son of a Macedonian peasant, he was one of the most significant of the early Byzantine emperors. He built Hagia Sophia and many other basilicas at Constantinople, Ravenna and elsewhere. He laid the foundation of the juridical basis of the empire with his revision, enlargement and rearrangement of the Theodosian Code. In it a distinction was drawn between the *imperium* (imperial authority) and the *sacerdotium* (the priesthood); interdependent, but neither subordinated to the other. The code of Justinian greatly influenced the development of canon law in the West. A strong defender of orthodoxy, he was unsuccessful in his endeavours to reconcile the Monophysites, but this led to the condemnation of the memory as well as the alleged doctrines of Origen.

p. 377. *Count Marcellinus*: Chancellor to Emperor Justinian (527–565).

p. 378. *Tria Capitula*: The three subjects condemned by an edict of the Emperor Justinian in 543–4, namely (1) the person and works of Theodore of Mopsuestia; (2) the writings of Theodoret against Cyril of Alexandria; and (3) the letter of Ibas of Edessa to Maris, all of which were considered sympathetic to Nestorianism. The Eastern Patriarchs assented but Pope Vigilius refused at first to approve the edict. On being summoned to Constantinople Vigilius eventually condemned the Three Chapters but upheld Chalcedon. The Fifth General Council which met at Constantinople in 553 condemned both the Three Chapters and (indirectly) Vigilius, who submitted the next year to the Council's decision. 'Justinian's policy, which was in fact an attack on the Antiochene theology and the decisions of Chalcedon, failed even of its purpose of reconciling the Monophysites' (*ODCC*, loc. cit.).

p. 378. *Fifth Ecumenical Council*: Victor Bishop of Tonno followed his earlier namesake, Victor Bishop of Vita (Vitensis), in recounting and defending the miracle of the confessors speaking after their tongues were cut out in the Vandal persecution under Hunneric.